STUDIES ON TWENTIETH-CENTURY SPANISH AND SPANISH AMERICAN LITERATURE

Kessel Schwartz

UNIVERSITY
PRESS OF
AMERICA

LANHAM • NEW YORK • LONDON

BEAVER COLLEGE LIBRARY.
GLENSIDE, PA. 19038

Copyright © 1983 by

University Press of America,™ Inc.

4720 Boston Way
Lanham, MD 20706

3 Henrietta Street
London WC2E 8LU England

All rights reserved
Printed in the United States of America

Library of Congress Cataloging in Publication Data

Schwartz, Kessel, 1920-
   Studies on twentieth-century Spanish and
Spanish American literature.

      Includes bibliographical references.
      1. Spanish literature--20th century--History
and criticism--Addresses, essays, lectures. 2.
Spanish American literature--20th century--History
and criticism--Addresses, essays, lectures. I.
Title.
PQ6072.S39   1983   860'.9'006   83-5793
ISBN 0-8191-3184-9
ISBN 0-8191-3185-7 (pbk.)

To Barbara

Acknowledgements

"Leviatán," Kentucky Foreign Language Quarterly, XVII, 3 (1970), 239-46.

"Madrid and Spanish Literature," Revista de Estudios Hispánicos, III, 1 (1969), 1-8.

"Literary Criticism and the Spanish Civil War," Hispania, LII, 2 (1969), 203-12.

"The Past as Prologue in Hora de España," Romance Notes, X, 1 (1968).

"Hora de España and the Poetry of Hope," Romance Notes, XV, 1 (1974).

"National and European Culture in the Contemporary Spanish Novel," The Cry of Home, University of Tennessee Press (1972), pp. 167-84.

"Thematic and Stylistic Constants in the Fiction of Alfonso Grosso," Revista de Estudios Hispánicos, X, 1 (1976), 112-23.

"Carlos Rojas Vila and An Act of Faith," Revista de Estudios Hispánicos, VII, 3 (1973), 349-59.

"El ingenioso hidalgo y poeta Federico García Lorca asciende a los infiernos," MLN, Vol. 97, No. 2 (1982), 443-47.

"Juan Goytisolo - Ambivalent Artist in Search of His Soul," Journal of Spanish Studies, Vol. 3, No. 3 (1975), 187-97.

"Motherhood and Incest in the Fiction of Juan Goytisolo," The American Hispanist, Vol. IV, Nos. 32-33 (1979), 23-25.

"Women in the Novels of Juan Goytisolo," Symposium (Winter, 1977), 357-67.

"Fauna in the Novels of Juan Goytisolo," Hispania, Vol. 64, No. 4 (1981), 540-49.

"Juan Goytisolo, Cultural Constraints and the Historical Vindication of Count Julian," Hispania, Vol. 54, No. 4 (1971), 960-66.

"Juan Goytisolo, Juan sin tierra, and the Anal Aesthetic," Hispania, Vol. 62, No. 1 (1979), 9-19.

"Language and Literature: Ricardo Palma and Juan

Goytisolo," The International Fiction Review (July, 1975), 138-42.

"Eros and Thanatos: The Poetry of Vicente Aleixandre--Surrealism or Freudianism?," Vicente Aleixandre: A Critical Appraisal (Ypsilanti: Bilingual Press, 1981), pp. 200-20.

"Symbolic Lips in the Early Poetry of Vicente Aleixandre," Revista Canadiense de Estudios Hispánicos, Vol. V, No. 2 (1981), 185-200.

"Posibilismo and Imposibilismo: The Buero Vallejo-Sastre Polemic," Revista Hispánica Moderna, Ano XXXIV, Nos. 1-2 (1968), 436-45.

"Verbum and Spanish Culture," Caribbean Studies, Vol. 15, No. 2 (1975), 153-55.

"Ciclón and Cuban Culture," Caribbean Studies, Vol. 14, No. 4 (1974), 151-61.

"Ciclón and the Castro Revolution," Hispania, Vol. 58, No. 4 (1975), 926-28.

"Themes, Trends, and Textures: The 1960's and the Spanish American Novel," Hispania, Vol. 55, No. 4 (1972), 817-31.

"The Theme of Suicide in Representative Spanish American Novels," Hispania, Vol., 58, No. 3 (1975), 442-53.

"Homosexuality as a Theme in Representative Contemporary Spanish American Novels," Kentucky Romance Quarterly, Vol. 22, No. 2 (1975), 247-57.

"From Prisoner to Warden in Twentieth-Century Spanish American Fiction," The American Hispanist, Vol. III, (Sept., 1978), 5-9.

"Two Faces of Feminism in the 1920's," Revista de Estudios Hispánicos (Oct., 1979), 461-71.

"Sexism in the Spanish American Novel (1965-1975)," The Pacific Quarterly (October, 1980), 522-29.

"The Whorehouse and the Whore in Spanish American Fiction of the 1960s," Journal of Interamerican Studies and World Affairs (Nov., 1973), 472-87.

"Antisemitism in Modern Argentine Fiction," Jewish Social

Studies, Vol. XL, No. 2 (1978), 131-40.

"The Jew in Twentieth-Century Argentine Fiction," The American Hispanist (Sept., 1977), 9-12.

TABLE OF CONTENTS

                                                                Page

INTRODUCTION   1

SPAIN

JOURNALS

Leviatán 13
Madrid and Spanish Literature 21
Literary Criticism and the Spanish Civil War 27
The Past as Prologue in Hora de España 43
Hora de España and the Poetry of Hope 49

FICTION

National and European Culture in the Contemporary
  Spanish Novel 55
Thematic and Stylistic Constants in the Fiction of
  Alfonso Grosso 73
Carlos Rojas Vila and an Act of Faith 81
El ingenioso hidalgo y poeta Federico García Lorca
  asciende a los infiernos 89
Juan Goytisolo - Ambivalent Artist in Search of
  His Soul 95
Motherhood and Incest in the Fiction of Juan
  Goytisolo 107
Women in the Novels of Juan Goytisolo 117
Fauna in the Novela of Juan Goytisolo 131
Juan Goytisolo, Cultural Constraints and the
  Historical Vindication of Count Julian. 149
Juan Goytisolo, Juan sin Tierra, and the Anal
  Aesthetic 161
Language and Literature: Ricardo Palma and
  Juan Goytisolo 177

POETRY

Eros and Thanatos: The Poetry of Vicente
  Aleixandre - Surrealism or Freudianism? 185
Symbolic Lips in the Early Poetry of Vicente
  Aleixandre 207

DRAMA

Posibilismo and Imposibilismo 225

Page

LATIN AMERICA

CUBAN LITERATURE

Verbum and Spanish Culture 241
Ciclón and Cuban Culture 245
Ciclón and the Castro Revolution 257

NOVEL

Themes, Trends, and Textures: The 1960's and the
    Spanish American Novel 263
The Theme of Suicide in Representative Spanish
    American Novels 287
Homosexuality as a Theme in Representative
    Contemporary Spanish American Novels 307
From Prisoner to Warden In Twentieth-Century
    Spanish American Fiction 319

FEMINISM

Two Faces of Feminism in the 1920's 333
Sexism in the Spanish American Novel (1965-1975) 341
The Whorehouse and the Whore in Spanish American
    Fiction of the 1960's 353

ANTISEMITISM

Antisemitism in Modern Argentine Fiction 367
The Jew in Twentieth-Century Argentine Fiction 379
Two Contemporary Hispanic Views of Israel and
    the Jews 393

INTRODUCTION

Most discussions of twentieth-century Spanish literature start with an analysis of the Generation of '98, originally labeled by Azorín the Generation of '96 but changed for the symbolic value of the later date. Its members, who reached their aesthetic and reformative peak between 1890 and 1905, continued to produce first-rate works in all genres during the first three decades of the twentieth century. Some, including supposed members, denied the very existence of such a generation; others could not agree on its membership which usually includes Miguel de Unamuno, José Martínez Ruiz, Ramiro de Maeztu, Pío Baroja, and Antonio Machado. While some members espoused eternal Spanish verities and traditions together with a profound soul-searching, others sought to reform Spain through Europeanization. A few writers endeavored to take excursions through time and space, engaging in existential exploration and the role of man in the universe. Although some members emphasized the skeptical and pessimistic, all generally concurred on the need for moral and spiritual regeneration together with a new view of aesthetics and reality.

Some of the same cultural, social, and political dichotomies showed up in a variety of journals in the 1930's, especially those published during the Spanish Civil War itself. Both sides contributed to journals, the Seville ABC, Jerarquía, and Escorial, on the one hand, and Madrid and Hora de España on the other. These journals reveal the inextricable interdependence of aesthetics and politics during those years. Even though the war resulted in the death of Antonio Machado and Federico García Lorca, and the escape from Spain of many outstanding poets such as Rafael Alberti and Pedro Salinas, dramatists like Jacinto Grau, and novelists like Ramón Sender, literary activity in Spain continued, dependent to a degree on the creative inheritance of '98.

Juan Goytisolo and members of his generation were also influenced at one time or another by writers like Pío Baroja. Nonetheless, Goytisolo attacked and disparaged the members of the Generation of '98, not only as ineffectual but also as a petrifying inheritance for new generations which had different problems. For him the cultural break represented by the Spanish Civil War resulted in a continuation of outmoded themes and techniques, a barrier against self-development almost as stultifying as twenty-five years of dictatorship. Writers of the 1960's and 1970's criticized not only Unamuno but also Ortega y Gasset, portrayed with devastating irony by Luis Martín Santos in Tiempo de silencio (1962).

But Goytisolo accepted traditional Spanish masterpieces such as the Libro de Buen Amor and La Celestina for what he believes to be their iconoclastic and subversive values; he praises even more highly Don Quijote de la Mancha, recognizing that Cervantes had explored virtually all of the latent possibilities in the novelistic genre used later by creative writers of fiction (including contemporary Spaniards). He himself incorporates semi-glosses from Don Quijote into Reivindicación del Conde Don Julián. As literary styles shifted from objectivism to formalism, from social content to aesthetic form, he and other writers of his generation stressed the need for a radical transformation in the relationship of Spain and European culture, since the war and censorship had contributed to Spanish literary isolation.

Spanish fiction has a distinguished twentieth-century register of names. Miguel de Unamuno in anguished "nivolas" searches for immortality, using the man of flesh and blood as a focal point for his dialectic between faith and doubt, life and death. José Martínez Ruiz (Azorín)'s autobiographical novels present impressionistic images and technical innovations but very little narration. Pío Baroja's illogical, disordered structures contain picaresque vagabonds who quite often fail; his abulic, pessimistic though often lyrical novels exemplify delusive values. Ramón María del Valle-Inclán, in his modernist phase, contributes artistic, musical, decadent fiction; his esperpento prose, on the other hand, involves a deformed and deforming aesthetic and a vision of life seen through a concave mirror. Ramón Pérez de Ayala, in ironic, intellectual, symbolic and psychological novels, whatever his conceptual metaphysics, comparison of art and life, and contrast between passive and active existence, shows a great tolerance for human folly.

Among that first generation of novelists born in the twentieth century, Ramón Sender (1902-1982) examines the horrors of war, the guilt of being human, the problems of adolescence, good versus evil, and the search for absolute justice. He often combines symbol and dream, reality and imagination in his existentially anguished quest for human values. Camilo José Cela, considered by some to be a member of the Generation of '36, was the rallying point for the renaissance of post-war Spanish fiction. His La familia de Pascual Duarte, the first important post-war novel, details the primitive reactions of a protagonist in a world without true moral values. The irrational and violent acts of Pascual may very well reflect the then current Spanish spiritual deficiencies. In other novels dealing with the Civil War, he examines Spanish victims of a cruel environment. A master stylist, he combines, in later fiction, temporal experimentation, existential exploration, and explicit sexual situations.

Many other novelists wrote during those years. Gómez de la Serna contributed intellectual, surrealistic, sensual, absurd, fantastic novels; Benjamín Jarnés experimented surrealistically with time, perspective, space, and myth; Gabriel Miró, with stylistic brillance which antedates the nouveau roman, achieved the peak of Modernist prose; Juan Antonio de Zunzunegui provided a more traditional realism.

Among those born after 1920, Miguel Delibes, Carmen Laforet, Ana María Matute, Luis Martín Santos, Juan Benet, and Juan Goytisolo stand out. Laforet's novel Nada (1944), the first Nadal prize winner, depicts a female protagonist immersed in a perverse environment of solitude, lack of communication and understanding. Delibes, who in early novels treats solitude, nature, death, and adolescence, later offers us Cinco horas con Mario (1966), which contrasts a traditional with a progressive view of life, and Parábola del náufrago (1969), which treats of violence, dehumanization, and the fate of the individual in a technological society. Ana María Matute concentrates on the Cain-Abel theme, the loss of innocence, loneliness, maternal feelings, and the interplay of reality and fantasy. Among her many impressive novels one may cite Primera memoria (1960). Juan Benet treats of the search for lost time, disintegration, degradation, ruin, guilt, loneliness, and the ambiguous world of violence, as he deliberately obfuscates the plot line in novels like Volverás a Región (1967).

After a period of social realism and an objectivism, best exemplified by Rafael Sánchez Ferlosio's El Jarama (1957), authors experimented more and more with form and aesthetics in order to create new imaginative realities. They employed linguistic codes, intertextuality, structuralism, and formalism. Some authors still utilized a kind of neo-realism, but Luis Martín Santos' Tiempo de silencio (1962) hastened the decline of this kind of literature. Pessimistic, ironic, humorous in turn, Martín Santos burlesques frustrated failures; but social implications cede to sexual and mythical ones as he stresses, especially, the importance of language, narrative consciousness, and point of view, an aesthetic change accelerated in the 1970's.

Many fine novelists, not emphasized in literary manuals as the very greatest, also deserve continuing critical attention. Among these one might include Alfonso Grosso and Carlos Rojas. Grosso derides some of the technical improvisations of his fellow novelists, failing to acknowledge Goytisolo and most of the Latin American writers as overwhelmingly important. In the 1970's, continuing to emphasize the themes of death, he simplified his baroque language, which resulted in a greater reading public for his works. Carlos Rojas wrote many prize-winning, imaginative novels on differing themes. Complex and independent, he constantly refines and experiments, but his intertextual and at times even metaphysical inclusions do not disguise his social conscience.

Juan Goytisolo, who through the years concerned himself with problems of writing and theories of the novel, started with the idea that literature and life are inextricably intertwined. Although exiled from Spain for many years and ignored by critics, Goytisolo, from earliest novels like Juegos de manos (1954) on, portrayed youngsters growing up, sick members in a sick society, products of the violence and hate associated with the Spanish Civil War and the post-war period. Goytisolo dedicated himself, perhaps as a kind of catharsis for his social conscience and his painful love for Spain, to the destruction of what he considered to be the myths of Spain, castigating the Catholic Church, government censorship, and the lack of literary creativity and courage among fellow writers. Although many of his early novels reveal themes and to an extent a style he was to use, refine, and make more complex with increasing mastery and the passing years, around 1965 he disavowed his somewhat monolithic support of social realism, objectivism, and verisimilitude for what he called "realist illusion." In many of his later novels Goytisolo employs Russian formalism and intertextuality, viewing his novels as both literature and a discourse on literature. His brilliant Reivindicación del Conde don Julián (1970) describes Spain as the mother of vices in need of destruction in order to find salvation. Juan sin tierra (1975) at the time seemed to be the final chapter in Goytisolo's aesthetic, psychological, and sociological search for meaning in his existence, as well as a final destruction of ordinary language and Spanish mythology. But Makbara (1980) blends literary allusions and linguistic forms with criticism of religious, political, social and sexual institutions as part of a persistent and sterile search for assuaging an imagined personal guilt.

The immediate impetus for twentieth-century poetic innovations came from the movement known as Modernism, defined in dozens of different ways. Among aspects cited one finds brevity, intensity, melancholy, vague and musical themes, renovation of form, evasion, French Symbolism, cosmopolitanism, and mythology. Largely skeptical and pessimistic, these poets were Hispanic participants in a universal crisis of letters and spirit which arose toward the end of the nineteenth century. Unamuno uncovered his soul in his contradictory, philosophical, religious, human and intellectual poetry, which also reflected his existential anguish. Antonio Machado, probably Spain's greatest twentieth-century poet, went beyond sound and color to reflect the spiritual and telluric aspects of his country in a poetry laced with religious uncertainties, existential anguish, and temporal preoccupations. Juan Ramón Jiménez served as a bridge between the Modernists and poets like León Felipe who searched for God, the meaning of life, and social justice in the humble everyday world. Jiménez' gossamer-like, intellectual, delicate, refined, and sad color-filled poetry emphasized a longing for beauty and perfection.

Undoubtedly the greatest poetic generation since the Golden Age was the so-called Generation of 1927 whose poets at first also flirted with the concept of pure poetry and intellectual aestheticism expressed by Jiménez. This generation contained giants like Jorge Guillén, who sang of the joys of life and later of existential preoccupations, and Pedro Salinas, who wrote abstract and conceptual poetry seeking form and substance over shadow and illusion. A poet preoccupied by ineffable beauty and love, he also wrote anguished existential works, searching always for the meaning of reality in a modern materialistic world in opposition to the reality of an inner spiritual one. Federico García Lorca utilized odd sensory combinations to offer us a primitive, childlike and yet sophisticated world and a harmonic, musical, symbolic poetry filled constantly with the brooding presence of death. Luis Cernuda dealt with destruction and death, the abyss between man and society, and the struggle to overcome sensual desires.

Vicente Aleixandre, the third Spaniard to win the Nobel Prize for Literature (Jacinto Benavente and Juan Ramón Jiménez were the others), combined the real and the unreal, struggling for a kind of transfiguration through an evocation of human and cosmic love. A master of chiaroscuro, he wrote somewhat hermetic poetry which yet communicated with the reader in spite of the pseudo-surrealistic imagery. His poetry may be viewed as a psychological journey from annihilation and despair to an affirmation of love and light, going from a world where the human ranked low in the scale of values to human preoccupations and later to the investigation of knowledge itself. His process of cosmic fusion combined the sensual and the metaphysical as he battled against reality, old age, and death, communicating in a contradictory way his poetic truth involving cosmic and human imperatives in a double poetic vision, the instinctive one of innocence and the experienced one of adult knowledge.

Linked to the generation of 1927 we have a series of poets such as Miguel Hernández, who fused the popular and the cultural in agonized, sensual, tormented love poetry preoccupied with death and the telluric. Among the members of the 1936 generation Luis Rosales discussed God, nature, youth, and family as he and others substituted the delicate phrases of the classic Garcilaso for the baroque and existential, creating somewhat repetitive and monotonous poetry. Blas de Otero, however, wrote of human solidarity, peace, and social justice. Of poets born shortly after 1920, José Hierro composed documentary and existential, hallucinatory poetry, rejecting isolated beauty but emphasizing love and tenderness, death and solitude. Carlos Bousoño wrote of life and death, hope and despair, going from the emotive to the intellectual. Among younger poets, José Angel Valente produced precise, intellectual poetry, seeing life as an adventure on the solitary road to death. Claudio Rodríguez, rejecting the social poetry of man and his problems so prevalent after the Second World War, and impressed by the joy and beauty of life, sought metaphysical truth and new visions of art, nature, and man in his discussion of the inanimate and the human.

The twentieth century witnessed the production of a number of plays, including some by that great novelist, Benito Pérez Galdós; by dramatists like Manuel Linares Rivas, a Catholic who worried about intransigence; by the Alvarez Quintero brothers who for three decades wrote pleasant prose dramas; by Eduardo Marquina, poetic, lyrical but possessing great epic force; by Gregorio Martínez Sierra, who wrote idealistic exaltations glorifying the maternal instinct, faith, and tenderness; by Miguel de Unamuno, who wrote skeletal drams about struggle and doubt; and by Valle-Inclán, who emphasized the ridiculous and grotesque in modern life. One must give a special place to Jacinto Benavente, author of ingenious, elegant dramas, at times empathic in spite of Benavente's general pessimism. He helped to refine the previously rhetorical expressions so common to Spanish drama of the nineteenth century. One may also mention Jacinto Grau, who wrote existential dramas involving spiritual and carnal human love; Enrique Jardiel Poncela and Miguel Mihura, comic and bizarre writers who exposed the hypocrisy of society; Alejandro Casona, a formidable playwright who combined reality and fantasy; and, of course, Federico García Lorca, who wrote poetic tragedies of elemental passions, blood, and death as well as experimental, surrealistic ones.

Among living contemporaries, Antonio Buero Vallejo (1916-) and his sometime antagonist Alfonso Sastre (1926-), are undoubtedly the best. Buero, who spent time in a Franco jail, has written historical dramas, various works evincing his special interest in blindness such as El concierto de San Ovidio (1962), and other dramas involving the interplay of light and darkness, fantasy and reality, human guilt and human values. Undoubtedly his Historia de una escalera (1950) marked the sharp change from previous sentimental dramatic expressions. Buero believes in witnessing the injustices of the world and recording them, as did playwrights who had been on the other side of the Spanish conflict like Joaquín Calvo Sotelo, a supporter of a

Catholic position, forgiving, although somewhat moralizing. But the great antagonist of Buero, insofar as theory and practice were concerned, was Alfonso Sastre. Sastre's dramatic voice declined in the 1970's, but Buero continued to produce significant works, overshadowing not only Sastre but younger writers like Carlos Muñiz.

Buero, essentially an existentialist, albeit an optimistic one, writes open-ended plays, but illusion and escape usually cede to practical possibilities without thereby ignoring the spiritual and political dilemmas of contemporary man. Buero nonetheless seeks to sublimate, to improve, rather than to relieve. He denies that doubt can lead to absolute despair but admits that faith can never be so certain as to leave no room for tragedy. Buero's defense of tragic hope stems from his desire for a better world as well as from his preoccupation with man's social and metaphysical fate. He believes that social works should promote catharsis but not at the expense of aesthetic concerns, for the ethical and the aesthetic should serve to reinforce one another. Social thought with no acceptance is useless, and during the Franco years Buero, acknowledging the impossibility of absolute freedom in writing, contented himself, unlike Sastre, more revolutionary and by Buero's standards less effective, with a philosophy of hope and the politics of the possible.

Twentieth century Spanish American fiction inherited, from the Modernist and Naturalist movements, aesthetic and poetic concerns combined with fatalistic elements involving man in a struggle with nature and with the injustices committed against his fellowman. Criollista novelists like Rómulo Gallegos in Doña Bárbara utilized modern stylistic techniques of various kinds. Ricardo Güiraldes presented in Don Segundo Sombra the beauty, color, and movement of the Argentine plains and man as part of cosmic forces. Other criollistas documented the struggle of man against cosmic forces, social tragedy, and the search for justice. In the 1930's and 1940's one nonetheless encounters brilliant technical, lyrical, and imaginative works like El Señor Presidente by Miguel Angel Asturias who utilized chiaroscuro, temporal experimentation, and imagery to convey the fear and repulsion, degradation and dehumanization, and the loss of human values involved in living under a dictatorship. Asturias' depiction of homosexuals, beggars, disease, and degeneracy combined with metaphoric experimentation, neologisms, and word-play serve as a bridge to contemporary fiction as does the brilliant novel of Juan Carlos Onetti, El pozo (1939) which many view as the first modern Spanish American novel because of its interplay of dream and reality, and in its creation of a continuing and profound sense of alienation.

Surprising social and aesthetic productions, given the size of the country, appeared in Cuba. From the beginning Cuban authors indulged in an anguished search for their roots and a definition of lo cubano. During the first four decades of the century, deploring the hypocrisy and evil they saw in their society, they portrayed the interplay of sincere with absurd values, the meaning of evil, and the potential for spiritual metamorphosis. Through an examination of Cuban deficiencies they hoped to be able to remedy them. They also oscillated between sympathy and repugnance, between the alienation from and yet adherence to an historic cultural matrix. Many of these authors constantly reinforced their need for symbol and message, since a political path to happiness seemed unattainable. Thus novelists like Carlos Loveira, José Antonio Ramos, Luis Felipe Rodríguez and Enrique Serpa portrayed the proletariat's anguish and aspirations, painting at the same time the problematic character of Cuban destiny.

Even the more aesthetic supposedly non-revolutionary contemporary novels of José Lezama Lima, Alejo Carpentier, and Severo Sarduy evoke symbols from the past; they seem unable to escape Cuban history or tradition and continue political-historical symbolism. In El reino de este mundo (1949) Carpentier insists that man has to impose tasks on himself to seek self-betterment for himself and suffering humanity. Lezama Lima, whatever his Taoism and baroque imagery, combines in Paradiso (1966) Afro-Cuban with metaphorical visions; Severo Sarduy in De donde son los cantantes (1967) creates a unique sense of history, contrasting Fidel Castro and Christ, Columbus and colonialism, and in this and other novels emphasizes symbolic transformations involving religion, politics, and sex to discover what it means to be Cuban and to solve the problem of finding happiness and salvation for a people apparently without them. And if Guillermo Cabrera Infante, in his recreation of prerevolutionary, bohemian Cuba in Tres tristes tigres (1967), reorients, destroys, and recreates language, he indulges also in mythic creation to create archetypes as does Carpentier in his vision of primitive America as Utopia. Carpentier's geographical, temporal, mythical transformations of the environment and poetic evocations of America join him to Gabriel García Márquez, Miguel Angel Asturias, and others as a master of magic realism. And, if reviews of the Grupo Minorista and later Avance were active in cultural reform, the same can be said of even later magazines and groups like Orígenes, Verbum, and Ciclón, which faced a special block in dealing with censorship and the relationship between political and revolutionary idealism and literary creativity and criticism.

Although, as we have seen, many of the earlier novels through prophetic vision, lyricism, or technical experimentation related closely to modern development, the 1960's produced an explosion of Latin American masterpieces. Contemporary novelists sought a new sensibility in a disintegrating society which they reflected through a destruction of novelistic chronology. They used subconscious symbols, multiplicity of planes, interior monologues, free association, counterpoint, simultaneous narration, gamesmanship, and temporal experimentation, combining existentialist despair with magic realism, dreams, nightmares, and metaphysics. In their view of reality as multi-dimensional, they fused the normal and the abnormal. For the most part their personal interpretations proved to be pessimistic visions of a disintegrating world where myth and magic, reality and fantasy, social and sexual problems seemed almost interchangeable in the face of cosmic absurdities. Part of the experimentation involved not only the relationship of the real and the fantastic but the creation of a new language to interpret these new realities. At times this linguistic revolution implied more than an escape from Nativism and promoted new ideologies. But many neo-realistic works, however new, could not shake free from the old themes of pathology, sexual preoccupations, and dictatorship, though these themes often appeared as part of a framework involving a disintegrating world filled with alienated beings. Many novelists who had previously published fine works in the 1940's, Eduardo Mallea and Agustín Yáñez among others, or in the 1950's, Juan Carlos Onetti, Alejo Carpentier, and Gabriel García Márquez (Juan Rulfo proved to be an exception) produced masterpieces in the 1960's and beyond.

Alejo Carpentier's El siglo de las luces (1962), using the French Revolution as a point of departure, portrays a warm, sensual, magic world in transformation. Carpentier continued to write fine novels in the 1970's, for example, La consagración de la primavera (1978). Juan Carlos Onetti wrote El astillero (1961) and Juntacadáveres (1964) about the absurd life of a frustrated protagonist, as alienated as other characters who search in vain for love and meaning in an unattractive world. Gabriel García Márquez' Cien años de soledad (1967), set in his mythical microcosm, Macondo, traces a family through seven generations. Civil wars as well as natural disasters bring about an eventual decay even in this surrealistic world of dreams, sex, and death. A masterpiece of magic realism, the novel may be viewed as a metaphysical inquiry into the origin of mankind, its birth and death, as symbolized by the Buendía family. Márquez gives us an oneiric-realistic view of a Spanish American dictator in El otoño del patriarca (1975); in Crónica de una muerte anunciada (1981), he combines solitary beings, casualty and destiny, through a mixture of memory, myth, and psychology.

Two among many outstanding Argentine novelists, Ernesto Sábato and Julio Cortázar, wrote brilliant novels in the 1960's. Sábato's Sobre héroes y tumbas (1962) mixes past and present, history and metaphysics in an unhappy and solitary Argentine world which shows the futility of attempting to escape the historical burden of the past, both good and evil. Julio Cortázar's Rayuela (1963) overshadows other novels he wrote during the 1960's and 1970's. A brilliant compendium of burlesque, metaphysics, and linguistic experimentation, it concerns the fruitless existential quest, in an absurd world, for meaning. The protagonist, since life is absurd, seeks to create his own reality in order to reach the ultimate square of his hopscotch game, an ontological undertaking impossible of fulfillment. Cortázar's use of foreign languages, semantic and semiphonetic word plays, slogans, and parodies helps destroy the false reality of traditional language in a search for truth.

Carlos Fuentes, Mexico's greatest novelist, in La muerte de Artemio Cruz (1962) evokes the revolutionary process, an existential quest, and the death of idealism in a materialistic world where corruption pays practical rewards. Artemio is Mexico itself, a victim of a decision to follow false material gods. Fuentes wrote several other novels in the 1960's and continued into the 1970's and 1980's, but not even his magnificent Terra nostra (1975) could match his 1962 masterpiece.

Mario Vargas Llosa's novels demythologized Peruvian institutions, the military in La ciudad y los perros (1963), as he exposed the decadence of the middle class and the frustrations and misery of the poor; in La Casa Verde (1965), filled with five interweaving stories involving multiple points of view, he creates an illusion of simultaneous time through a masterful use of retrospective dialogues, dual narration, fusing two unrelated scenes into a single narrative unit, and stream of consciousness. He may be the leader of linguistic manipulation among contemporaries, as he contrasts primitive and civilized forces unable to communicate. In addition to other novels in the 1960's and 1970's (among them the unusual Pantaleón y las visitadoras, 1973, about providing whores for army units), Vargas Llosa, in 1981, produced what he calls his best novel, La guerra del fin del mundo, which abandons Peruvian settings.

José Donoso's El lugar sin límites (1966), though excellent, cannot match his masterpiece, El obsceno pájaro de la noche (1970), a combination of the erotic, mythic, and magical which reflects the decay and disintegration of the modern world, a world of nightmare visions which supports the author's ironic pessimism about man's destiny. Casa de campo (1978) and El jardín de al lado (1981) also emphasize his remarkable exploration of the conflict between interior and exterior reality.

In many of these novels the preoccupation with the erotic, the aberrant, and the sexual, an integral aspect of Spanish American fiction throughout the twentieth century, reflects the continuing influence of the Terrible Mother archetype in terms of ego birth, the dragon fight of the hero, and other elements in Spanish American fiction. Spanish American males seem unable to conquer the malevolent goddess with whom they constantly struggle. This, in part, explains the masculine attitude in a matriarchal society with regard to feminism, sexism, and the treatment of women in general, whatever the protestations of contemporary novelists about being liberated or progressive.

Finally, although Latin America has produced some brilliant Jewish writers, Albert Gerchunoff and José Chudnovsky of Argentina and Isaac Goldemberg of Peru; and although famous writers like Gabriela Mistral and Jorge Luis Borges, who admits the enormous influence of Jewish mysticism on his works, extolled the merits of the Jew in Latin American life; the old dichotomies inherited from Spain, Catholicism, and the Spanish Inquisition maintain their force in Latin America. Antisemitism, not a major leitmotif in Latin American literature, nonetheless, persists as part of the fabric of literary productions into the 1980's.

LEVIATAN

Leviatán, a socialist review subtitled "Revista Mensual de Hechos e Ideas," has been largely forgotten, but its political and literary pronouncements resemble closely those of some Spanish writers born in the 1930's when the journal was first published and may be of more than archeological concern to students of contemporary literature. The first number appeared on May 1, 1934, shortly after the socialist strike in Barcelona. It understandably ceased publication in July, 1936. Its director, Luis Araquistáin, was a novelist, dramatist, and political essayist who wrote extensively on the dangers of what he called United States imperialism. His collection of essays published posthumously, El pensamiento español contemporáneo, contains extensive material on Krausismo in Spain and bolsters his contention that Spain has always been the victim of executioners, both foreign and domestic. Araquistáin had been the director of the weekly journal, España, supposedly the progenitor of Leviatán, which he viewed as its continuation, and España also served as a fertilizing agent in the formation of El Sol, possibly Spain's leading paper. Araquistáin had also taken part in the writing of the Republican constitution.

The title, Leviathan, refers both to the Biblical monster and Hobbes' use of it as a symbol of the state. More specifically it was chosen to promote Engels' idea of the fusion of the concept of the proletariat with that of socialism. Supposedly dedicated to a pure interpretation of Marx and Engels, uncontaminated by later unorthodoxies, Leviatán deliberately eschewed literary matters to concentrate on politics, socialism, anarchism, labor unions, the economic situation of the world, life in Russia, the perils of European fascism, and agrarian reform. In spite of its announced goal of examination of civilization in the hope of contributing to a new world and giving space to writers "censored by the capitalistic world press," and its intention to concentrate on social injustice and government ineptitude, the journal included matters of literary concern to reveal a continuing interrelationship of political commitment and literary endeavor in the twentieth century. Among its contributors were John Strachey, Fernando de los Ríos, Ramón Sender, Jean Cassou, and Andrés Iduarte.

As a contemporary instrument the journal examined the philosophical bases of the Spanish Republic and its noble dream, the opposition of the Spanish middle class, allied with the Church, the military, and the monarchists, to social reform, and the possibility of incoporating the proletariat into the government. One can see clearly the forces tearing Spain apart, the germs of revolution already inherent in Seville and elsewhere (Araquistáin foretells as inevitable the battle to the death between the two ideologies), the in-fighting among various groups, the fleeting coalitions, the hardening of political lines, and the conflict between revolutionists and evolutionists.

Among the literary matters discussed in the journal are the essays of Ortega y Gasset, the Generation of 1898, the esperpentos of Valle-Inclán, the twentieth-century novel, and the then current theater. Indirect involvements show the impossibility in Spain of divorcing literature from social and political matters. Francisco Pina, the secretary of Leviatán and a friend of the poet, Miguel Hernández, introduced him to Ramón Sender who attempted to have Rafael Alberti publish Hernández' poetry in his journal, Octubre, a communist review. Alberti, for some reason, turned Hernández down, and the latter then established a satisfactory association with José Bergamín and his Cruz y Raya.[1]

Araquistáin takes exception to philosophical ideas expressed by Ortega y Gasset and contends that Ortega indulges in a monotonous reiteration of a limited number of ideas, one of the principal ones being that reason serves life and not life reason. He examines Ortega's brief flirtation with Republicanism and his even briefer one with socialism (for Ortega a new kind of aristocracy), a point of view he soon rejected (in 1914) in favor of capitalism. Ortega was fairly true to his own principles, but he promoted a perhaps unconscious hypocrisy in his sterile prophecy of the revolt of the masses, in reality "anhelo profundo de su espíritu."[2] In a continuation of his article (January, 1935), Araquistáin finds Ortega's work to be improvised and contradictory. He attempts to refute Ortega's contention that Bolshevism and Fascism are identical and typical movements of mass men directed by mediocre ones. Elsewhere he praises Ortega's recognition of Russia's revolution as "espléndido carácter de magnífica empresa." Araquistáin, himself carried away by his defense of Russia, insists that she will serve as a bulwark for Europe against the "yellow peril," an interesting observation in view of Russo-Chinese clashes in the 1960's.

F. Carmona Nenclores examines the Generation of 1898 and the dichotomy implicit in their original system of values and their activity as human beings. Nietzschean supermen and the rehispanicizing or Europeanizing of Spain seem remote in the 1930's, and members of the Generation of 1898 and their rebellion against their time have no meaning for the current (1930's) generation. Writers living in the 1960's and born about the time Leviatán was being published also evaluate the meaning of the Generation of 1898, and surprisingly their evaluations strongly resemble those forgotten ones in the socialist journal of 1935, understandably more personal (the members of the Generation of 1898 were still living) and emotional.

In the Leviatán articles Pío Baroja is evoked as a man of inhibitions and permanent resentments, an "egoísta químicamente puro y por eso se limita a encogerse de hombros ante los enigmas de la hora."[3] The then opposition to Baroja may appear strange in view of his sympathy for enemies of the status quo, but he rejected social reform as a solution to human problems, and his later anti-Semitic overtures under Nazi pressures reflect the accuracy of the 1935 analysis. Fear and feelings of impotence determine his character, and he belongs more clearly to the nineteenth than to the twentieth century. Unamuno, also narcissistic, seeks desperately through his contradictions and paradoxes to straddle ideological fences. Maeztu, whom some regard as having changed his viewpoint, was always a terrorist. When he was an anarchist "su terrorismo era rojo: bombas y atentados personales; ahora amenaza con el fuego del infierno. Pero lo permanente y esencial es el terrorismo."[4] In any event his Christianity is but a pose, for his hatred of man and human beings must represent the very opposite of the Christian message. As for Azorín, he has always been a spectator, unmoved by events. His ethos seems to involve a pure intellectualism which is comparable to "un estado de castración pura."[5] Almost inhuman or non-human, he represents but the shadow of a man who exists in reality only through the elements of pen and ink. With the exception of Azorín, the others are blinded by history and unable to view the contemporary world. They are frozen into a static equation (literatura-individuo-masturbación), and, as comfortable rebels, belong to the past with absolutely no relevance or ties to current writers.

In the 1960's Luis Cernuda, Juan Goytisolo, and others have attempted to put into perspective critical judgments about the Generation of 1898, and they marvel at the unanimity of praise for its members by the Establishment into the decade of the 1960's. For them the writers of 1898 are sterile representatives of the repressive weight of outmoded tradition. With the vacuum created by the Spanish Civil War and the loss of almost an entire literary generation, Unamuno and others were resurrected to give some continuity to Spanish culture which civil war and other events had irrevocably mutilated. By 1955, however, with the arrival of the so-called "generación del medio siglo," criticisms of the Generation of 1898 by young writers were considered sacrilege, an inescapable irony when one considers the response members of the Generation of 1898 had elicited with their own attacks on the then status quo. In the 1960's Unamuno, Azorín, Pío Baroja, and their friends were encased like classic museum pieces, indeed, enshrined, and acceptance of their writings and their values became almost a theological question of faith. Critics became cult members and, instead of serving as bridge to the future, the Generation of 1898 had become a wall against it. Spain, currently a neocapitalistic nation, differs from the world known by Unamuno, and so his literary work can not serve in the current culture. Each generation must be prepared to make its own errors and avoid the crutch of a doubtful respectability by not aspiring to the officially exalted positions of the literary inquisitors and theologians.[6]

Valle-Inclán, on the other hand, elicited the continuing admiration of Leviatán writers. After his early sensual skepticism and almost exclusive esthetic preoccupation, he gradually came to see Spain as a deformation of Europe in two dimensions (tragedy and caricature). He viewed Spain itself as an esperpento, the product of a mirror deformed by internal pressures. Spain, for him, was a grotesque victim of ignorance, hunger, and Catholicism. Valle-Inclán thus represents a long line of Spanish writers with such special vision, beginning with Juan Ruiz. Unlike the members of the Generation of '98 who became trapped in a senile bourgeois farce, he was constantly rejuvenated. His esperpentos offer "una visión de tipo revolucionario. En una palabra anti-clasista."[7] Far from being socially ineffective and impotent to face the future, Valle-Inclán died with his faith in the proletariat and its creative potential intact.

Ramón Sender contributed two articles, one on the novel and one on the theater. He examines briefly the outworn metaphysics and middle class values of a whole generation of novelists in the first third of the twentieth century, their lack of vital spirit, and their presentation of conflicts based on artificial problems. For Sender, at that moment in time, the vital principle of literature involved creation in common and the representation of collective aspirations through social literature. He believed that the disinterest of the proletariat represented the only guarantee for man's future. Great Spanish writers had always been the product of revolutionary currents which helped create new tensions in man. This vital principle (a property of the proletariat) must be isolated as a basis for one's work, controlled only by the novelist's critical sense. Psychology and technique may play a role, but great art is beyond formula or school, and preoccupation with mysticism or spiritual manifestations does nothing for human progress. Sender sees the difference between bourgeois reality and the socialist one as a conflict between viewing it ideally or dialectically. One should not seek answers in utopian literature nor in surrealism with its torturous path extending from pure instinct to spirit. From this wedding of the subconscious and the spirit was born the religious art of the Middle Ages, itself an evasion of responsibility. A true novelist will be satisfied with what Sender terms "percepción ganglionar y la razón."[8] His identification with the masses will be achieved, not through his head, but through the ganglion. By becoming a part of the mass one may, through it, translate its essence into words.

With some exceptions, even into the 1960's, the Spanish novel is rooted in social realism, and novelists, like Juan Goytisolo, whatever their techniques or aesthetic preoccupations, continue to conceive of the novelist's mission as a predominantly, perhaps exclusively, human one. Sender has always been interested in social problems, a theme which runs through most of his novels as does his passion for social justice, although he later took a more objective view about the nobility of the proletariat as opposed to the ignobleness of the bourgeoisie. He has always maintained a highly subjective but provocative view of Unamuno and Pío Baroja. Shortly after his contributions to Leviatán, he became completely disillusioned by the communists and abandoned his peripheral if for a time serious acceptance of their ideology. A revolutionary, Sender was an individualist with a strong mind of his own and a moral sense transcending specific ideology.

In his article on the theater Sender stresses that the social worth of the contents is all-important. He urges the creation of a drama relevant to the contemporary scene and attributes the decadence of the theater to the stupid themes written almost exclusively for the middle class and artificially sprinkled with comic situations and outmoded naturalism. Arniches, the Alvarez Quintero brothers, and Pedro Muñoz Seca serve only to distract the audience from problems of social unrest, the destruction of old moral values, and the class struggle, an anesthesia and obfuscation willingly endured. The only real theater of the 1930's lies in the conscious reconstruction of life through art, but without formulas. The best hope for a new theater lies with Casona in works like Nuestra Natacha, but, says Sender, Lorca may abandon, eventually, his popular-cultural fusion and "se incorporará impetuosamente a esa misma corriente."[9]

Although Leviatán had little direct effect on future literary development and although most of its political ideas reflect an unfortunately monolithic confrontation between two philosophies of life, for Spaniards it still has an important historical relevance. In reflecting the eternal dichotomy which has always afflicted Spain, the journal reveals an absence of the tender, the delicate, and the moderate, more than matched by the savage fascist writings of the time. It shows an intransigence which the vicissitudes of history have not softened, but unlike fascist journals Leviatán shows a continuing concern for human beings. Apparently the past thirty-four years have not really changed anything essential about Spain, and an examination of these cultural themes of the 1930's may enable us to look at contemporary ones in a new way.

Notes

[1] See Marcelino C. Peñuelas, Conversaciones con Ramón J. Sender (Madrid, 1970), p. 193.

[2] Luis Araquistáin, "José Ortega y Gasset: Profeta del fracaso de las masas," Leviatán (December, 1934), 22.

[3] F. Carmona Nenclores, "La generación del '98 y nuestro momento histórico," Leviatán (March, 1935), 12.

[4] Ibid., p. 13.

[5] Ibid., p. 14.

[6] Juan Goytisolo, El furgón de cola (Paris, 1967), pp. 78-84.

[7] F. Carmona Nenclores, "Genealogía de los esperpentos de Valle-Inclán," Leviatán (February, 1936), 58.

[8] Ramón Sender, "El novelista y las masas," Leviatán (May, 1936), 40.

[9] Ramón Sender, "El teatro nuevo," Leviatán (June, 1936), 51.

MADRID AND SPANISH LITERATURE

The general feeling among Spanish scholars seems to be that little of literary value was produced during the Spanish Civil War. Yet a number of reviews such as Hora de España, of two years duration, and ephemeral ones such as Madrid, published twice (February and May, 1937) in Valencia show that while the terrible war years had affected they had not desiccated either the creativity or the idealism of Spanish intellectuals. Madrid was the journal of the members of the Casa de la Cultura of Valencia, supported by the Ministry of Public Instruction and Fine Arts. They chose the title Madrid because they felt "Madrid es lo que nos une a todos. Si de Madrid arranca nuestra labor, a ella y en homenaje a ella ha de ir dirigidos todos los trabajos que aquí se publiquen."[1]

A rather unique journal, it might never have had its variety of contributors and subject matter except for the war. The critics, musicians, poets, painters, psychiatrists, and professors who wrote for it presented a wide range of literary and scientific articles to show they believed in the free development and historical continuity of culture which, they felt, ". . . solo es compatible con la libre determinación política y social de los pueblos."[2] They wanted to contribute to the spiritual prestige of Spain, and, although they evinced a demotic ideology, they sought to maintain cultural values by balancing past and present and discovering the one in the other. In their representation of Spanish culture they saw not an escape into abstractions or Utopia but a defense of the intellectual and moral values of their society. More ironic than irate in their view of current events and history, they could not escape completely the effects of the conflict, reflected, at times, by a consuming nostalgia or moral passion, but their sensitivity enabled them to evaluate professionally, even in the midst of obviously painful and destructive events.

Not all the writers, of course, could be equally objective, Juan de la Encina claims that he abandoned his career as literary critic on the night of July 20, 1936, because he realized that for a long time to come, "nada tenía ya que hacer en ese oficio y menester que venía cultivando con pasión, con espíritu de justicia y desinterés, durante un cuarto de siglo. Dio por periclitada su labor y por infecunda su siembra. Sin embargo, todo esto, con ser mucho para su vida particular, le pareció nonada, bagatela, insignificancia sin remisión, cosa en fin despreciable, ante el dolor que en aquella hora presentía para su patria." Only through the mirror of truth which the painter, Arturo Souto, held up to him could he return, if only for an instant, "a un oficio y a una acción que tenía por desuso casi olvidados."[3] In another article Encina evokes a Valencian bridge from which, after descriptions of water, sky, and countryside, he makes excursions into history and time. Caliban, the brute force of the earth, the first born of History, evolved not through literature but through blood; yet, perhaps, if Prospero lives, he may make Caliban offer more than sorrow and pain.[4] Only one other article deals with the Civil War. In "Tres evocaciones de Madrid," Angel Ossorio y Gallardo recalls Madrid in 1933, 1936 and 1937.

The contributors treat a wide range of scientific subjects, among them chemical compounds, electrical conductivity, binocular vision, gases, and vitamins. The authors defended Spanish science, as Padre del Río Hortega elaborates in his analaysis of the spiritual and scientific values of Spanish culture, for "Los cien millones de españoles e hispanoamericanos debemos aspirar a que nuestra literatura científica nos enorgullezca o, a lo menos, no nos sonroje."[5] The nonscientific writers include José Bergamín, who writes on Rousseau; Pedro Sanjuán, a musician; Ricardo de Orueta, who studies Visigothic sculpture; and José Moreno Villa, who deals with palace paintings in the Golden Age.

Four poets contributed literary articles. León Felipe attempts to define poetry in "Poesía integral," part of a course he once gave at the University of Panama and never before published. He feels that Spanish poetry may be viewed in a "línea paralela y congruente con la Historia y política de España."[6] The poet of the future will differ from present ones whose poetry is only "un sistema luminoso de señales, hogueras que encendemos aquí abajo, entre tinieblas encontradas para que alguien nos vea, para que no nos olviden . . . Poeta, para mí, es aquel hombre que tiene la virtud o la gracia de saltar rápidamente, en un momento determinado, de lo doméstico a lo épico, de lo euclidiano a lo místico, de lo contingente a lo esencial, de lo temporal a lo eterno, de lo sórdido a lo limpiamente ético."[7] He labels poetry, not by schools (for him the principal error in the study of literary history is the view that poets are anchored and unmoveable islands without continuity), but as aristrocratic, popular, or integral. Aristocratic poetry, the poetry of minorities and largely of foreign origin, is erudite, hermetic and novel. Popular poetry is national, communal, clear, simple, human and realistic. León Felipe finds in certain episodes in Don Quijote a key to the Spanish character, "los caminos bifurcados del poeta y del pueblo, de la épica y de la Historia."[8] The highest poetry, "poesía integral," is that by a known author who adapts the traditional efforts of his predecessors. An integral poet attempts to clarify and communicate a universal message to all mankind. Jorge Manrique is such a poet in his Coplas, a general integration of disarticulated and diverse elements, which represents the final triumph of a series of traditional efforts. A real poet destroys both time and space by overcoming the barriers imposed on him by historical man, but in the final analysis even the poet cannot explain his work: "Un poema no se explica nunca. Un poema se explica él mismo y explica muchas cosas. No hay que tener una llave para abrir un poema. Un poema debe ser una llave, el mismo que abra algo que estaba cerrado u olvidado en un mundo."[9] Life, as poetry reveals, is a consequential process, not "a tale told by an idiot full of sound and fury," and the poet, therefore reflects optimistic idealism at the possibility of a morally, socially, and intellectually free society.

Antonio Machado attempts to interpret Spain as more than history and tradition. Man carries history within himself, both the knowledge of the past and the hope and fear of the future, but his most essential characteristic is mortality, which only a true person can face. Machado praised Unamuno, "el que menos habló de resignarse a ella [death]. Tal fué la nota antisenequista original y españolisima, no obstante de este incansable poeta de la angustia española."[10] He views Unamuno as a precursor of European existentialism.

Juan José Domenchina, yet another poet, cites the importance of distinguishing the characteristics of Valle-Inclán from his characterizations. He refutes Valle-Inclán's reputation for virulence, condemnation and "terrible absolutes," finding his statements lacking in "intención dañosa, tal vez constituyese. . .unos generosos escapes de la generosidad valleinclanesca, que tendía a enaltecer, paradójicamente, monstruosamente la insignificancia o la pobre significación de sus prójimos."[11] The creator of the esperpento, which consists of contradictions, Valle-Inclán in his attacks carries no conviction, refusing to accept anything seriously. Rather than slander he offers a special kind of heroic, inoffensive truth: "Don Ramón jamás se propuso ofender o denigrar con sus barrocas y espléndidas calumnias. Por el contrario, el designio que le movía. . . era un designio de altura: Magnificar con hipérboles de sevicia, con graciosas y generosas atribuciones de perversidad--en las que nadie, y el menos que nadie, podía creer--la insignificancia de sus semejantes."[12]

José Moreno Villa finds, in the buffoon and the palace fool, the mysteriously simple and monstrous aspects of nature which have always attracted mankind. Golden Age dramatists included these "locos de Palacio" in their works, but we do not know what they were really like and how they talked. Only through the theater, whose gracioso tried to make Spaniards laugh, can we glimpse this aspect of courtly life. Dwarfs do not appear in the dramas, probably because appropriately realistic actors were unavailable. Moreno Villa feels certain that Lope de Vega would have loved to have them in his plays, for in a theater like his, ". . . animado y coloro, esencialmente pintoresco, los enanos hubieran puesto su nota de contraste, tan esencial para las grandes figuras como la del gracioso u hombre de placer."[13] He wonders whether Cervantes was not influenced by the court jesters in portraying Don Quijote as a loco and Sancho Panza as a kind of dwarf.

Elsewhere Moreno Villa recalls Lorca, his "alegrías y perfumes," his fabulous stories, and his folklore. He sees him as "un manojo de cintas de colores, pero también una honda guitarra y un chato de manzanilla."[14]

Tomás Navarro Tomás examines the literary relationships involved in the intonation and physiognomic aspects of the voice. An emotional tone may convey understanding without meaningful words. In La hermana San Sulpicio, Puig's companions were unable to understand him, but "'Solo por la entonación y por las furiosas miradas que alguna vez nos dirigía, sabíamos que nos estaba poniendo como trapos.'" In La ruta de don Quijote Juana María's voice, rising above the crowd, elicits "'Quién tiene esta entonación tan dulce, tan suave, tan acariciadora . . .'" In El tablado de Arlequín, Pío Baroja's sick man cannot move his audience because he cannot find "'la inflexión de voz propia del momento.'"[15] The voice tone often reveals the true emotional state which words seek to hide or, on the other hand, helps feign what one does not feel, common techniques among the picaresque heroes of the Golden Age. At times the intonation itself diguises the emotion (firmness and calmness during an emotional scene or irritation hidden beneath soft words), a technique employed by Padre Coloma, Palacio Valdés, Juan Valera, Valle-Inclán, and especially Blasco Ibáñez. Among older writers Cervantes evinced great interest in voice properties, seeking to specify the exact emotional degree with expressions such as, "'voz turbada o alterada,' 'voz turbada y temerosa,' or 'voz turbada y lengua presurosa.'"[16] One must admit, nevertheless, that, in the broad panorama of Spanish literature, allusions to voice intonation are comparatively rare.

Physiognomic values are more commonly employed by Spanish authors. Belarmino tries to hear the voice of his beloved Angustias among the chorus of those at the convent, "'. . . hacía esfuerzos por desenredar la voz azul de Angustias de entre la madeja policroma del coro.'" The voice represents personality, as blind men in Pedro de Urdemalas by Cervantes and in Flor de Santidad by Valle-Inclán testify. Navarro Tomás examines briefly the relationship of man and animal voices in literature, citing Quijote's recognition of Sancho through the braying of his ass, "'Famoso testigo . . . el rebuzno conozco como si lo pariera, y tu voz oigo, Sancho amigo,'"[17] Although other Golden Age writers like Céspedes y Meneses, Lope de Vega, Vélez de Guevara and Tirso de Molina adjectivally described voices as "soft" or "sweet," only Cervantes recognized the full measure of importance of voice quality in its real and human aspects and for the development of literary action. Modern writers more easily understand the evocative power of the voice, especially Azorín, Pérez de Ayala, and Valle-Inclán.

The Civil War intellectuals of Madrid avoided manifestoes. Elsewhere they repudiated the to them repugnant beliefs of the Fascists, but neither antipathy toward Franco nor justification or vindication of the Republican political position played a significant part in Madrid, in spite of its government subsidy. Without turbulence or tragic pose, vanity or naiveté regarding their importance in the scheme of things as exclusive defenders of Culture, they continued their scholarly activities, certain of the necessity of cultural continuity as the beginning of wisdom for man in his hope for a free society where human aspiration need not be defeated.

Notes

[1] *Madrid* (February, 1937), preface.

[2] *Madrid* (May, 1937), preface.

[3] Juan de la Encina, "Arturo Souto o la vocación" (May, 1937). p. 156.

[4] Juan de la Encina, "En el puente de la Trinidad" (February 1937), pp. 143-148.

[5] Padre del Río Hortega, "La ciencia y el idioma" (February, 1937), p. 68.

[6] León Felipe, "Poesía integral" (February, 1937), p. 119, fn. 1.

[7] Ibid., p. 119.

[8] Ibid., p. 122.

[9] Ibid., p. 125.

[10] Antonio Machado, "Notas de actualidad" (February, 1937), p. 10.

[11] Juan José Domenchina, "Genio y paradoja de D. Ramón del Valle-Inclán" (February, 1937), p. 59.

[12] Ibid., p. 60.

[13] José Moreno Villa, "Locos, enanos y negros en la Corte de los Austrias" (February 1937), p. 117.

[14] José Moreno Villa, "Recuerdo a Federico García Lorca" (February, 1937), p. 149.

[15] Tomás Navarro Tomás, "Citas literarias sobre entonación emocional" (February, 1937), pp. 26-27.

[16] Ibid., p. 31.

[17] Tomás Navarro Tomás, "Datos literarios sobre el valor fisionómico de la voz" (May, 1937), p. 128.

LITERARY CRITICISM AND THE SPANISH CIVIL WAR

From January 1937 though October 1938, many of the outstanding intellectuals on the Republican side contributed essays, poetry, fiction, and drama to Hora de España, a journal first published in Valencia and then in Barcelona. The editors were Manuel Altolaguirre, Rafael Dieste, Antonio Sánchez Barbudo, and J. Gil-Albert. Later, María Zambrano, José María Quiroga Pla, Emilio Prados, and Rafael Alberti joined the original editorial board. Contributing collaborators of the journal included León Felipe, José Moreno Villa, Antonio Machado, José Bergamín, Rafael Alberti, José F. Montesinos, and Dámaso Alonso, all of whom wished to prove to the outside world that "España prosigue su vida intelectual o de creación artística en medio del conflicto gigantesco en que se debate."[1]

As was to be expected, the journal contained many propaganda pieces, political documents and journalistic descriptions of the war, fascist terror, and the suffering of the pueblo which the intellectuals viewed as their progenitor. They attacked the Catholic Church, extolled the merits of the "Cause" and the "boys" in the trenches; but they also produced some perceptive and informational essays on literature from the Middle Ages on as well as original works of occasional merit. Poets like Emilio Prados and Miguel Hernández hoped to express in their literary works the same human values which workers and warriors affirmed with their sacrifice, but they, along with the other writers, rejected propaganda as well as the concept of art for art's sake because "efectivamente somos humanistas pero del humanismo éste que se produce en España hoy" (August 1937, 84-92).

Antonio Machado (August 1936, 11-14), José Bergamín, and Antonio Sánchez Barbudo, in stressing the ties of the intellectual to the people, deny that they are writing propaganda. Bergamín, denigrating intellectual personalism, considers the writer's basic concern to be "la de su comunicación o comunión humana" (August 1937, 33); Antonio Sánchez Barbudo, through an understanding of surrealism ("la patada en la calma, el deseo inoportuno, la transformación sorprendente . . . lo irracional, lo que está más allá de la previsión lógica; lo ilógico . . . rompe las cadenas de la mentira y hace ostentoso el hastío"), in its relationship to left wing political movements (January 1937, 46), arrives at a definition of social realism which involves not only literary renovation but also that of society, "porque para nosotros arte o literatura es verdad, poesía, drama y no juego; es hombre, libertad" (July 1937, 74-75). He concludes that the Spaniard's hope for a better world, reflected in the Civil War, began with the psychological and philosophical travail of great writers who showed symptoms of political concern (June 1938, 68). Hopefully, the present may presage a future spiritual unity of Spain's double vision of the real and the ideal, of literary phenomena and political desires. Juan Gil-Albert rejects realistic art in the hope of a "tension total que convierte la realidad en epopeya" (February 1937, 35); and Ramón Gaya rejects both collective art and deshumanización, insisting that the true writer needs humanity, tenderness, and kindness (June 1938, 25-26).

Creative contributions include poetry by foreign writers like Stephen Spender and Spanish works by Antonio Machado, León Felipe, Miguel Hernández and most of the other well known poets. The romances, sonnets, and elegies treat of religion, the war, love for a ravaged Spain, a remembrance of things past, a search for one's poetic soul, the need, in the reality of the moment, to choose heroism over happiness, and other aspects of human suffering, passion, and joy. The theatrical contributions, some of dubious distinction in their propagandistic fervor, include Rafael Dieste's Nuevo retablo de las maravillas, a parody of Cervantes' famous work. Here only those "que no estén tocados de marxismo, sindicalismo, anarquismo y demás plagas," can see the traveling troupe's performance (January 1937, 71). Among other dramas are a fragment of García Lorca's Así que pasen cinco años (November 1937) and Max Aub's auto, Pedro López García, full of dream dialogue and symbolic appearances. Fiction contributors are Benjamín Jarnés, Juan José Domenchina, Juan de la Cabada, Enrique Diez Canedo, Lino Novás Calvo, Ernestina de Champourcin, and Antonio Sánchez Barbudo.

Among critical essays on foreign literature are those of Manuel Valldeperes who discusses the decadent aspects of Catalan theater after the deaths of Guimerá and Rusiñol (July 1938); José María Capdevila, who analyzes the work of Joaquín Ruyra, Catalan novelist and poet (September 1938); Nicolás Guillén, who writes on Cuban literature (November 1937); and Andrés Iduarte, who studies César Vallejo, his heroic death, and his works (August 1938).

Philosophical, cultural, and sociological articles alternate with the more purely literary ones. Joaquín Xirau examines various philosophical interpretations of reality (October 1938); Julián Marías discusses the problem of God in modern metaphysics (October 1938), the nature of citizenship, the role of the stoic, the rise of internationalism, and totalitarian states (December 1937, 47). Rosa Chacel warns of a pseudo culture which may dissipate itself in historical interpretations instead of facing living reality (January 1937, 14); finally, José Bergamín attacks the Spanish clergy and excoriates the Church for their support of and "inmoral convivencia" with the Spanish fascists (January 1937, 27).

Hora de España gives us an insight into the thoughts, hopes and daily despairs of the war years, and the culture of a time, whatever its merits, which in one way or another has continued to determine almost all contemporary Spanish literature. The writers themselves also sought their cultural roots in older literary periods. Antonio Porrás writes on the Arcipreste de Hita (April 1938) and on the Caballero del Verde Gabán (July, 1938); Dámaso Alonso discusses social injustice in Spanish literature from Juan Ruiz on (February 1937); Máximo José Kahn details the contributions of Spanish Jews to the language and literature of Spain (March, April 1937, and May 1938); Rafael Dieste (February, 1937) and Max Aub (May 1937) write on Cervantes; Juan González del Valle analyzes Golden Age realism (March, 1938). José Bergamín (November 1937) and Antonio Machado (December, 1937) write on Mariano José de Larra; Ernestina de Champourcin on Rosalía de Castro (February 1938); Manuel Altolaguirre on Armando Palacio Valdés (February, 1938); and Rosa Chacel (February 1937) and María Zambrano (September 1937 and 1938) on Benito Pérez Galdós.

The critics were not overly confident about the value of their contributions. Antonio Machado, stressing the validity of kindly criticism in analyzing creative works (October 1938, 13), explains the lack of literary evaluation of major cultural contributions: "se explica por la casi inexistencia de una crítica española, y se disculparía, si esta crítica existiera, por las circunstancias de nuestra vida actual, sobradamente angustiosas" (September 1938, 5). Yet, as one reads the literary essays of Hora de España, one sees that Machado's own generation evokes much critical comment in its anguish which resembles that of the Civil War, "un grito de una razón de dentro" (February 1937, 51), in spite of María Zambrano's accusation that the Generation of '98 confused the ghost of history with history itself. The traditionalists and intellectuals identified themselves with Spain: "caso típico D. Miguel de Unamuno; creía que él era España y por eso no temía equivocarse ni creyó que tendría que dar cuentas a nadie" (April 1937, 26-27).

Miguel de Unamuno receives most of the critical attention. The editors consider him to be a man "a quien todos hemos amado y combatido . . . El, como nadie, se habrá llevado a la tumba el frío de una España triste, poseída por mercenarios" (January 1937, 33). Several writers discuss Unamuno's apparently ambivalent political attitudes. José María Quiroga Pla venerates his memory and insists he will always be remembered as "hombre y poeta de España" (March 1938, 24). Antonio Machado also rejects completely the contention that Unamuno betrayed the Spanish people, stating, "No lo he creído nunca ni lo creeré jamás" (April 1937, 9). José F. Montesinos agrees with Machado and considers absurd the notion that Unamuno's work "podría oírse jamás, con coherencia verdadera, en boca de fascistas--de los fascistas que tanto odió Unamuno hasta el día de su muerte . . . su obra perdurable se revolverá siempre contra esa grotesca intentona seudo-fascista que no aspira sino a una segunda Restauración" (April 1937, 20). Montesinos, nevertheless, acknowledges that Unamuno will be a polemical topic for generations to come because his literary contradictions are apparent from his earliest writings, as he seeks to discover the Spanish soul and dreams of the resurgence of Spanish countries everywhere. More than any other Spaniard it was he "que más de propósito ha procurado suscitar discrepancias, y allá en los años de su juventud consiguió realmente apasionar con lo que llamaron sus paradojas y sus simbolismos--formando entre los dos últimos siglos, contradicción y hecha carne. Asiente y disiente, aboga por lo mismo que combate. Parece como si sintiera el halago de casi todo aquello que le repele, y que necesitara del antagonista para afirmarse a sí mismo" (April 1937, 14-17).

His work was understood in different ways, depending on the orientation of the critic. Rosa Chacel declares that Unamuno's philosophy was "fundamentalmente, por encima de toda opinión, anarquista" (July 1937, 14). Arturo Serrano Plaja points out, on the contrary, that Unamuno rejected excessive individualism: "ese mismo individualismo que se hace impositivo nos llevó al dogmatismo que nos corroe" (July 1937, 42). Antonio Machado views Unamuno as the precursor of contemporary existentialism in Europe: "coincidiendo con los últimos años de Unamuno, florece en Europa toda una metafísica existencialista, profundamente humana, que tiene a Unamuno, no solo entre sus adeptos, sino también--digámoslo sin rebozo--entre sus precursores" (April 1937, 8).

Montesinos, conceding the tragic and dramatic aspects of Unamuno's works, sees them, in their religious, ascetic, mystic and theological inclinations, as nineteenth rather than twentieth century productions. Unamuno's literature, as a moral force, became identified with the destiny of Spain itself, and the author shares "con los hombres del '98 esa preocupación española, pero difiere de ellos en la actitud. Por la actitud está más cerca de Ganivet que de Azorín o Baroja" (April 1937, 16-17). Although he was a traditionalist rather than a revolutionary, the questions Unamuno raised are basic to any political or social program intellectuals envisage for Spain's future. The Civil War may not change revolution into literature, but unless its authors strive for a moral and ethical integrity, like Unamuno's generation, they may fail. Above all they need "la valentía del pensamiento y la valentía de la generosidad (April 1937, 21).

Antonio Machado, a principal contributor to Hora de España, is himself analyzed by other critics. José Bergamín considers him to be the direct heir of Bécquer, Luis de León, San Juan de la Cruz, Lope de Vega, Jorge Manrique, and Juan Ruiz. As such he is the deep, pure voice of Castilian lyric poetry, "música cadenciosa y dilatada, sombría y clara como voz de agua; que es de mar o de lluvia, o de gotear en la piedra; de llanto y risa; de súplica, de rezo, de gozo; de amor y de nostalgia. Voz que dice el más puro y más hondo pensamiento, el que siente, el que canta. Voz de la sangre. Misiva de corazón y estrella. Callada voz de España" (September, 1938, 23). María Zambrano stresses Machado's love for the Spanish people. Combining reason, philosophical thought, a social conscience, and poetic knowledge of love and death, Machado ethically, morally, and poetically faces with the pueblo a shared battle and a common destiny (December 1937, 74).

Rafael Dieste comments on the hispanidad of Valle-Inclán as well as on his cult of the grotesque, the bizarre, the irrational, the terrible but penetrating view of reality he promotes. Valle-Inclán's puppets are not "clownescos . . . sino de caracterizadora y terrible inspiración española (May 1937, 31).

Post Generation of '98 figures also received critical attention. Rosa Chacel views Ortega y Gasset as "el primer maestro español que crea una escuela pulcra, coherente y tenaz; no ha podido pasarle lo que al gran Unamuno, que la sucesión de su obra excelsa se ha corrompido pronto en el discipulaje, minando por la impostura, y no ha podido sucederle porque recurriendo a la definición anterior, su verdad es luminosa y brutal" (April 1937, 48). Ortega's truth is reason, a living cult, and he tries to live reason and think life, fully aware that the mission of living is a final and principal consequence (April 1937, 49).

The critics in Hora de España consider poetry the genre which best expresses the human equation and the Republic. The Civil War reorients poets toward life and away from classic form and content. Returning to the world of man, his joys, sorrow, and pain, the new poets, intensely personal and yet social, blur distinctions between epic and lyric forms, renovate the romance, and revindicate its former social function by redefining man as part of that world (January 1937, 54-56). Romances are difficult to write in current times because crude truth is not a good source for the juglar. Painful, immediate events remove the grandeur and the heroic projection. Yet, states Benjamín Jarnés, the true voice of the people "son los romances que responden a una verdadera necesidad de cantar. No a la vanidad de cantar" (June 1938, 64).

León Felipe, objecting to dehumanized art for Spaniards experiencing a unique Civil War, feels that poets surviving the war will have a unique language not easily matched by those of other countries. Yet neither technique nor style is of central importance. A harbinger of hope and a transition poet, he stresses the human message: "mi voz aun no es nueva y mi lenguaje no es tampoco el que ha de venir. No soy más que la semilla de un poeta que apenas empieza a romper la costra primera de la tierra. Una promesa. Mañana, detrás de mí, detrás de nosotros, vendrá la palabra y la canción madura que todos estamos ayudando a florecer (February 1938, 31). He claims that critics of the past, preferring Celtic contributions (vagueness, melancholy, sentiment) criticized poets like Jorge Manrique for their lack of personal sadness. But in the Coplas form, theme, and sorrow, in forming an amalgam of history and poetry, do not disguise the intimate, painful rhythm which runs through the poem, although its tears are for all men. As literature progressed from the national to the universal, the Castilian used his very españolismo to escape to the human, the ecumenical, and the transcendent. Civil War poets, facing a bare reality, are involved in the same struggle for light which saved Juan Ramón Jiménez from becoming another melancholy Becquer. The struggle for land and the Civil War are to preserve the light of Castile, "empeños de lucha por la luz," which will remain to underline the poet's cry for justice, vengeance, and reconquest (June 1937, 20-22).

Among still other critics, María Zambrano contends that poetry is the most revolutionary genre, "al menos de determinado tipo de crisis históricas o revoluciones, pues ambos términos los tomamos aquí como equivalentes" (June 1938, 48); Luis Cernuda exclaims over the rapid appearance of new poets in all corners of Spain, denying that his generation is depersonalized, and stressing the immediate popularity of Lorca and Alberti. Many other poets became known through Gerardo Diego's 1932 anthology, and Manuel Altolaguirre and his wife, Concha Méndez, helped popularize the new poets in England where Altolaguirre edited a paper which included some of their poetry. When Alberti returned from Moscow, almost all his fellow poets published in his journal, Octubre, in 1933. Not only are these poets not dehumanized, but each is a revolutionary, "un revolucionario con plena conciencia de su responsabilidad. Rigor en su trabajo y disciplina en su actitud; esto aprendieron los actuales líricos españoles de sus maestros en poesía a través de los siglos" (June 1937, 65).

Of all the twentieth century poets Federico García Lorca receives the greatest attention. Pablo Neruda feels that Lorca best symbolizes those who have fallen in the defense of liberty because he was a victim of the "other" Spain, the traditional, dynastic, ecclesiatical Spain which saw him as a progressive, democratic, living spirit. Spaniards will continue to defend themselves with his songs, and he will remain forever in the minds of men. Since the time of Góngora and Lope nobody had as much creative force, so much mobility of form and language, nor such "seducción popular tan inmensa dirigida a un poeta" (March 1937, 70). Everything he touched, even the mysterious or the esthetic, was filled with sounds which reached the multitudes. He brought to poetry and drama the human and tempestuous without renouncing poetic mysteries. A magician, he carried happiness wherever he went. Neruda recalls an Extremaduran village at dawn. Federico, watching the sun rise in an abandoned feudal mansion, saw a little white lamb devoured by six or seven black pigs. Perhaps, says Neruda, this incident which impressed Lorca greatly was a forewarning that Lorca was to be the victim of a crime which Latin American poets can neither forget nor forgive: "No lo olvidaremos ni lo perdonaremos nunca. Nunca" (March 1937, 78).

Antonio Machado blames the citizens of Granada for Lorca's death, for they might easily have proved "a los verdugos del fascio, que Lorca era políticamente innocuo, y que el pueblo que Federico amaba y cuyas canciones recogia no era precisamente el que canta la Internacional" (April 1937, 9-10). The fascists, amazingly, also tried to claim Lorca as their own. The falangist newspaper of San Sebastian, <u>Unidad</u>, held the "reds" responsible for his death: "A la España imperial le han asesinado su mejor poeta . . . Yo afirmo que ni la Falange Española ni el Ejército de España tomaron parte en tu muerte . . . Tus sentimientos eran los de la Falange, querías Patria, Pan y Justicia para todos" (Luis Hurtado, May 1937, 71).

Vicente Aleixandre, in a much reprinted essay, comments that critics have seen Lorca, as variable as nature herself, as water, a rock, an angel, or a jungle. Lorca meant morning, clear, merry laughter, fresh fields, slopes and meadows, and green olives on yellow earth; yet at times, with his feet sunk in the depths of time, in the remote roots of the Spanish soil, he was more ancient than child, an indefinable elemental. Innocent as a shell on the beach, he was also "ardiente en sus deseos como un ser nacido para la libertad . . . En Federico todo era inspiración, y su vida, tan hermosamente de acuerdo con su obra, fue el triunfo de la libertad, y entre su vida y su obra hay un intercambio espiritual y físico tan constante, tan apasionado y fecundo, que las hace eternamente inseparables e individibles" (July, 1937), 44). Lorca was capable of merriment, but his capacity for love and suffering, never fully understood, are clearly revealed in Sonetos del amor oscuro, a lost work full of torment, flesh, soul, and the heart of the poet.

Luis Cernuda feels that no other poet of his generation was as "pura y hondamente popular," as Lorca (September 1937, 67). Painfully, Cernuda recalls his friend in 1927 in Seville; in 1930 in Vicente Aleixandre's house where Lorca played the piano, recited poetry, and sang songs; at Cernuda's home in July, 1936 when Lorca read La casa de Bernarda Alba, discussed with Cernuda his latest work, Sonetos del amor oscuro, and planned a projected Mexican trip. At three in the morning Lorca was anxious to get home so that the light of day might not strike him, "como si esa primera claridad lívida y descompuesta no anunciara una nueva vida sino una muerte; tránsito entre tinieblas y luz que los hombres no pueden contemplar sin riesgo" (June 1938, 17). Lorca was not a messianic bard, but his poetry needs no posthumous deformation to incarnate, as it does, the deepest and most inspired voice of the Spanish people. Lorca, a poet of love and death, in his poetry, free and spontaneous as a natural force, reached the public which accepted it joyfully. Yet Lorca knew pain and sorrow, and even in his moments of joy felt "el roce de una espina oculta. Esa es una de las raíces más hondas de su poesía; él muerde la raíz amarga que en diferentes formas y ocasiones vuelve como tema de ella" (June 1938, 18).

Among other commentators on Lorca, Juan Gil-Albert discusses his universal impact and his significance for his fellow poets for whom he was "la gracia, el ritmo, y la desbordada pasión; también ellos le vieron los últimos días de una amistad que nadie pensaba enterrar tan prematuramente, cuando su viaje hacia Granada decide . . . inexorable de su vuelo (March 1938, 90).

Emilio Prados, Luis Cernuda, and Rafael Alberti dedicate poetry to Lorca. Prados sings of Lorca in "Estancia en la muerte con Federico García Lorca," as "El hombre en las cenizas del mundo se deshace; / y su nombre queda entero bajo el sueño del aire" (July 1937, 54). Luis Cernuda exclaims in an elegy:

> Por eso te mataron, porque eras
> Verdor en nuestra tierra árida
> Y azul en nuestro oscuro aire.
> (March, 1938, 94)

Rafael Alberti writes: "No tuviste en muerte/ la que a ti te tocaba" (March 1938, 92).

Other poets receiving critical attention are León Felipe, José Bergamín, Arturo Serrano Plaja, Emilio Prados, Rafael Alberti, and Miguel Hernández. León Felipe best sums up the spirit of the day. He distinguishes heroic epic man from the domesticated variety, dream from reality, fusing the epic with history and the pueblo with poets to eliminate both dragons and merchants. León Felipe fits his own definition that the complete poet will be the one who "recoja todos los malos heroísmos, la oculta intimidad y la belleza del mundo, todos los gestos perdidos de los seres anonimos y exalte los valores populares--misterios y realidades--en el gran poema del futuro" (February 1937, 52). Antonio Machado considers sonnets by José Bergamín, especially "A Cristo Crucificado" and "Ante el Mar," as worthy of inclusion "en los mejores florilegios de nuestra lírica . . . la poesía de Bergamín se encrespa y aborrasca--las cuadernas del soneto crugen, pero no ceden--con sobrada tormenta para el vaso barroco (October 1938, 11-13). Machado, wondering why life dies and for whom death sings in the first sonnet, witnesses the triumph of an agonizing Christ who faces the sea in the second.

María Zambrano contends that Arturo Serrano Plaja is the most revolutionary contemporary poet: "no canta la revolución dándola por cierta y sabida, sino que se propone ante todo saberla, desentrañarla, apurar su sentido; vivir, en suma, poéticamente de ella y sobre ella" (June 1938, 49). The poet, unable to avoid a certain separation between his revolutionary zeal and poetic dedication, lacked the maturity to translate his testimony poetically until, in El hombre y el trabajo, which he began writing before the July 1936 uprising, he finally faced reality. Poets often suffer from "una incomunicación con las fuentes más íntimas no sólo del conocimiento sino del amor," but the indispensable social awareness, confrontation with reality, and love of truth are found in good measure in the poetry of Serrano Plaja (June 1938, 52).

Bernardo Clariana considers Emilio Prados' war poetry the most telling and the poet as "uno de sus primeros poetas militantes" (October 1937, 75). Altolaguirre agrees that Emilio Prados is "el verdadero iniciador de nuestro romancero de la guerra civil" (April 1937).

Most of Rafael Alberti's De un momento a otro, written between 1932 and 1937, had already appeared in reviews before its publication in book form. Antonio Sánchez Barbudo states that it is "un índice de la poesía dramática y apasionante, viva en la historia de nuestros últimos años, historia de presagios y dolores, de esperanzas dibujadas sobre un mapa de oscuras realidades; y la historia al mismo tiempo, de la evolución de un poeta, la historia de la poesía de Alberti en los años citados, su historia propia, la historia de un alma" (October 1937, 66). Imprecation and tenderness alternate with agitation and memories of things past, the world of childhood, the cause of the pueblo, a trip to the United States and Central America, tropical animals, plants, Americanisms, sadness, humor, hope, and redemption. The poems of the last series, the fifth, are dedicated to a variety of people, and in their sadness and deep feeling recall the sadness of Quevedo. Melancholy and moral preoccupations, they are an affirmation of the cause of the people.

Criticism, even of favorite fellow intellectuals, was not always affirmative. Miguel Hernández, in spite of his intermittent dignity and daring, reveals through his technical facility and exuberance, that in the depths of his soul he is still "un levantino, muy levantino; y lleva en sí lo que de peligro esto representa, aunque también lo que de riqueza, de gustosidad, de vida carnosa significa . . . Todo fue a él, todo lo que escribiera Miguel Hernández en arranque de poeta verdadero, pero también lo que trazara a su sola mano, su mano de versificador tan tremendamente fácil que logra formar a veces infinidad de versos, no ya sin contenido alguno, sino sin nada sin palabra siquiera, tan solo con sílabas y acentos" (Ramón Gaya, May 1938, 45-47). Levantine writers, so accustomed to passionate delivery, may end by conveying only the appearance rather than the substance of inspiration and fire. Since Hernández was one of the most exposed to the war, his poetry on the conflict would naturally be truthful, but Gaya questions whether the first thrust of emotion can convey art. Viento del pueblo, written under trying circumstances, had to be of uneven merit, and in it one finds lines as perfect as Garcilaso's followed by verse journalistic in tone. Although his poetry contains pure truth and pure form, neither, of themselves, can be true art, and in the lack of perfect fusion lies the principal defect of his work. Altolaguirre and others, not unmindful of Hernández' poetic contributions, are more immediately impressed by his fighting on the Andalusian front and his sacrifices (April 1937).

Theater also interested the critics of Hora de España. Enrique Diez-Canedo contributed to the April 1938 issue, "Panorama del teatro español desde 1914 hasta 1936," to be published in English as part of The Theater in a Changing Europe. Starting with Echegaray, "jefe indiscutible de la generación neo-romántica que siente las primeras acometidas del realismo (p. 14), he discusses the Catalan Jose Feliú y Codina as a forerunner of realism; Joaquín Dicenta, Selles, and Leopoldo Cano, students of Echegaray; and Benito Pérez Galdós who made few concessions to current taste in his theater of "alta poesía en el concepto, desarrollado por sendero de verdad;

pudo ser, y no lo fué, el gran modelo de teatro realista en España" (p. 16). Galdós lacked in his plays the popular acclaim he achieved as a novelist, and his liberal philosophy which stressed the equality of all beings, failed to arouse the bourgeois audiences of his day.

Jacinto Benavente, while destroying the hypocritical masks of Spanish society with his European manner, remained "un espíritu netamente español, no ajeno a las tradiciones de la picaresca" (p. 18). By the time of La ciudad alegre y confiada, however, his españolismo had disappeared, and the First World War "le halló como decidido germanófilo" (p. 19). As the years passed Benavente became a defender of order, a professional nationalist, and a reactionary, never completely able in dramas such as Pepe Doncel, 1928, to reject his more turbulent and open past. Much of Benavente's success on the Spanish stage corresponded to that of the pair of great comedians, María Guerrero and Fernando Díaz de Mendoza, who worked with him.

Other playwrights include Manuel Linares Rivas; the brothers Serafín and Joaquín Alvarez Quintero, graceful, superficially brilliant, and optimistically simple; and Gregorio Martínez Sierra, optimistically tender, whose theater descended at times to rhetoric: "pero que en el sentido transcendental de su teatro, que proclama la fe en el poder del ensueño . . . tiene su dominio propio y su peculiar manera" (p. 24). Martínez Sierra also contributed to theatrical development, as did Eduardo Marquina with his historical themes and love intrigues. The theatrical attempts of poets such as Cristobal de Castro, Ramon de Godoy, Enrique López Alarcón, Francisco Villaespesa, Luis Fernández Ardaván, Joaquín Montaner, and Joaquín Dicenta, hijo, were less effective. Among the few successful collaborations was that of Antonio and Manuel Machado in works such as Juan de Mañara, 1927, about a penitent mocker, and Las adelfas, 1928, a psychoanalytic play. Carlos Arniches created comic and grotesque dramas, and Pedro Muñoz Seca briefly offered the astrakán which he unfortunately abandoned for dramas defending his ultraconservative political ideas. Jacinto Grau, on the other hand, missed being a first rate figure because his realizations could not match his aspirations. Finally, Benavente had his disciples such as Enrique Suárez de Deza and Francisco Serrano Anguita while Eduardo Marquina influenced, among others, José María Pemán.

In current theater, states Diez Canedo, Unamuno and Valle-Inclán, the former with his "formas escuetas, diálogos bruscos, vueltas de pensamiento inesperados" (p. 34), and the latter with an opulent rhetoric, refined sensuality and popular rebellion are renovators. If Unamuno proved philosophical, Valle-Inclán waxed poetic. Also of supreme importance are groups such as the Misiones pedagógicas in their resurrection of Golden Age drama, the surrealistic theater of Azorín and Gómez de la Serna, and Manuel Azaña, especially in his first rate play, La corona, 1932. Other renovators include Cipriano Rivas Cherif, the poetess Josefina de la Torre, Claudio de la Torre, Paulino Masip, and Alejandro Casona. Rivas Cherif impressed Diez-Canedo with his ingenuity in Un sueño de la razón; as an interpreter of classical and foreign theater; as an actor, director, and advisor in the Teatro Español from 1928 to 1935; as the founder of the Estudio Dramático del Teatro Español and also the Teatro Escuela de Arte whose participants had to exhibit a perfect discipline. Finally, Diez-Canedo praises the dramas of Rafael Alberti and García Lorca as "hoy la más clara realidad de un nuevo teatro español" (p. 44), and the activities of La Barraca, aided by writers like Eduardo Ugarte.

Manuel Altolaguirre, holding a somewhat lower opinion of the Spanish theater, suggested that it had returned to a more primitive state when the bobo and rufián reigned supreme, so that it might serve propadanda purposes or for the distraction of workers and peasants. He felt that writers were producing dialogued romances, farces and anti-Fascist theater of great simplicity of form "para que pueda ser captado por un pueblo que no entiende de sutilezas literarias" (September 1927, 29-30). Altolaguirre admits, nevertheless, that the same public applauded the Teatro Universitario La Barraca and the Guignol theater of Miguel Prieto, aided by the young poets Pérez Infante and Camarero. He praises Rafael Alberti, Ramón Sender, Emilio Prados, Miguel Hernández and others for attempted innovations such as children's theater. Without denigrating the theater of Arniches, Benavente, and the Quintero brothers, he finds it less important than that of Azorín, Grau, the Machado brothers, or Gómez de la Serna, all prevented by the times from writing great theater. Only two, in his judgment, succeed as playwrights, Federico García Lorca and Ramón María del Valle-Inclán. The latter's theater (Celtic, refined, sensual), in spite of certain defects "llenará una época muy próxima de nuestra vida teatral" (September 1937, 42). Altolaguirre was to have directed three of Valle-Inclán's dramas: La cabeza del Bautista, La rosa de papel, and Farsa y licencia de la reina castiza, which he liked best for its deformation of the courtesan atmosphere, erudition and fantasy. For him it is a "magnífico esperpento, cuya presentación exigirá en el director una enorme capacidad de trabajo" (September 1937, 32). As for Lorca, Altolaguirre recalls that when his Bodas de sangre was performed "veíamos en el al nuevo Lope de Vega del Teatro Español. En su Zapatera prodigiosa sentíamos a Molière que revivía. En Yerma, Séneca y García Lorca se encontraron" (September 1927, 63). Lorca apparently planned a Greek tragedy about a rich Cordovan farmer murdered by a maddened son, but he never wrote the work. Lorca read <u>La casa de Bernarda Alba</u>, originally called <u>Las hijas de Bernarda Alba</u> to a group of friends, stressing that he hoped he had achieved "severidad y sencillez" in his work.

Altolaguirre's own play, <u>El triunfo de las Germanías</u>, written in collaboration with José Bergamín, in spite of its popular overtones, received bad reviews because it contained too many propaganda speeches (February 1937). Other plays were constantly reviewed and analyzed. Antonio Sánchez Barbudo, commenting on a <u>zarzuela</u> theater group, Grupo Arte y Propaganda, headed by María Teresa León and aided by Alberti, hopes that the actors and writers will achieve their goals, "contribuyendo así a abrir caminos más holgados a la sórdida vida de nuestro teatro actual" (October 1937, 76). Juan Gil-Albert notes performances by La Barraca of three entremeses by Cervantes, finding in them a new emotional depth projected through the actors' experience in acting at combat fronts and hospitals (October 1937).

Criteria separating literary criticism from propaganda may depend on the fashion of the moment. When one reads <u>Hora de España</u>'s criticism some three decades later, it may appear didactic in attempting to determine a work's validity through demonstrating its truth or degree of compliance with or reconcialition to "reality" or a special social ambience. Some will find the criticism sensitive, spontaneous, and sincere, perhaps with valid insights and criteria. Others may label it emotional, subjective, and aggressive. Most will, at least, be willing to concede that the writers convey, articulately, insights, whether reasoned or intuitive, into the effects the emotional nature of a war experience had on convictions of quality. The journal's critical contributions are only occasionally sharply definitive or perceptive since the writers stress circumstantial, external, and symbolic values as a logical unity, exclaiming that the Republican intellectual is the voice of the people. While their conclusions are neither always illuminating nor clearly cogent, the critics, in their search for justice, while not dispassionate nor morally neutral, are often objective, revealing both independence and integrity. Concern and conviction, passion and nostalgia, and a conflict between reasoned and instinctive judgments, provide constant empathic if not intellectual stimulation and satisfaction. In some instances, obviously, the critics allow the reality of the moment to alter their critical criteria, but for the most part they avoid an irrational accretion in support of an identity of interest, approaching the critical process both intuitively and intellectually and comparing tradition to the current scene. In the criticism of a culture at war, we glimpse the conscience and the intellectual and psychological resources of critics and creative artists, neither despondent nor indifferent, who helped determine the entire course of contemporary Spanish literature, and we receive a reminder of continuing commitments and the fruitlessness of trying to forget what cannot be forgotten.

Notes

[1] *Hora de España* (January 1937), 6. Further page references in the text are all to this journal.

[2] The *Misiones pedagógicas*, formed on May 29, 1931, became active in September of that same year. By March 15, 1934 the workers had gone on seventy missions to about 298 towns and had created 3,506 new libraries.

THE PAST AS PROLOGUE IN HORA DE ESPANA

Hora de España, a journal published by Republican intellectuals between January, 1937 and October, 1938, sought to promote the view that "España prosigue su vida intelectual o de creación artística en medio del conflicto gigantesco en que se debate."[1] Among its contributors were Emilio Prados, Dámaso Alonso, León Felipe, Miguel Hernández, Antonio Machado, and Rafael Alberti. In addition to poetry and drama Hora de España published a series of perceptive essays on contemporary literature, but its writers also sought their cultural heritage in the past, viewing the current conflict as a continuation of the age old struggle of the "dos Españas." Indeed, for them, as for the fascists, Spanish culture implied a kind of hispanidad, and the editors welcomed articles dealing with Spanish America.[2]

A few contributors, showing a spurious and superficial Marxian tone, hoped to avoid either pure art or pure propaganda as they faced the "reality" of the moment. Others attempted a somewhat idiosyncratic approach to the past. Most, in relating history, past literature and current life, without being moralists, stressed a regenerative spirit and a new humanism. Whatever their political persuasion (most in spite of their gratitude to Russia were not Communists), they often appeared frustrated Romantics as they sought identity with the past, both recent and remote.

Máximo José Kahn traces the contributions of Spanish Jews who, he postulates, may have been the Iberians, the "ebreos" or "iberim". Commenting on the correspondence of many Basque terms to equivalent Hebrew ones, he also relates the sudden appearance of the cult of the bull in Egypt, where the Hebrews served as artisans for three generations, to the Sephardic Jews. Jewish teachers, philosophers, astronomers, and poets, among them the greatest lyric voice of all Judaism, Yehuda Halevi, influenced the vocabulary of Spanish Christians. Desmazalado is obviously related to the Hebrew mazal or good luck, and Cante Jondo (not deep song as many contend but rather holiday song), is a corruption of the Hebrew Cante Yomtob (March, 1937). The philosophic Judaic-Hispanic vision of Salomon ibn Gabirol (Avicebron), Maimonides, and Leon Abravanel (León Ebreo), created the possibility of a Spanish Golden Age. Through the constant rebirth of Judaism, Sephardic Jews came to provide also the germs of a European Renaissance (April, 1937). Kahn concludes that Spain, in spite of the contributions of its Jewish intellectuals, was: "Antes de la Republica. . . un país antisemita que no solo no tenía interes por sus judíos, sino que les despreciaba" (May, 1938, 31).

43

The writers consider the Cid, as a man of the people, to belong to the Republic, and view the Arcipreste de Hita as a proponent of "una línea vitalista . . . la exaltación de lo vital . . . todo lo que nos es más inmediato a los sentidos que es lo que Hita revela y valora aquí."[3] They read the Libro de buen amor as literature of social protest, "un grito de rebeldía contra aquella sociedad, contra el orden social de aquella época."[4]

Juan González del Valle, concerned with the Golden Age, discusses Cervantine space and perspective and Quevedo's urgency and haste (March, 1938). Rafael Dieste, one of many interested in Cervantes, examines that writer's position in the light of the Civil War (February, 1937); and Max Aub compares the political and military situation of Numancia to the current scene (May, 1937). Republicans especially liked the episode of the Caballero del Verde Gabán from which they learned a lesson of brotherhood: "Convivir; relacionarse con el prójimo; poner todos los medios para que las vidas individuales se suplan unas con otras y entre ellas se establezcan corrientes de inteligencia . . . la más cabal y espléndida de todo el Quijote y, acaso, la más interesante de nuestra literatura . . ."[5]

María Zambrano sees don Quijote's clear and perfect will as showing the historical failure of Spain. If exceptional beings "llegasen al nivel de lo histórico, no se produciría la novela; lo que no llega a ser historia por carecer de realidad, de conexión con el resto de los acontecimientos, por no estar engranado con ellos, y sin embargo, es--no llega a ser elemento de la historia, pero tiene un ser--, es protagonista de su propia vida, es un ente de novela . . . es en ella donde hemos de ver lo que el español veía y sabía y también lo que el español era. También de lo que carecía."[6] Don Quijote, reflecting the poverty of the Spanish State, had to take refuge in his madness to save his high and perfect love. Sancho, through his convivencia with don Quijote, reveals that the latter's roots lie in the pueblo which fights the isolation of man from his neighbor. Thus, don Quijote . . . lleva clara e inequívoca la noción del semejante en el centro de su espíritu; está solo en su empeño, pero esencialmente acompanado por el mejor de cada hombre que vive en él. Es la nobleza esencial del hombre lo que don Quijote cree y crea, la mutua confianza y reconocimiento (September, 1937, 23).

Mariano José de Larra was one of the nineteenth century authors who received critical attention. Rosa Chacel admires his vision of Spain and sees him as a precursor "de todo lo que llenó nuestro próximo pasado y de lo que aun habiendo llegado a su madurez, no es todavía más que un futuro incalculablemente poderoso . . . (March 1937, 55); Machado exclaims that

Larra's romantic mission was to promulgate a great truth, that "el hombre es la medida de todas las cosas, menos la de los hombres y la de los pueblos" (December, 1937, 9). Larra's <u>costumbrismo</u> may have been the pretext for irony; his <u>romanticism</u> for agony, as perhaps his resurrection by the Generation of '98 revealed. The newspapers of Larra's day apparently made little of his suicide, but now one can see his importance for the present and the fulfillment of his destiny.[7]

To acquire courage in the current struggle along with a vision of a better Spain, the intellectuals tried to relive the epic of Spain's disasters, her faith and her anguish, found in the novels of Benito Pérez Galdós. They discovered, in addition to heroism, "confianza . . . un esperanzado desprendimiento de las razones que nos harían desconfiar, una íntima paradoja, un alegre secreto que nadie podrá quitarnos ni siquiera aquellos que puedan quitarnos la vida."[8] In contemplating Spain's vicissitudes, Galdós eternalized the passionate moment in a simple, natural style, but he never attempted to guide Spanish minds even in his thesis novels where his political philosophy and attitude toward society are so clearly revealed.[9]

Galdós portrays the obscure, generic life of city and country districts, and through the intimate, daily activities of anonymous Spaniards, shows us the fabric from which historical events emerge, "El protoplasma hispánico impreso de mil huellas, mas también hirviendo de nuevos gérmenes . . . el sujeto único, en sus innumerables caras, de la novela galdosiana" (September, 1938, 31). One can comprehend the profound awareness of things Spanish in his novels only through a realization that Spanish realism is, more than a quality of style, an intuitive knowledge of humble beings and things.

Life triumphs over the intellectual in the rich, complex world of Galdós which reveals the dichotomy between the man of ideas and the poet. A mysterious poetry emanates from his descriptions of humble characters like Benigna and Fortunata, both of whom are ". . . puro pueblo . . . Fortunata nos ofrece el misterio de la maternidad imponiendo su ley--Misericordia nos muestra otro misterio, el de la fuerza de cohesión de un pueblo más alla de la locura, y de la prudencia, sacando su fuerza de su prodigalidad, su esplendor, de su miseria" (September, 1938, 36). <u>Misericordia</u> shows us the tragic duality of a Spain suffering from a deficient assimilation of racial, religious ingredients of the <u>pueblo</u> and reveals people living in a dream world, unable, like Benigna, to face reality without the burden of a petrified and deformed past. As the representative of the people, Benigna, offering hunger and hope, accepts the dreams of others without living by them.

Ernestina de Champourcin finds Rosalía de Castro in her A las orillas del Sar, more literary and preoccupied with form and rare metrical combinations than she is in her more intimate and spontaneous regional works. Although Rosalía de Castro was considered a typical writer of Galicia, "lo que sus versos tienen de subjetivo o sea de universales, le hacen rebasar el marco en que críticos y apologistas la encerraron" (February, 1938, 17). She treats of humble victims of social injustice, their poverty and sorrow, and had she lived in the present time she would have supported the pueblo; for literature belongs to all and "aunque no hable de ellos, se deja impregnar por los vaivenes de la historia, recibiendo su huella y conservándola a través de siglos y generaciones" (February, 1938, 19).

The critics mentioned other nineteenth century writers, among them Armando Palacio Valdés with whose death ". . . pierde la literatura española un famoso novelista y la democracia uno de sus defensores" (February, 1938, 90), and whose prologue to the Majos de Cadiz Ramón del Valle-Inclán considered to be "todo un tratado de estética" (February, 1938, 90).

We have seen, then, the somewhat remarkable spectacle of writers in the midst of a terrible Civil War, who in their writing, not only sowed the seeds of a future literature but looked to the past for the progenitors of their spiritual, moral and literary values, finding there the inspiration for their battle in defense of liberty and intellectual freedom.

Notes

[1] Hora de España (January, 1937), 6. Further citations in the text will be from this journal.

[2] Typical is the article by Nicolás Guillén on the mestizo aspects of Cuban poetry (November 1937), 42-43.

[3] Antonio Porrás, "Razón de hoy," (April, 1938), 56-62.

[4] Dámaso Alonso, "La injusticia social en la literatura española," (February, 1937), 14-15.

[5] Antonio Porrás, "Introducción a un apocalipsis de Cervantes," (July, 1938), 28.

[6] María Zambrano "La reforma del entendimiento español," (September, 1937), 20-21.

[7] José Bergamín, "Larra, peregrino en su patria," (November, 1937), 17-23.

[8] Rosa Chacel, "Un nombre al frente," (February, 1937), 49-50.

[9] María Zambrano, "La reforma del entendimiento español," p. 26.

HORA DE ESPAÑA
AND THE POETRY OF HOPE

During the Spanish Civil War the Republican journal, Hora de España, published between January, 1937, and October, 1938, promoted a continuing intellectual activity involving literary and historical criticsm.[1] In addition to the numerous essays and some propagandistic poetry about proletarian solidarity, the journal published poetic contributions which sought to reaffirm human values and the sacrifices involved in fighting for an ideal. The leitmotif, in what was after all a fratricidal war, was principally love and hope instead of hate and denunciation. The poets gave personal testimony, inevitably products of their social and historical situation, but within this somewhat restricted cultural context, their poems possess special textures and recurring imagery which reflect their authors' identification with universal imperatives. Juan José Domenchina tries to define the concept of literary structure itself:

> Pero la difícil ciencia
> de nuestro esclarecer el oscuro
> dominio, pero el seguro
> distinguir, pero el exacto
> decir y el divino tacto
> del poeta. . . ¡qué agonía
> de lucidez, qué porfía
> de propósito en el acto!
> (January, 1938)

Considering themselves, in their solitude and anguish, more than instruments of a social philosophy, the poets optimistically anticipated a better future where good would triumph, leaving evil unfulfilled. Some of their poetry was also published elsewhere, but many poems appeared only in Hora de España. Among contributors to the journal were some of the most famous stars in the Spanish poetic constellation: Antonio Machado, Emilio Prados, Rafael Alberti, Miguel Hernández, Luis Cernuda, León Felipe, José Moreno Villa, and Germán Bleiberg. In addition to expressing their doubts and uncertainties, their loneliness and despair in the face of devastation and disaster, the poets lovingly identified themselves with their country as it had been, as it was, and as it might someday be. Emilio Prados, generally considered by his fellow poets to have been the initiator of Spanish war poetry (April 1937; October 1937, p. 75), in "Tres Cantos en el Destierro," longing for an invisible reality faintly illuminated in his subconscious, a lost dream of happiness, exclaims:

> Aquí vivo, cantando la voz que ya me queda,
> aquí vivo, y mi canto conduzco por el tiempo,

> y si mi voz se nubla por tanta lejanía
> que confundida al llanto luce bajo mi angustia,
> sólo es dulce nostalgia de la oculta presencia
> que el azar de la guerra fugazmente me obliga. . .
> (October 1937, pp. 83-84)

As he recalls the tender hills, the sedge, and the olive and fig trees of his beloved Spain, the poet is tormented by the loss of loved ones whom he wants to join in death:

> Abril, en guerra o paz,
> siempre me encuentras
> deconocida en medio del combate,
> junto a las hojas de mi muerte, trémulo,
> aguardando su eterna flor desnudo.
> ("Sombra de abril," June 1938)

As time passes and love and even joy are forgotten, man can still hope amidst the surrounding ghosts, for "entre fantasmas vive mi esperanza" (p. 24).

The poets reflect on the seasons of the year and geography, extolling the beauties of nature. Miguel Hernández recalls:

> El sabor de la tierra se enriquece y madura:
> caen las copas del llanto laborioso y oliente,
> mana de los varones y de la agricultura,
> bebida de mi frente.
> ("Visión de Sevilla," September 1937, p. 49)

Ramon Gaya, in a variety of poems, among them "Hermosura en la guerra," sees with a painter's eye that Spring will always return, a painful beauty not without its consolation. Antonio Machado, turning from Juan de Mairena's musings on death, time and immortality, writes poems to Lister, to Federico de Onís, to a dead boy, and to dawn in Valencia. In his well-known "La primavera" he associates war and the eternal land:

> Mas fuerte que la guerra--espanto y grima--
> cuando con torpe vuelo de avutarda
> el minoso trimotor se encima
> y sobre el vano techo se retarda
> . . . .
> Soria pura, entre montes de violeta
> di tú, avión marcial, si el alto Duero
> a donde vas recuerda a su poeta
> (June 1938, pp. 5-6)

The poets assert positively that their moral anxiety will be alleviated, whatever the truth or reality of the moment, as their country's future becomes their ultimate concern and metaphorical truth. León Felipe contends that life is heroism rather than happiness and that bloodshed may be justified only through the concomitant hopes for brotherhood and peace which it may, perhaps, bring in its wake ("La Insignia," May 1937). Arturo Serrano Plaja, in "Canto a la libertad," stresses that from ruin and death a new life can be born, for although men, families, and even towns may die, liberty will survive (April 1937, p. 35). Reaffirming his faith in love and destiny, in spite of the war, he believes that man learns though suffering and that Spain will someday be free (May 1938). Germán Bleiberg, a lieutenant in the popular army, also declares for freedom and a future (January 1938).

This theme of continuity and eternity recurs constantly. Juan Gil-Albert's "Poemas de Revolución" describe a world which seems to march toward an implacable destiny, without room for peace or tranquility. Yet, although the year has brought destruction and death, it foreshadows the threshold of a period in which Spain "inicia su esperanza de continuidad / sobre unos campos abandonados, / sobre sus ciudades deshechas" (January 1937, pp. 42-44). Manuel Altolaguirre, accepting the prospect of personal annihilation and a country overwhelmed by hate and death, sees hope for rebirth and a new future through the continuing existence of the land itself (March 1937, p., 31). Emilio Prados, even in his most militant war poetry or that of immediate motivation such as "Elegía a Francisco Blanco," a sailor missing on the southern front, reiterates the central concern that from sacrifice and even death may come a new light and hope (April 1937, p. 35).

The most complicated contributor, Luis Cernuda, believes in the inherent nobility and dignity of man, avoiding, for the most part, the post-war bitterness so much a part of his poetry and engendered by the very Civil War experiences, which did not result in a new Spain, he was undergoing at the time he was writing for Hora de España. In this poetry he appears still to accept what he later terms a Spanish myth, as he dreams of spiritual fulfillment. In "Elegía Española," an integral part of his complete works, Cernuda seeks the mysterious essence of the Spaniard and Mother Spain. Traitors and cowards deny her, but her children cannot forget her. Spain is the past and yet she is also a promise for the new dawn. Only through her survival, whatever the sacrifices, can there be a hope for the future:

        Y su odio, su crueldad, su lucha
        ante ti vanos son como sus vidas,

>   porque tú eres eterna
>   y solo los creaste
>   para la paz y gloria de su estirpe.
>   (April 1937, p. 32)

Even in his two most negative poems, "Lamento y Esperanza," and "Scherzo para un Elfo," evoking the suffering of the Spanish pueblo on a continent of "mercaderes y de histriones al acecho," he announces that dreams still remain: "El sueño es una nube de la que el hombre es viento. / ¿Quién podrá el pensamiento separarlo del sueño?" (November 1937, pp. 31-32). The poet withholds judgment, waiting and hoping that Spain will live and not die, a far cry from his publications in later years in which he views Spain as a wicked stepmother, chained by ignorance and intolerance and the masks of a dead past.

The world of then and the world of now, one can see, involve essential human problems unchanged in their totality. The poetic affirmations of dignity, patriotism, and love maintain their importance through all the political vicissitudes which have ensued. These partisans, whatever their transitory doubts, found transcendental meaning in their lives, beyond the truth of the moment, half glimpsing, perhaps even creating, something beyond their immediate reality and what their sense and reason imposed upon them. Committed to an ideal, a reflection of man's aspirations, they based their poetic vision on their illusion of an over-confidence in man's inherent goodness and nobility of spirit. Yet, even at this late date, their message of hope is one which contemporary Spaniards would do well to acknowledge.

Notes

[1] See Angel Sánchez-Gijón, "Le reviste letterarie nella guerra civile spagnola: Hora de España," Carte Segrete 1 (1967), 121-38; Kessel Schwartz, "The Past as Prologue in Hora de España," RomN, X (1969), 15-19; "Literary Criticism and the Spanish Civil War," Hispania, 52 (1969), 203-212; and "The 'Pueblo', the Intellectuals and the Spanish Civil War," Kentucky Romance Quarterly, XIV, 4 (1969), 299-310.

NATIONAL AND EUROPEAN CULTURE IN THE CONTEMPORARY SPANISH NOVEL

From the Middle Ages on, as Erasmian and Krausist[1] conflicts with the establishment testify, Spain has both accepted and rejected foreign cultural elements in conflict with its own traditional ones. Spaniards have had to struggle against the limitations of their intellectual life since the Counter Reformation isolated them from the mainstream of European through. Spain has almost always suffered a cultural lag in accepting literary movements, often trying them briefly first, rejecting them in reactionary fashion, and finally accepting them after they have almost run their course elsewhere. In the early twentieth century Manuel Bartolomé Cossío fostered the esthetic and spiritual revaluation of the artist, and Joaquín Costa, the "Apostle of Europeanization," encouraged Spaniards to copy European culture and economics. The "Generation of 1898,"[2] profoundly influenced by Nietzsche, among others, searched for new values to replace traditional ones. At the same time the Modernists emphasized, in a continuing Apollonian-Dionysian conflict, exotic cosmopolitan and universal concerns along with a dedication to the remote past. In the first three decades of the twentieth century, Miguel de Unamuno created novelistic "agonists" who searched for immortality, Pío Baroja lamented the irrational and illogical universe of delusive moral values, and Pérez de Ayala documented the relationships between life and art, tempering his metaphysical yearnings by an intellectual approach to life.

Unamuno, hoping to "Hispanicize" Europe, rejected European science and culture and anathematized those who wanted to bring the Western industrial world to Spain. Yet he knew German, French, Italian, and Danish and was keenly aware of European philosophical and literary currents. Ortega y Gasset, on the other hand, through the Revista de Occidente, promoted from 1923 on, as he had been doing in essays since 1910, the thought that "Regeneration is inseparable from Europeanization . . . Truly from the beginning it was quite clear that Spain was the problem and Europe the solution."[3]

Ortega believed that the novel was a kind of hermetic exercise which should stress form and refinements of techniques. He seemed to define the novel as something dehumanized, cold, and objective. Pío Baroja, whose vision of the world was as chaotic as life itself, held that the novel is an instrument of communication and representative of life and that form and technique are relatively unimportant. In the prologue to La nave de los locos (1925) he describes the novel as multiformed and states that every novel has its own type of skeletal structure, although some, biologically, appear to be more invertebrate than vertebrate.

Ortega encouraged Benjamín Jarnés, Gómez de la Serna, and Francisco Ayala in their adherence to European avant-garde movements. The first two novelists mentioned followed the French surrealists and wrote esthetic, somewhat mannered, and intellectual novels, copying from foreign rather than from national models. Ayala experimented with first-and second-person narrative, although he did not immediately succumb to vanguard attitudes. In general, formal renovation and the search for new forms along with a determination to follow European art, poetry, and fiction seemed to control novelists of the day.[4]

Juan Luis Alborg, in Hora actual de la novela española (1958), suggests that post-Civil War Spanish novelists broke with the Generation of 1898 and with all predominant Western cultural currents. Although the novelists of the 1940's and early 1950's wanted to escape their heritage, few really understood the technical innovations of the modern novel, even those which had been in use for more than a quarter of a century. Spaniards traditionally reject extreme manifestations of literary movements and, as Ricardo Gullón, points out, have "customarily taken from foreign currents that part which is best attuned to their intrinsic nature and to their particular modes of expression. . . ."[5]

In a polemic with Julián Marías, Robert G. Mead, Jr., excepting the "Generation of the Emigres," referred to the geographic and spiritual isolation from liberal currents of European thought suffered by Spaniards. Marías insisted, a message he has kept repeating to the present, that "Spain is in Europe."[6] José María Gironella, on the other hand, contended that "our novel has enclosed itself within an hermetic world, ignoring the great universal problems with a certain self-satisfied provincialism."[7] He believed that obsessive interest in localism, exaggerated sentimentalism, and superficial characterization were typical of the Spanish novel.

Writers born between 1922 and 1936, according to José María Castellet, belong to what he calls the "Mid-Century Generation." He distinguishes these writers from earlier ones like Camilo José Cela and Miguel Delibes because of their social compromise, collective heroes, subjective experience of misery to convey reality, and especially their "profound sense . . . of the dynamics of history."[8] Also called a "wounded generation" and "innocent generation" (because of their lack of direct involvement in the Spanish Civil War), these novelists witnessed and denounced Spanish social injustice, an attitude which became so fixed that it became petrified and in itself provincial in the early 1960's after a decade of such writing. Although they were largely not European-oriented, they used European techniques at times to carry out their tasks.

Contemporary Spanish novelists discuss most frequently the influences of the Italian neo-realists, French existentialists, and the nouveau roman. They learned from Italian neo-realists to confront reality while avoiding unidimensional and emotive involvement in their concentration on the poor and the proletariat. The Italians believed that the novelist might modify society, but they avoided stereotyped realities of a single truth. In the 1950's young French writers stressed uncommitted description in their nouveau roman, believing that the novel was a sufficient statement of its own reality which the reader had to interpret. The objectivists borrowed from the movies and radio in attempting to create a pure novel whose reality was neither absurd nor significant. Other European novelists combined essay, painting, music, literary criticism, and biography in new ways. Existentialist anguish continued, but some novelists seemed more concerned with technique than meaning and employed strange symbols to appeal to multilevel perceptions of readers. They superimposed simultaneous structural levels involving circular time, the multiple view, and various esthetic devices which served more to hide than to convey. Style became disjunctive as though metaphor no longer sufficed to carry the burden of guilt of the modern world. Man, a finite being, lived more and more in the present in the face of the knowledge of his certain death and the absurdity of the world.

Around 1965 a younger Spanish generation, born in the 1940's, moved away from more traditional literary values and from objectivism and the nouveau roman. Some members of the innocent generation also became more discriminating in their mastery of European culture. Rejecting old traditions which seemed to be irrelevant in a computerized world, these novelists despairingly search for meaning in a disintegrating society whose chaos they convey through the destruction of normal chronology. Spanish novelists continue to express varieties of Sartrean existentialism and have produced lyrical and sexual experience together with an esthetic exercise in twisted time and ruptured novelistic structures to avoid old dimensions and to modify the novel's structure to fit their own reality. As Guillermo de Torre states: "Today nothing is foreign to fiction: not metaphysics, nor most concrete brutal deeds. No territory is forbidden to it; no shadow of ancient taboos survives. Everything may be included within its incredibly elastic limits."[9]

It must be remembered that Spanish novelists were isolated

for fifteen or twenty years from European intellectual sources, and only recently have they begun to overcome the tragic heritage of the Spanish Civil War and its political consequences. As Francisco Ayala says: "In Spain many writers who have lived segregated from the rest of the world are now discovering Europe. . . . I believe that in the last ten years this confinement has ceased . . . and that Spanish literature is beginning to lose its provincial character."[10] The Civil War destroyed even the lines of communication previously established by the <u>Revista de Occidente</u> in the 1920's, and for many years readers were all but limited to expensive and scarce Argentine editions. Even in the 1960's, as one of the young writers states, novels by Cesare Pavese, Vasco Pratolini, or Henry Miller were prohibitively priced and "among young Spaniards interested in literature, how many have read Proust, Henry James, D. H. Lawrence, or Virginia Woolf?"[11] At the same time the novelists were deprived of the stylistic and literary progress made by their own countrymen, since most of the good novelists were living in exile. Deprived of European cross-fertilization for so long, once channels of communication were opened, Spanish novelists eagerly examined the heterogeneous mixtures of almost half a century of European fictional experimentation, which accounts for the strange jumble of influences from several distinct generations (all new for these writers). Among them are Marcel Proust, Franz Kafka, James Joyce, Alberto Moravia, Aldous Huxley, André Gide, Virginia Woolf, Jean-Paul Sartre, Thomas Mann, William Faulkner, and Alain Robbe-Grillet and his contemporaries. Many give lip service to even later antinovelistic novels, but few understand them.

In 1956 the suspension of the Congress of University Writers triggered attempts to use new techniques to describe the Civil War, childhood memories, rural and city life, and social and political events. Because of censorship novelists had to convey their ideas indirectly, especially in the 1950's, in order to escape charges of doctrinal deviation, and they encouraged the reader to penetrate their surface view of reality and draw conclusions which they could not more openly endorse. The European Community of Writers, founded in 1960 by G.B. Angioletti to promote contact among all European writers, had about one hundred Spanish members. In 1959, 1960, and 1961 a number of internationally known novelists like Michel Butor and Alberto Moravia participated in the colloquia on the novel held in Formentor, Majorca. Spanish novelists, among them Cela and Goytisolo, participated in the discussions and debates on technique, form, and fictional realism. Butor had been translated previously into Spanish, but he was known only to a few intellectuals. The Formentor experience helped bring him, Max Frisch, Marguerite Duras, and others to the attention of

Spanish novelists. In the 1963 Madrid coloquium on the new novel, essentially a debate between social realists and objectivists, the Spaniards, for the most part, defended social realism.

Almost all the European novelists began to be translated with some regularity into Spanish in the 1960's. Insula published reviews of European works in their column, "The Foreign Novel in Spain," with commentary by Domingo Pérez Minik and news from European centers by J. Corrales Egea and others, in order to keep readers abreast of cultural movements. The Revista de Occidente, Papeles de Son Armadans, and other journals also followed European cultural activity. A cursory glance at a few issues of Insula reveals, among novels translated and commented upon, those of Leonardo Sciascia, Julian Mitchell, Alain Robbe-Grillet, Claude Simon, Marguerite Duras, Yuri Kazakov, Yuri Nagibin, Elizabeth Bowen, Ivy Compton-Burnett, Graham Greene, Jean Cau, Friederich Dürenmatt, Elio Vittorini, Italo Calvino, Cesare Pavese, Vasco Pratolini, Edmunde Charles-Roux, Christiane Rochefort, José Cabanis, Lawrence Durrell, Nathalie Sarraute, Iris Murdock, Angus Wilson, Günter Grass, Heinrich Böll, and Witold Gombrowicz. For the most part, however, these novels were known only to critics and not read by Spanish novelists. Critics also knew the Marxist theories of Lucien Goldmann and George Lukacs, but few novelists read their works, and fewer yet, having read them, had digested their theories or applied them. Even among critics only a limited number knew about the new European novel: "There are so few of us Spanish critics who preoccupy ourselves with the contemporary non-Spanish novel."[12]

Spanish novels were also published in many foreign languages. Juan García Hortelano's works have been translated into a dozen languages. Ignacio Aldecoa has appeared in German, Italian, Swedish, and Polish. Ana María Matute is also much translated, and Juan Goytisolo's novels have sometimes been published in French before they appear in Spanish. Yet, until about 1965, the Spanish novel was largely provincial, reflecting the legacy of Pío Baroja, Valle-Inclán, and even Pérez Galdós, basically a nineteenth-century realist.

The Spanish Civil War has never fully lost its impact as a unique event involving human values and sacrifice and impelling many writers, through their own brand of social realism, to attempt to rejuvenate and transform their society in the hope of future spiritual unity. The Spanish novelists wanted to define their reality and at the same time to serve their society. They could not easily divorce themselves from content and from their moral miseries, and they lacked the freedom of other European countries to represent their true feelings. In the post-Civil

War period French youth had a free choice between moral suicide as defined by Albert Camus and a new system of values based on their war experience, occupation, and concentration camps. Frenchmen had their country and their enemy. Spaniards, on the contrary, lacked ideas in common, facing, not a foreign enemy, but their own blood relatives.[13]

Themes of the exploited peasant, underpaid worker, and slumdweller[14] took precedence over European theoretical and formal advances. Some of the novelists, in their descriptive expositions of social reality without exegesis, analysis, or explanation, ignored formalistic and esthetic preoccupation almost completely, which confined them to the excessively narrow limits of the present, "naturally extraordinarily ephemeral,"[15] and explains their recent relative silence. As the members of the "innocent" generation examined man's isolation, his anguish, and his inability to communicate, along with social factors, they often combined their satirical view of society and the metaphysical role of man in the world within a traditional framework; and with the rarest of exceptions only those novels concerned with social man and contemporary Spanish reality had much success.

As we have seen, the nouveau roman was known in Spain, but the Spanish novelists could not avoid social commitments or accept the individual's loss of self-determination and lack of emotional association. Objective accounts of ordinary people were common in the 1950's, but Spanish novelists rejected efforts to replace words by images to reflect reality. They could not completely abandon plot and character development in the name of structure and style nor could they understand the often contradictory explanations emanating from French novelists about objectivity, subjectivity, and infra-realism.[16] Although Spaniards accepted visual description and respected Michel Butor's desire to force the reader to make interpretations (the anonymous narrator enabled them to penetrate the reality of appearance in their hypocritical country), they were more influenced by Italian neo-realists like Pratolini.

It must be remembered that members of former generations continue to publish in the current decade. Ramón Sender (1902-), possibly the greatest living Spanish novelist (almost unknown to contemporary Spanish writers until about 1965), had given a direct view of Spanish reality in Imán (1930) which was unmatched by later social novelists. Together with Arturo Barea and Max Aub he created the only outstanding fiction about the Spanish Civil War. In most of his novels Sender shows a compassionate love for human beings as he combines the metaphysical, mystical, lyrical, and sensual with an existential search for self. One finds Kafka's sense of nightmare and Joyce's subconscious flow, but even more in his works one sense the presence of Ramón de Valle-Inclán. In his idealistic and humanitarian concerns Sender seems to be the direct heir of Pérez Galdós; and his realistic literature, "of a social and testificatory nature," foreshadows the newer generations' literary interest.[17]

Among his novels of the 1960's are, Crónica del alba (1967), whose definite version he elaborated for a quarter of a century and which examines the awakening conscience and moral formation involved in becoming a man; Las criaturas saturnianas (1967), a historical novel about Cagliostro and a Russian princess, which combines epic, farcical, and literary historical elements; En la vida de Ignacio Morel (1969), winner of the Planeta Prize; and Nocturno de los 14 (1969), which deals with suicide, reality, fantasy, and literature. Sender is a unique and intuitive writer not easily classified. Some of his novels deliberately defy a level of logical association in the surrealistic tradition. Others, almost parables or allegories, stress man's place in the universe and his need for self-knowledge. In his examination of the interrelationships of the real world and creative imagination, in his search for harmonic visions of human brotherhood, and in his existential search for immortality, he represents the best traditions of the Spanish novel. Although his primary preoccupation is with freedom and responsibility for one's fellow man, the Spanish problem has never been far removed from his work.

Camilo José Cela (1916-), himself influenced by Pío Baroja and Valle-Inclán, owes more to them than to European literature, although he anticipates current novelists in his emphasis on language and structure. He was among the earliest Spanish novelists to experiment with Bertolt Brecht's Verfremdungs-effekte, a distancing which made the familiar remote. Uncommitted to any specific form, Cela through the years has contended that it is impossible to define what a novel is. La familia de Pascual Duarte (1942) probably encouraged "authors and titles . . . that promise to make Spain, if not a leader in the European novel, at least part of European trends";[18] but as Robert Kirsner shows, preoccupation with Spain and the cruelty which is an inherent part of Spanish life constitute the predominant themes of his novels.[19] La colmena (1951), a complex documentary reflecting the counterpoint of Aldous Huxley, opens the formal aspects of style and esthetic treatment of social preoccupations, and Mrs. Caldwell habla con su hijo (1953) resembles the nouveau roman. Other novels are Tobogán de hambrientos (1962), which contains cinematographic views concerning the relationships of one hundred people, and La

61

familia del héroe (1965), a burlesque monologue on Spanish pride which seems inspired by the European novel. Cela, then, has been influenced by European culture but not to the extent of betraying his Spanish ancestry. He exposes the smells, sounds, and cruelty of Spain, and in his portrayal of people trapped by life, death, and violence, as victims of sexuality, existential anguish, and despair, he is traditionally Spanish.

Miguel Delibes (1920-), in his glorification of rural life, seems to reflect Ortega y Gasset's gloomy prediction that the modern novelist will resemble a talented woodcutter in the Sahara desert, refraining from great plots because "a bit of tension and movement suffice."[20] Delibes, in his themes of alienation, preoccupation with youth, and his gray world of ordinary people, reveals his relationship to the "mid-century generation." He believes that the novelist must be true to his time and avoid forms which do not answer urgent artistic needs. In the prologue to his Obras completas (1966) he admits that he started as an unconscious or intuitive rather than intellectual writer, stressing simplicity of style and attempting to escape the unpleasant contemporary world through the evocation of childhood. In the prologue to the third volume (1968) he notes that there is more intellectual content and existentialism in his works than he had realized, although childhood, death, and nature are continuing themes. He rejects the social novel, but he agrees that Spanish society urgently needs revision. Above all he stresses the need for what he calls "the sentiment of one's fellow man," a concern for the human situation. One critic states that a definite change of style from the traditional to a more introspective analysis occurs in Delibes's works from about 1950 on, as the author places the reader in contact with "the common people", an apparent objectivity which disguises what in reality is a clearly subjective portrayal.[21] In Cinco horas con Mario (1966) Delibes's psychological penetration is substantiated through the long monologue of the woman before her husband's corpse, but the novel reflects equally clearly an external reality fashioned by stupidity, injustice, and ignorance.

Ignacio Aldecoa (1925-1969), probably Spain's best contemporary short-story writer, rejects esthetics, although he admires Malraux. Among his Spanish literary ancestors he acknowledges Valle-Inclán and Gómez de la Serna, both aloof and "aristocratic," but his protagonists are humble folk, truck drivers, gypsies, transient farmers, and fishermen, little people fenced in by life but striving for human dignity. In their solitude as victims of fate they typify the Spanish pueblo and what Aldecoa himself once called "immutable Spain." He stated that "what moves me above all is the conviction that there is a Spanish reality, crude and tender at the same time, which is almost unpublished in our novel."[22] Among his novels are Gran sol (1957), about fishing boats, life on board, and the monotony and fatalistic resignation of the fishermen, and Parte de una historia (1967), about the effect of foreign tourists on a fishing village.

Ana María Matute (1926-) concentrates on alienation, violence, love, hate, pain, cruelty, death, the passage of time, solitude, and nature, which often reflect her pessimistic view of mankind. Largely lyrical and subjective, she differs from the pseudo-objectivists of her generation through her special talent "in extracting the invisible reality of the external world . . . and 'eternal Spain.'"[23] At times, with a childlike view of magic and mystery, she recalls the Mansilla region of her youth, but she cannot escape the contemporary world of fear, suspicion, cruelty, and tormented children in need of love. Her pessimism, revealed also through her Cain-Abel confrontations, undoubtedly a reflection of the tragic fratricidal Spanish struggle which she cannot forget, is only occasionally relieved by a religious awareness of the need for redemption. She refuses to exclude herself from the sorrow of Spain, believing that in addition to portraying national reality the novel should wound the conscience of readers.

She uses a diversity of stylistic techniques, "lush and poetic . . . harsh and realistically detailed . . . in fact, an intentional effort to fuse the manner of expression with the development of the material."[24] She also shows a predilection for oneiric symbols, interior monologue, flashback, and temporal experimentation. When asked in 1960 about European contacts Matute stated that "as a novelist my critical freedom is limited to society and its vital forms and not to literature written because of the same critical function of other creators,"[25] but she admits that her European favorites are Sartre, Camus, Pratolini, Vittorini, and Pavese. Her trilogy Los mercaderes, set in Mallorca, is at times a bitter allegory. Primera memoria (1960), the first volume, records the passage from childhood to adolescence. Los soldados lloran de noche (1964), the second volume, shows man as a victim of his world, and La trampa (1968), a tender and poetic novel, reveals a continuing existential preoccupation with loneliness, the meaning of human freedom, and man's inability to adapt to the real world in which he himself has perverted the Christian message.

The objectivist pattern in Spain was shaken in 1962 with the publication of Tiempo de silencio by Luis Martín Santos (1924-1964). Martín Santos wanted the reader to assume "mentally the situations described through a new procedure: it is no longer a question of submerging directly--as all forms of recent realism have done--into an objectivity which is offered in a direct way, but of capturing and introducing him to it by the magic of the verbal form."[26] The novel's antirhetorical language, interior monologues, and linguistic subjectivity reveal the author's indebtedness to European novelists like Mann, Proust, and his favorite, Joyce. But unlike Joyce he attempts to interpret his reality and use his mythology in a social framework. He stated that "the new French novel seems sterile and precious to me. Italian realism is breathing its last. I believe that one may rely on a German renovation of a romantic, intellectual nature, one might say Kafkaen. . . ."[27] Martín Santos evinced great interest in the existentialist philosophy of Sartre and read Martin Heidegger, Wilhelm Dilthey, and Oswald Spengler.

In his novel Martín Santos, through the failure of his young doctor protagonist, shows us alienated man in a cruel and tragic Spain, the social sores, and the shortcomings of the Catholic Church in his country, where one can live only in "the time of silence" because society rejects and frustrates the individual who criticizes the status quo. Yet man will continue to struggle with his inability to communicate, ensuing loneliness and anguish, and with a variety of other spiritual problems.

Juan Goytisolo (1931-) combines the traditional picaresque novel with interior monologue, reportorial, temporal, or cinematographic techniques to treat the fate of the postwar generations. Extracting incidents from his own experience and contrasting the indifference and cynicism resulting from the death and destruction caused by the Spanish Civil War with an innocent world of make-believe, of fairy tales and fables, he finds in the actions of children, torn apart by adult emotions of love and hate in a poverty-stricken world of violence and hunger, a microcosm of adult life.

Goytisolo's favorite novelists are the Americans: John Dos Passos, Carson McCullers, Truman Capote, William Styron, and William Faulkner; but he was also impressed by French writers like André Malraux, Proust, and especially Gide, and by the Italians Pavese and Vittorini.[28] At first he seemed almost a disciple of Robbe-Grillet, but since 1959 he has rejected the latter's excessive objectivity, stressing his lack of lyrical and esthetic intent, unity of form and content, and uncertain value system. Goytisolo cannot accept Robbe-Grillet's contention that literature may not serve a political cause,[29] nor can he escape his role in attempting to further justice.

Goytisolo held Ortega y Gasset as primarily responsible for having created a situation in which Spanish readers found more in foreign novels than in national ones to satisfy their sentimental and moral needs, unfulfilled by the stylized efforts of Ortega's aristocratic followers. In spite of Goytisolo's own insistence on a national novel, he has borrowed extensively from European sources, experimenting with narrative rhythms, abrupt transitions from past to future, and impressionistic portrayals of groups of people whom he joins and abandons and whose lives intersect briefly in parallel and contrapuntal plots. Some of his characters seem devoid of real humanity, but all have relevance to the total structural complexities he creates. He later came to believe that in molding the material of his novel to a specific form and by using cinematic techniques he had indulged in an intellectual exercise because in his search for a structured originality he had deformed authenticity of situation and character.

Juegos de manos (1954), a beautiful description of adolescent hate, love, and rebellion, bears a definite relationship to Gide's Les faux-monnayeurs; Duelo en el Paraíso (1955) resembles both William Golding's Lord of the Flies (1954) and Les Enfants Terribles by Jean Cocteau, showing us the tragedy which ensues when children act out adult roles. In these tales of defeated and disillusioned victims of society Goytisolo, along with his characters, indulges in an idealistic search for a viable future.

In La resaca (1958), more clearly a reportorial novel about religious and political factors in Spain, he uses focus shifts and objective description. La isla (1961) continues his indictment of society, emphasizing Spanish sexuality in a grotesque and self-righteous country dedicated to self-destructive hedonism and alienated from the world of the spirit. The reader of these novels can only conclude that the wicked world will always frustrate the noble and good.

In Señas de identidad (1966), an outspoken attack on the Franco police state, Goytisolo describes Spain as a "dark river bed of suffering, an immense sea where no ray of light has touched or ever would: a barefoot, empty-handed and broken life of millions and millions of countrymen, frustrated in their personal essence, relegated, humiliated, sold, a suffering mass of beings entering the world without apparent logic. . . ."[30] Imposed intellectual conformity is so strong that soon a secret police will no longer be necessary for the thirty million Spaniards who welcome millions of European and American tourists to enjoy the local sun. Alvaro Mendiola, the protagonist, searches for himself through documents and memory recall, exploring historical, geographical, temporal, and spatial relationships in a search for Spain's signs and their meaning.

Goytisolo's mature novels intensify the faithful transcription of Spanish society, but his detailed documentation does not detract from his identification with his creations in a world where normal passions and the quality of being human are frustrated. Goytisolo projects reality through strange symbols and structures which appeal to a reader's multilevel perceptions. He extracts esthetic possibilities from ordinary life to achieve a combination with his ethical preoccupations. Always keenly aware of European literary movements and the infinite possibilities of artistic creation, he has not functioned absolutely within the esthetic limitations imposed by any movement.

Goytisolo's generation, in attacking Ortega y Gasset and Unamuno, wanted not to destroy but to modify their literary inheritance in conformity with their new culture. In 1965, when France had ceased for almost thirty years to concentrate on Gide or Valéry, Spanish critics still operated around the writers of the Generation of Ninety-Eight. Goytisolo himself feels more at home with university positivism, Marxist criticism, existentialist theories, and structural or formalist criticism than do most of his fellow novelists. He firmly believes that Spaniards, in keeping with new findings in anthropology, sociology, and psychology, should no longer limit themselves to a single monolithic and dogmatic level. Tradition is an unmoving force, and culture cannot be exclusively inherited; it must be forged by each new generation.

In spite of the apparent immobility of its political superstructure, Spain, in accepting the modern industrial world, is undergoing concomitant moral and cultural changes. The nobility and loyalty which supposedly characterized Spaniards have disappeared, along with "the sentimental and moral reasons for our adhesion to the pueblo, so brave during the Civil War but responsible, because or its pasivity, for the present government."[31] Europeans in their esthetic admiration of "backward Spain" help support its old structures and to petrify its history, although tourists have opened Spanish eyes to the possibility of a new monetary religion. In copying the superficial aspects of foreign models without having had the requisite social education and training, Spaniards have created the caricature of a Western society. Before Spain can recreate itself it must be willing to face its reality, uncover the hypocrisy and egotism beneath its masks of pride, and reinforce the cause of human aspiration in its populace which has deteriorated into the "shadow of a people."

As one examines other well-known contemporary Spanish novelists one finds that some are traditional, some reveal older European influences, some relate new techniques to traditional matter, and a very few experiment with a universal thematic and structural matrix. Antonio Ferres (1925-) subordinates technique to ideology and a direct transcription of unpleasant reality in La piqueta (1959) and other novels. He likes Pavese, Pratolini, and Moravia and is familiar with Butor's works, but he believes that foreign models will have to be greatly modified before they can influence Spanish contemporaries interested in reflecting their own time and culture.[32] Antonio Martínez-Menchén (1930-) follows Proust, Joyce, and Kafka. His Cinco variaciones (1963) is a sociological exposé combining themes of alienation and sexual frustration. Daniel Sueiro (1931-), in La criba (1961), also shows the influences of Kafka, and reveals the sordid life of journalists in Madrid. Corte de corteza (1969), a realistic science-fiction novel about a near future world, deals with an increasing awareness of universal problems and man's alienation in an industrialized and technical society. The author explores the moral and ethical problems involved in brain transplants as the protagonist, given a new body, cannot accept the joys of love or beauty in an otherwise cynical and hypocritical world.

Some readers profess to find in the contemporary Spanish novel "a radical liquidation of tradition . . . their effort transcended the limits of previous renovations, giving them an amplitude, a universality which has only rarely been seen in their literature."[33] More reasonably, Edmund Stephen Urbanski believes that the "cultural environment of Spain of today gives witness to certain intellectual phenomena which seem to indicate a change in the evaluation of its culture and in the revision of its orthodox thought toward the foreign."[34] The younger novelists are abandoning social realism as they become more and more absorbed by the world around them, intensifying and magnifying reality through shaping its infinite possibilities rather than its mere reproduction. A few have been educated in European cultural centers or have been in close contact with European authors. Jesús Torbado (1942-), who has traveled all over Europe as a kind of vagabond, tells of corrupting factors in modern life, sings of the corruptibility of one's faith in God, man, and self, and follows Sartre, Joyce, and Hermann Hesse in Las corrupciones (1966); but his protagonist, José Antonio Fernández, seems straight out of a novel by Pío Baroja. La construcción del odio (1968), inspired by Kafka, protests against the establishment and man's lack of freedom. Torbado's Historia de amor (1969), has a timeless setting in its exposure of man's hypocrisy and deceit and the self-deception in which he lives. Torbado believes that solitude, which usually invites despair or stoicism, may imply hope and become the key to modern man's existence. José María Guelbenzú (1944-) in El mercurio, in which he himself is a character, relies on the technique of stream-of-consciousness, creating a mosaic of illogical and absurd situations, strange obsessions, word tricks, and literary allusions, especially to his favorite, James Joyce. Germán Sánchez Espeso, a young Jesuit professor of theology, breaks completely with Spanish tradition in Experimento en Génesis (1967), a detailed and stylized intellectual description filled with cinematographic imagery, geometric forms, and interior monologue. His protagonist, an alienated writer who has been abandoned by a girl and a young criminal he has protected, serves as a point of departure for an allegorical elaboration of biblical themes. Juan Benet Goitia (1927-), fond of Melville, Faulkner, and Henry James, in Volverás a Región (1967) uses a ninety-page first chapter to introduce the historical and geographical background and two alternating monologues to convey a pessimistic vision of contemporary life. Región serves as a focal center for a symbolic re-creation of tragic Civil War events. Una meditación (1969), a long discourse, the living memory of a man, his motivations and sentiments which he himself analyses, reinforces the author's view that existence is an enigma in an unknown universe.

Allegorical, lyrical, introspective, and existentialist novels exist in contemporary Spain, but one still encounters more commonly autobiographical and cathartic novels about the restrictive and gray Spanish world. After 1965 Spanish novelists at times show a more sophisticated involvement with European trends, but essentially themes are traditionally Spanish. Other countries have economic and cultural environments largely foreign to the Spanish way of life, and European culture has had much more effect on Spanish critics than on its novelists. Some novelists, as we have seen, rejected the traditional modes but without ending their alienation from Europe which has no validity for their private search for authenticity. Others have created artificial but unoriginal visions of the world. As life becomes more industrialized and the economic level rises, the feeling of alienation, entrapment, and discontent grows, but Spanish fiction has not been fundamentally altered. The novel continues to fulfill its political, social, and journalistic function because today one is still severely limited by censorship in Spain. In the novelist's continuing concern with his society and commitment to social change, he employs new forms but reflects, in the given moments of the contemporary scene, old philosophies. Few Spaniards can convey or utilize a three-dimensional experience to communicate in an ever-shifting and changing world. Realism, fantasy, and the quest for authentic values in a society without them have created a confused jumble in the novelist's mind. Whereas in other parts of Europe novelists express their own visions and obsessions, their own reality, Spanish novelists still, by and large, continue to describe a country where old myths survive, even though they have lost their functional powers in a nation which has stopped being truly Spanish without ever having become European.

Notes

[1] Christian F. Krause (1781-1832) was a Kantian who taught philosophy at Heidelberg. Sanz del Río, who held a scholarship at this university, returned to his native Spain imbued with Krause's ideas and began what was later termed the "Krausista" movement in Spain. This actually turned more into a humanistic and harmonious style of life than a philosophy, but it became an active element in the endless struggle between liberals and conservatives, Krause himself remains virtually unknown in philosophical circles, but his influence on Spanish thought shows once again how completely Spain was isolated from the European mainstream and how strongly the Spanish intellectual reacts when brought into contact with the outside world.

[2] The most important members were Unamuno, Baroja, Azorín, Valle-Inclán, A. Machado, and Maeztu.

[3] José Ortega y Gasset, *Obras completas* (Madrid, 1957), I:543.

[4] Guillermo de Torre, "Hacia un más allá del realismo novelesco," *Revista de Occidente* 4 (July 1963), 106-14.

[5] "The Modern Spanish Novel," *Texas Quarterly* 4 (1961), 83.

[6] See Robert G. Mead, Jr., "Dictatorship and Literature in the Spanish World," *Books Abroad* 25 (1951), 223-26; also see Julián Marías, *Books Abroad* 26 (1952), 232-36, and *Meditaciones sobre la sociedad española* (Madrid, 1966), 36.

[7] "Por que el mundo desconoce la novela española," *Estudios Americanos* 10, no. 47 (1955), 139-66.

[8] *Sur* 284 (Sept.-Oct. 1963), 51; and "Juan Goytisolo y la novela española actual," *La Torre* 9, no. 33 (1961), 132.

[9] *El espejo y el camino* (Madrid, 1968), 12.

[10] María Embeita, "Francisco Ayala y la novela," *Insula* 22 (March 1967), 6.

[11] Andrés Amorós, "Novelas y novelistas," *Revista de Occidente* 5, no. 47 (1967), 240-46.

[12] Andrés Amorós, *Insula* 24 (Jan. 1969), 6.

[13] Manuel Lamana, *Literatura de posguerra* (Buenos Aires, 1961), 36.

[14] Pablo Gil Casado, La novela social española, 1942-1968 (Barcelona, 1968).

[15] J. Corrales Egea, "Crisis de la nueva literatura," Insula 20 (June 1965), 10.

[16] Infra-realism: the novel is its own reality, and the imaginary therein becomes more real than exterior reality and thus goes beyond it.

[17] José R. Marra López, "Ramón J. Sender, novelista español," Insula 19 (April 1964), 5.

[18] David Foster, Forms of the Novel in the Works of Camilo José Cela (Columbia, Mo., 1967), 158-59.

[19] The Novels and Travels of Camilo José Cela (Chapel Hill, N.C., 1963), 182.

[20] José Ortega y Gasset, Obras completas (Madrid, 1957), 3:416.

[21] Ramón Buckley, Problemas formales de la novela española contemporánea (Barcelona, 1968), 85-136.

[22] Juan Luis Alborg, Hora actual de la novela española (Madrid, 1958), 263.

[23] Geoge Wythe, "The World of Ana María Matute," Books Abroad 40 (1966), 19.

[24] Margaret Jones, "Antipathetic Fallacy: The Hostile World of Ana María Matute's Novels," Kentucky Foreign Language Quarterly 13 (1967), 6.

[25] Insula 15 (March 1960) 4.

[26] José Antonio Gómez Marín, "Literatura y política. Del tremendismo a la nueva narrativa," Cuadernos Hispanoamericanos 45, no. 193 (1966), 112-13.

[27] Janet Winecoff, "Luis Martín Santos and the Contemporary Spanish Novel," Hispania 51 (May 1968), 230-38.

[28] Letter to Maurice Coindreau, 29 June 1955 in Jeux de Mains (Paris, 1956), xx.

[29] Juan Goytisolo, "Formalismo y compromismo literario," Casa de las Américas 4, no. 26 (1964), 149.

[30] Juan Goytisolo, Señas de identidad (Mexico, 1966), 376-77.

[31] Juan Goytisolo, El furgón de cola (Paris, 1967), 4.

[32] Insula 22 (March 1967), 6.

[33] Juan Carlos Curutchet, Introducción a la novela española de posguerra (Montevideo, 1966), 10-11.

[34] "El revisionismo en la valoración de las letras y cultura contemporánea de España," Hispania 48 (1965), 816.

THEMATIC AND STYLISTIC CONSTANTS IN THE
FICTION OF ALFONSO GROSSO

Alfonso Grosso (1928-), born in Seville, lost both parents when he was only nineteen years of age. The concomitant financial and emotional pressures to which he was subjected, undoubtedly affecting his development as both artist and man, reinforced his tragic sense of life. After working for the government of Spain for a number of years, Grosso began writing seriously only in 1956, winning the Sesamo prize for "Carboneo," a short story later included in Germinal y otros relatos (1963). His first novel, La zanja (1961), finished second to Ana María Matute's Primera Memoria in the Nadal competition of 1959. Guarnición de silla won the Critics' Prize for 1970. In between these two prize-winning novels, Grosso produced Un cielo difícilmente azul (1961), Testa de copo (1963), El capirote (1966), and Inés Just Coming (1968). Forbidden in Spain, De romería, which together with Testa de copo and El capirote was to have formed a trilogy under the title A la izquierda del sol, has not yet been published. Inés Just Coming, subtitled "compás de espera de un ciclón en el Caribe," is the first volume of a promised trilogy, Legados y capitulaciones. In addition to his novels Grosso has written religious poetry and has co-authored several travel works.

Grosso's physical world regularly reflects two classes of society, the very rich and the very poor. Delighting in the microcosm of life afforded by small cafés and tavems, he denounces poverty and corrupt politics, essential parts of his world, and excoriates the execrable system of Spanish justice, police procedures, and jails. His lower-class fictional creations, who for the most part lead gray and hopeless lives, together with his upper-class characters, who suffer empty ones apparently devoid of principles of social significance, try to evade the pressures of the world through obsessive absorption in sex, cars, or hunting and fishing. Grosso, as a setting for this febrile human activity, provides us with lyrical descriptions of beautiful natural phenomena: sunrises, sunsets, magnificent starry skies, and the sea, which above all holds an irresistible attraction for him.

In Grosso's fictional universe, men without work and victims of various governmental inequities exist under substandard conditions. One of the "underdogs" of La zanja, Pedro, typically, lives in a "pobre mísera y triste casa excavada en la tierra."[1] Carlos, the lamplighter, coughs up bloody sputum as he awaits his inevitable fate. Attempts at labor organization and human solidarity fail because the workers are unable to unite effectively against the establishment. Accustomed to bad treatment and hoping for any relief, the men cannot trust one another, unsure as to who may be a company spy. In Un cielo difícilmente azul, peopled by truck drivers, washer women, carpenters, and grave diggers, the poor in the chabolas experience a life of poverty and unforgotten Civil War antagonisms. One of the truckers, Angel, recognizes a Republican friend from twenty years before who through disguise and good luck had managed to achieve a kind of success. Not so fortunate are most of the others, even though the younger generations talk of redeeming the worker. For them life is grim; death is more positive: "El estado se preocupa de los muertos, Es una ventaja. Algo es algo."[2]

These same poverty-stricken citizens appear in later stories and novels. In Germinal we see hunger, depressed times, and black market operations. In Testa de copo the fishermen attempt in vain to preserve their traditional percentages received from the fishing company. Marcelo, a small man, through his false arrest, shows us how victimized modern man can be. In El capirote, the figure of Christ Crucified offers no salvation for hapless workers who belong to society's infrastructure. Grosso, in contrasting the life of rich and poor, contends that workers of the entire world suffer hunger, cold, and deprivation, but Juan's longing for a small plot of land symbolizes a fantasy never to be fulfilled by most Spaniards. Grosso, in his American scenes of Inés just Coming, filled with cubanismos, English, and French, admits that life under Fidel Castro means the lack of coffee, cigarettes, and night clubs. It also implies a complete change in social acceptance of the unfortunate of the world. Helena, nostalgically recalling the former good life, never dreamed that "una guajira y un asiático pudieran sentarse frente a ella en un restaurante, dormir en una habitación de su mismo hotel u ocupar un apartamento frontero al suyo . . . discutir tú a tú con el vecino del Norte; sentarse en los pupitres--o en los estrados--de las aulas universitarias . . . bañarse en las aguas de las mismas piscinas que ella frecuenta."[3] Yet even in a supposed worker's paradise poor Chino must find money so that his wife and child may have lodging for the night. Guarnición de silla reveals the other side of the coin, a conspicuous consumption by ladies and aristrocrats who worry about archeology, castles, masked balls, and five o'clock teas.

Grosso knows police and their methods in Spain. In Testa de copo Marcelo, unjustly arrested, is classified as a schizophrenic and committed to an insane asylum because he rebels against his incarceration. Juan, of El capirote, is falsely accused of stealing a golden chain by the woman whose advances he rejected. After six months in jail awaiting trial, suffering cold and illness (he cannot receive state clothes since he is not officially a prisoner), he is freed, without

74

explanation or recompense, when the missing object turns up. Grosso portrays the procedures, transfers, false confessions under torture, declarations and depositions, and jail life itself, all affronts to human decency.

In Grosso's novels aroused and frustrated women make advances to men, a number of whom, in turn, accost a variety of women. Promiscuity, prostitution, homosexuality, lesbianism, and extra-marital affairs represent an exploding sensuality and sexuality (a constant in Grosso's novels) which reach fruition in Inés Just Coming, filled with loose and half-naked women, whores, adulterous wives, complacent husbands, ready to share their spouses' favors with other men, defloration, and masturbation. The women professionals perform for perfume and fine clothes, which in Cuba are far more precious than money. In Guarnición de silla the love affairs continue, a sexuality reemphasized by a homosexual attachment and a seduction by a priest.

Automobiles, especially sports cars, appear to mesmerize Grosso, who fills his novels with a machine world of trucks, Land Rovers, and Ferraris. They represent for him an instrument of fatality, responsible for the denouement in a number of novels and the deaths of various characters. In La zanja a tourist driver hits and kills Garabito, a truck driver recalls war and death, and characters become concerned with the number of cars produced in the Citroën factory. Cars, carrying man on his road of life, which leads to death, thus become the instruments or vehicles, both literally and figuratively, of that life or death. Grosso delights in detailed descriptions of trucks and cars, recalling, almost lovingly, "la suavidad táctil del volante de un Ferrari."[4] Miguel Angel, of Guarnición de silla, is an expert collector of old cars, and the entire novel builds to the inevitable crash of Ignacio's sports car with a truck and a Land Rover.

Nature, as has been stated, is important for Grosso, who depicts the varying moods of the sea, rolling waves, ships, sea gulls, and schools of fish. The sea may be kind or cruel, but it has its own beauty. Every novel contains positive nature descriptions which contrast with human miasmas, symbolized often by the corresponding interaction of light and darkness, for man despoils God's creations. Nature's interplay of colors seems to fascinate Grosso: "La tierra negra y esponjada de las huertas rebrilla con la luz nueva; con la luz nueva reverbera la tierra calma, que se tornasola de ocres y de azules en los surcos donde la flor blanca del algodón, húmeda de blancura, se despereza";[5] "el cielo se ha tornado gris mate, verdoso por oriente; pero hay un resto de añil sobre el monte bajo, sobre los canchales de piedra. . .";[6] "La noche era pura y azul . . . llegaba el aroma del azahar."[7]

Many of Grosso's characters are tragic rather than wicked, living creatures who know pain, suffer, love, and hate. Others are hypocritical and dishonest, believing in nothing but survival. At times their primordial instincts fuse with primitive prejudice and rebellion; at others they are the ordinary people we might encounter anywhere. Pilete, the old traveling musician; Mrs. Humphrey, the garden lover; Rosarito, loving mother; Eugenio, who dreams of love and marriage; Doña Edugivis, retired owner of several whorehouses, who passes her days playing cards and reminiscing with an old servant; and don Roque Prado, a civil guard lieutenant, more than pale reflections of fictional humanity, lend a special dimension of life to La zanja. Angel and Remigio, the truck drivers, and Pedro and Nacho, the would-be criminals in Un cielo difícilmente azul, and Germinal, a young man from the short story by that name, live in a world where deceit and counter-deceits, masks against life, seem necessary to survive. Marcelo's friends, in Testa de copo, know he is innocent but refuse to get involved. They are as much victims of society as he himself is a psychological victim of the nullity imposed upon him. Helena, of Inés Just Coming, suffering from personal estrangement, misses hand-made clothes as much as love. In Guarnición de silla Grosso attempts to add a philosophical introspection to the meaning of being a man in an existential universe. Ignacio, who had abandoned the city thirty-two years before, comes back to search for himself and his memories. As with most of the other characters in this novel, a trivial group on the periphery of life who substitute sex and empty activity for values, he exudes a pervasive air of unreality.

Grosso throughout implies that life has little purpose in the face of ineluctable fate. In La zanja Carlos makes his rounds in the rain, knowing that just as the mud has spattered the laundry his mother has washed for the American colony, so will blood stain his clothes and end his life. Pedro, realizing that we die little by little, believes, nonetheless, that one must keep on living. Totó feels that his life has no purpose beyond temporary sexual relief in Rosario's hut, and he lives "con el miedo clavándosele como una aguja en la garganta."[8] Romero even more disillusioned, states: "Estoy ya cansado de soñar y dejo pasar los días por tal de seguir viviendo, aunque mi vida sea una vida que no merezca ser vivida."[9]

In Un cielo difícilmente azul Grosso more directly attacks the problem of man's temporality, the mystery of existence, and the tragic dimensions of life which inevitably lead to death.

He promotes a kind of predestination involving inevitable future events over which man has no control. The unexpected, the lethal, and the liability to disaster comprise the complex of antecedents whose interaction precludes the possibility of any other end. From the moment that Nacho steals the cartridges at the police station, it becomes inevitable that he will kill the man who saw him. Frustrated in their robbery attempt, Pedro and Nacho force Remigio to drive them in his truck, which takes a curve at too much speed, crashes, and kills them all. Yet, Grosso seems to say, free will might prevail, if characters only knew how to choose wisely. Angel and Remigio, after bringing the altar to the local church, instead of returning, stay over to take on an unauthorized load of coal for money, with fatal consequences. Similarly, in Germinal y otros cuentos, Rodrigo, attempting to hide some stolen watches in a honeycomb, is stung to death by bees,

Although it may be argued that existentially choice of some kind is always involved, Grosso in his later novels of implacable fate, not so directly involved with this freedom, seems to say that in an absurd world all choices end badly. Doubt, disenchantment, and boredom are the fate of modern man, unable to cope with his daily life and destiny. Made aware of the passing time by constant tolling hours, Marcelo, in Testa de copo, constantly fears his inevitable end. His father had died in a drunken stupor in a puddle of water, and he knows that someday he too will succumb to a liquid death: "Siempre la muerte a la mar, o frente a ella, o para el inevitable holocausto dentro de ella, y, por tanto más muerte de hombre que de mujer, menos temida por esperada ya desde el nacimiento. o a lo sumo, desde el momento del raciocinio. . . ."[10] When he slips and falls on the boat hook, in the testa de copo he had abandoned five years earlier, he has fulfilled what destiny had in store for him. Passing time is also important in El capirote. Juan's appointment with death is measured off by striking bells and tower clocks. He suffers, waits, and hopes in vain. Obtaining a job as helper in carrying the heavy religious statue, he is crushed to death under the feet of his fellow workers, most of whom, small men, too, have only temporarily escaped Juan's doom.

In Inés Just Coming and Guarnición de silla, where disparate and apparently unrelated figures meet to fulfill fate's decree, Grosso emphasizes how intertwined human lives are. In the end, historical fatality will bring people and hurricane or people and cars together, and nobody will win. The members of Ignacio's family had mostly met tragic deaths of various kinds, as will he in his little red sports car, which collides with a truck and the Land Rover driven by Jaime. Burnt beyond recognition, Ignacio will not achieve, even in death, his heart's desire, burial in the family pantheon. Historical and legendary evocations supply a counterpoint for tragedy, frustration, and false hopes, as Grosso's characters futilely attempt to escape their fate.

Grosso presents his themes and situations through fleeting exposures and a kind of baroque counterpoint, leading to a final synthesis. Alternating stories and characters, without apparent immediate connection, interspersed dialogue and interior monologues combined with time jumps, flashbacks and memories triggered by objects such as a wine glass, are elements of his style, In <u>Inés Just Coming</u> Grosso deliberately imitates Guillermo Cabrera Infante and other Spanish American novelists of the moment, intensifying experimental techniques such as alternating recalls, chains of association, interior monologue, and fragmented explanations of conversation and action. The author gives incredibly detailed delineations of every little act, simulating psychic flow with broken and unpunctuated chains of associations. He includes, at the beginning of each interior monologue or free association, an enumeration of diverse objects. Typical is a trip to the airport by Helena to meet her husband: "Máscaras, caretas, apliques, lámparas, bolsas de rafia, abanicos, sombreros de yarey; albos pañolicos de cabeza, collares jaspeados, ceniceros de Isla de Pinos, manteletas de hilo con lentejuela; tumbadoras, maracas, pulseras de madera . . . Se persigna Bartolomé de las Casas en un reclinatorio de caña güin. . .Los tacones tamborilean el aluminio. En la diagonal la medalla de la Caridad del Cobre muestra su reverso: En fila india, entarjetados de cartulinas verdes y rosas, hacia el DC-8 que huele a perfume de Dana, caminan los 'gusanos.' . . .Y, a fin de cuentas, ¿puede saberse por qué me voy?"[11]

In <u>Guarnición de silla</u> an even greater intensification of stylistic techniques occurs, involving the recall of one hundred and fifty-two years of family history, the time of Joseph Bonaparte, and sugar mills and slavery in Cuba. Much of this recall is triggered by photo albums or by objects as diverse as grapevines, a train, or sculptures, described in great detail. Begga falls asleep while reading the history of the house of Trastamara; in a kind of stupor she witnesses the family chronicle. Through interior monologue and dialogue within her mind, along with alternating third person recalls, we shift from character to character and time to time. Claudia, the dying nun, also threads associations and third person description into her recall, as does Ignacio. Grosso employs exhaustive depiction and metaphorical outbursts throughout: "como el barquito cabeceante agrandando por la óptica, el cetáceo de acero, lustroso y ya despreñado, que acaba de levar anclas después de vaciar su opulento vientre concebido allende los mares por el priapo del tubo anillado, falo del submarino oleoducto proveedor, tropical serpiente de los espigones petroleros de Oruba, enfila vacío, alto de borda, ebrio de cotas, hinchado ya de nada como un globo de seda--playero balón de cascos rojigualdos . . . junto a los mosaicos romanos, las ánforas griegas, las medallas de Licinio y Salamina, las monedas de Jano, los bronces de Gordiano y Nerón . . . Y las hachas obsidianas y los diminutos falos de jaspe hallados en las necrópolis ibéricas de Jadramil, dispuesto sobre los estratificados de cuarcita--en las vidrieras de la sala capitular: amiantos, alberos, argentíferas partículas, rosadas transparencias, arenas ocres, sienas y azules salpicadas de ramalazos cárdenos o desvaídos de añiles y verdes marítimos, frente a las mazas de plata, los sombreros de alas anchas de terciopelo rojo con moños de seda carmín y las capas pluviales ribeteadas de galones dorados y marchitos, y las otras piedras. . . ."[12]

In his early work Grosso attempted to follow the documentary realism so popular in the 1950's, later verging toward a more aesthetic kind of realism, without thereby denying social imperatives. In his later novels which emphasize the aristocratic and jet set over workers and fishermen, he states things in a different way but continues to analyze problems from which, as a Spaniard, he cannot remain aloof, even though he situates them in a more cosmopolitan framework. He attempts to use language in a new way, inevitably creating a certain ambiguity for the reader accustomed to older forms in which, superficially, the author seems to express himself more clearly. Undoubtedly a social realist, he nonetheless seeks to explore the infinite possibilities this reality affords instead of merely reproducing it. His philosophy that existence is an enigma is not new, but he attempts to express it through a stylistic synthesis of the spiritual and physical. Grosso, an imaginative and forceful novelist, uniting the political and the poetic, combines a mature technical artistry with social and moral imperatives and a firm knowledge of the emotions and experiences of human beings. Having created his own special view of man's suffering in a world of chance, without magic or miracles, where most players are doomed to lose, he reinforces this feeling of alienation through his implication that only death gives a final solution and freedom from implacable fate.

Notes

[1] Alfonso Grosso, La zanja (Barcelona, 1961), p. 225.

[2] Alfonso Grosso, Un cielo difícilmente azul (Barcelona, 1961), p. 129.

[3] Alfonso Grosso, Inés Just Coming (Barcelona, 1968), p. 144.

[4] Ibid., p. 15.

[5] La zanja, p. 26.

[6] Un cielo difícilmente azul, p. 58.

[7] Alfonso Grosso, El capirote (Mexico, 1966), p. 9.

[8] La zanja. pp. 226-27.

[9] Ibid., p. 223.

[10] Alfonso Grosso, Testa de copo (Barcelona, 1963), pp. 34-35.

[11] Inés Just Coming, pp. 145-47.

[12] Alfonso Grosso, Guarnición de silla (Barcelona, 1970), pp. 10, 14.

CARLOS ROJAS VILA AND AN ACT OF FAITH

Carlos Rojas, the author of several previous novels, in *Auto de fe* (1968) has produced what *Spain Today*, impressed by the novel's magic, gripping atmosphere, calls "one of the high points of modern fiction. . ."[1] As in his earlier works, Rojas deals with the meaning of faith and Christ's sacrifice on the cross, but the novel's two intertwining plots concentrate on the resurrection of Lazarus and events in the court of Carlos II, *el hechizado*. Lazarus, a fictional recreation in *El autillo de Lázaro*, a theatrical piece written by the king, also awakens in the contemporary world of the court of Carlos to share in the dreams and real life situations.

Rojas' bewildered reader is gradually drawn into the novel's creation and supplies many of the links before they appear. Using infinite shades and contrasts, multiple exposures and perspectives, Rojas both shows us the interior life of his tormented protagonist and parodies it. He uses a mixture of allegorical, theological, ontological, and archetypal symbols to convey his religious allegory, but in spite of his temporal jumps and anachronisms, he creates the effect of a linear development rather than that of superimposed structural levels. He mixes dreams, demons, witchcraft, and a baroque simulation of reality which seems more real than reality itself.

Baroque fragments which later fuse into a viable whole are accompanied by minute observations, and an apparent superimposed sameness, with countless subtle variations of the repeated accumulation of events and memories shared by various people. The same scenes are repeated over and over again from different points of view by different characters who take over the narration within the novel to achieve a special kind of deflected reality. We learn of Lazarus' death not only from the *Autillo's* prologue but from the king himself. Hernando Lapuente, the father of twin girls, and the king both recall the buffoon's death. The king, the queen, Viviana, the jester's mother, and Baltasar, the inquisitor, describe the *auto de fe* in which Felipe Próspero, the jester's brother, dies. A number of leitmotifs recur throughout. Three drops of blood appear after the jester's night with the twins and in the queen's nightmare vision of the *auto de fe*. Thirty pieces of silver are given to Judas by Lazarus to encompass his death, by Lapuente to the dwarf to cure Elvira, his wife, of her unending menstrual flow, and by Judas's dog to Lazarus as his price of love for humanity. Other motifs include the light reflecting from the glasses of the dwarf and Lazarus, the allergic reaction of the king to cold, and the herd of pigs at the *auto de fe*.

A series of parallel events involving a sometimes puzzling circular completion repeat not only vocabulary and imagery but the central idea of resurrection and death. We see Jesus on the cross, Felipe Próspero on the cross, Lazarus resurrected, the buffoon resurrected. Dream and reality become confused, and narrators, both real and imagined, from real life and from the plays by Felipe and the king, offer a constantly changing focus and perspective along with alternating levels of consciousness. The twins, in their madness, want to conceive Felipe again and create an immortal, exactly as the daughter of Jairo of Capernaum in Lazarus' time, after she had been resurrected by Jesus, hoped for an eternal daughter. The king's monkey functions as the devil in the court of Carlos II as does Judas's dog in an earlier age. Essentially, these are the two principal time levels involved, but backward and forward sweeps in time through the jester's and Lazarus's mind occur constantly, as the latter, for example, recalls his sister's pleas, his first meeting with Christ, with Judas, and with Basamat, the leper girl. Rojas shows us that the past is an integral part of the present and inseparable from it, and in revealing what was and what is, stresses the fleeting quality of existence and the continuing acceptance of responsibility, guilt, and love to enhance and articulate his theme of resurrection.

The play written by the king, as a record of his dreams, and the actuality of Lazarus becomes intertwined until it is almost impossible to separate one from the other, the reality from the creation or the characters' dreams from those in the play. All have double roles. The dwarf becomes Lazarus, the king, Judas, and Lazarus, Jesus. As the play becomes part of the novel so do the dwarf's dreams and those of the created Lazarus. The stories fuse, and Lazarus of Bethany, resurrected, will dream that he is a dead jester, a nightmare within a nightmare. Is the jester dreamed by Lazarus or is Lazarus dreamed by the jester? Alternating between humor and pathos, history and invention, Rojas offers us dreams within dreams and metaphysical preoccupations which are simply another form of reality. The worlds we dream are no more unreal than our own, and we can never be sure whether we ourselves are not perhaps the products of another's dream, for all realities are paradoxes, And one of the central questions asked by Lazarus, by the buffoon, by the king, and by Felipe Próspero is: "Who art thou?".

This question concerning the reality of existence and the quest for identity is constantly reiterated, implemented by multiple use of the doppelgänger where two versions of personality are equal and interchangeable and by a kind of Unamunian use of "el otro" where ego fragments may be aware of themselves in the world and undergo ego transformations, which results in an alternative personality.² Lázaro learns: "Siempre hay otro detrás de cada acto que el hombre dice libre. Los otros son tú, Lázaro el necio. Te conciben, te paren, te aborrecen, te matan, te recuerdan, y tú no puedes ni siquiera negarte a concebirlos, parirlos, aborrecerlos, quererlos, matarlos, o recordarlos. Uno no es nadie."³ The dwarf shares the dreams of Lazarus who dreamed him in the same way that the dwarf dreamed Lazarus. The jester tries to wash away his brother's kiss as Lazarus had tried to remove the one Jesus gave him. He realizes that he may not be the parody of the Lazarus of the play but that Lazarus may be his own parody. Neither can abide the suffering of living when the one who gave him life has died. In the jester's death trance he has a son who is identical to his brother Felipe (Viviana comes to believe that the buffoon himself is her son Felipe) who in his dream died much in the way he had been killed on earth, and precisely for having given him life. The characters struggle to become, in flux, instead of being complete. When one twin becomes pregnant the other suffers a false pregnancy, for neither can survive alone or be distinguished through a solid identity.

The characters use a confused type of interior monologue of recalled history or a previous event in the mind, drawing ever closer to consciousness. Rojas reintroduces a passage almost verbatim, previously recorded within the novel as a memory. He usually uses italics or parentheses in shifting from the court of Carlos II to Lazarus and from conscious to subconscious passages, but at times he introduces material from earlier pages more directly. "Bufoncito, amigo . . . -Dime, Hernando. - ¿Te gustó el cantar de las mellizas?" Asombrado por cuestión tan imprevista me puse como la grana. Quise evitar recuerdo de mis pecados; pero las voces de las mozas hacían eco de la memoria. "Bufón, ¿duermes o vives? -Bufón, ¿Vives o mueres? -Vive. -Se le van los ojos de tus teticas a las mías, pasando la mirada por la luna. . . ."⁴ Rojas uses repetition skillfully to give an almost Cervantine flavor to his dialogue. "Llueve. -¿Llueve? Sí, mira--extendió la palma y mostróme una gota entre las rayas . . . Llegó la tormenta--musitó mi voz, en parte liberada. -Llegó--asintió el monarca. . . .Regresemos al coche antes de que arrecie. --Regresemos, entonces. Me miró a los ojos, a punto de volverse. ¿De veras es memoria el infierno? --Solo memoria, mi rey. --¿Lo juras? --Lo juro. . . ."⁵

The novel deals with several minor theological matters and a number of evangelical themes such as Christ's acceptance of man's collective guilt, the resurrection of Lazarus, Judas's betrayal of Jesus, the meaning of immortality and salvation, and the relationship of Christ's sacrifice to the universality of our contemporary life. On another level, through the eyes of the dwarf court jester, in addition to metaphysical inquiry about life, solitude, and death, we are given some insight into what customs in the court of Carlos II must have been. Yet the novel is only incidentally historical in spite of the accurate references about Carlos, the influence of certain priests, the attempts by the Church to exorcise his demons, and the various court intrigues. Characters alternate between the skepticism and doubt inherent in humanity and a desire for faith and belief in immortality. Judas is portrayed, in an unusual role, as a defender of society. Yet his doubts and passion make him literally and figuratively blind and lead him to destruction. He contends that he loved Jesus and followed Him of his own volition, even though Jesus had always insisted that the only will was that of His father in heaven. Judas committed suicide because he finally realized that he had not betrayed Jesus out of free will. He sold Jesus, it seemed to him, because his soul belonged to people on earth and not to heaven; he could not believe in a liberty which they lacked on earth and in a future justice promised, without betraying them. Judas laments that neither Lazarus nor Jesus, through their resurrection, were able to free man from his slavery. Yet he wants Jesus alive again because he is convinced that "sin el Hijo de Dios no hay justicia, y sin justicia no hay Dios."[6]

Lazarus agrees that Jesus, in order to fulfill prophecy, arranged to have Judas sell Him. Lazarus also understands Judas's hatred of oppressors and injustice. The dwarf writes that according to his immolated brother, Felipe, Judas sold Jesus because he believed that He had defrauded the people by offering them glory in death instead of life on earth and had thus sold man's liberty in exchange for eternal life. Judas argues with Lazarus (in the role of Christ) as to whether justice is possible and whether he was resurrected for the good of all or for the living dead. He believes that those who suffer persecution in the cause of justice will eventually own the earth, but he is not certain whether man will make his paradise on earth or in heaven. He admits that while there is one slave in the world all men are slaves. Only when the world belongs to all men will humanity enter the kingdom of heaven and Jesus's love for mankind be fulfilled.

Lazarus, in his dialogue with Judas's dog, states that Jesus's kingdom was not of this earth. The dog replies that it ought to be if Jesus (Lazarus) truly merited the title of "hijo de hombre." Lazarus has no easy answer when the sick of Bethany plead with him to bring back Jesus, for "no pudo fenecer y abandonarnos entre tanto sufrimiento y tanta desesperación."[7] Baltasar, the Chruch inquisitor, disputes Felipe's thesis that when all power dies man will be resurrected, but the dwarf (Lazarus) finally understands that hate, fear, egotism, and pride are what separate and isolate man like death itself. Love may be the answer which will revive our humanity and enable us to share in the resurrection and eternal life when death itself has died. Jesus, removed from hate and love, ignored the passions of mortality because he conceived of an authentic life only in the eternal glory of heaven.

In his nightmare Lazarus sees himself nailed on a cross on Golgotha and realizes that some may die so that others may live. He views Jesus as an enemy who gave him the poison of eternity with a kiss of friendship, but unwilling to accept Jesus as scapegoat or sacrificial lamb, he is not convinced that Jesus did not triumph through conceding his immortality to him. Since only Jesus, now dead, could have removed his gift, Lazarus, alone and mad, is condemned to suffer his immortality eternally, like death itself. As an eternal being, even though he tries to reject both heaven and earth in favor of death, he cannot escape his culpability at living at the expense of the deaths of others and thus may be more guilty than Judas.

According to Baltasar, the devil brought death, the denial of eternal existence, into the world. If Christ is resurrection, man by definition must also believe in Hell or be damned forever. The dwarf contends, nonetheless, that the only hell is one's memory. To be a man is to suffer alone, a suffering mitigated through love and compassion for one's fellow man through whose death Christ's sacrifice is relived. When piety becomes love and Jesus has returned to his father, Lazarus may obtain his peace, one which Judas hopes he may share through Lazarus's kiss. Lazarus rejects Judas's belief that the only life is the mortal one; mortality is a figment, and Christ has no meaning beyond that of resurrection and life. Although man faces the knowledge of certain death, he must govern his acts justly in the face of the possibility of eternal life. The dwarf wonders how future historians will treat Carlos II and his court, but he knows that it will involve the eternal story of Lazarus, death, and resurrection. Rojas, apparently following Nikos Kazantzakis's lead, stresses the unchanging moral imperative linking modern man with Christ's sacrifice.

<u>Auto</u> <u>de</u> <u>fe</u> contains a number of prophetic and oneiric visions more often part of a metaphysical and religious world than of a subconscious one. The author utilizes dreams and new ways of looking at time and space as he concretizes and accepts the absurd, transcending irrational experiences to reflect the moral dilemma of his world, and revealing its absurdity by making the central player a dwarf court jester. At times real events are recalled and recreated in dreams and prophecy. Viviana foretells the end of the king and the misfortunes to overtake his house, the death of his queen, his remarriage, his lack of heirs, and the loss of his throne to strangers from

across the mountain. When Lazarus falls asleep, after drinking a special wine, he finds himself in a patio which he has never seen before. He hears a voice calling him forth and encounters Felipe Próspero who asks him who he is. And Lazarus realizes that he is another person, born in Bethany of a dead mother and reborn as the jester of Carlos II. He sees the auto de fe, views the king as Judas, shifting in his dream from scene to scene, as he reenacts the events already described in the novel.

The king's resurrected monkey appears a number of times to create visions for the jester who recalls the performance of the king's play, his role as Lazarus, and his death. In his trance the monkey turns him into the very image of Carlos and grants him immortality on the condition that he neither love nor hate. When he lies with the queen in his double identity of dwarf and Carlos, he falls in love and becomes a dwarf once more. When the monkey gives him another chance, the queen dies giving birth to Felipe Próspero, his son, whom he begins to hate. On another occasion, as he talks to the queen he slips into an earlier vision of the nude queen, who kisses him to prove it is not a dream, and he identifies with the king in memory and reenacts past scenes to the tune of the monkey's flute.

In another dream the dwarf sees Felipe fly to the top of the acacia tree. The court climbs the tree and Felipe, wrapped in a sheet, falls to the courtyard. When the jester opens the sheet he finds only flowers which turn to ashes at his touch. In yet another vision the jester recalls a puppet show in which the king asked pardon for having been born and received the penance of having to keep on living, a scene which fuses with the guilty king's visit to ask him for help in escaping his devils, a possession which occurred after Felipe's execution. In a subsequent chimera the jester rides in the king's carriage, and the latter recalls his own father who had taken him on a similar ride many years before. The jester, with an inner vision, also recalls similar past scenes. They see once more a procession of chanters which the queen describes as part of the auto de fe. The jester understands the chanters' references about the purification of the soul as applying to the king's culpability in engendering Felipe in another man's wife, but the king attributes all to the work of the devil-monkey and his flute. And so the jester dreams on, realizing that men are like blind demons who can believe in God but never see him. Before his death the king prophesies the loss of Spain to foreigners and sees his monkey with Judas's dog on its back and a black coach loaded with his family dead.

These dreams are augmented by the grotesque situations in the novel. The tribunal argues over aphrodisiacs and diet in attempting to determine the king's paternity. Baltasar, who envisions Christ as the devil, himself hungry for death, plans to go to Bethany disguised as a woman in order to search for Satan. The jester baptizes his dead son with the bloody water in which the doctor had washed his hands. The king attempts to force from a dead man the extent of his own eternal punishment. As the king's exorcism proceeds, he suffers an erection (the jester recalls a similar occurrence when his father hanged himself) which the priest, believing it to be the work of the devil, kicks down with his shoe. The priests force the king to lie on the ground on the theory that he is closer to Hell there than in his bed and that the devil might find it more palatable to make the trip from there.[8]

Rojas uses parody, humor, the grotesque, and the ultrarational in his metaphysical visions to transmute rather than transmit reality. He converts a historical reality into a mythic one with a tormented self-created order all its own, where fantasy and reality, ordinary events and a magic world are but different views of the same existence. Mixing the lyric and the literary in his ontological and metaphysical treatment, Rojas ponders the meaning of reality versus illusion, the ultimate nature of man, and the Christian's lonely confrontation with his destiny whose meaning can be deduced only through the positive power of love and the concomitant unraveling of Christ's sacrifice and resurrection.

Notes

[1] *Spain Today*, 2 (Madrid, April, 1970), 30. Less impressed, Andrés Amorós, *Revista de Occidente*, 74 (May, 1969), 259, finds it to be "novela interesante, pero no lograda."

[2] See Unamuno, *Creator and Creation*, Ed. José R. Barcia and M. H. Zeitlin (Berkeley, 1967), pp. 72-78.

[3] Carlos Rojas, *Auto de fe* (Madrid, 1968), p. 197.

[4] Ibid., p. 287. The memory is repeated verbatim from page 223.

[5] Ibid., p. 252.

[6] Ibid., p. 64.

[7] Ibid., p. 295.

[8] These and other scenes from the novel fulfill the criteria established by Wolfgang Kayser, *The Grotesque in Art and Literature* (Bloomington, 1963), p. 184, that "Suddenness and surprise are essential elements of the grotesque."

EL INGENIOSO HIDALGO Y POETA FEDERICO GARCIA LORCA ASCIENDE A LOS INFIERNOS

Carlos Rojas, in previous novels like Azaña, recreated the existential imperative of his protagonist's life through a contradictory creative process inherited from Cervantes. In his 1980 fictional recreation of Lorca's life and death (a Nadal prize winner), he details once again the price of ignorance, incomprehension, and prejudice. In the presentation of events, real and imagined, Rojas, giving equal creative weight to both, divulges Lorca's life through that poet's own memories, through the dream reality of a possible author of the very events recorded in the novel, and through an elderly Lorca's dream. The various lives, authentic and fictional, occupy the same plane in Rojas' novel much as the madmen Cardenio and Don Quijote confront one another on the same level of existence in Cervantes' masterpiece. Rojas uses an apparently antithetical but unified mosaic of reality to reveal, little by little, the existential essence of what we assume to be the truth about Lorca, what we imagine to be the truth about Lorca, and what, given individual political, ethical, and moral persuasions, we might have wanted to be the truth about Lorca, Rojas' "ingenioso hidalgo."

Federico, in a spiral arm of an individual hell, composed of infinite numbers of stages for the dead, condemned to be who they were and fully conscious throughout eternity, recalls, through repetitive memory fragments, his own life and works. Isolated on his stage, confronting the mirror of his memories and condemned to a solitude he cannot bear, Lorca prefers any kind of life to his present immortal state in his mnemonic hell. His salvation, if it comes, will release him from remembering, will provide the peace of forgetfullness in his post-mortem world, as absurd and logic-free as his previous existence, and will clear the stage for the newly dead.

In the four chapters of the novel, which serve as the four theaters of Lorca's first person narrative performance, both he and the other characters muse on the meaning of reality and ponder whether we exist independently or as creatures in another's dream. Rojas reproduces admirably the process of memory through an anaphoric technique, an echolalia involving fragments of all the events of Lorca's many possible lives: the imaginary Lorca who stayed in Madrid, the one who remained in the Rosales's house, or the one who became a professor in the United States. The many memories include the lights in the night sky at Lake Edem Mills, de Falla's anger at the dedication of the "Oda al Santísimo Sacramento del Altar," the avoidance at a train station of Ramón Ruiz Alonso, the deputy from Granada, and meetings with Ignacio Sánchez Mejías. Rojas, when the event is not real, supports its recall through a third person memory. In his metaphorical statement or mental fabrication of this fictional and yet vividly real Lorca, he reconstructs memories much as Proust recalls his pictorial and verbal past; indeed Rojas cites the influence of the French novelist much as he credits that of the author of Don Quijote de la Mancha.

From his spiral hell Lorca overhears an interview between a fictional Sandro Vasari and Ramón Ruiz Alonso. Vasari, dreaming Lorca's hell as well as his own theatrical stage, relates the same events remembered by Lorca of his trip from Madrid. Later Lorca encounters an alter ego who passed the many years on the second floor of the Rosales's house and for whom his younger version is simply a figment of his own dream. Much as Cervantes credited Cide Hamete Benengeli with the authorship of his great work, Rojas also serves as a kind of translator for Vasari who wrote the novel in four sections so that his lover, Marina, might compose a musical sonata which would fuse the themes of Lorca's life and works.

Although the alternative lives of Lorca, based on his not having taken the train to Granada, project a literary reality as powerful as truth--in one episode he rejects the Nobel Prize for Literature--and the impinging characters like the green-eyed bisexual whose father had raped her seem as authentic as Lorca's real friends and enemies, a historical if embellished biography serves as the novel's cornerstone. Lorca, recollecting the events leading up to his friend Ignacio Sánchez Mejías' death in 1934, realizes: "cuán claras fueron entonces las señales de la gran tragedia en espera de nuestro pueblo y cuán ciegos fuimos nosotros al ignorarlas."[1] One of the most moving events in Lorca's life was the loss of his friend in the bull ring. He recalls their friendship with the dancer la Argentinita who, says Lorca, felt a maternal and sisterly affection for him and, in a reference to his homosexuality which made his relationship with his father so difficult, "por los hombres como yo" (p. 32). The dancer, jealous of the matador's lovers, called Lorca daily to complain, one reason for his departure for Granada, "porque jamás toleré mi propia impotencia ante el dolor ajeno" (p. 33). Elsewhere he states it was to celebrate a traditional brithday party with his family. Lorca associates his terror of death with loss of identity and with his homosexuality, relating an obscure love failure and attempt at suicide with his visit to Columbia University and Vermont in 1929-30.

Among other key incidents in his life, he reviews what happened during his last day in Madrid on July 16, 1936 just before the outbreak of the war and includes a prophetic dream of death. In his theatrical sphere Lorca believes that what ensued that Thursday had occurred previously, that for him the experience had already been lived. Once in Granada, he took refuge in the Rosales's home.

Part of Lorca's retrospection concerns his religious preoccupations, his love for the gypsies, and his many friends, among them Alberti, Buñuel, Salinas, Gerardo Diego, Dalí, and de Falla. In the process he includes literary references to the works of Góngora, Valle-Inclán, Ortega y Gasset, and others, reproducing one imaginary scene of a childhood encounter with Antonio Machado and that poet's evacuation from Madrid to Valencia during the war.

But in addition to literary friendships and influences, Lorca discusses his own works, especially as autobiography. His poetry, whatever its rhythm and musicality, tells the story of his life, the counterpart of the death present as its basic element. Quoting from many of his works, he recalls the ballad of the Emplazado as a kind of prognostication, sees the "Romance Sonámbulo" as his own story, and identifies with the death of Antonio de Camborio and the horseman who will never get to Córdoba. Lorca also recalls specific aspects of his work from El maleficio de la mariposa, acted by La Argentinita, through El público, which he considered to be far ahead of its time and which he asked his friend Rafael Martínez Nadal to destroy: "destruir en seguida el original de El público . . . Si muero, El público no tiene razón de ser para los demás" (pp. 50, 127); from his famous lament for Ignacio Sánchez Mejías, whose genesis he relates, to the Poeta en Nueva York and "la multitud que vomita." Lorca also planned a drama, La destrucción de Sodoma, a kind of allegory of the Spanish Civil War.

But fascinating as Lorca may be as a creative genius, the circumstances surrounding his death attract through their variety and mystery more than the conditions concerning his life. Rojas resurrects and recreates all of the theories (those of Ian Gibson and Jean Louis Schonberg, among others) concerning Lorca's death, involving factors such as homosexuality, jealousy, and the impact of Lorca's writing. Even before leaving Madrid Lorca suffered a series of presentiments about Granada.

In the overheard interview between Vasari, taking notes for the novel of Lorca's life, and Ramón Ruiz Alonso, Lorca learns that the governor of Granada had ordered his detainment. While denying responsibility and justifying himself, Ruiz emphatically denies theories about homosexual jealousy. Lorca, on the other hand, remembers his "miedo irracional. . .supuesto pánico del afeminado a la muerte. . ." (p. 29), and the reality of his death: "Luego sin juzgarme, me matarían a tiros por el trasero, llamándome maricón" (pp. 151, 158). Ruiz Alonso recalls how he kept a soldier from mistreating Lorca when his squad took him from the Rosales' house: " ¿Cómo te atreves, miserable? En mi presencia . . ." (pp. 85, 119, 187, 216), but Vasari extracts from Ruiz the admission that Lorca died because the authorities feared his writings.

The ambivalent relationship between the Rosales boys and Lorca has never been fully explained. As an official of the Falangist party, the older brother, Pepe, supposedly had great authority. In the novel Luis Rosales thought Lorca might be safer at Manuel de Falla's house, but Lorca stated that the musician would never pardon him for a supposedly blasphemous poem. Luis also considered escorting Lorca to the Republican lines. In any event, once taken prisoner by Ruiz Alonso, Lorca received repeated assurances from Pepe that he would be set free.

As for the governor, in the novel he had supposedly long ago witnessed and envied the relationship between Lorca and Sánchez Mejías. Dying of cancer, the governor also assures Lorca that he will not be harmed. In the final analysis, when the soldiers take Lorca to his death in an old Buick, we do not fully understand who was responsible. We must rely on the poets' father: "Tú morirás la (death) que te impongan los otros porque en este país de infamia y de desdicha, quienes no eligen su muerte están destinados a que los maten los imbéciles. La estupidez es nuestra inocencia" (p. 118).

Since the narrative line derives from a technique of multiple viewpoints constantly reinforced, the author reemphasizes the key points and relationships of the Lorca who was and who might have been. Thus he recognizes the old man's dream of hell, the second floor of the Rosales home with its Proust volumes and Salinas translations (pp. 105, 144, 146); he implies that Lorca died because some believed that he caused "más daño con la pluma que otros con la pistola" (pp. 86, 114, 121-22, 167, 202, 215); or he recognizes that a feigned madness might have saved Lorca: "Porque no te finges loco para ser absuelto" (pp. 122, 125, 127, 130, 133, 136, 147, 161, 175, 179-80, 183). Some of these chains serve almost as epic tags, repeated refrains which seem associative memory flashes and which serve to emphasize aspects of the protagonist.

Throughout, Rojas uses these and longer memory slices, with subtle changes, to construct his mosaic of repeated thought fragments which touch the conscious surface of Lorca's mind.

One of these involves the aurora borealis which so impressed Lorca in Vermont at Lake Edem Mills: "para convertirse pasado mañana en los peces del lago Edem Mills que encendía la aurora boreal" (p. 15); "la aurora boreal sobre el lago Edem Mills, encendiendo bancos de peces rojos . . ." (p. 11); "resplandor de aquella aurora, que prende la noche y los peces con su rojez más ardiente" (p. 12); "la noche anterior a la aurora boreal. . ." (p. 224); "antes de presenciar la aurora boreal sobre el lago Edem Mills" (p. 243). Another involves contact with his father" ". . . hijo, por ti lo daría todo, incluidos tu madre y tus hermanas! ¡Que Dios me perdone! Ten mucha prudencia! Tú no puedes faltarme nunca, nunca, nunca!" (pp. 108, 111, 118, 135, 178). The list of these repeated chains could be extended indefinitely, since the entire novel, like a jigsaw puzzle, depends on these disparate pieces. One key point in the protagonist's life occurs at the railroad station in Madrid, when he begs his friend Martínez Nadal to leave so that he can escape the attention of Ramón Ruiz Alonso. This long scene, viewed by Lorca, by Ruiz, and as a third person reflection (pp. 66-67, 149, 158, 177), remains fused in Lorca's mind with the painting by Monet, "La Gare Saint Lazare" which, accompanied by his father, he saw as a child. The transitory contacts with his friend, his father, and with his executioner become a kind of single temporal unit. Monet's train becomes Lorca's train to Andalusia. One enters Saint Lazare, and the other leaves from Madrid to carry Lorca to an irrevocable death.

Carlos Rojas delays the denouement as he builds his novelistic structure brick by brick with facts, suppositions, conjectures, and the poet's works. He puts into concrete and conscious form a series of Lorca's reflections through a kind of vicarious memory, drawing forth, in almost psychoanalytic fashion, direct and indirect memories of remembered or near remembered situations and sensations disguised at times by inappropriately imagined events. Often in this process of recall, Rojas utilizes paintings in addition to writing to convey the visual, pictorial qualities of the event, thus lending veracity and dramatic impact to his novel about a poet who conveyed so beautifully (in visual terms) the fantastic and symbolic values of our everyday world and whose tragic and senseless death continues to intrigue students of Spanish literature.

Notes

[1] Carlos Rojas, *El ingenioso hidalgo y poeta Federico García Lorca asciende a los infiernos* (Barcelona: Ediciones Destino, 1980), p. 27. Further citations in the text are to this edition.

JUAN GOYTISOLO - AMBIVALENT ARTIST IN
SEARCH OF HIS SOUL

Juan Goytisolo, who claims that he has remained constant in his belief that he needs artistic freedom, states: "y puedo, permitirme el lujo de escribir lo que pienso . . . Para mí el ejercicio de mi inteligencia no puede disociarse del ejercicio de la libertad. . . ."[1] In the 1970's, refining his position, he insists that "el escritor debería liberarse de todo aquello que le identifica y define, le da una etiqueta. . . ."[2]

As part of his declaration of artistic independence, Goytisolo, on numerous occasions, declared that he had to desert documentary realism, whatever his civic responsibility as a citizen of a dictatorship, because the realistic novel "distaba mucho de responder a las exigencias artísticas, culturales del mundo moderno."[3] Furthermore, since, in a Spain without political liberty, literature had to assume some of the functions of a free press, some writers, through a false idealism, by giving witness to social reality, in essence indulged in a new kind of evasion because "la littérature tient alors le rôle que devrait remplir la presse."[4] The only solution for the Spaniard (i.e. Goytisolo) who wanted to write literature was to leave the country because "el intelectual español ha sido siempre en potencia un candidato a la emigración."[5] Through his self-imposed exile Goytisolo could then attack his society, which, following Claude Lévi Strauss's theories, he held to be simply a collection of myths. In the process he substituted (and zealously defended) his own "truth" for "myths" he ferociously assailed.

The thesis of this paper is that, whatever his reiterated position about his need of freedom to search for truth behind Spain's hypocritical masks, Goytisolo, through his voluntary exile, far from attempting to achieve artistic freedom and liberty, has engaged in a self-deception and caused himself unending suffering. His condition is like that of his alter-ego, Julián, in Reivindicación del Conde don Julián, who cannot escape his temporal memory trap and must over and over again repeat his self-torture: "mañana será otro día, la invasión recomenzará."[6] The key to Goytisolo's writing is that his soul and psyche are inextricably interwoven with both his aesthetic and political-socioeconomic pronouncements and that the autobiographical and recreated elements of his novels are therapeutic in nature, an abreaction to bring repressed material to the conscious level so that through its examination the author may relieve the tension of continuing subconscious conflicts.

Goytisolo, who has constantly expanded his credo of liberty, shows a certain ambivalence about the artist's role in society. He believes that the writer must choose between romantic rebellion and being a functionary in a capitalistic society whose technological advances reduce the sphere of action for the intellectual. Nonetheless, even though one with a social conscience can try only "pura y simplemente . . . de no enloquecer,"[7] he must do his utmost to resolve the conflict between aesthetics and morality, action and contemplation, even though political and literary inconformity differ considerably. The true artist needs freedom to look at things in a new way, as he struggles against the status quo and runs after a constantly changing Spanish reality (for him primarily mythical). Thus, if the artist tries to transform mankind only, he is not producing literature. What matters is the internal violence of a unique experience which may justify the transformation on aesthetic grounds.[8] In the same way, his protagonists try to participate in a decisive act to give meaning to their lives and resolve inner turmoil.

It is not sufficient to fight, says Goytisolo; one has to fight well, "conjugar belleza y riesgo . . . para mí el objetivo primordial de la creación literaria."[9] What he fails to add is that his creativity is overwhelmingly cathartic; his admission that it is easier to be a spectator than an agent of social transformation and to view a country's past and future from an aesthetic and intellectual rather than from a moral perspective masks the constant relationship in his fiction between social and private repression. Although he claims aesthetic motivation, he cannot refrain from attacking what he considers to be an anesthetized society which seeks to defend its ossified respectability against artists like Goytisolo. But the fact that Goytisolo thinly disguises that he is still a social realist who believes that the artist must somehow tie in revolutionary ideology, admit his responsibility to humanity, and expose everything which may impede revolutionary progress, masks yet another truth, conveyed constantly, as will shortly be demonstrated, by his combinations of metaphor, symbol, and myth.

In all of his novels Goytisolo analyzes the socioeconomic structure of Spanish society and promotes the idea of revolutionary change through a destruction of the old corruptions of humanity. The basic difference between Goytisolo and other social realists is that he seems to care little about the greatest good for the greatest number or even about the Spanish people. His primary concern is Juan Goytisolo, a man unable to escape emotional, romantically tinged ties to a former existence and the traumatic events of his youth. Much as a thwarted child might react, he rekindles repressed desires both of omnipotence and defiance, as even a casual perusal of any of his anti-social protagonists demonstrates, As he continues to protest his need for current artistic freedom, he at the same time remains enslaved by the constructs of the past. From his first novel to his last Goytisolo plays a dual role; he is both David and Agustín in Juegos de manos and Julián and Alvarito in Reivindicación del Conde don Julián. As such he must accept the fatal consequences of passivity and culpability on the one hand and activity and guilt on the other; throughout his novels characters destroy that which they most love. In murdering David, whom he loves, Agustín has killed himself, knowing full well that the worst thing in life "es la carencia del amor, la soledad, el vacío."[10] Agustín immolates himself, much as Goytisolo, who has subconsciously carried on a life-long love affair with Spain, seeks consciously in his writing to deny a reality or its intrapsychic representation which might cause him pain. Agustín claims that nothing links his generation to the past and that many times he faces the new day, not knowing what to do, that he is "buscando una respuesta, y en realidad ni siquiera conozco la pregunta."[11] Sixteen years later Julián's only answer is to relive once more his destructive dream and hope for regeneration through Alvarito whose "amor consentido puede todavia regenerarme,"[12] but whom he may also destroy: "un día te mataré, oyes. . . ."[13] And Alvarito, the boy (Little Red Riding Hood) who would normally become an orthodox Spanish citizen, is sodomized in a role reversal by Julián dressed as the legendary grandmother. In Señas de identidad Alvaro dreams that Jerónimo will kill him and that his executioner will use a knife. Whereas the grandmother in Señas rejects Alvaro, in Reivindicación she uses a knife against him in one of the graphic destructions she visits upon him. Admittedly, differing conjectures about the symbolism involved can be entertained. Alvarito might be any number of people (Franco, whose African connections are well-known, appears elsewhere in the novel as Tonelete, Ubicuo, and Figurón), if one wishes to indulge in mental subtleties; but no excessive stretching of the imagination is required for the thesis of this paper.

Having lost his mother at an early age, Goytisolo seems to fill his novels with a sexuality which involves incestuous implications and which helps his characters refute or deny that relationship. In addition to encounters with implicit homosexuals, both hardy and weak (Gorila, Raimundo, Jerónimo, Tariq, Uribe, Benjamín), and sadistic situations, his novels are filled with a physical or mental transvestism and with mothers, represented as negative archetypes, who have ambivalent sexual relationships with their children, often involving a conscious hatred or denigration of the woman by the male involved. All of Goytisolo's novels are the same novel, reviewing the same situations, the same characters and protagonists in search of themselves who, their innocence lost, feel nausea at their own impotence and sense of constant betrayal. Having lost his mother Luisa in a bombardment by General Franco's forces, Goytisolo, then seven, could not accept the loss of love and subconsciously thirsted for vengeance, with a concomitant self-torment. These ambiguous novelistic relationships, by definition destructive, recur constantly as in the case of Agustín and his mother in Juegos de manos and Doña Estanislaa and her son "Romano bien amado" in Duelo en el Paraíso. Indirectly responsible for his death, she dresses him as a girl and dreams of impossible achievements for him. At times the mother-son tie is a sadistic one; thus Agustín comes to hate his mother; and Arturo in Fiestas actively despises his; a character in Para vivir aquí considers his to be a whore; and Julián, the adult, will force Alvarito, the child, to bring his mother to him for sexual purposes, The boy "idolatrado e idólatra de su madre,"[14] will steal from her, lie to her, and as he contemplates her degradation promised by Julián: "la entrega el líquido desdén, los latigazos: y tú estarás delante y mirarás; tu mamacita y la culebra, la culebra y tu mamacita . . ."[15], will feel inordinately guilty.

Death is often a part of this relationship. When Abel (Goytisolo) loses Dora, the teacher in Duelo en el Paraíso, his surrogate mother, he becomes the blood sacrifice for the role-playing children, much as David and his other alter-ego protagonists also serve as propitiatory immolator-victim of his own projected guilt feelings which can no longer be masked by innocence. As Frederic Wertham has written: "excessive attachment toward the mother can be transformed directly into a violent hostility towards her,"[16] which shields the child from unconscious incestuous wishes. Thus Goytisolo's wish to destroy, in a sense murder Spain, suggests that he wishes to have sexual intercourse with her, his mother country. Through the love-hate equation and defense mechanism he establishes, he seeks to negate the very thing he holds Spain (and his memory of his mother) to be. His mother country, for him symbolized as a nun (chaste, pure) but suggestively clad in black silk pajamas, may thus be reentered by don Julián through her vaginal canal, as he brandishes his "serpent," an instrument of rape for a prostitute country; but he also defines himself as Orpheus searching for Eurydice.

Womb fantasies occur in many of Goytisolo's novels, in Señas de identidad, when he is making love to Dolores, Alvaro describes the act in terms of "buscar un refugio, perderte en su hondura, reintegrar tu prehistoria materna y fetal. Ojalá te decías, no hubieras salido nunca."[17] In Reivindicación del Conde don Julián, the protagonist's vaginal voyage also reflects guilt together with a kind of castration fantasy and a wish to be devoured. His return to mother Spain seems to be an identification with the phallus of the father in an oedipal situation,[18] and his activities assume both Goytisolo's creative and emotional roles. At the beginning of the novel he clearly states: "unido tú a la otra orilla como el feto al útero sangriento de la madre, el cordón umbilical entre los dos como una larga y ondulante serpentina," but later in the novel, now himself the serpent, he seeks to break the tie: "al nacer, rompe las yjares de la madre: tu vientre liso ignora la infamia del ombligo."[19] The protagonist, overcome with anxiety, feels trapped, digested, and expelled, and shortly thereafter, comforted, enveloped by the pacifying fetal shadows as he gropes about the room, his own soothing womb. Goytisolo employs a defense fantasy connected with being a child inside his mother; once expelled or born, he feels extreme anxiety at being forced from her, possibly a reconstructed screen memory of parental coitus.

Agreeing with Mario Vargas Llosa that one must mistrust those intellectuals who speak well of their country, Goytisolo defines literature as an expression of discontent, believing that the critical function of its creator, whatever his society, is just as necessary as the apologetics of the patriotic soldier or government official: ". . . ambas son en efecto complementarias y opuestas y si la sociedad sin funcionarios no es concebible, una en la que los funcionarios silencian a los escritores se converte rápidamente en infierno."[20] The writer must keep mankind unhappy with itself, and stimulate unceasingly "la voluntad del cambio y de mejora, aun cuando para ello debe emplear las armas mas hirientes y nocivas. . . ."[21]

Goytisolo expresses this negativism and deforming image of Spain, supposedly based on his literary theories, in many ways. He insists on bodily excretions, defecation, urination, at time on objects, at times on people, the destruction of cats whose deaths in almost all his novels seem to delight him, a constant emphasis on flies and lizards, an emphasis on the negative or stormy aspects of nature, a great hatred toward women, described in denigrating terms, horrible diseases in many of his novels, the death of young children, and many other similar descriptions in a world in which scorpions kill grasshoppers, and men, each other.[22] His overuse of transvestism, but one kind of mask, the hiding of his protagonists behind various disguises, afraid to show themselves as they really are and ready to make up for their supposed shortcomings and guilt feelings through self-immolation and attempted violence, and his negativism in general reveal his feelings about himself as much as about society. As the school teacher, Quintana, in <u>Duelo</u> en <u>el</u> <u>Paraíso</u> stated about war orphans (Goytisolo's own case), "A esos niños que no tienen ni padre ni madre es como si les hubiesen estafado la infancia."[23] Goytisolo reiterates constantly that he wants especially to attack the myths of his country but allows his mask to fall as he admits: "lo cual sería igualmente una forma de reconocerse parte de él, de manifestar a rebours su deuda con el mismo."[24] In rejecting the Spanish reality which he defines as mythical, in order to reaffirm his own mythology, Goytisolo seeks to escape painful memories. The realization that his rejection is a mechanism of denial seems apparent in all his works but especially in <u>Señas</u> <u>de</u> <u>identidad</u> whose Alvaro Mendiola becomes a totally anguished protagonist of <u>Reivindicación</u> <u>del</u> <u>Conde</u> <u>don</u> <u>Julián</u>. All of his characters are Goytisolo; by rejecting and hating their family ties they believe they have achieved freedom: El odio que se agolpaba en su garganta me devolvía la identidad."[25]

In a sense, then, Goytisolo, while rejecting romantic rebellion and the nineteenth century view that fiction can serve as a vehicle for protest and the shaping of national consciousness, recreates those very ideas (old concepts in a new shape) in his need to protest social injustice and defy bourgeois values and traditions, as represented by Spanish institutions, and Spain's moral and puritanical sexual codes. This romantic attitude is especially apparent in his travel narrations such as <u>Campos</u> <u>de</u> <u>Níjar</u>. The world for him, too cruel to face, becomes a make-believe entity. A host of his characters, among them Uribe, Utah, Abel, and Julián, live in a fantasy universe of their own. Unable to face reality, Goytisolo must deny it and substitute his own more pleasant possibilities.

Goytisolo, who also resembles these writers like Huidobro of an earlier generation who attacked values through experimentation with new form, insists that the novelist has to reject language as something inherited or definitive. If a work is artistically valid, it must pitilessly destroy historical, cultural, and linguistic myths, for the duty of the modern writer is "la de ser mitoclasta'"[26] Goytisolo's style, then, becomes part of his own personal mythology and serves as the building material of his social and human vision of a new world which starts with the subversion and destruction of the old. Spanish intellectuals are victims, trapped by their inherited language which belongs to another age and another world, far removed from the real universe which "reclama de ellos un lenguaje inédito, liberado de los clisés y las fórmulas que por rutina formal, aún imitan."[27] Society, and not grammarians, creates language, and what many call incorrect expressions may very well be a new way of viewing the universe and freeing the inherent and latent forces operating within language itself. For the Spanish novelist who wants to violate syntax in his siege against orthodox expression, the breakdown of his language may also symbolize the self-destructive processes. It may well be, as Roland Barthes says, that literature as a system of signs predominates over any message,[28] but in Goytisolo's case so interwoven is the author with his material that by destroying traditional language instead of escaping from national myths he in reality is only trying to flee from himself and to exorcise the demons of his past. In any event, "la destrucción de los viejos mitos . . . tendría que partir de una análisis y denuncia de lenguaje. . ."[29] something Goytisolo almost achieves through his occasional lyricism, multi-level linguistic games, parodies, phonetic tricks, and comic alliterations but which corresponds to the conflictive interactions between Goytisolo and his society and between Goytisolo and himself, an interdependence which exacerbates tensions.

But in addition to demolishing linguistic myths, the subversive power of the imagination should also be employed, says Goytisolo, in political situations, for, whether it be in capitalistic or soviet bureaucracies, "frente a inquisidores y comisarios, la literatura debe campar por sus respetos."[30] Goytisolo, at first drawn to the socialist movement, later changed his view about formal Marxist ideology, finding it as limiting as the chains imposed by a capitalistic society. Rejecting the reduction of culture to the category of a product of the socio-economic system and the socialist ideological message about the social function of art, he attacks governmental and cultural institutions of his country together with the pueblo which benignly allows them to continue their existence. Goytisolo fears that the modern writer, discovering that old gods have feet of clay, may join Marxism or some equally fallible movement which, without affording either the liberty of the moral and aesthetic identification needed, will merely substitute one heavy official orthodoxy for another.

In his apparently reasoned definition of his literary and cultural system, Goytisolo shows that he is unable to bridge the gap between myth and reality, inner psyche and political reality, as he inadvertently continues to reveal what one might call the real Goytisolo, for whom, like the Unamuno he scorns, "le duele España." He professes to hate that which, in reality, appears to be a long lost love object. His constant references to death and sexuality, so much a part of all his novels, whatever their importance as statements about Spain's frozen religio-sexual codes, mask a pathognomic state which reflects anxieties and fantasies and unresolved, unconscious conflicts which he projects in symbolic form. An examination of his fiction reveals that, from beginning to end, he has not changed the essential elements of his pessimistic social vision nor his preoccupation with Spanish culture. Whatever his artistry, suggestive contours, or luminous verities, his novels continue to be didactic and his art a means to an end. His use of vocabulary and strange symbols, which have an almost hallucinatory intensity at times, seems to be a screen for his own search for ultimate values and feelings of guilt and inadequacy shared, in some form or another, by all of his protagonists from David and Agustín to Julián and Alvarito.

By developing his creative possibilities to the maximum and by rejecting the interests of political power which temporarily control him, the artist, declares Goytisolo, serves his country best. Yet, as he himself admits, all artistic and literary work consists of a web of factors which partly escape the will of their creator. When favorable circumstances in which to grow are lacking, the duty of the creator "será buscar entonces el clima propicio sin el cual su obra no existiría."[31] Goytisolo's insistence on his need to be away from Spain and his political and aesthetic explanations for that need appear to be somewhat hollow, nonetheless, in the face of his elaborate construct of dual realities. Alvaro in Señas de identidad admits that his search is: "Familia, clase social, comunidad, tierra: Tu vida no podía ser otra cosa . . . que un lento y difícil camino de ruptura y disposesión."[32] Julián, in the next novel, states: "consciente de que el laberinto está en ti: que tú eres el laberinto: . . . juntamente verdugo y víctima."[33] Julián of the ballads took revenge and suffered because of his daughter; Goytisolo, the modern Julián, because of his mother. In his latest novel, Goytisolo, the protagonist-narrator, is still lying to himself and to the world as he renounces his country of disparate masks and tries to conceal the true nature of his sensory processes, which reveal that he is inextricably a part of the very cultural framework he rejects. In his attempt to disguise relationships between symbol and meaning at subconscious levels, he conveys his continuing dialogue between himself and his circumstances, his own guilt feelings and the need to expiate, in some final cathartic manner, his unresolved feelings about Spain, in part stemming from the Civil War which had such tragic personal consequences for him. His deliberate betrayal of his country as a fictional don Julián masks subconscious feelings that he is in reality guilty, much as Jews living in the United States during the Holocaust, however innocent and unable to change the course of events in Germany, assumed a guilt from which many have not yet escaped.

Goytisolo's artistic and intellectual impulses differ subtly but concretely from his emotional ones. Though in both cases he seems to be pleading for individual freedoms, he knows that he has used the one (authentic artistic endeavor), in which he has been fearless, to disguise his deficiencies in the other (political and social progress). In turn these mask a neurotic ambivalence which continues, nonetheless, to surface as a rift in the whole cloth of his moral and ethical persuasions, as he constantly attacks what he perpetually seeks.

Throughout his writing one senses Goytisolo's feelings of frustration and guilt at his own impotence with respect to his country and the fulfillment of authentic human needs. He can never be sure, even on a conscious level, that emigration, which by default abandons the fight to those who remain, is a noble or idealistic course to take. His self-justifications and aesthetic pretensions and revindication as a defender of artistic purity are less than convincing, for if the world Goytisolo portrays contains only executioners and victims, he should not only hope but also fight for a free and just society which would allow his creative gifts to flourish. In the final analysis, Goytisolo uses creativity as a weapon against his loveless universe, for he cannot acknowledge that, in truth, he needs his Spanish soil. And so, alienated and estranged, he consciously denies that he desperately wants, subconsciously, the very love and acceptance he so cavalierly rejects.

Notes

[1] See interview in <u>Mundo Nuevo</u> (June, 1967), p. 54.

[2] Juan Goytisolo, <u>Obra inglesa de José María Blanco White</u> (Buenos Aires, 1972), p. 97.

[3] See "Declaración de Juan Goytisolo. . .," <u>Norte</u>, XII, 4-6 (1972), p. 91.

[4] See interview with Jacqueline Platier, <u>Le Monde</u> (July 25, 1962).

[5] <u>Obra inglesa</u>, p. 23.

[6] <u>Reivindicación del Conde don Julian</u> (Mexico, 1970), p. 240.

[7] Juan Goytisolo, <u>El furgón de cola</u> (Paris, 1967), p. 19.

[8] Ibid., pp. 51-55.

[9] Ibid., pp. 35-36.

[10] Juan Goytisolo, <u>Juegos de manos</u> (Barcelona, 1954), p. 256.

[11] Ibid., p. 143.

[12] <u>Reivindicación del Conde don Julian</u>, p. 220.

[13] Ibid., p. 227.

[14] Ibid., p. 215.

[15] Ibid., p. 229.

[16] "The Matriarchal Impulse," in <u>Dark Legend. A Study of Murder</u> (New York, 1966), p. 134.

[17] Juan Goytisolo, <u>Señas de identidad</u> (Mexico, 1966), p. 164.

[18] See Bertram D. Lewin, "The Body as Phallus," <u>The Psychoanalytic Quarterly</u>, I, no. 2 (1932), pp. 24-47.

[19] <u>Reivindicación</u>, pp. 13, 126.

[20] <u>Obra inglesa</u>, p. 93.

²¹Mario Vargas Llosa, "La literatura es una forma de insurrección permanente," *Revista Nacional de Cultura*, XXIX (July-September, 1967), p. 101.

²²For a further discussion see Kessel Schwartz, "Stylistic and Psychosexual Constants in the Work of Juan Goytisolo," *Norte* (July-Dec., nos. 4-6, 1972).

²³*Duelo en el Paraíso* (Barcelona, 1960), p. 137.

²⁴*Obra inglesa*, p. 97.

²⁵*Juegos de manos*, p. 151.

²⁶"Declaración de Juan Goytisolo. . .," *Norte*, p. 93.

²⁷*El furgón de cola*, p. 48. See also *New York Times Book Review* (March 31, 1974) in which Goytisolo reiterates that writers who choose to stay in Spain must heroically continue to resist intellectual castration.

²⁸"Qu'est ce que la critique," *Essais critiques* (Paris, 1964), p. 256.

²⁹*El furgón de cola*, p. 183.

³⁹*Obra inglesa*, p. 64.

³¹*Obra Inglesa*, pp. 94-96. Also see *New York Times Book Review* (March 31, 1974) in which Goytisolo states that he must live in an atmosphere which "permits his work to exist."

³²*Señas de identidad*. p. 55.

³³*Reivindicación*, p. 52.

MOTHERHOOD AND INCEST IN
THE FICTION OF JUAN GOYTISOLO

Unamuno claims that "en la mujer todo amor es maternal,"[1] although in her pursuit of motherhood she may be a virtual monster by reason of sexual repression.[2] Camilo José Cela's Pascual Duarte can find relief for his ambivalent feelings toward his terrible mother only through matricide; in Mrs. Caldwell habla con su hijo, that predatory and possessive lady seems more lover than mother. Juan Goytisolo, though not creating a single character to match his predecessors' mother figures, makes clear through his thematic material that mother love may be the most important single element in his work.

Having lost his mother in an air raid, Goytisolo recalled that event twenty years later while working on a film about that very bombing, and, overcome by the remote but horrible possibility that he might see her in some of the photographic material being used, he agonizes: "un sudor frío embebió todo su cuerpo. . ."[3] In his autobiographical notes Goytisolo also admits that the death of the family servant Eulalia, his surrogate mother, affected him more than that of his father (JG, p. 21). Disclaiming an absolute relationship between his own life and that of his characters, he nonetheless concedes that certain protagonists reflect "una serie de vivencias personales" (JG, pp. 115-116).

His mother pervades all his works, consciously or unconsciously. In Duelo en el Paraíso Abel associates music with his lost mother; Dora, a mother figure to the orphan school children, dies in an air raid. The school master Quintana asserts that it was as though "los hubiesen estafado la infancia."[4] In Reivindicación del Conde Don Julián we meet young Alvaro, the conscientious student, "idolatrado e idólatra de su madre."[5] Alvaro Mendiola, in Señas de identidad, visits his mother's grave; he claims that she has faded from his memory, but recalls her blue eyes, being served breakfast, and a visit with her to his senile grandmother.[6] The author reverses reality here; Alvaro's father dies when he is seven; his mother only disappears (SI, p. 119).

In his conscious aggression against what he he considers to be the antiquated sexual and religious codes of the Western world, Goytisolo also presents personal conflicts in symbolic form. David loves Estanislaa, supports her against his father, and exclaims: "Mamá, mamá querida, yo sólo te quiero a ti" (DP, p. 145). Mendiola feels sexually attracted toward Sergio's mother. At first Sergio wants him to sleep with her to betray his father: "Me gustaría que hicieses cornudo a mi padre" (SI, p. 91), but when they kiss he becomes uncontrollably jealous.

In Reivindicación del Conde don Julián, Alvaro associates his own sexual drives with the feelings of mother Isabel la Católica, "pecador no, muerto le quiere. . ." (RJ, p. 224). But he and Julián can destroy the mother country by changing her incarnation, Isabel, into the erotic dancer whose vaginal canal can be entered. In Juan sin Tierra Alvaro links the Pareja Reproductora with the primal scene and the husband's impotence with the incest barrier. Furthermore most of Goytisolo's masculine characters, ambivalent about their sexual roles, seek to be somebody else in order to find relief from their illicit desires. Changó has incestuous relationships with his mother, and the narrator, a reincarnation of Changó, will then possess "a la impoluta Madre Común en la más peregrina de las posturas."[7] Alvaro, the Christ figure, violates his mother and thus becomes his own father.

Mothers return this incestuous feeling. Abel's great aunt Estanislaa refuses to leave David at night and remains next to his bed whispering words "de ternura y confianza" (DP, p. 142). She loves her other son Romano even more, and they constanly seek each other's company away from her husband, "en los rincones y escondrijos de la casa" (DP, p. 159). When Romano brings Claude home, his mother, feeling an almost irrational jealousy, forces her to leave. She then weeps for joy at the thought that her son will now never leave el Paraíso: "Allí . . . se convertiría en el sostén de su madre" (DP, p. 168). The wife of the imaginero in La resaca scorns her impotent husband. Obsessed with the thought of Antonio, a surrogate son, she allows her sexual fantasies to become a reality. Antonio realizes, both sad and relieved, "que su niñez había muerto y que, en adelante, jamás podría escaparse."[8] Sergio's mother, jealous of his girlfriend, fights with him "como si fuera su amante" (SI, p. 92). In Juan sin Tierra, when the mother substitute offers her backside to the protagonist, neither is frightened at the thought of incest: "sin mostrar repugnancia al incesto . . . ofrendándole sus posterioridades enjundiosas" (JT, p. 56).

The characters reveal their forbidden feelings, often identifying with society's outcasts. Like Alvarito in Juan sin Tierra they may have descended to this world to redeem all the pariahs from sin, ". . . a través del cuerpo de su Madre, tomando de su carne y de su sangre, sin romper ni disminuir su inmaculada y virginal pureza. . ." (JT, p. 53). The deliberate distortion of normal family relationships takes on nightmarish proportions of destructive animosity, and the son, feeling his own ego threatened by his unvoiceable guilt, denies it through his fantasy of controlling ravaging tribes, of brutalizing, sodomizing, and then killing to revenge himself for the primal scene: "sorprendí siendo niño . . . me hizo concebir un odio violento, insaciable. . ." (JT, p. 155).

This frustration and guilt, concerning a mother one misses and yet betrays, may explain the protagonist's claustrophobia experienced in the dispensary in Reivindicación del Conde don Julián. Returning to the past implies being with Mother, especially when combined with his sense of déjà vu. The fear of entering an enclosed space also comprises "among its latent ideas the one that the enclosure is the mother's body."[9] Alvaro alters his personality, becoming another Julián in order to resolve his inflated identification with his mother. Distracting himself from incestuous thoughts and resorting to sadistic and masochistic attempts to sublimate painful intrapsychic representatives of reality, he gives in to Julián's serpent, the father figure waiting to enjoy Alvaro's mother. We know that in many dreams and phobias the "ravenous animal . . . is the greedy and jealous father, intruding with his claim" (BL, p. 200).

Constant references to the vaginal orifice and the uterus imply being with his beloved mother figure and a "forma de liberación, de retorno a la madre, motivo relacionado con la preocupación central del protagonista."[10] The womb then can be a place of refuge, a paradise, and Goytisolo's works abound with fantasies where it serves as a protective enclosure: "buscar un refugio, perderte en su hondura, reintegrar tu prehistoria maternal y fetal" (SI, p. 164). In Reivindicación del Conde don Julián the youth takes refuge under Putifar's skirts, "Me escondí allí dentro hasta que él se fue" (RJ, p. 72). Julián explains his situation as that of a fetus tied to the mother's blood-engorged womb, the umbilical cord between them coiling sinuously: "unido tú a la otra orilla como el feto al útero sangriento de la madre" (RJ, p. 13). He specifically comments on the reassuring fetal shadows in the soothing womb, "la apaciguadora penumbra fetal" (RJ, p. 15).

But the womb can also be dangerous to the life force. Julián cannot really enjoy it "por ser todo este lugar algo irreal, sin vida" (JO, p. 95), which helps explain also Alvaro's psychological disorientation and death fears. The deadly female, represented by Medusa, Medea, and Circe, among others, is, both in her sexual and maternal aspects, as old as myth itself. Sigmund Freud states the obvious by defining the mother as the baby's (and since the child is father to the man) and man's first object of desire. In remote times, he says in Totem and Taboo, men lived in small bands dominated by a single father who had access to all the women and power.[11] This jealous father, much to be feared, could kill the offending child. In Goytisolo's Reivindicación del Conde don Julián, entry into the sacred grotto implies the fantasy of coitus with mother. By turning his whole body into a penis, "the individual is swallowed in toto . . . related to the well-known fantasy of the vagina dentata" (BL, pp. 35-36). Although the fear of being devoured may arise from other than genital wishes, in this novel the protagonist serves as a sexual organ swallowed by Mother Spain's sex and becomes his father's phallus in what clearly seems to be an oedipal situation. In the vaginal orifice he serves as an "oveja inmolada a la madre. . ." (RJ, p. 168). As a child grows, inevitable sexual attachment brings on feelings of guilt, and in some cases women continue to represent for him ambivalent pleasure and pain, life and death,[12] both as a terrible mother figure and as the mate of a punishing father.

Fire and carrion birds are both classic death symbols. In psychiatric literature Prometheus, the fire bringer, devoured by the carrion bird, offers a kind of post mortem identification with the lost mother: "the patient dreams of clinging to a rock or cliff which represents the mother, while the place below is described in strikingly oral terms: there is a pool or lake which will 'swallow her up', or there is a 'yawning' or 'gaping' chasm or canyon. More elaborately the dreamer may be threatened by the jaws of death . . . or by the mouth of Hell" (BL, p. 135). Goytisolo uses this exact association: "Prometeo robó el fuego del Olimpo . . . tal vez es el cuadro angustioso del adolescente que encendió en sí mismo el fuego de la lujuria . . .", relating it to the picture of a horseman on a bridge over an abyss on whose other side stands a lascivious woman. The rider falls, and "el Averno le espera con las fauces abiertas" (RJ, pp. 105-106). Goytisolo later shows Alvaro trying to cross a bridge to find the provocative woman (mother) on the shore, but: "abajo le aguarda el abismo con las fauces abiertas" (RJ, p. 213).[13] These emotional dependencies frustrate the child. Manuel Durán states that "la madre, en este caso España, es un obstáculo a la vida verdadera del hijo, impide con su obsesionante presencia que el hijo madure y llegue a ser el que tiene que ser. Si es preciso . . . hay que llegar hasta la destrucción de la madre."[14] This needs to be free, based in part then on the mother's power to forbid instinctual needs, causes Agustín in Juegos de manos to encourage his father to be unfaithful to his mother whose love overwhelmed him: "me envolvía como un ropaje excesivamente prieto. Mis confesiones, por desvergonzadas que fuesen, le procuraban un motivo de amor . . . sin caer en la cuenta de que era precisamente esa aceptación la que más nos distanciaba."[15] Julián, together with the other coalescing identities in Reivindicación del Conde don Julián, ends up by rejecting his authentic progenitor. Alvaro deceives his mother to satisfy the demands of the enchanter (father) and serpent, thus removing the possibility of being loved, the very thing he wants.

An anxiety for love, sensitivity to rejection, and an ensuing self-torment may easily turn to hate. Most of the characters in Juegos de manos hate their parents. Agustín, by refusing his mother's help, finally feels free: ". . . el odio que se agolpaba en mi garganta me devolvía la identidad" (JM, p. 151). Similarly, Arturo in Fiestas loathes his mother Cecilia. Pregnancy and childbirth, consequences of motherhood, produce sad results. In Duelo en el Paraíso Abel's mother dies with his unborn sibling inside; Dora also dies pregnant. In Señas de identidad Alvaro forces Dolores to have an abortion, claiming at the same time that "mi pasado eres tú" (SI, p. 341). In Reivindicación del Conde don Julián the viper rips its mother's entrails to shreds, her smooth belly untainted: "tu vientre liso ignora la infamia del ombligo" (RJ, p. 126). This need to abort, to destroy the mother's body and the concept of maternity, may also possibly relate to the rage evoked by her power to impede instinctual activities.[16]

One may find varying degrees of oedipal fantasies in Goytisolo's novels. In Juan sin Tierra Alvaro equates the retention of his feces with being good and in a paradisiacal state. Projecting destructive jealousy against his father, he desires but also hates his mother for her lack of purity, proved by her part in the previously mentioned primal scene. He regresses to an anal-sadistic level, torn between soiling and retaining, for those he loves he also hates. Because of his incestuous longings he must change his mother into a bad object, fecal matter subject to expulsion: "la idea de la profanación sacrílega le abrumaba de tal modo que instintivamente su abdomen se contraía y la materia fecal no alcanzaba a abrirse paso. . .(JT, p. 220). The protagonist also associates his hatred of women with their sexual desires, their lascivious reaction to the masculine attributes of King Kong: "soñadoramente contemplan la fabulosa dimensión de sus atributos" (JT, p. 75). The incestuous Changó, the narrator, and King Kong become synonymous through the fornication with a whore, known as Queen Kong. But huge Kong cannot satisfy the sexual longings of the women. Reversing the equation, Alvaro believes that his mother wants a large penis, his father's. Jealously realizing that he does not have such an organ and that he cannot satisfy her, he punishes her anally.

A boy's feeling of inadequacy at the thought of his genital in relationship to his mother, his wounded self-image, and the shame and guilt stemming from his emotional attachment, may render him incapable of any feeling at all for the opposite sex because "all women are as forbidden as his mother. This may declare itself . . . in actual homosexuality."[17] Alvaro of Señas de identidad, beyond his own homosexuality, easily identifies with Frederic, whose mother had died prematurely and who is timid and anguished near people with "un respeto excesivo hacia el bello sexo, resultado de la muerte cruel y prematura de la madre" (SI, p. 336). He recalls his own happiness, on first meeting Dolores, because she looked like a boy. Doctor Vosk in Juan sin Tierra elicits from the narrator that he had indulged in homosexual acts which, together with the relationship, in Reivindicación del Conde don Julián, between Julián and Tariq and Julián and Alvarito represent the culmination of a long series of conscious and unconscious homosexual attachments among characters who cannot accept their masculine role. Jerónimo, Benjamín, Tanger, Alvaro, Alvarito, David, Agustín, Pipo, and Gorila reflect an obvious dualism which seems involved with bisexual or homosexual tendencies.

For all the preceding reasons, then, the little boy, badly hurt by being abandoned by his mother, transforms love into a vindictive need to hurt and destroy. Since the author-narrator relates mother and country: "la patria es la madre de todos los vicios" (RJ, 134); "los españoles llevamos . . . la envidia y la mala leche en la sangre" (SI, p. 288); he may obtain erotic freedom from his own guilt feelings by turning frigid Spain into a hot number, an untouchable nun into an obtainable whore, who must then be punished for her transgression. Mrs. Putifar is first besmirched by the boys who urinate in her vagina, a common fantasy of children wishing to destroy mother and by extension father.[18] Alvaro will be his mother's pimp, delivering her to the Arabic phallic serpent: "tu madre y la culebra, la culebra y tu madre: ella también es curiosa y la quiere conocer . . . tu querida madre es como las otras. . ." (RJ, pp. 228-229). The final punishment, of course, is death. Jesus, the boy doll, kills the transformed Virgin, she having previously been maimed by having her ringed fingers cut off. In the "happening" Mrs. Putifar is also killed. Goytisolo's novels contain a variety of women suffering from brain tumors or cancer, an obvious reflection of childish fears of death. But such sadistic attacks and death wishes backfire. Though by equating mother and prostitute one may visualize a relationship, the repressed wish to be with mother results in a kind of degradation and disenfranchisement of self which deflect death wishes inwardly. Alvaro himself is forced into sodomy and suicide as Caperucito Rojo, for only through displacing mother as the sacrifice can he sever the umbilical cord and be truly free: "el ombligo desollado y sin voz. . ." (RJ, p. 210).

Again the Goytisolian incidents seem to reflect Freudian theories. The cannibal has a devouring affection for his enemies and only devours people of whom he is fond, and an expression of tenderness toward one's mother may represent also a wish to destroy her. Furthermore, nobody commits suicide unless in doing so he is at the same time killing an object with whom he has identified; thus he turns against himself a death wish really directed against someone else.[19]

Doubtless Goytisolo's apparent radicalism masks a deep emotion and strong feelings about his society whose mores and rectitude he outwardly rejects. Obviously successful as a novelist, he appears nonetheless to be a deracinated being who, unable to accept old Spain, cannot find comfort in the new. His vehemence reflects an inchoate attempt to escape the personal demons of his past, but far from showing, by his denial of sexual conventions, an insensitivity to Spanish traditions, he reveals how much that culture means to him. One does not dedicate a literary life to the destruction of something which means nothing. The repetitive refrains to Goytisolo's novels seem to this reader to be a reflection of the author's ambivalence, on both a personal and political level, which masks a longing for love and acceptance by the very Mother Spain he professes to despise.

Notes

¹Miguel de Unamuno, Del sentimiento trágico de la vida (Madrid: Editorial Plenitud, 1966), p. 107.

²Leon Livingstone, "Unamuno and the Aesthetics of the Novel," Hispania, 24 (1941), 449. See also Ricardo Gullón, "La voluntad de dominio en la madre unamuniana," Asomante, 17 (1961), 41-59.

³Juan Goytisolo, ed. Julián Ríos (Madrid: Editorial Fundamentos, 1975), p. 10. Further references in the text are to this edition hereafter noted as JG.

⁴Juan Goytisolo, Duelo en el Paraíso (Barcelona: Destino, 1960), p. 137. Further citations in the text are to this edition hereafter noted as DP.

⁵Juan Goytisolo, Reivindicación del Conde don Julián (Mexico: Joaquín Mortiz, 1970), p. 94. Further citations in the text are to this edition hereafter noted as RJ.

⁶Juan Goytisolo, Señas de identidad (Mexico: Joaquín Mortiz, 1966), p. 86. Further references in the text are to this edition hereafter cited as SI.

⁷Juan Goytisolo, Juan sin Tierra (Barcelona: Editorial Seix Barral, 1975), p. 117. Further references in the text are to this edition hereafter cited as JT.

⁸Juan Goytisolo, La resaca (Paris: Club del Libro Español, 1958), p. 250.

⁹Bertram D. Lewin, Selected Writings of Bertram D. Lewin, ed. Jacob Arlow (New York: The Psychoanalytic Quarterly, 1973), p. 53. Further citations in the text are to the edition hereafter noted as BL.

¹⁰José Ortega, Juan Goytisolo, alienación y agresión en Señas de identidad y Reivindicación del Conde don Julián (New York: Eliseo Torres, 1972), p. 106. Further citations in the text are to this edition hereafter referred to as JO.

¹¹Sigmund Freud, The Basic Writings of Sigmund Freud (New York: Modern Library, 1938), p. 88.

¹²Herbert Marcuse, Eros and Civilization: A Philosophical Inquiry into Freud (New York: Random House, 1962), p. 69.

[13] For a further elucidation of bridge symbolism see: Paul Friedman, "The Bridge: A Study of Symbolism," Psychoanalytic Quarterly, 21 (1952), 49-80.

[14] Manuel Durán, "El lenguaje de Juan Goytisolo," Cuadernos Americanos, 19 (1970), 169.

[15] Juan Goytisolo, Juegos de manos (Barcelona: Ediciones Destino, 1960), p. 148. Further citations in the text are to this edition hereafter noted as JM.

[16] Karen Horney, Feminine Psychology (New York: Norton, 1973), p. 141.

[17] Ernest Jones, Hamlet and Oedipus (New York: Doubleday, 1954), p. 89.

[18] See Melanie Klein, "Early Development of Conscience in the Child," in Psychoanalysis Today, ed. Sandor Lorand (New York: International University Press, 1944), pp. 70-71.

[19] Sigmund Freud, The Standard Edition, ed. James Strachey (London: Hogarth, 1955), XVIII, 105.

WOMEN IN THE NOVELS OF JUAN GOYTISOLO

In twentieth-century Spanish fiction, female characters, victimized by circumscribing traditional social values, suffer in a masculine world which views them as maternal, subservient or destructive.[1]

Among members of the Generation of '98 Unamuno, admitting that "el autor no sabe hacer mujeres, no lo ha sabido nunca,"[2] concentrates on the maternal. Azorín's pure and innocent women symbolize perfect harmony, married bliss, and consolation;[3] yet Iluminada reduces her husband to an object: "La mujer es la que lo dispone todo [. . .] Azorín deja hacer, y vive, vive como una cosa."[4] Carmen Laforet claims that Pío Baroja may not merit his anti-feminist reputation attributed to him because "no ha retratado a sus heroinas en un momento de pasión."[5] Gloria Durán also believes that "no se puede calificar a Baroja de antifeminista."[6] The author himself states that "toda la psicología de los psicólogos de la mujer está basada en [. . .] la incoherencia y en la contradicción."[7] Yet, in Paradox Rey, he satirizes both the unattractive Amazon, Dora and the feminist Miss Pich who insists: "Los hombres son seres inferiores [. . .]. El rey David también era mujer."[8] Ramón Pérez de Ayala descibes a gallery of negative women in Belarmino y Apolonio, the shrew Xuantipa, the fuzzy headed romantic, Felicitá, the domineering duchess of Somovia, the timid Angustias, and the foolish doña Basilisa. In La pata de la reposa, although Alberto sees Fina as an innocent ideal, he decides in favor of sensuality.

Ramón Sender, on the contrary, usually stresses feminine innocence in a masculine world; for example, Niña Lucha in El epitalamio del prieto Trinidad, the innocent non-mother with an instinctive faith in life, the Duchess in El rey y la reina, a transcendental ideal, and Valentina, Pepe's spiritual love in Crónica del alba. But other twentieth-century novelists are less charitable. Pipia Sánchez in La catira, naked in front of a mirror, proclaims that inside her may be hiding "una mujer cruel."[9] In the same novel the Indian María avenges herself on Trinidad Pamplona, leaving his corpse in the field so the buzzards can pluck out his eyes. Miguel Delibes' women characters are less than admirable. Typical females include: the self-righteous and puritanical "La guindilla mayor" (El camino), the inquisitorial "el undécimo mandamiento" (Las ratas), the narrow-minded, vulgar, and bigoted Carmen (Cinco horas con Mario), and Adela, whose husband wanted only her "apetitosa anatomía."[10] Luis Martín Santos shows women to be sexually subordinate. Muecas dominates his wife completely and impregnates one of his daughters. Dorita's mother explains the lover's situation "ante el rugido masculino la osadía de una orden de mando que dice 'deseadme'[. . .] fin para el que el cuerpo de la hembra ha sido fabricado y hacia el que incesantemente tiende."[11] In Juan Benet's world of adulterous women, Gamallo's daughter reflects that her early loves "no tuvieron otro efecto que lanzarme fuera de mi edad a una suerte de anacrónica y lasciva ingravidez."[12]

At first glance, when compared with his fellow novelists, Goytisolo affords women a minor role in his works. Further consideration leads one to conclude that in spite of the disproportionate attention given Alvaro Mendiola, Count Julian, Juan sin Tierra, David, Agustín, Utah, and a host of other masculine protagonists, women may well be the narrative psychological raison d' être of much of Goytisolo's fiction. Several critics have already written about the maternal in Goytisolo,[13] so I shall not treat that aspect of his novels here.

Goytisolo's women, trapped by life and history, offer us a deformed and grotesque glimpse of what is generally accepted as the feminine essence. Part of this vision relates to the author's rejection of a reality and morality belonging to the middle class; but in the process of destroying institutions he also destroys relationships involving women. In spite of his male protagonists' cool detachment from "happenings," they react solipsistically, using women as passive entities through which they can project their own modifications and thus attempt to free themselves from some tormenting problem. Whether or not woman adheres to outmoded Spanish codes, she serves as a kind of backdrop against which the action occurs, though she herself may be victim, oppressor, lover, mother, dream image, or whore.

Goytisolo's male protagonists, sadistic and negative, employ pejorative descriptions which reflect the lack of spiritual implications involved in their reaction to women. Though Goytisolo accepts, up to a point, the medieval idea that woman must be either saint or whore (in Reivindicación del Conde don Julián we find Isabel la Católica and the Virgin Mary but also Mrs. Putifar and the mulatto dancer), all of them are sex objects to be entered. His characters reflect unconscious and obscure anxieties, and his scenes involve sexual organs, castration-like decapitations, and anal intercourse. In his cacographic scenes of urinating on the sex of the Daughter of the American Revolution, he goes far beyond what we think of as Spanish machismo. Attempting to degrade woman and the entire sexual process, he rejects that aspect of hypermanliness which views the feminine archetype as fragile, submissive, and obedient. His women may be vain, empty, things to be used, to take vengeance upon, to be destroyed, but they are also potentially dangerous and destructive. Woman the castrator, the death dealer, becomes very real in his novels.

Fernando Díaz Plaja claims that "todo español es, realmente, un posible don Juan [. . .] y en general más apto al amor físico que en otros países,"[14] another concept which Goytisolo constantly refutes. Thus in Reivindicación del Conde don Julián the Spaniards' organs are limp lettuce leaves, and the women prefer the Arabs' phallic serpent which can bring them joy: "robusta culebra suplantará su concepto mísero y lechuguino."[15] At the same time he shows clearly that Spaniards view women almost exclusively as sex objects. In "Suburbios" from Para vivir aquí the boys talk of a woman who "tiene tetas que no le caben en la blusa," whom they would like to favor with their attentions immediately.[16] They are also avidly interested in the thought that African women "se afeitan entre las piernas" (PVA, p. 27). Don Julio in El circo makes improper advances to Celia. The Gorila in Fiestas has a permanent liaison with Juana and a native mistress. Bruno, in Fin de fiesta has a French mistress and a temporary affair with Gloria. Ricardo and Artigas use two blond Danish pick-ups in Señas de identidad to satisfy their urges. Even the young boys in La resaca think of girls only in sexual terms. Elsewhere, a man on a bus "feels up" the woman next to him (RJ, p. 235); graffiti exclaim: "I fuck all girls from 7 to 75" (RJ, p. 59); and even nature invites the assumption of man the actor, as the author describes the sand: "dunas suaves como núbiles pechos o juveniles caderas" (RJ, p. 70). Women need nothing to fulfill their role. Man must always prove his manhood. The Spanish males in the crowd fix on a young girl, her innocent jutting breasts, her zealously guarded treasure. Saliva drooling, they are totally absorbed by the possible assault on her crypt: "en la brusca y candorosa insurgencia de los pechos, en el bien guardado tesoro [. . .] imaginarios espeleólogos de la cripta, de las cavidades recónditas" (RJ, pp. 27-28). The men represent a collective animal aggression, even though the sensual Arabs and their serpents are the true machos. The point is that woman is sexual property, a vagina to be possessed, violated, and destroyed if it suits one's purpose; hence the gigantic cave of the nun's vaginal orifice and the ensuing sexual orgy. Alvaro, in Señas de identidad indulges in "el ya clásico amancebamiento con la hija de una notoria personalidad del exilio."[17] He forces Dolores to have an abortion, leading to her own sexual revenge as she runs off with Enrique, affronting Alvaro's machismo. Enrique, in La isla, impotent and angry at his own deficiency, turns on Claudia, making her feel like a whore.

Most of Goytisolo's masculine protagonists in their search for love echo David, in Juegos de manos. Passive where women are concerned, he knows that they want men to dominate them. Even potential homosexual relationships involve the concept of machismo: "virilidad ruda y silvestre de aquellos hombres (SI, p. 174). In spite of his need for Dolores, Alvaro succumbs to this type of man. In Fin de fiesta "Isabelo tenia muy buena planta [. . .] y por la manera de expresarse, comprendí que estaba celoso de su virilidad."[18] Count Julian, disguised as Granny, will sodomize Alvarito; for Juan sin Tierra sodomy will be the norm.

To satisfy their belief in their own powers, men invent the myth of female phallic worship, the ultimate consequence of Freudian penis envy. The women in Reivindicación del Conde don Julián worship the male serpent which can satisfy them. In Juan sin Tierra, the women, kidnapped by King Kong, contemplate the fabulous dimensions of his masculine attributes. Sadly having to renounce their madness because of the dimensions involved, they will curse "a gritos la angustia de un destino irrisorio que les priva de la forma superior del conocimiento: del bíblico, el total, el inmediato: imposible."[19]

Women need men in various degrees. In El circo, inventing a liaison with Beremundo that never existed, Flora uses her fantasies about a man to ease her frustration. Celia, too, lives a vicarious love through romantic illusions. Gloria steals stamps from her father in Juegos de manos to free her lover from prison. Claudia, in La isla, when Enrique touches her, says, "no sé lo que me hago. Ten piedad de mí."[20] Dolores' desire for love is difficult to satiate, and she flirts with others before making desperate love with Alvaro. Sara begs Alvaro: "Haz conmigo lo que haces con las demás mujeres. En seguida, ¿me oyes?"(SI, pp. 453). When he refuses, she immediately goes to bed with another man to wipe the desire for Alvaro from her system.

The women's insatiable sexual drives accompany negative descriptions. Mrs. Putifar has smeared lipstick, a provocative neckline (RJ, p. 48), and, in her reincarnation as the flower-seller, shows scabrous, provocative breasts as she grabs the boy and forces his penis into her vaginal opening (RJ, pp. 99-101). The challenge to perform is always present. She asks him if he knows what her anatomical parts are called and then tells him laughing to go and ask his mother. All though Spain, women, even impatient virgins, want phallic satisfaction: "casadas, solteras, y hasta vírgenes [. . .] una rubita, con unos pechines así, que no me dejaba a sol ni a sombra [. . .] encapricha con mi menda una cosa mala" (RJ, p. 154-55).

Rejecting her form as Isabel la Católica, Alvaro Peranzules' daughter breaks out her silk black pajamas and offers herself in a suggestive dance, whipping herself with slow, persistent rotary motions, pleading for masculine help (RJ, p. 164), much as an earlier incarnation, lips voracious and red, ready to swallow down the salt of the earth in one gulp, flaunted her body, "invocando masculina ayuda con labios sedientos" (RJ, pp. 76-77). Throughout, the women are described as ardorous, with custard-like hips, jutting breasts, insatiable, and wild. Viewing these sexual demands as abnormal, two impotent men among many, the husband of the Pareja Reproductora in Juan sin Tierra and Enrique of La isla blame the woman. On the other hand, a refusal to meet his sexual needs leads the male character to view as abnormal a state of purity which he must somehow denigrate.

Goytisolo stresses that erotic behavior is a positive quality of Arab life absent from Spain.[21] One of Julián's principal tasks in his campaign of vengeance is to undo the virginal state and eroticize Spanish life and literature, destroying tradition, language, and sacred myths: "Se puede entender la presentación del sexo femenino como otro lugar insólito creado en la imaginación del narrador para parodiar el mito de la virginidad."[22] Goytisolo himself points out that the Pícara Justina, who indulged in a thousand shady tricks and episodes, always insisted: "Yo bien sabía mi entereza y que mi virginidad daría de sí señal honrosa, esmaltando con los corrientes rubíes la blanca plata de las sábanas nupciales" (FC, p. 73). And through Fuensanta, in La resaca, he stresses the Spanish belief that "Las mujeres deben casarse enteras."[23] Proclaiming that he was definitely attacking the myth of feminine virginity imposed by the Spanish Catholic Church which prevailed upon Rome to promulgate the dogma of the Immaculate Conception, Goytisolo discussed publicly the pathological hatred of sex exhibited by many Spanish writers, the sexual crime which supposedly caused the invasion of Spain by the Arabs, and the consequent attacks on "la España sagrada."[24] Although one may accept the explanation that his novels are a response to a repressive society and a Church that fights natural instincts in a studied recoil from sexual realities, what emerges is constant derogation of women and a literal wish to degrade them. This attitude extends far beyond the concept of virginity to include other potential positive characteristics they may have, but since the pundonor of the seventeenth century fits in so well with his literary attacks, it serves at the same time to mask a psychological one.

Lourdes teaches Alvaro a kind of religious masochism as she describes the torture of a young girl, later to be a saint, and associates death with virginity (SI, pp. 19-31). With unerring accuracy, Goytisolo's narrator wards off a series of fantasies dangerous to his ego as he extols the virtues of rude caresses and expert love-making like a Mohammedan he-goat "lejos de vuestras santas mujeres y sus sagrarios bien guardados" (RJ, p. 44). We see a spinster prima donna with her phallic umbrella and menopausal hot flash reading chapter after chapter about the expert maneuvers that the heroine of a best seller uses to defend her virginity. The unforgettable excursion into the "sacred grotto" attacks both Spain and woman, for the narrator describes feminine organs as belonging to the dark domain of Pluto. The interior itself is described as hideous, poisonous, nauseating, oozing "miasmas mefíticas de una musgosa y húmeda expansión [. . .] mundo rezumante y viscoso" (RJ, pp. 163-71). The author repeats the same negative description of woman's sexual apparatus as a hellish place, the womb "rugoso y cubierto de cicatrices" (RJ, pp. 99-101). Not content with this destruction, to express his feelings Julián insists on an extensive word play on "coño" in all its possible linguistic derivatives.

Men want women pliant and aroused but at the same time timid and pure. Goytisolo's ambivalence becomes abundantly clear, if one reads his work as a whole. On the one hand he pokes fun at virginity. On the other, he views women negatively because they indulge in sensual activities. In "Otoño en el puerto cuando llovizna" one of the characters claims: "A las mujeres les gustan los hombres sucios, cuanto más mejor" (PVA, p. 37). In "Suburbios" in the same collection, Laura, pregnant, may be abandoned because she has gone out with other men. Similarly, in Campos de Níjar the Swedish couple's sexual freedom causes commentary and scandal.[25] In Fiestas the Gorilla, while having sex with a woman on the beach, recalls his wife's infidelity with his own brother: "la muy cochina."[26] In La isla Claudia Estrada returns after an absence of six years to become a part of the gross Spanish world of animal instincts. Her cynical diary, covering eleven days, reveals women as negative sensual creatures. For the taxi driver who first meets her, women are whores and, as he says: "Las extranjeras nos tienen mal acostumbrados. Vienen únicamente para esto" (I, p. 11). Miss Bentley is known for her savage body; Betty, a seventy-two-year-old grandmother, for her sexual activity with fishermen. Sensuality and sexuality triumph as virginity disappears from the map. Laura, the eternal whore, sleeps with everyone. Rafael's mistress, a French model, in turn has a lover, an Italian aristocrat. In Fin de fiesta the marital relationships all involve infidelity, affairs, or seductions. In Reivindicación del Conde don Julián the female bigots, driven mad by the drugs, rend their garments, masturbate, and try to copulate with one another. One of Goytisolo's more pejorative pictures, whatever its civil rights connotations, reveals "la hembra que se abre y defeca, la negra que orina, las nalgas al aire" (JT, p. 7).

Women, then, not only figuratively but literally, become whores. In Para vivir aquí most of the stories revolve around these types and houses of prostitution. As one character states: "Aquí no tenemos más que las putas [. . .] las putas y las casadas [. . .] Lo fastidioso es que con las casadas tienes que darte prisa" (PVA, p. 130). In the same collection circus girls are forced to act as prostitutes to a frustrated town. In La chanca we meet Almerian prostitutes; in La resaca Coral, a sixteen-year-old prostitute. Alvaro learns about sex from a whore and recalls his fear that she might know he was a virgin (SI, p. 77). The protagonist of Reivindicación del Conde don Julián had also learned from the "labios de la mujerzuela experta" (RJ, p. 220), and he finds a Cinderella of easy virtue to share his bed. At one point we meet an international marketplace of prostitutes: "si la francesa no te gusta, tengo también una españolita: un verdadero terremoto [. . .] petite fille? fraulein to fuck" (RJ, pp. 155-56).

In any event, real love is difficult for protagonists filled with compulsions and frustration which lead them to prefer the physical to the spiritual, prostitutes over virgins, homosexuals over heterosexuals, and nymphomaniacs over chaste women. In Fin de fiesta the four variations clearly show the instability of any man-woman relationships. Similarly, Alvaro Mendiola believes that he and Dolores cannot help one another, that their love is futile, and that his feeling for her is narcissistic (SI, p. 331). Dolores herself feels soiled by Alvaro and his homosexual incidents.

Unable to obtain their impossible dream, the protagonists blame their impotence, syphilis, or homosexuality on women, who must then be punished for their inability to give man what he wants. Juan sin Tierra's glorification of anal intercourse makes clear its antifeminist attack, debasing the female genital through anal representation. In Señas de identidad we meet "la guapaza española típica hasta la náusea" (SI, p. 98). In Reivindicación del Conde don Julián a little girl will make a jump rope of the old woman's intestines (RJ, p. 147). Even more graphically, in the dream sequence involving Mrs. Putifar, once she is on the ground, little Arab boys steal her jewels and with obscene irreverence "levantan la falda y se arriman a orinar a la gruta" (RJ, p. 68).[27] Women, then, are not accepted for their own sexuality, as free. Goytisolo's masculine protagonists, manifesting a constant neurotic hostility involving sodomizing, destructive impulses, cannot accept man-woman union on a spiritual level.

In addition to viewing woman as degraded, the protagonists fear her for her castrating potential. On a psychological level, even the simplest woman is aware of her sexual power. As Fuensanta says: "A los hombres hay que tenerlos un poco a raya" (LR, p. 179). In <u>Juegos de manos</u> David's first sweetheart, Gloria, uses him only to further her own plans. Ana, who wants to kill Guarner for real or fancied slights, recalls that her mother browbeat her father and always spoke in negative terms of "tu pobre padre [. . .] daba por entendida la exclusión de papá."[28] David recalls his early fear of women and his aunt's attack on the priests by deliberately sending them laxative-laced chocolates. In <u>Duelo en el Paraíso</u>, Angela and Lucía delight in their brother Jordi's impotence: "muy por encima de la vileza y suciedades de los humanos."[29]

Alvaro Mendiola, looking for his roots, recalls how he felt imprisoned by his dominating Aunt Mercedes. He also knows he cannot really possess Dolores, freely admitting that in their love-making he is usually afraid. When she asks him whether her body disgusts him, he gives her a somewhat ambiguous answer, "me ahogo en él" (SI, p. 342), significant in view of his previously expressed fear. He recalls her as "lejana, hostil, apasionada, amante" (SI, p. 348), and his homosexual encounters may well have been motivated by a desire to escape her female genital.[30] He forces her into an abortion, but she avenges herself.

In <u>Reivindicación del Conde don Julián</u>, Mrs. Putifar violates the child sexually, much as he later will be sodomized by the serpent, and, in the wake of her sexual revelation, Pandora brings a persistent syphilis difficult to cure. Men console themselves by viewing women as needing to ease the fever between their legs, but man loses in the end. Mrs. Putifar forces the boy to penetrate her vagina, which ultimately may lead to his death. Indeed, women's sexual apparatus, as we have seen, is always described in extremely negative and almost repulsive terms as congested with blood. Once the traveler enters he discovers that he is "ahogándose, ahogándose" (RJ, pp. 99-101). Karen Horney claims that the bloody manifestations of womanhood are doubly sinister and thus defloration, for example, "involves the utmost danger to man" (FP, p. 135). Penetration of the vagina, then, is a perilous undertaking. Once inside the Spanish grotto, man himself becomes a prisoner, and his only hope for escape is to destroy it from within. It is a place from whose jaws few travelers have ever returned, hideous, poisonous, nauseating, an interior similar to Medusa's poisoned snakes (RJ, pp. 163-71).

The obvious fear of castration equates the loss of the organ with a kind of real death. Alvaro had been encouraged by his teacher, Miss Lourdes, in his desire to be a virginal martyr, and he associates the act of intercourse constantly with death: "No era acaso el orgasmo una pequeña muerte" (SI, p. 126). Recalling his first sexual experience, he again equates it with death: "que te había devuelto a la vida tras aquellos segundos inacabables de olvido, de muerte" (SI, p. 78). We may well ask, as Karen Horney does, whether side by side with his desire to conquer man does not have a simultaneous longing for extinction in the act of reunion with the woman—a longing underlying the death instinct (FP, pp. 138-39). Although this fear may not stem exclusively from the genital area but rather from a pregenital nursing situation, Goytisolo stresses the equation that sex equals death. Even the soldier and the girl making love relate their act to death (DP, pp. 188-89).

This aggression against man's sexual possibilities (including castration fears) recurs over and over. Alvaro's grandmother uses a knife against him. In the Rodrigo ballad which contributed to La Cava's reputation as a whorish type, the king suffers a special punishment by being bitten on his offending organ by a serpent, suffering a castration resulting in death. One conclusion to be drawn therefore is that coitus with females may result in death—a repeated thread in Reivindicación del Conde don Julián. Several times we see a horseman try to cross an abyss, eyes riveted on the provocative figure of a lascivious woman—described as was Mrs. Putifar, pleading for masculine help, torso writhing, hips swaying. And in a moment the rider will fall to his death: "el Averno le espera con las fauces abiertas" (RJ, pp. 105-6). Trying to cross the bridge, Alvaro also falls into the water at the foot of the cliff, the primal feminine element which will swallow him up: "pasa un puente sobre el abismo un puente que va estrechándose hasta quedar reducido a una tabla escueta [. . .] no ve la sima no ve el vacío sólo ve al otro lado la destructora y provocante figura de una lasciva mujer la Muerte [. . .] abajo le aguarda el abismo con las fauces abiertas" (RJ, pp. 212-13).

Whatever their sensuality, the women in Goytisolo's novels have bad characters. In Juegos de manos David's great aunt is infantile and egotistical; Celeste is shallow and hypocritical; Ana's mother is also an egostistical social climber. Estanislaa, the aunt in Duelo en el Paraíso, is overbearing. Doña Francisca in Fiestas is sadistic. Trinidad, in La resaca, is prepared to denounce her husband Giner to the police and turns his sons against him. In El circo Vicky and her sister hate each other and their parents.

Goytisolo almost always paints his females in somber tones. Antonia, the servant in Fiestas, is dying of cancer of the brain. The grandmother is senile. Doña Cecilia, living in a dream world, is also dying of cancer. Piluca attempts unsuccessfully to live vicariously through her cousin Pira's fantasies. Juana of El circo is bored with life. The women of Fin de fiesta manage to survive but at the price of forgiving infidelity, foregoing passion, and aging. In Juan sin Tierra the narrator dwells lovingly on the menstrual flow of young girls, extols soiled Kotex, and in general degrades woman's natural physical and psychological functions.

Although a few good women exist in Goytisolo's novels, they are for the most part peripheral to the central action and usually meet a tragic end. Pira, the child-woman in Fiestas, is raped and killed. In Juegos de manos Alicia serves as a temporary dream image for the effeminate Tanger and Juana as a transient symbol of purity for David. In Fin de fiesta Mara gives her husband strength, and Elisa, of El circo, a happy masochist, thinks only of Utah's welfare. Goytisolo portrays servants most positively. In his autobiographical notes he recalls that the death of Eulalia, the family servant, who looked after the children "con el amor y solicitud de una madre,"[31] affected him more than that of his father. Pipo loves Antonia, but the latter develops cancer of the brain. Filomena, the servant in Duelo en el Paraíso, kind to Abel, had lost five children. But even this positive archetype must be besmirched, for in Reivindicación del Conde don Julián, although the "anciana y devota sirvienta" serves him chocolate on a tray and reads him the story of Little Red Riding Hood, Alvaro must betray her to Julian and falsely accuse that selfless lady of stealing (RJ, p. 97).

Where women are concerned Goytisolo seems unable to escape the traumatic events of his youth, and in their portrayal he seems to rekindle repressed desires of various kinds. In his total attack on Spanish culture and the portrayal of scandalous scenes which do not disguise his deadly seriousness, he focuses on woman as a negative archetype, perhaps an ambivalent reflection of what he always wanted and could apparently never find: warmth, generosity, sympathy, and an affirmation of the redeeming power of love.

Notes

¹See Rosalina R. Rovira, "La función de la mujer en la literatura contemporánea española," Explicación de textos literarios, 20, I (1974), 21-24. See also María Aurelia Capmany, El feminismo ibérico (Barcelona: Oikos-Tau, 1970), for a study of feminine alienation in Spain.

²Miguel de Unamuno, Amor y pedagogía (Madrid: Espasa-Calpe, 1959), p. 11.

³Marguerite C. Rand, "Azorín y Eros," Revista Hispánica Moderna, 19 (1963), 218-33.

⁴José Martínez Ruiz, La voluntad, Obras completas, I (Madrid: Aguilar, 1947), 983.

⁵See Fernando Baeza, Baroja y su mundo (Madrid: Ediciones Arion, 1961), II, 383-85.

⁶Gloria Durán, "Baroja, antifeminista?", Insula, 27 (1972), p. 8.

⁷Pío Baroja, El mundo es ansí (Madrid: Rafael Caro Raggio, 1930), p. 106.

⁸Pío Baroja, Paradox Rey (Madrid: Espasa-Calpe, 1934), pp. 66-67.

⁹Camilo José Cela, La Catira (Barcelona: Ed. Noguer, 1955), p. 346.

¹⁰Miguel Delibes, Mi idolatrado hijo Sisi, Obras completas, I (Barcelona: Ed. Destino, 1964), p. 466.

¹¹Luis Martín Santos, Tiempo de silencio (Barcelona: Ed. Seix Barral, 1971), p. 221.

¹²Juan Benet, Volverás a Región (Barcelona: Ed. Destino, 1967), p. 297.

¹³See Manuel Durán, "El lenguaje de Juan Goytisolo," Cuadernos Americanos (November, 1970), 167-79; José Ortega, Juan Goytisolo, Alienación y Agresión en Señas de identidad y Reivindicación del Conde don Julián (New York: Eliseo Torres, 1972), pp. 91-99; Kessel Schwartz, "Juan Goytisolo, Ambivalent Artist in Search of his Soul," Journal of Spanish Studies: Twentieth Century, 3 (1975), 187-97.

[14] Fernando Díaz Plaja, El español y los siete pecados capitales (Madrid: Alianza Editorial, 1969), p. 136.

[15] Juan Goytisolo, Reivindicación del Conde don Julián (Mexico: Joaquín Mortiz, S.A., 1970), p. 127. Further citations in the text are to this edition, hereafter noted as RJ.

[16] Juan Goytisolo, Para vivir aquí (Buenos Aires: Sur, 1960), p. 22. Further citations in the text are to this edition, hereafter noted as PVA.

[17] Juan Goytisolo, Señas de identidad (Mexico: Joaquín Mortiz, S.A., 1966), p. 9. Further citations in the text are to this edition, hereafter noted as SI.

[18] Juan Goytisolo, Fin de fiesta (Barcelona: Editorial Seix Barral, 1961), p. 91.

[19] Juan Goytisolo, Juan sin Tierra (Barcelona: Editorial Seix Barral, 1975), p. 75. Further citations in the text are to this edition, hereafter cited as JT.

[20] Juan Goytisolo, La isla (Barcelona: Editorial Seix Barral, 1961), p. 149. Further citations in the text are to this edition, hereafter noted as I.

[21] Typical is his statement in El furgón de cola (Paris: Ruedo Ibérico, 1967), p. 76 that, "Cada vez que el erotismo español se manifiesta lo hace bajo la influencia árabe." Further citations in the text are to this edition, hereafter noted as FC.

[22] Linda Gould Levine, Goytisolo: La destrucción creadora (Mexico: Joaquín Mortiz, S.A., 1976), p. 135.

[23] Juan Goytisolo, La resaca (Paris: Club del libro español, 1958), p. 179. Further citations in the text are to this edition, hereafter noted as LR.

[24] Juan Goytisolo, "Declaración de Juan Goytisolo de la mesa redonda celebrada en la Universidad de Wisconsin-Parkside," Norte, 13, 4-6 (1962), 92-93.

[25] Juan Goytisolo, Campos de Níjar (Barcelona: Editorial Seix Barral, 1960), p. 90.

[26] Juan Goytisolo, Fiestas (New York: Dell, 1964), p. 158.

[27] According to Emil Arthur Gutheil, The Language of the Dream (New York: Macmillan, 1939), p. 54, symbolically "all

secretions and excretions [. . .] equal [. . .] each other [. . .] of interchangeable value are: blood, urine, pus, water, semen. . . . " Thus urinating may equal intercourse.

[28] Juan Goytisolo, Juegos de manos (Barcelona: Ediciones Destino, 1960), pp. 93-94. Further citations in the text are to this edition, hereafter noted as JM.

[29] Juan Goytisolo, Duelo en el Paraíso (Barcelona: Ediciones Destino, 1960), p. 27. Further citations in the text are to this edition, hereafter noted as DP.

[30] See Karen Horney, Feminine Psychology (New York: Norton, 1973), p. 137. Further citations in the text are to this edition, hereafter noted ad FP.

[31] Juan Goytisolo, ed. Julián Ríos (Madrid: Editorial Fundamentos, 1975), pp. 12-21.

FAUNA IN THE NOVELS OF JUAN GOYTISOLO

Real and imagined resemblances and relationships between animals and human beings have preoccupied writers from earliest times, and they have utilized animal imagery constantly throughout literature for derogatory, satirical, or sympathetic purposes. In contemporary Hispanic literature Ramón Sender, Juan José Arreola, and Julio Cortázar, among others, have concentrated on the theme; but none has so consistently used animals iconoclastically as Juan Goytisolo.

Goytisolo no doubt believes that Spanish society is a menagerie, a kind of backward jungle, inhabited by herds of sheep easily victimized by dictatorship, capitalism, tourism, the Catholic Church, and sexual frustrations. Spaniards suffer all of the savage aspects of animalistic living without any of the positive benefits to be derived from a more primitive and forceful life containing sexual and sadistic elements which help one to cope with a cruel and violent world. If the atmosphere of Spain is bestial, it is only natural that animals reside there. As the author ridicules the pretensions to cultural dignity and intellectuality of Spanish society, he uses animal characterizations, using beasts to show us the absurdity of human life, and indicating a variety of zoomorphic and emotional relationships which involve aggression, death, danger, sex, hunger, politics, and religion.

Animal imagery, anthropomorphism, and zoomorphism exist from his first through his latest novels, with a continuing intensification, starting with Señas de identidad, of cultural, psychological, and sexual connections. At times he attributes animal characteristics or qualities to humans. At others he ascribes human motivations to non-human beings. Additionally, he uses imagery involving bats, dogs, cats, goats, monkeys, tigers, rabbits, lizards, fish, snails, frogs and, in reality, an entire galaxy of animals from apes to vultures.[1] In over a hundred instances Goytisolo employs animal imagery as a stylistic device without any species designation. Human beings and animals often lead mutually dependent lives, and pets reward the affection of their masters (JM$_2$, p. 67). Although he at times refers to "astucia animal,"[2] or "me araño como una fiera" (F., p. 125), for the most part Goytisolo, through his human-animal comparisons, views the latter as a victim of humanity's worst inhuman instincts: "Jadeaba como un animal perseguido" (JM, p. 207); "como un animal acorrolado" (DP, p. 104); "timorato e incierto . . . animal doméstico" (SI, p. 75).[3] When Alvaro suffers his heart attack, the crowd ignores his pain, and he is "el animal indefenso que jadeaba a sus pies, acechando la llegada de la ambulancia . . ." (SI, p. 59). In general Goytisolo places humans far down the zoological scale, even below parasites.[4]

Before treating the seven types of animals used most persistently by Goytisolo, let us examine some of his general themes. Given his interest in the self-destructive politics of his country, his attacks on the imposed and accepted intellectual conformity, and his search, not only for his own marks of identity but the signs and meanings of Spanish society, it is not surprising that he uses animals to portray the immobility of the Spanish political superstructure and its denial of human life and dignity.[5] Goytisolo describes the animalization of a society through the metaphoric roles of his characters. Alvaro, for example, alone and feeling almost invisible, associates the croaking of frogs and the noise of crickets to past events, recalling Spain as a cradle of heroes, saints, madmen, and inquisitors, "toda la extraña fauna ibera . . ." (SI, pp. 164-65). Goytisolo uses this concept of a general herd to criticize the status quo, seeing the defenders of reason taking animal advantage over fellow countrymen, herds of oxen eating the fodder provided them, "triste rebaño de bueyes . . . pasta de aprovechados," and composes his documentary "sobre la grey española expulsada de su tierra por la opresión . . . el hambre la injusticia" (SI, pp. 104, 237, 355).[6] When Alvaro attends Prof. Ayuso's funeral, he compares the new Barcelona society to "fauna española" and proposes that traditional shacks might disappear without the new capitalism, which brings more than its share of new problems.

Goytisolo, utilizing a variety of animal connotations to convey important characteristics, evokes Spain as "la habitación natural de la fauna española . . . grey silvestre," condemned to disappear with animal-like resignation before the tourists' onslaught (SI, p. 64). Aside from the "happening" involving the American tourist, "Hija de la Revolución Americana" (CJ, pp. 65-68), the narrator describes a tourist excursion bus, huge as a whale and having a snout like a shark (CJ, p. 46). Elsewhere, hordes of tourists take shelter, "cobijados bajo el ala de clueca de un oficioso" (JT, pp. 103-04).[7] The tourists conclude that European districts are much cleaner, for in Spain abstract mongrels search for food amidst clouds of flies, "negras, velludas, pringosas" (CJ, p. 45).

Contrasts with other countries involve a continuing denigrating description of the misery and poverty in Spain, "perro esquelético . . . basuras . . . oleadas de moscas tornasoladas y perezosas . . . entre aquellos despojos . . . corrupción del aire. . ." (DP, pp. 52-53). These comparisons, then, reflect an indolent and degraded State where animals prowl garbage-laden heaps, part of the environment in which Spaniards live.

Political comparisons inevitably lead to cultural ones. Alvaro associates Venice with birds (SI, pp. 362-63), Amsterdam with butterflies (SI, p. 346), and Cuba with animals wandering through the fields (SI, pp. 425-27). This evocation of foreign climes allows him more objectively to visualize his own culture, which he sees as a superficial adoption of foreign models which in no way alter hidebound Spanish traditions. The only solution involves their complete cultural destruction, visualized by the narrator of Reivindicación del Conde don Julián and Juan sin Tierra.

The Moors, transformed into frightening submarine fauna, will take over (CJ, p. 84), a process which Goytisolo intensifies with hallucinatory evocations and drug stupors, as through animal symbols, he replaces Spanish with Arabic culture. In Nubian territory, abandoning the promiscuous herd, riveted on "los gestos felinos de tu mentor," he falls "entre las fauces abiertas del cavernoso mastín," before once more imagining himself "entre tu antigua fauna," now incarnated as Alvaro Krupp but acknowledging that "el subsuelo africano te basta . . ." (JT, pp. 131-33). Thanks to his special use of pronouns, the narrator manages to travel the Moslem world. In analyzing his language, Vosk complains that the narrator is trying to sell him a cat for a hare and receives as a response to "¿qué mosca le ha picado?," the reply that it might be a common housefly or a tsetse fly (JT, p. 303). Dissatisfied, the narrator will in the future use another language (Arabic), his gift curling back on itself like the tail of a scorpion. And so he transforms himself like a larva into an insect and, like a frog, mocking and mocked, puts down on the white paper sheets bits and pieces of his former personality (pp. 318-19). The narrator abandons all of his traditional literary symbols. One of the Vosk incarnations enchants the birds and the beasts, but is surprised to find the beautiful literary heroine in a deserted place, populated, "por lo común de alimañas y otras temibles fieras. . ." (JT, pp. 268-69). After a mocking rejection of the shibboleths of literary tradition and an exploration of writing, which he likens to a bird hunting for prey (JT, p. 298), the narrator realizes that he will never have his statue in a public square, that birds will not alight on it nor dogs stain its pedestal; in this way he will avoid an obscene symbiosis with the land he hates (JT, p. 317).

Part of Goytisolo's reservations about Spanish culture and tradition involves his continuing and long-standing aggression toward the Catholic Church. These attacks, related to animals, occur in several novels. In satirical auto da fe scenes, some victims go to their deaths on a donkey, and the president of the Society for the Prevention of Cruelty to Animals fails to take into account the cathartic nature of the ceremony which will protect humans from acting like "los más brutos animales" (JT, pp. 195-96). In a savage attack on the Virgin Mary and a parody of the birth of the Christ child, Goytisolo has a "perro esquelético" sniff at him and associates his homage with "pie de culebra, pelos de macho cabrío . . ." (CJ, p. 237). In <u>Juan sin Tierra</u> the attack, if possible, is even more ferocious. The dove in mythology symbolizes love; in Matthew 10, innocence. But, according to an old Christian legend it also represents the word of the angel which, as the breath of a dove, entered Mary's ear, obviously with phallic power.[8] In Goytisolo's novel the bird pecks the canary seed, and excites Yemayá, captivating her. When Changó appears on a Moorish horse, his moustache like a lizard's tail, he kills and devours the bird but also metamorphoses as the Dove. Yemayá, eager to face his masculine organ, pictures it as a wild beast, "hosco y dañino animal" which she is eager to liberate from between his legs (JT, pp. 56-57).

Goytisolo's concern for the Spanish religious strait jacket leads him to the concomitant topic of sexuality. Goytisolo's protagonists struggle for ego identity, and his heroes suffer from a variety of neurotic manifestations and fantasies involving castration, a return to mother, other womb fantasies, fetishism, sadism, and masochism as they encounter bizarre situations and incidents.[9] Sibling rivalries, incest, impotence, bestialism, homosexuality, masturbation, and various neurotic and hallucinatory sexual states and parent-child relationships comprise some of the carnal, sensual, animal symbolism. As usual Goytisolo employs animals specifically and generally. Peranzules's daughter displays her thighs which "la hispánica grey" holds in awe (CJ, p. 164). Men take their sexual pleasures "gozando como brutos animales," and convicts are allowed their "pecado bestial" (JT, pp. 29, 201). Parodying the white man's view of blacks' sexual activities, Goytisolo proclaims that "ni las fieras ni animales del monte son tan desenfrenados" (JT, p. 38).[10] As the narrator views the primal scene he dreams of the charge of wild beasts who will destroy his parents (JT, p. 156). A child will condense into one image the primal scene and his own union with his mother. A situation causing separation means anxiety and aggression. When he sees his parents in bed together, the child wants to separate them and punish his mother's infidelity represented by the primal scene.[11]

Animals, many times, reflect human emotional states involving love, fear, hate, and especially aggression, which quite often leads to death, a mortality portrayed through the zoological connection. In Juegos de manos Agustín kills David whose motionless feet "imitaban la aleta de un gran pez" (JM, p. 244), Goytisolo here employs a symbolic symmetry, for earlier in the novel David recalls how in his childhood he saved, with the help of other children, some fish which were suffocating; how don Angel caused him to drop some, but how happy he felt with "la visión de los peces, ebrios de la vida" (JM, p. 178). In Duelo en el Paraíso, Abel, about to die in the forest, "oscura como un presagio de muerte," listens to the frightened birds and croaking of crows, and Elósegui relates the song of the birds before Abel's death to their silence after it (DP, p. 16). In Señas de identidad Alvaro matches animals with natural death sequences, for example, in the cementery where a hoopee symbolically skims the tops of the tombs.[12]

In his reflections on humanity and its social, cultural, religious, and sexual constructs, Goytisolo prefers certain animal organisms in order to reflect negative bestial, sensual, or physical attributes but also to demonstrate the superiority of animality over humanity. These include serpents, birds, insects, cats, bulls, apes, and dogs. The serpent, of course, has been traditionally hated and feared, and Goytisolo refers to its connection with Christianity and its victims. Venemous serpents will accompany Alvaro's flirtation with Hell (JT, p. 292), and the serpent will tempt him despite the protestations of Alvaro's guardian angel about his incipient defecation. When Alvaro eliminates without sound or fury, the serpent flees. Viewed in its aggressive, poisonous, mythological attributes, the serpent throughout will adopt a threatening posture. The Arabs, and not the Spaniards, can use it, exercising their power with "enigmática violencia . . . la sierpe hambrienta se apercibe al ataque" (CJ, pp. 135-36, 144). The tiger-eyed Julián will sodomize Alvarito with his serpent, strangle him, and inject its poison, "el líquido mortífero". Additionally, the "cuerpo rígido" of a lifeless cat, hanging by its neck from one of the trees, will accompany that death (CJ, pp. 209-18). The serpent also kills Mrs. Putifar in a "happening" and on birth destroys the inside of his mother (CJ, p. 126). Yet, reptiles are superior entities. In Manhattan sewers crododiles, lizards and iguanas will produce a new amphibious species, the envy of men who would be like them, large, flexible, and with a talent for swimming.

As man descends the animal scale, he will, paradoxically, ascend, exalting "los encantadores de serpientes," disputing propaganda about serpents' poisonous fangs, and exploring the hiding places of the crafty reptile with hopes of domesticating it (JT, pp. 79-81).

Goytisolo uses serpent imagery in many ways: "la carretera zigzaguea como una víbora . . . (JT, p. 115), but concentrates on their sexual and phallic power.[13] Anxious females await an attack: "el pasivo serrallo acogerá con júbilo la robusta culebra"; "mujeres de toda laya . . . rehusando el lechuguino concepto invocan en sueños la arábiga sierpe" (CJ, pp. 127, 149). Count Julián violates the grotto of Spanish purity but traps himself, his serpent becoming a stone blade. Goytisolo depicts the reptile ecstasy of Arab asps as the damsels surrender to Tariq's men "con docilidad bestial, a sus cobras tenaces e imperiosas culebras" (CJ, p. 172). His description includes mention of the Medusa, whose head horrified and turned men to stone, a symbolic rigidity easily equated with phallic prowess.[14] Alvarito, fascinated by Julián's asp, evokes in his mind all kinds of sexual activity and dangerous beasts, matching his excitement to Julián's snake's arousal. He succumbs to the "cobra barrocamente erguida . . . triunfal . . . abraza, estrangula, asfixia . . ." Unwilling and resisting at first, the boy later submits to the sodomy, enslaved by and kneeling to the serpent to "implorar el perdón" (CJ, pp. 219-25). The serpent also involves the mother figure, pictured as good, kind, and protective. Julián orders Alvarito to bring her to be victimized by the snake, "tu madre y la culebra, la culebra y tu madre. . . ." And through sodomy and suicide, "serpiente troglodita . . . en simbiosis fulminea . . . tú mismo al fin, único, en el fondo de tu animalidad herida . . ." (CJ, pp. 228-30), Julián and Alvarito become one; Julián, thus, liberates himself through the sexual instinct represented by the snake. In a sense this incident may be equated with a symbolic dragon fight in mythological terms, for the hero's fate portrays that of the ego and the danger of being swallowed by the maternal unconsciousness. A successful dragon fight results in the marriage of the hero and the female captive in order to found a new kingdom. When this fails to occur it implies a strong unconscious tie to the Great Mother.[15]

In Juan sin Tierra the narrator relates the power he feels to "serpentina presencia que subyuga y que castra . . ." (p. 125). He comments on the clandestine cult toward lascivious reptiles, as a shameless convict admits his "execrable devoción a la sierpe" (p. 205). Receiving fraternal care, insuring their reproduction, they may infiltrate the conjugal bed itself (p. 249).

The serpent also fuses with the snake charmer, Julián, and the story of Little Red Riding Hood, in almost identically reproduced versions of the same event at different stages of Reivindicación del Conde don Julián, although the author alters the apparent superimposed sameness through countless subtle variations. The narrator states, "érase una vez un precioso niño," complete with fetishes, snake, wolf, and blood (p. 13). Alvarito takes the role of Caperucito, and Julián, disguised as grandmother, will receive him. The author associates the fairy tale with illicit sexual relations of neighbors, their mongoloid child, and the violation of Alvarito by the flower seller. Interspersed with the plot line,". . . soy Caperucita Roja y traigo unas tortas . . .," we find the gossip of the flower seller and her lover (pp. 94-98). Alvarito Peranzules, transformed into Little Red Riding Hood, will carry the goodies to Granny, will get into bed with her, and, discovering that she is a sharp-clawed Moor, will exclaim: "qué bicho tan grande tienes" (pp. 209-10). Alvarito "busca y acata la serpiente" (pp. 224-25), implying that he wants the wolf to follow him to grandmother's house, to have Julián wound (sodomize) him with the serpent.[16]

Interestingly enough, in view of the identification of Julián with Alvarito, Géza Roheim postulates that the wolf, grandmother, and Little Red Riding Hood are the same person. She is swallowed into her own "sleep-womb," the same as the inside of her mother. The hunter is the father figure; his knife, the penis. Julián then represents the father, but Roheim states that the infant desires and is the original aggressor; aggression and regression combine as the cannibal child creates a cannibal mother.[17] Julián tells himself to flee from his people in order to be safe in his adopted African land. Clearly he connects his own people with parents and Alvarito, as we have seen, for "víbora, reptilia o serpiente enconada que al nacer, rompe los yjares de la madre: tu vientre liso ignora la infamia del ombligo . . . el niño vuelve del colegio con la cartera a la espalda . . . el niño fascinado por el aspid y tú, Julián, avanzando. . ." (p. 126). Grandmother may also be mother, and the story explains an oedipal situation. The wolf, both good and bad, gives and takes, since the sexual object is both desired and feared.[18] Of course, if mother and grandmother are one, a child would not want to harm her, but if a wolf killed her (Julián's alter-ego Tariq is called el lobo), the child could hate and fear the wolf without feeling responsibility. Nonetheless, the child is involved because he can consummate his sexual desires only by proxy, in a symbolic rape.[19]

Avian imagery may convey both pleasant and unpleasant situations as the author refers to bird-like motions and mannerisms of a number of his characters. David's great aunt, Lucía, "corría de un lado a otro como un pajarillo" (JM, p. 180), and the woman searching for her father sticks her head out "como la de un pájaro recién arrancado de su nido" (SI, p. 392).[20] One characteristic of Goytisolo's description of birds involves their comparison with material objects; birds flying overhead are "como flechas" (JM, p. 124); banana trees are forsaken black-winged birds (F. p. 156). He uses them also to reproduce political situations. In Señas de identidad Alvaro's aunts "como loros" reject newspaper accounts of the Spanish situation as lies (SI, p. 320); in Reivindicación del Conde don Julián the hombre carpeto is "la gallina"(CJ, p. 115), and the Falangist fighters who ended the possibility of a Spanish rebirth are "aguerridos y escandalosos gallos de marzo" (CJ, pp. 124, 137).

Birds play an important sexual role in Goytisolo's novels. Antonio's introduction to sex takes place in the presence of birds.[21] The bird, of course, has always been a phallic symbol, and in the popular speech of many languages is a synonym for the masculine organ. In La isla Claudia's sister-in-law shows her a canary in a cage, hungrily examined by a cat which flees upon her approach, much as her own appearance incapacitates Enrique. When Rafael attempts to make love to her she resists and, on going down stairs, finds the canary cage on its side and the bird gone. Her own feelings of frustration and alienation are thus reinforced. Meanwhile, the children watch the cage in hope of punishing the cat.[22] Quite often sexual and religious connotations occur together. Lourdes, recounting tales of martyrdom, links the virginal spirit of one martyr to the dove: "se vio salir de su boca una paloma blanca" (SI, p. 22). In Juan sin Tierra the savage attacks include a sexually aroused fat girl who waits for a visit from the Dove or Holy Spirit. Blessed fruit of the womb, the girl on the record jacket performs delicate needlework picturing a gentle ox, a donkey, and a little lamb while she scrutinizes the sky, waiting for "el raudo y ligero visitador" (p. 54). Chango's violation of his mother and concomitant destruction of the Dove, a continuation of the parody, intensifies the sexual elements involved. He himself becomes the Dove and, as the Christ child, his own father.

Human beings identify their own emotional states with the presence of birds. Antonia's parrot in Fiestas imitates the lady upstairs while its mistress holds the bird to her breast, petting and kissing it. When Pipo awakens to a new day to the sound of birds, he realizes that butterflies had once been caterpillars, linking their change with his own coming of age and the release by the authorities of thousands of pigeons with his own emotional maturity (F.,pp. 218-19). Pablo and his friend Atila react to the ferocity of the cockfight, the former with aversion, the latter with identification: "participaba en el combate con los cinco sentidos. . . . Estaba excitado todavía por la tensión de la riña" (EC, pp. 35-37). The fugitives, carrying birds, open the cage door to set the doves free, connecting their own plight with that of the birds (DP, p. 11).

Alvaro's recall blends with the noise of crickets and a bird moving out to sea. As he talks to Dolores, a blackbird alights on the eaves. When he awakens "los pájaros gorjean en las ramas . . . las golondrinas son infinitamente sutiles." He associates his new tranquility with "el vuelo irreal de las aves"; his relationship with Dolores and self-discovery with cats and birds: "los gatos negros y las palomas blancas . . . os devolvía poco, a ti y a ella, a vuestra remota extraviada identidad." Once more in the present, he holds Dolores's hand, the silence composed of an infinity of tiny sounds, the croaking of frogs, the hum of the crickets and "el vuelo conciso, ceñido, de los pájaros" (SI, pp. 348-49, 399, 465, 476, 332, 398). Paris for Alvaro also means a battle between an old man feeding pigeons and a woman who tries to chase them away, symbolic of his own inner turmoil between artistry and action (SI, pp. 379-81).

At times the instinctive forces found in children, adults, and animals reveal themselves through aggressive acts, the killing of a cat, or a rooster, with which Julián identifies, like him pursued and related to the rabies-carrying dog as a destructive force.[23] A casual examination reveals a persistent, sadistic, and aggressive animal symbolism related to human activity in all of Goytisolo's novels. Luis and Gloria "ponían trampas a los pájaros y cemento en la boca de los hormigureos" (JM, p. 68); more than cruelty, their action symbolizes their general rebellion against society's rules. The children in Duelo en el Paraíso exercise the power to torment smaller children and animals not only to compensate for their own feelings of impotence in the face of superior adult strength but also as a reflection of the savage environment and reality. The little ones learn to kill birds with "cargas de dinamita" (p. 20), and bands of boys knock down their nests "a pedradas" (p. 224). Abel also shatters the birds' eggs, forgetting the love Estanislaa had taught him to feel for birds (DP, pp. 20, 224, 240-41, 116-17, 233, 229-30). As noted previously, birds also symbolize human death. Elósegui hears of Dora's death to the accompaniment of a "chillido siniestro y lejano de un ave" (DP, p. 58), and Alvaro, as he views nature, sees "auroras tiñosas . . . sobre el esqueleto de los automóviles. . . .Un aroma de muerte y putrefacción impregna agudamente el paisaje" (SI, pp. 441, 465).

Cats also play a large role in Goytisolo's menagerie. One of the characters in La resaca is Hombre-Gato; in other novels characters have "ojos brillantes de felino" (DP, p. 123), "mirada felina" (JT, p. 108), or "felinos ojos" (CJ, p. 89). Mendiola recalls a variety of black cats, one belonging to Professor Ayuso, another belonging to Madame de Heredia, and still another in Madame Berger's French cafe (SI, pp. 81, 332, 335-36). In Juan sin Tierra the narrator passes a symposium of starving cats performing their concert of mournful meows under the Toscaninian baton of a splendid tiger-striped specimen, "insolente, matón, con superiores aires de chulo" (p. 114). As with other animal symbols, Goytisolo uses cats to demonstrate human aggression. In Duelo en el Paraíso Pablo and Abel dream of the bullets with which they will pierce Lucía's cat (pp. 240-41), throw rocks at it (pp. 116-17), and drop a paving stone on another one, which makes Abel feel, "por vez primera la ilusión de ser hombre" (p. 233). In Señas de identidad children also stone a cat, and in Reivindicación del Conde don Julián they pursue a cat, "pelón y tiñoso," and kill and bury it (pp. 51-52, 239).

Cats have almost always served as an erotic symbol; quite often they may represent the "evil mother." An unconscious dislike for women and a fear of aggressive erotic components, may, nonetheless, cause one to think of the cat as male rather than female. In any event, antipathy towards cats is always symbolic.[24] Abel insists on knowing the precise relationship in the birth process between cats and people. The answer that one comes into the world to seek purity angers him, and the relationships of cats and birth, seen as unpleasant, triggers a train of associations concerning his stillborn brother and jealousy at the intimacy that the unborn child had with his mother (DP, p. 112). Cora, for the sexually aroused soldier, is "mi gatita" (LR, p. 125), and Laura, removing her clothes, rubs against Román like a cat (I, p. 112). The cat, pursued by the boys who beat its dead body, in spite of its difficult life had lived nights of love and erotic meowing (CJ, pp. 18, 239).[25]

The ape and monkeys play an important role in some of Goytisolo's novels. One of the chief characters in Fiestas is the huge muscled Gorila; in Señas de identidad one of the supposed spies is also named Gorila. Spain, for Álvaro in Señas de identidad, means a monkey on a platform, angry at the noise and the crowds which drive him wild (SI, p. 370). Aside from extended use of imagery, Goytisolo uses the gorila designation either seriously to convey similarities or as a continuing source of burlesque and parody. Thus in Juegos de manos the term gorila epitomizes women both pejoratively and positively.[26] The ape, also, has given rise to sexual myths, and, a virtual caricature of man, has represented man's evil impulses.[27] Goytisolo fuses the erotic with religious impulses. In Juan sin Tierra, after Chango possesses his mother, he converts to King Kong, the totemic animal of the narrator. His apparition creates frustration among moaning damsels who admire, in vain, his tremendous artefact, a symbol of amorous potency denied humans. The characters undergo a variety of changes to "orangután victorioso" and then to a gorilla, "onírica metamorfosis" (JT, pp. 76, 159). The

140

zoo, in reality a whorehouse inhabited by four-handed hominids, gives Kong, newly reincarnated as Changó, the chance to possess the backsides of Queen Kong, the Visitada and principal whore of Istanbul. . . . The excommunicators try to excommunicate all ophidians, but they fly to Africa in search of an avenging King Kong. In a desert filled with wild beasts, "prado lleno de serpientes, ora pro nobis . . . verdadera Queen Kong," the narrator realizes that the thought of Hell should terrorize him, as he peruses an old manual of piety (pp. 290-92). Goytisolo's implication that the Church is a whorehouse and that the metamorphosed Queen-Kong, a whore, is the Virgin Mary, carries his attack to its ultimate possibilities.

As Linda Gould Levine has shown, Goytisolo makes no distinction between cruelty to man and toward animals.[28] The defeat of idealism by animalistic guards who torture peasants much as onlookers torture a bull offers a good example: "hay que prolongar el juego hasta el límite, apurar su agonía hasta la hez" (SI, pp. 152-53). Thus the spectators throw stones at a young bull while others cut him with a knife. The bull, for Goytisolo, also exemplifies the sexual process, a rather standard indentification. In Cretan culture bulls represented fertility; in our culture they reflect masculine virility. But, as we have seen, for Goytisolo they may also be victims. When Claudia sees the bull fight, she muses on the absurdity of life, and her alienation takes on an almost physical presence (I, p. 79). In addition to the emptiness she feels, she accepts Dolores's symbolic interpretation, linking the spectators with a lack of sexual prowess. As in Enrique's case, this identification creates the reverse of machismo (I, p. 135). On the other hand, when Gorila visits the whorehouses, he begins to bellow like a bull (F., p. 148).

Dogs, man's best friends, reflect that relationship as well as the more aggressive and bloodthirsty instincts of man. From the moment Abel arrives at Paraíso, the dog seem to understand him and licks his hands. Abel plans to go off to war but not without Lucero whom he believes to be "más listo que muchas personas. . ."(DP, p. 55). Gorila claims his female dog loves him as much as he loves her: "es mi única mujer" (F, p. 138). But hungry dogs and bloody wolves also represent aggression; a dog's teeth become a hypodermic needle (CJ, pp. 104-05, 210, 35); and the intestines of the disemboweled little donkey, Platero, will make a jump rope for a little girl, who herself will die of rabies (p. 147). Dogs then become associated with death. When Elósegui hears the news of Dora's death, he restrains a crazy impulse to run to her room and smell her bed "como un perro" (DP, p. 58). And, of course, the author links dogs with sexual contact. Julián associates his syphilis with "perros hambrientos," and the dog who bit him licks up the decapitated cock's blood from the floor (CJ, pp. 103-05). The rooster, its severed head a displacement from below,[29] implies, in addition to castration, impotence versus virility. Other incidents involving dogs occur in LR (p. 193), SI (p. 126) and JT (pp. 25, 151).

In Reivindicación del Conde don Julián insects appear as a symbol of human life and especially of children,[30] as we can see in the time trip taken in the dispensary (CJ, pp. 64, 107-08). Insect imagery, a constant in Goytisolo's novels, concerns adults also. In El circo Utah meets a woman in a bar who "evolucionaba en la pista como un insecto aturdido por la luz"(EC, p. 18). In Señas de identidad Antonio's friend's wife looks at him "como a un insecto de especie . . . inclasificable" (SI, p. 211).[31] Goytisolo also reinforces his descriptions of inanimate objects through insect imagery: "la gramola continuó girando como un insecto torpe" (JM, p. 68); "Los farolillos . . . emitían destellos de luciérnaga. . . ." (DP, p. 141).[32]

In attacking the capitalistic system, an artificial Spanish graft, Goytisolo also castigates, in zoological terms, the influx of tourists and the United States presence. The narrator of Juan sin Tierra wonders whether the grasshopper or the locust benefits most from the surplus value of the ant, though he admits that some blame the bumblebee, dragonfly, glowworm, or even the ant itself, because of its love for work which causes the surplus value. Statistically, without applying an elitist criterion to the various fauna, he gives equal opportunities to all species, including bedbugs, lice, and other parasites (JT, pp. 246-47).

The political-insect relationship occurs in most of his novels. Arturo gives the same attention to Murcian shacks and their inhabitants that Paco affords his ants, and for the same reason, because they attack the beauty of the status quo: "Para sacudirse las pulgas necesitan entrar en mi cuarto." Francisco compares them to flies, and Arturo, associating them with ants, believes that the police should whisk them all into a bag "como cucarachas" (F. pp. 22, 114, 174, 181). The young apprentice weavers, condemned to work for a master spider who lays eggs in her victims to feed the next spider generation, are trapped insects, who, paralyzed by the poison, wait helplessly as the spider "pone sus huevos. . ." (CJ, pp. 63-64).[33] When Mozart's Requiem stops, the silence is broken only by the "canto de los grillos y el sonoro croar de alguna rana," a most persistent image, but the Requiem, in a sense, is also a funeral for Spain; the croaking frogs and chirping crickets reflect the empty words of Alvaro's relatives in attempting to justify their actions, much as moths become associated in Alvaro's mind with

142

Eulogio's passion for the stars, "entre la polilla y telaraña" (SI, pp. 32, 34).

Goytisolo's most aggressive attacks involving insects occur in Reivindicación del Conde don Julián, and they are both executioners and victims. Julián slaghters insects in preparation for his attack on Spanish culture, and insects, themselves victims of carnivorous plants, help in the destruction of Peranzules. Julián smashes the sponger-centipede (p. 235). Goytisolo attacks the stultifying effects of the Generation of '98, the Senecan inheritance, and the Spanish readiness to herd together in masses. Seneca, incarnated as a bullfighter, has his supporters, "enjambres, como abejitas" (CJ, p. 120), and, ironically, insects will later destroy his other incarnation. Goytisolo associates insects, done in by insecticides, with Spanish literature, as Julián collects flies, ants, beetles, horseflies, bees, and cockroaches which he duly deposits in selected volumes of Spanish classics. Alvaro Peranzules, observing the pointless existence of hominids and invertebrate masses and, able to identify a true "capra hispánica" by the smell of its dung (CJ, pp. 81-82), matches his firm principles with his crustacean appearance. A cross between a mammal and a medieval warrior, he recites a crustacean sonnet, evoking the tradition of Castile against a background of attacking dogs (CJ, pp. 160-162), and as he continues with the classics, he discovers crushed flies spattered over the drama. He tries desperately to choose other volumes for his declamations and evocation of Spanish tradition as insects buzz around him, but they escape in swarms from the book, multiply, and result in the death of Alvaro and the "capra hispánica" (CJ, pp. 179-84).

Although Alvaro, in Señas de identidad, constantly associates the works of men with insects, we see the connection more clearly in Reivindicación del Conde don Julián. The narrator, in the dispensary, mentally returning to his Natural Sciences class some twenty-five years earlier, relates the morphology of the scorpion and the arachnids, and, viewing a defenseless grasshopper trapped in a jar, recalls his horror when his teacher grasped him by the collar and obliged him to watch (pp. 91-93). Creative writing and day dreams substitute for what was once the play of childhood, a constant Freudian implication in the novel. Unlike conscious memories during maturity, "childhood memories are not fixed at the moment of being experienced and afterwards repeated, but are only elicited at a later age when childhood is already past; in the process they are altered and falsified, and are put into the service of later trends, so that generally speaking they cannot be sharply distinguished from phantasies."[34] Antonio identifies sexual relations as a way of dying, and in his relationship with the whore, a bad woman and a dangerous object to love, associates the act with a spider, symbolic both of danger and mother (SI, p. 214). He also links the death of his father to "el hondo zumbido de las cigarras" (SI, p. 115), an image repeated exactly later (p. 160).

Throughout Duelo en el Paraíso the author emphasizes human moods through animal imagery. El Arcángel destroys the reflection of the gray tadpole because of his self guilt; the advancing soldiers encounter butterflies, bees, and a fleeing cat, and Sergeant Santos imagines snakes, lizards with fly eyes, fearful rabbits, "todo un mundo de animalejos . . . hormigas, grillos, cigarras, cucarachas, insectos hostiles. . ." (p. 122). The soldier guarding Abel's body feels horror at the fly buzzing about the bullet hole (DP, p. 183). El Gallego senses that "las mariposas, los hombres que marchaban acoplados, no eran otra cosa que un turbio impulso hacia la muerte" (DP, p. 189).

In his moral commitment which he phrases in frustrated and at times nightmarish terms, Goytisolo uses animals to reflect negatively the entire range of moral, idealistic, psychological, and physical characteristics of the Spanish people, their religion, machismo, stoicism, literature, hymenolatry, honor, and language. He refuses to acknowledge his country except in subservient or destructive terms, as he attacks the values which he feels have circumscribed it and prevented its maturation as an important member of the world scene.

Notes

[1] Among dozens of such references, found in all of his novels, are a young man's "ojos de gacela," Señas de identidad (Mexico: Joaquín Mortiz, 1966), p. 270, hereafter cited as SI; Tariq's "mirada implacable de un tigre," Reivindicación del Conde Don Julián (Mexico: Joaquín Mortiz, 1970), p. 136, hereafter cited as CJ. Further samples in his earlier works include: "El recuerdo se había posado en su cerebro como un murciélago," Juegos de manos (Barcelona: Ediciones Destino, 1960), p. 261, hereafter cited as JM; "parecía un pájaro oscuro, un grajo extraño," Duelo en el Paraíso (Barcelona: Ediciones Destino, 1960), p. 22, hereafter cited as DP; and "ronroneaba igual que un gato," Fiestas (Buenos Aires, Emece, 1958), p. 45, hereafter cited as F.

[2] La resaca (Paris: Club del Libro Español, 1958), p. 94. Further references in the text are to this edition, hereafter cited as LR.

[3] Among many other such images we find "con la dulzura de un animal manso" (JM, p. 107); "como un animal cogido en una trampa" (SI, p. 163).

[4] See Juan sin Tierra (Barcelona: Editorial Seix Barral, 1975), p. 173. Further citations in the text are to this edition, hereafter referred to as JT.

[5] In Señas de identidad, for example, Alvaro links the death of the Yeste peasants with the running of the bulls, vultures, and dogs, and a crowing rooster (pp. 122, 149-51, 143). Lucas's death is specifically related to the noise of frogs (p. 157); and prisoners, awaiting execution, identify with a flock of birds in the sky (p. 477).

[6] He employs the same image in other novels, for example, "aletargada fauna" (CJ, p. 17) and "peninsular fauna" (JT, p. 179).

[7] In Señas de identidad tourists profane the land; one reads the Cid's poem on the back of a camel (p. 205); elsewhere they swarm "como moscas." See El circo (Barcelona: Destino, 1957), p. 29. Further references in the text are to this edition, hereafter cited as EC.

[8] See Ernest Jones, "The Madonna's Conception Through the Ear," Essays in Applied Psychoanalysis (London: Hogarth Press, 1951). pp 312ff. See also F.L. Wells, "A Summary of Material on the Topical Community of Primitive and Pathological Symbols,"

Psychoanalytic Review, 4 (1917), 46-63, who explains that the dove, supposedly proceeding from Joseph's genitals, lighted on his head to designate him as the future husband of Mary, and also symbolizes the Dove or Holy Ghost, bringer of children.

[9] See Kessel Schwartz, "Stylistic and Psychosexual Constants in the Novels of Juan Goytisolo," Norte, Nos. 4-6 (1972), 123.

[10] In Juan sin Tierra the Pareja Reproductora comes to Church in a coach drawn by two stallions as the impotent husband wanders amid the "fauna cerril de Manhattan" and the fat whale of a lady, awaiting sexual contact, utters 'rugidos de fiera" (pp. 73, 24-25).

[11] See Géza Roheim, "Teiresias and Other Seers," Psychoanalytic Review, 33 (1946), 320.

[12] Other death associations involving animals may be found in JM, pp. 46, 47; F, pp. 156, 171; and DP, pp. 112, 114, 117, 183, 261, 266, 268, 292, 293.

[13] See Treasury of Snake Lore, ed. by Brandt Aymar (New York: Greenberg, 1956), p. 44.

[14] The Medusa also involves the fear of castration, mitigated by the fantasy of supplying the female with a male organ, for if she has one the male need not fear the loss of his own. See Jacques Schnier, "Morphology of a Symbol: The Octopus, " American Imago, 13 (1956), 3-31.

[15] See Erich Neumann, The Origins and History of Consciousness (New York: Pantheon Books, 1954), pp. 150, 160, 206.

[16] See Linda Gould Levine, Juan Goytisolo: La destrucción creadora (Mexico: Joaquín Mortiz, 1976), p. 292, f.n. 29.

[17] Géza Roheim, "Fairy Tale and Dream," The Psychoanalytic Study of the Child, 8 (1953), 394-403.

[18] See Elizabeth Crawford, "The Wolf as Condensation," American Imago, 12 (1955), 306.

[19] See Robert Gorham Davis, "Art and Anxiety," Partisan Review, 12 (1945), 310-21.

[20] Among a number of such avian designations we find Luz Divina "como un pájaro apuñado" (EC, p. 45); Uribe as a "paloma blanca," Planas as "un ave bondadosa" (JM, pp. 134; 261); Angela

and Lucía as "un par de loros," Estanislaa as a "paloma" (DP, pp. 211, 291); and similar imagery in DP, pp. 108, 165, 292; F, pp. 57, 93; and SI, pp. 433, 455.

[21] See La resaca (Paris: Club del Libro Español, 1958), p. 94. Further references in the text are to this edition, hereafter cited as LR.

[22] La isla (Barcelona: Editorial Seix Barral, 1961), pp. 46, 126. Further references in the text are to this edition, hereafter cited as I.

[23] José Ortega, Juan Goytisolo, alienación y agresión en "Señas de identidad" y "Reivindicación del Conde don Julián" (New York: Eliseo Torres, 1972), pp. 85-87. Similar cruelties occur in other novels, for example in LR, p. 116 and JT, p. 115.

[24] Nelson A. Crawford, "Cats Holy and Profane," Psychoanalytic Review, 21 (1934), 168-79.

[25] Ortega, Juan Goytisolo, alienación. . .,p. 107, refers to "animal que encarna el maleficio y la pasión sexual."

[26] For example, "gorilas hembras," (pp. 14, 56, 154; "gorila," pp. 23, 125, 161; "linda gorila," pp. 39, 108; and "gorila muy fea," p. 57.

[27] Arthur Brenner, "The Ape: Simia que similis," American Imago, 11 (1954), 306-27.

[28] Linda Gould Levine, Juan Goytisolo: La destrucción creadora, pp. 62-63.

[29] J.C. Flugel, "Polyphallic Symbolism and the Castration Complex," International Journal of Psychoanalysis, 5 (1924), 155-96.

[30] Linda Gould Levine, p. 290, f.n. 4.

[31] Similar imagery involving butterflies, bees, ants, and crickets may be found in JM, p. 40; DP, p. 159; EC, pp. 124, 197; F, p. 108; LR, pp. 72, 254, 262; ; I, p. 40; and SI, pp. 66, 211.

[32] In El circo, he compares party lights and fireflies (p. 186); in Señas de identidad, helicopters with butterflies (p. 445); and in Juan sin Tierra, a flashlight and a firefly (p. 17).

³³Among the many other animal associations of hungry, naked shanty children, garbage, and people living an animal life, see F, p. 178; LR, p. 43; SI, pp. 65, 90, 382; CJ, pp. 107-08; DP, pp. 273-74; and JT, pp. 15, 18.

³⁴Sigmund Freud, The Standard Edition of the Complete Psychological Works of Freud, tr. and ed. James Strachey and Anna Freud et al. (London: Hogarth Press, 1906-08), IX, 83, 152.

JUAN GOYTISOLO, CULTURAL CONSTRAINTS AND THE HISTORICAL VINDICATION OF COUNT JULIAN

Juan Goytisolo's novel, Reivindicación del Conde don Julián (Mexico: Joaquín Mortiz, 1970. 242 pp.) solidifies his already significant position as one of Spain's leading contemporary novelists, even though the country he represents has chosen, for political reasons, to ignore or downgrade his contributions as much as possible. In his latest novel Goytisolo takes his full measure of revenge while continuing his merciless exposure of the foibles and falsifications of Spanish culture.

The novel, hovering between dream and reality and involving mythology and metaphysical doubts as it recreates the absurd in Spanish tradition, serves as a solipsistic attempt to prove that only Goytisolo's modifications and states are true existence. In its grotesque vision of the world, this work combines essay and literary criticism, viewing reality through strange symbols and structures and utilizing free association, dream, reverie, and double personality. The author (Goytisolo-Julián), the protagonist-narrator, renounces his country of disparate masks, but he cannot escape its cultural ties completely. The narrator becomes the alter-ego of Count Julián, the Visigothic governor of Ceuta, who according to legend betrayed king and country and handed Spain over to the Arabs. A concomitant character component in the novel, Tarik ibn Zaid, the Berber invader of Spain who supposedly helped depose Rodrigo, the last Visigothic ruler, and for whom Gibraltar, because of his landing there, is presumably named, complements Count Julián as historical figure, dream figment and contemporary. According to legend Rodrigo, overwhelmed by the charms of Julián's daughter, La Cava or Florinda, made improper advances and then forced himself on her. For the Spanish losers, La Cava (from the Arabic kahbah) was a wanton or harlot, but Goytisolo neatly reverses the equation.

Making use of legend, myth, history, poetry, and the subconscious, Goytisolo gives us a kind of personal history of Spanish culture and a very clever critical review of its representatives and shibboleths. He shifts in his mind from one time level of subconscious recall to yet another, employing an apparent stream of consciousness as he moves from past to present reality and comes ever closer to consciousness and historical narrative. As in his previous novels, we encounter strange types, excellently portrayed by his keen photographic eye, and a continuing burlesque of official Spain.

In a sense the novel has no plot but is based around a series of primary encounters with reality, at times impossible to separate from fantasy and reverie. Indeed, the entire novel may be viewed as a dream while falling asleep or awakening.

Goytisolo uses symbols in his communication which deliberately or unconsciously also give us insights into himself and into human beings in general in their painful struggle to achieve ego identity and to escape the agonies of life. A kind of fictional memoir, La Reivindicación del Conde don Julián uses a melange of daily increments to build an artistic conceptualization of an inner and outer world, but it is a daily reality seen, at times, half asleep or half awake, as Goytisolo intertwines the hallucinatory with the physical surroundings of the moment. Even a literal interpretation of events does not affect the impact of the novel on the imagination.

The novel opens to Julián's dreams of vengeance and the Arabic invasion to come. A knife sharpener's call summons up classical portraits of pastoral flute and Pan which in turn dissolve into a flow of associations involving a children's game in a vacant lot, a dead cat, whose postulated suffering and sexual activities remind him of his own desires, and the flight of Spanish refugees. Lighting a cigarette and thinking of food bring on other associations involving everything from DDT to Pompey and the Temple of Isis. As Julián contemplates the remains of food, cockroaches and other victims of his insecticide, he sweeps the insects into a bag to take with him.

He wanders into a dispensary with its variety of medicines and suffers a claustrophobic reaction to the dingy room. Returning to a former class of Natural Sciences without explanation or time interval, Julián recalls an unfortunate arthropod of articulated body and limbs whose torture he was forced to view in class a quarter of a century before. Leaving the dispensary as one born again, he pays his daily visit to the library whose exterior reality of door, steps, and people leads him again into a series of introspections and cultural queries, as he comments on aspects of Spanish literature from Berceo to García Lorca. Removing some insects from his sack, he places them, in turn, in appropriate classical literary volumes and smashes them between the pages. He leaves the library and becomes immersed in the crowds each component of which, lottery seller, street vendors, or a boy playing a transistor radio, triggers a series of endlessly elaborating elements and associations.

In a café he suffers a kind of hallucinatiory syzygy in which he faces his self of twenty-five years before as a boy. To escape the unwanted attention of a reporter he leaves but not before visiting the men's room where he indulges in a loving description of the process of urinating (an act which apparently has fascinated Goytisolo from Juegos de manos on), but this time, unfortunately, on an unseen victim occupying the place destined to receive his "rubio desdén fluido." Fleeing again,

Julián recalls himself at nine in Spain, accepts the services of his boy guide for a tour through the Kasbah which he himself knows so intimately, and among other incidents, has an involved encounter with a sponger, meets a group of tourists, a Spanish journalist, a lawyer, and various reincarnations of Seneca. Finally he returns to the same room furnished with two chairs, a night table and a chandelier with two burnt out bulbs, and to bed to dream again for "mañana será otro día, la invasión recomenzará" (p. 240).

Aside from the incidents or what appears to "happen" in the novel, in what amounts to a deliberate projection of unconscious conflicts transmitted from childhood and school in a new form, Goytisolo indulges in a kind of autistic mental process free from logical constraint, at times triggered by outer stimuli and at others apparently spontaneously generated. In one scene he sees a snake charmer who is performing for a group of tourists. Two tourists pose with him for pictures. One, a "Hija de la Revolución Americana," a gross projection of everything Goytisolo hates about the United States, poses with the snake on her shoulders. It bites her on the cheek, she dies, and the youngsters of the Zoco Grande rob her, lift her skirt, and urinate on her private parts. The funeral cart arrives to put an end to what Goytisolo self-indulgently mocks as a "macabre happening." The "Daughter of the American Revolution" alias Mrs. Putifar (as we later find out, a true counterpart of her Old Testament namesake) is an imposing woman liberated by psychoanalysis from her inhibitions. Julián's guide disappears, and he contemplates the enemy shore line of distant Gibraltar. The "Daughter of the American Revolution," fully recovered from her death and profanation, joins the other tourists, a departing plague of "Martians."

The narrator slips into and out of sleep and through different states of consciousness as he re-experiences in dream-like symbolic representations, distorted, recaptured, and resynthesized content. He has memories of a naked woman and first sexual encounter, and an ensuing remorse intensified by his Spanish Catholic background; he himself becomes a sexual organ as he takes a vaginal journey and is swallowed by the womb. Real and imagined scenes, recurring themes, the encounter with the sponger, the dispensary, the toilet, a class of Natural Sciences, combine half-conscious associations, confusing images and fused destructive and libidinal instincts. He loses consciousness, is one with his mother, dies, is transcended and mythified. A neurotic and limited group of fantasies, which he somehow associates with a need for rejecting Spain, recur constantly. Aside from his condemnation of his culture, Goytisolo presents disguised relationships between symbol and meaning at subconscious levels and involving psychological connotations rooted in the painful dynamic of human life.

Many of these processes, admittedly surrealistic and stylistic in nature, also bear a close relationship to Freudian thinking. In the manifest content of a dream, for example, the penis may be represented by the dreamer's own body, a fantasy often involving a return to the mother. A genitally colored regressive variant of the Chronos myth, this return, a passive feminine fantasy, and a distortion of the idea of being devoured and the fear thereof, offers a version of a castration fantasy.[1] Other incidents in the novel may well represent screen memories. Some seem capable of being equated with the infant's satiation at the breast and a subsequent falling asleep, memory traces of which lend content to the second wish of the oral triad (the wish to devour, to be devoured, and to sleep) and which also appears in various forms of claustrophobia.[2]

Goytisolo's novel, a constant dialogue between himself and his circumstances, combines the commonplace with neurotic states and fantasies which promote a Freudian interpretation. We see a cock, its neck almost cut in two, chased by a band of boys and a dog who licks up the spilled blood (in his paranoid state this image triggers thoughts of treason and the destruction of Sacred Spain). The dog licking the blood, boys urinating on a woman's private parts, and a boy, (himself) forced to view the death agonies of an insect are elements among infinite variations on the theme of vengeance and hatred of the past. The spurious child (Julián-Alvaro-Goytisolo), as he was twenty-five years earlier, represents that past and must suffer repeated and ritual deaths of various kinds, facing the consequences of his confrontation with his other self, the adult Julián and his serpent companion (an inversion of the Rodrigo romance). Throughout, the narrator returns to school days, classes in Natural Sciences, memories of a servant and hot chocolate, and a personal version of the story of Little Red Riding Hood. Adult and boy confront each other, talk, merge, and separate, and on one level of interpretation it may be argued that Goytisolo appears to reject reality for a regression to the past where his sexual fantasies operated more freely. At the same time subconscious recall is projected onto the state of actuality (illicit affairs, a hydrocephalic child), and as the narrator obeys a sign in Tangiers to give blood and save a life we see the psychological relationship between immediate present, shortly elapsed present, and the past.

Julián gladly gives blood to consummate his vengeance (it contains infectious material, rabies, for his fellow Spaniards). Bitten by the dog who licked up the blood of the cock (at this time the floor is covered with decapitated roosters), he, safe from reprisal, waits for the symptoms to take effect. These seemingly classic concentrations of guilt feelings and anxious states give way to the Church confessional and communion. Given wafers mixed with hashish, the parishioners indulge in a frenzied sexual orgy, as damsels fall penetrated by the Arabs' serpents and Julián personally despoils the statue of the Virgin and Child. The Church itself tumbles down among its human groups, covered with blood, sweat, and semen, as they pant and fornicate.

The repetitive motifs of vaginal voyage, materializations of Seneca as various people, the bug smashing, and the snake charmer involve a special style and technique. Associations within associations, ever shifting, ever returning in kaleidoscopic frenzy, with lengthy devotion (within the memory) to detailed descriptions are done as tachistoscopic images flashing on a screen. But some are given in slow motion. The novel is surrealistic in its relating of the unrelated and in the interplay of reality and sub-reality, a juxtaposition of dissimilarities which leads to disorientation. Adapting free association, the narrator's mind moves without deliberate preconceptions from thought to thought, feeling to feeling, spontaneously sifting analogues and apparently unrelated impressions to form new combinations of the same symbols, a process aided by a masterful use of second person address throughout. Time is a series of over-lapping fragments, part of a multi-dimensional framework, and so the narrator enters any moment without consideration of chronology to create a series of simultaneous superimposed memories and multitudinous planes of meaning involving literary criticism, poetry, and music.

An opening scene establishes one aspect of Goytisolo's style, giving us an admirable glimpse of a dreaming-waking state of associative chains, from geography to friends, past and present, as the new day dawns:

> la angustia te invade: sudor frío, aleteos del corazón, palpitaciones: atrapado, preso, capsulado, digerido, expulsado: el consabido ciclo vital por los pasillos y túneles del aparato digestivo-reproductor, destino último de la célula, de todo organismo vivo: abres un ojo: techo encamado por la húmedad, paredes vacuas, el día que aguarda tras la cortina, caja de Pandora: maniatado bajo la guillotina: un minuto más, señor verdugo: un petit instant: inventar, componer, mentir, fabular: repetir la proeza de Sherezada . . . érase una vez un precioso niño . . .: Caperucito Rojo y el lobo feroz, nueva versión sicoanalítica con mutilaciones, fetichismo, sangre: despierto ya del

> todo: ojos abiertos, vista atenta a los juegos y trampantojos de la luz en el cielorraso: un leve esfuerzo: tres metros, incorporarse, calzar las babuchas, tirar de la correa de la persiana: y: silencio, caballeros, se alza el telón: la representación empieza: el decorado es sobrio, esquemático: rocas, esqustos, granito, piedra . . . años atrás, en los limbos de tu vasto destierro, habías considerado el alejamiento como el peor de los castigos. . .(p. 13).

And, after a string of associations and memories, we are again with "tres metros, incorporarse, calzar las babuchas, tirar la correa de la persiana."

Stylistically reminiscent at times of the "nouveau roman" with which Goytisolo was so intimately acquainted, the novel arranges itself as a theatrical set filled with symbolically significant city streets, buildings, cafes, and rooms. And so the drama opens, as the venetian blind opens to let in the light, to a recall of Julián's long exile, an estrangement which he first considered the worst of punishments but to which he later became indifferent as he sought for other certainties in Africa, separated from his culture by the sea. Without transition we take an inventory of his room, the chairs, the clothes, a dirty handkerchief, a lamp, a chandelier with two burnt-out bulbs, a minute examination of his billfold and its contents, to be particles of his fantasies, and again to thoughts of his country with a romantic farewell to its outworn culture: "lermontovianamente recitas el negro ensalmo: adiós Madrastra inmunda, país de siervos y señores: adiós tricornios de charol, y tú, pueblo que los soportas. . ." (p. 15). On one level Goytisolo creates the impression of obsessive repetition. On another he maneuvers subtle differences in the imagery involved to portray the illusive properties of memory itself.

One of Goytisolo's common techniques is to break up a dialogue by other action and associative chains. A vaguely familiar Spanish journalist seeks to obtain the narrator's attention, but the latter deliberately reads his newspaper. As he reads the announcements and advertisements, the journalist insists on conversing with him:

> Grandes Facilidades de Pago: inútil, inútil: el homo hispanicus no se da por vencido y carrespea y mira y mira y carrespea y orienta hacia ti la silla . . . preparando mentalmente su discurso . . . hablando ya perdone chimenea de hogar bajo en salón, cocina totalmente instalada con muebles de fórmica y muebles de unión con salón-comedor, carpintería de

madera . . . bidé con surtidor central perdone Barato:
Un Verdadero Sueño creo que nos conocemos Rolex
Oyster Day-Date: 116'5 gramos con pulsera de 18
quilates: automático, antimagnético y blindado lo vi
una vez en Paris andaba usted acompañado su señora
supongo no una mujer morena en el barrio latino o en
Saint-Germain se confunde usted buceando en su
memoria, cerca, muy cerca de la diana: con sonrisa de
galán de cine español de los años cuarenta: estólido
y tenaz preparaba usted un documental le repito que se
confunde no es usted reportero?. . . (pp. 57-58).

At times the narrative is lineal but elliptical as each image starts a series of subimages:

Buscando con la mirada el cartel descolorido del
Croissant Rouge: al oreo de la lluvia y el viento,
pero visible aún: Donnez votre sang, sauvez une vie:
y precipitándote al despensario más próximo: en la
tiniebla propicia del anochecer: con las gafas
ahumadas y un bigote postizo: savia rica, espesa,
bienhechora: embotellada, distribuida, inyectada:
movimientos ondulatorios por las pléyades
ganglionares, apoteosis florida: torciendo al fin por
la primera bocacalle y colándote por la puerta
entreabierta: habitación rectangular con los estantes
llenos de productos etiquetados, parada obligada en tu
paseo sin rumbo por la ciudad: consuelos y alivios
. . .(p. 29).

In an advertencia Goytisolo acknowledges the contributions of a host of Spanish literary figures from Alfonso el Sabio to Ortega y Gasset and especially the assistance of the Spanish American novelists, Carlos Fuentes, Julio Cortázar, and Guillermo Cabrera Infante. Quoting from sources as disparate as Vergil and Ian Fleming, employing mythological and classical references, and utilizing everybody from Kipling to General Pershing, Goytisolo mocks his fellow Spanish writers, parodying Góngora and Rubén Darío and annihilating Juan Ramón Jiménez whose Platero he considers the epitome of modern vulgarity. In satirizing literary patterns Goytisolo, usually ironic rather than cynical, penetrates Spanish chauvinism and attempts to deflate the outdated devotion to a meaningless tradition represented by excessively praised national authors. As he offers a literary and historical interpretation of his culture he inculcates his own lyric vein so noticeable in all his works. Goytisolo most closely resembles, of all those mentioned in the advertencia, Guillermo Cabrera Infante in his parodies of serious literature, malicious portraits, variety of puns, and examination of various sexual taboos and fantasies. His guided tour of Tangiers matches Cabrera's through night-time Havana in Tres tristes tigres. Goytisolo also shares the Cuban's devotion to lavatory graffiti and involvement with various foreign languages.

One may view Reivindicación del Conde Don Julián as a kind of musical composition (many actual musical compositions, musical instruments, rhythms are recurring notes in the novel) complete with variations, counterthemes, coda and recapitulation. But one can never quite come to grips with the abstract in this work (technique and content seem indistinguishable at times), and one is unable to separate illusion from perception or to penetrate the superimposed heterogeneous and homogeneous layers which comprise simultaneously existing states of consciousness in which, for example, man equals insect and both change and yet remain.

From a purely technical viewpoint, however, Goytisolo's most remarkable contribution seems to be the language itself, a leitmotif of the composition endlessly foreshadowed and fitfully fulfilled as the novel proceeds. Each word and even part of a word impels one to additional semantic and phonetic investigation. Goytisolo inserts English, French, Latin, Italian and Arabic, uses clichés and bad puns and at the same time mocks them, "O tempora! O Moros!" At times the process resembles the preverbal one of infants but involves, in reality, sophisticated artistic connections. As Emir Rodríguez Monegal stated, in a discussion about the Spanish American novel of recent times, the central issue in the use of words is not to say something in particular but to transform the narrative linguistic reality itself. This transformation is what "la novela 'dice' y no lo que se suele discutir in extenso: trama, personaje, anécdota, mensaje, denuncia."[3] The novel is an open anticultural work whose center of gravity "no es ya el determinismo de los temas sino las raciones del yo y sus rostros, la conjugación de las formas y el juego en un espacio cuyo sentido está dado por la necesidad de crear nuevas relaciones entre la modificación del individuo y la modificación de la realidad."[4]

In using a new kind of language, almost the message itself rather than its vehicle and an entity apart from the fantasy, reality, criticism or content involved, Goytisolo creates special situations, such as a delicate description of Seneca defecating or an elaborate view of feminine reproductive organs. Since the subconscious, which knows no social or cultural conventions, is talking, Goytisolo employs a lexical congeries which, even in 1970, some would find offensive and coarse. At times Goytisolo uses semantic-phonetic combinations deliberately solecistic but which like the rest of the book plays with phonetic nuances, ambivalence, and accumulation.

Julián may reject his Spanish language, "feliz de olvidar por unos instantes el último lazo que a tu pesar, te une irreductiblemente a la tribu: idioma mirífico del Poeta, vehículo necesario de la traición, hermosa lengua tuya" (p. 70), but only momentarily, for in spite of his triumphs over Catholicism, literature, and other aspects of Spanish culture, he cannot destroy the language. He seeks to paralyze its circulation, suck out its sap, take out words one by one until the tower of language, bloodless, falls like a castle made of cards. As part of his attack he burlesques that most august of institutions, the Royal Academy, and its entrance speeches: "y en cada parte de la oración y en cada oración del período, qué elipsis, transiciones, giros! qué movimiento, pasion, entusiasmo . . . tropos, sinecdoques, metonimias, metáforas se suceden vertiginosamente como un suntuoso castillo de fuegos de artificio: hipérboles, silepsis, antítesis, repeticiones que subraya con su bella voz de bajo mientras sus manos fusiles recorren los estantes de las librerías y apartan el ejemplar de rústica de algún exquisito drama de honor . . ." (p. 177). As Alvaro declaims, insects arise to accomplish his destruction, and he calls in vain for help from books of chivalry, from the Cid, and from Seneca. The insects copulate, reproduce, devour the paper, corrupt the style, and destroy the ideas. Alvaro's mask dissolves and he is reduced to cu-cu-cu, cuna, culebra, culpa, cupletista, cubil, curandero, as he dies, a victim of a moribund and absurd historical weight. But sadly the narrator realizes that Gredos, the countryside, and even traditions may disappear, but never the language.

Existentially, the narrator seems to accept Heidegger's conclusion that the ordinary mode of being with others is impersonal, debased, and unauthentic. Heidegger stresses the "debasement of others to mere tools by the rare men of character who had risen to the level of a richer genuine existence."[5] Julián expresses a sense of dread and potentiality denied and unmaterialized, nor can he escape a sense of guilt, of feeling superfluous, of not belonging, which accounts in part for the constant interplay of the will to dominate and to be dominated, indeterminate protagonists and projections of his own split personality as he struggles to create his own values. Chained to Spain and humiliated by her, he feels that he must destroy her in order to be free; at the same time he can appropriate and possess her, a Sartrian mold of masochistic and sadistic interplay. He also seems to believe with Sartre that reality lies in action in the present, for the past is gone and the future is a nonexistent now not yet here. The narrator, disoriented, seeks within the labyrinth of self for the meaning of existence. Victim and executioner at the same time, he endures a conflict of being as more and more he confronts the abyss between what he hoped to accomplish and what he can, between a reality envisioned and and an actuality.

One must not assume, nevertheless, that imagery, subconscious flow, temporal flights, hallucinations, and a kind of existential Odyssey undertaken by the narrator in which only his own modifications and states exist as he pits his potential against the world, keep the novelist from his specific social and political concerns. Following Lukacs's advice, Goytisolo avoids a subjective introspection without support in reality which would breed a disintegration of human personality.[6] He protests Spanish social and political conditions and, in an ever-shifting and changing world where reality and fantasy are no longer enemies, he seeks to express his reality and not just a reality.[7]

Goytisolo is both witness and participant in the cultural, social, and political history he describes, that of a regime dedicated to tradition and opposed to progress which nonetheless, paradoxically, welcomes industrial capitalism. The Franco government has destroyed Spain's special charm without generating the liberties enjoyed by more advanced countries, for the Civil Guard continues its brutalizing work and the pueblo spinelessly accepts the status quo. Goytisolo rails against archaic systems and falsifications about so-called progress which has brought motels, service stations, foreigners in bikinis, and combined new concepts of marketing the latest household appliance or detergent with bulls, guitars, and flamenco. Goytisolo shows what happens in a society of conspicuous consumption, summing up the impact of widely diverse segments of the population in the lament of the perpetual sponger, willing to relate to his public the illness and difficulties of "decent" citizens who do their share of praying at the mosque. Through Julián we see young apprentices condemned to work as victims of a master spider who lays eggs in the victims who will serve as food for the next generation of spiders. We learn of the role of the exile, trapped by an uncertain present, fairly pleasant for some, austere and difficult for most, a geological layer composed of solid and liquid men, and especially men whom Larra so aptly classified as "hombre globo." In a Spain of streets choked with automobiles, skyscrapers, and American hotels, Julián replaces a religious penitent who carries a cross weighing a hundred kilos, made from a telephone pole. Catholicism has no validity in contemporary Spanish culture. But Spain is but a part of the problem, and Goytisolo manages to attack the United States, the Ku-Klux-Klan, the tortures and persecution of natives in Mississippi and Alabama, the almighty dollar, napalm, the consumer approach to life, and especially the American tourist. Descriptions of Arab and Spanish scenes fuse, and one knows only that Goytisolo, in what to him at least is a profound moral truth, tries to exorcise and expose contemporary evil which his conscience must repel.

Spain, then, however betrayed, is the mother of all vices, and only by betraying her, something which defines and identifies him, can he shed his individual mask. Julián flees the bourgeois and imperialistic pretensions of his own culture, hoping in an Arab one of drugs to find the vehicle for his vengeance against his "tierra ingrata," a monotonous, wounded land of false masks. Goytisolo utilizes a concoction of Greek mythology and Spanish geographical features, comparing Spain to a vaginal entrance to be violated, easy prey for the Arab invasion now that the "rancios valores" of the Cid and his ilk have succumbed to modern industry, to "el deslumbrante progreso industrial, la mirífica sociedad de consumo . . ." (p. 136).

In his fantasy Julián would eliminate the "tierra enjuta y desnuda" of Castile and substitute for its typical flora and fauna entities which would eliminate all those elements so soulfully described by the Generation of Ninety-Eight, installed now as members of the established pantheon. Goytisolo reserves his most telling blows for the cultural patterns fixed by that generation of writers. He criticizes Spanish histrionics and lack of humor and mocks the Spanish preoccupation with death, a false image for those who consider themselves and their pundonor as superior to the rest of humanity. Some Spaniards claim that Spanish culture is a combination of Senecan stoicism and bullfighting (in writing like bullfighting only strict adherence to tradition can circumvent censorship). Alvaro Peranzules, the Spanish lawyer, represents the formal and false aspects of Spanish imperialistic thought, the Mystics, and heroic Castile. He is a modern reincarnation of Seneca, born not in Cordoba but in Gredos. Unfortunately, the role of Seneca and stoicism in Spanish life, the meaning of eternal Spain and Castile, have been fixed by the Generation of Ninety Eight, creators of false myths. So, in addition to taking vengeance on Spanish masterpieces, "obra de algún intocable," and interweaving effortlessly Francisco de Quevedo and Santa Teresa, Goytisolo reserves his special barbs for Unamuno and his fellow writers, their rhetorical figures and abuse of expressions such as "me duele España," and their creation of a mental attitude fixed by tradition and routine, a concept of an archaic Spain which has nothing to do with reality and which the new generations must eradicate if they are ever to become contributing members of the contemporary world.

Notes

[1] See Bertram D. Lewin, "The Body as Phallus," *The Psychoanalytic Quarterly*, 2 (1932), 24-47.

[2] Bertram D. Lewin, "Phobic Symptoms and Dream Interpretation," *The Psychoanalytic Quarterly*, 21, 3 (July 1952), 295-322.

[3] Emir Rodríguez Monegal, "Diario de Caracas," *Mundo Nuevo* 17 (1964), 22-23.

[4] The description given by Julio Ortega of the Argentine novelist, Nestor Sánchez, and his technique. See Julio Ortega, "Nestor Sánchez: La novela del lenguaje," *Imagen* 30 (August 15, 1968), 6-7.

[5] Marjorie Green, *Dreadful Freedom* (Chicago, 1948), p. 70.

[6] See George Lukacs, *Realism in Our Time* (New York, 1965), p. 35.

[7] In this connection see Mario Vargas Llosa, *Times Literary Supplement*, 3 (November 14, 1968).

JUAN GOYTISOLO, JUAN SIN TIERRA, AND THE ANAL AESTHETIC

Juan sin tierra, begun in 1972 and finished in 1974, a recall by Goytisolo of his real and fictional world, is an image best understood through a psychoanalytic anamorphoscope, for his novel, a distorted mirror or esperpento, reflects life and the world in anal terms.

In spite of his own statements about the various developmental stages in his fiction, Goytisolo repeats once more the constants of his earlier work,[1] expanding and resharpening them with greater understanding of his own personal and social interaction with the rest of humanity. In this personal process Goytisolo exhibits a continuing self-pity and rage evoked at his own guilt, suffering, and betrayal, but redirects his conscious and subconscious hostilities to an earlier stage where his social preoccupations (which he never really abandoned) were allowed freer expression. His feelings about the negative role of Catholicism in Hispanic life and his ambivalent view of the lower classes combine with a continuing sexual emphasis and need to refocus his own inescapable guilt concerning his family, the Civil War, and Spain. Goytisolo, a kind of archetypal hero in his novel, indulges subconsciously in an act of contrition and purification. In classic psychoanalytic style, he expels, literally, in the feces of his writing (he himself makes the obvious comparison between print and body waste), the introjected mother and father, the guilt they inherited and passed on to him, and his own accumulated filth brought on by the process of living; in other words, he gets it out of his system.

During his spatial, temporal, and fantastic travelogue, he visits Cuba and the world of slaves which together with his exposure to the Arabic experience reflect factors from previous works. In Paris, Tangiers, Istanbul, the Nile, the Nubian desert or the Sahara, the protagonist attempts to despoil whatever values he finds, to degrade them, to flee and to continue his existence as a kind of Wandering Jew in unacknowledged atonement for some unnamed but imagined sin which may be obsessively and repetitively written or traveled out of existence. Whether he is sodomizing, emulating pillar-dwelling Christian anchorites, fighting against the Turkish army, experiencing martyrdom, or crossing the desert, he lives in solitude and estrangement from a linguistic, cultural, and political inheritance he wants to destroy. He claims that for him Spain, "país que ha dejado de ser el tuyo,"[2] is simply a place on a map, a route elsewhere, but he continues to excoriate the falseness of its classical literary values, its bestiality, its sexual taboos, and its religious bigotry which he wishes continuously to betray and reject. He also rewrites and deforms history so that its villains become heroes, as he discredits morality, patriotism, and the family.

By implication, his destruction of the literary, religious, political, and social processes of Spain includes that of personal authority. Thus he indulges in erotic and linguistic aggressions and phallic rituals which involve the process of reproduction and creation, in more grotesque form than ever before, penetrating, not so much the vagina or uterus as in Reivindicación del Conde don Julián, but in violent incestuous transgression, the backside of mother, father, and the world. Goytisolo seems to want to shock his readers and himself by an ever more challenging and limitless effrontery. In his previous novel, by degrading parental relationship, he sought escape from the last moral prohibitions which still united him, however loosely, to his past. In Juan sin tierra, not content with the complete elimination of these prohibitions, the narrator wishes to commit an act so terrible that it will forever put him beyond any possibility of pardon or mercy. With a cold, cruel, and loveless lust, giving free rein to his erotic fancies and destructive urges largely anal in character, he hopes that the sadistic impulses he releases will continue indefinitely to cause general disorder.

Goytisolo, through his characters, indulges in a long session of self-analysis in which he drags to his conscious mind all of the associations, repressions, and neurotic states of a lifetime in one final attempt at catharsis, partly though not fully achieved in his previous works. A kind of anguished monologue which weaves in and out of the conscious and unconscious mind of the narrator(s), the novel evokes primitive figures of fantasy and myths, through which, apparently, the characters hope to be able to alleviate torturing erotic impulses. The protagonist wants to destroy his parents whose primal activity reproaches him for his own unvoiceable wishes. In order to relieve his frustration both through the slavery and degradation of his own body and the debasement of others, he employs sexual aggression as a kind of reinforcement for an uncertain masculinity. He concentrates on destruction, subversion, and sadism, with an obsessive insistence on the perverse from sodomy to bestialism, and on a host of sexual fantasies involving dwarfs, animals, and various objects, the more degrading the more desired. Although this aggression consciously concerns an attack on Spain's (and the Western Capitalistic World) frozen religio-social codes, language and culture, it also masks unresolved anxieties and unconscious conflicts projected in symbolic form.

In this latest novel, Goytisolo's creations seem to indulge in a regression from the genital to a pregenital anal-sadistic level. The narrator, not precise as to where or whence he flees, clearly feels he has been exiled and expelled from Spain, an external reality. From Tangiers, filled with the smells and tastes of that city, he watches, as Count Julián and Alvaro before him, the coastline of his country from which the Jews were expelled in 1492 and the Arabs in 1609. Goytisolo feels a double loss, the Cuba of his ancestors and the Spain of his parents.

From <u>Juegos</u> <u>de</u> <u>manos</u> through <u>Reivindicación del Conde don Julián</u> the author lovingly described the act of defecation. In <u>Juan sin tierra</u> he broadens his preoccupation and identification with bodily secretions and excretions found in his other novels (involving also vomiting as an upward displacement from excretory functions) to include his writing, another part of him. He also dwells compulsively on every variety of sodomizing experience. Julián, metamorphosed as Little Red Riding Hood's grandmother, had sodomized Alvarito in <u>Reivindicación del Conde don Julián</u>, but the anal experience is omnipresent in <u>Juan sin tierra</u>.

Every neurotic adult contains at the core of his unconscious mind a howling and enraged child who is aggressive to himself as well as to the outside world. Alvaro recalls his own early religious training concerning the corrupt aspects of the human body and his shame at the daily act of "defecar en su primoroso orinal de porcelana esmaltada. . ." (p. 220). His refusal to perform and his resistance to medical appeals and strong laxatives cause him to suffer extreme constipation, willingly endured because he wants to emulate saints by excreting only pleasant emanations from his pores, a family perfume exemplifying spiritual progress. Part of his continuing anal aggression involves his mother, represented by the symbolic sodomizing of the Virgin as well as by Changó's devouring of the Paloma and incestuous possession of his mother Yemayá. The author, in describing the portable outhouse, brought to Cuba in the nineteenth century, implies its maternal qualities. The supreme satisfaction, summed up subvocally by his great grandmother in "el egregio watercloset automático," relates the maternal to the anal as she exclaims: "he cagado como una reina" (p. 20).

The entire novel centers around the defecatory process and its relationship to the psychological, social, and religious manifestations, both private and public, which affect the author. One leitmotif in <u>Juan sin tierra</u> involves a recurring public anal evacuation by a group of slaves: "al alcance de su vista pero no de su olfato, se dispone a recibir las dádivas de una veintena de individuos de ambos sexos . . . a un metro de distancia uno de otro, conforme a las normas de una rígida disciplina castrense, ofrendando en cuclillas a la fraterna asamblea esas partes carirredondas, joviales. . ." (pp. 16-17). Goytisolo imagines the postcard scene of multiple performers as an orchestra, directed according to the related sounds produced by woodwinds, flutes, oboes, or saxophones; on the other hand, he describes the individual act and deposits of his ancestors in the watercloset in terms which give his tableau the dimensions of a religious ceremony.

Since Juan's "neurotic" (and creative) purpose depends almost exclusively on hate, when confronted by genital guilt he regresses to an anal-sadistic level which substitutes pregenital strivings. Quite often this type of regression "causes impulses to soil or debase to appear . . . the libidinal relations of the compulsion neurotic . . . are ambivalent; those he loves, he also hates. The overmoral and overaesthetic character traits or symptoms built up to help ward off the anal, erotic and sadistic urges, represent in some way the opposite of these, and are reaction-formations or overcompensations for them."[4] Goytisolo's creation equates spiritual advances and emotional satisfaction with anal acts, much as a child who defecates, controls his own environment. Aside from the pleasure, the act allows him to express himself as a free and independent being and to show his resistance and contempt for rules which are foreign to his primitive nature.[5]

Throughout Juan sin tierra, pathological aggression toward humans and animals and sadistic desires to hurt and torture mask various sexual urges and the displacement from one erogenous zone to another. These destructive impulses, represented in the unconscious by means of anal-expulsive imagery. "in its most primitive form equates the act of defecation with the act of destruction or murder"[6] The obsessive interest in excretory processes (in feces and the anus) in Juan sin tierra together with the destructive urges relate also to other sexual activities. Alvaro's fear of performing may point specifically to his identification with the penis which permits the "undoing of the castration . . . which may in itself be a source of anal-sadistic gratification. The daily act of parting with his feces . . . in a child may serve as a model for fear of parting with his penis, made acceptable by knowing that the following day there will be more feces and the loss will be undone."[7] Lewin has shown that the whole body may be a penis and another's body may also equal one's own penis.[8] Juan's descent upon various unsuspecting nations and peoples and Ebeh's aggression also seem to fit this equation: "degollando a la víctima de

164

un solo tajo: . . . recibiendo en el rostro el impacto lustral de la sangre: la dureza mineral de sus rasgos asume una puridad cristalina y a delicious warmth swells through you a la vista del recio espectáculo. . ." (p. 161).

Anal eroticism contains two opposite pleasurable tendencies which involve sadistic impulses: "The evacuation of the bowels calls forth a pleasurable excitation of the anal zone. To this primitive form of pleasurable experience there is presently added another, based on a reverse process--the retention of the feces."9 Goytisolo provides us with a savage parody of the relationship between the spiritual and defecatory impulses which he equates with the sins of the flesh. Good Christians must struggle against defecation, although they inevitably succumb, in the hope that "un día cualquiera, inopinadamente, acaecerá el milagro: dejarás de cagar! de golpe desaparecerán tus ansias, apreturas, retortijones, angustias: una quietud fisiológica y síquica, una serenidad corpórea y espiritual embeberán lentamente tu ánimo. . . "(p. 217).

Someone who is possessive of another may treat the object of his desire as he does his own private property, that is his feces. The threatened or real loss of an object signifies "to the unconscious mind . . . an expulsion of that object in the sense of a physical expulsion of feces."10 In Juan sin tierra the separation from mother to establish an independent ego (body and mind) later gives way to an anal-stage analogue, that is the separation of feces from the body. The author seems to allow parts of his subconscious to become independent. Alvaro divided himself in Reivindicación del Conde don Julián. In Juan sin tierra this personification, in part, seems to have been exercised on intestinal parasites, which will dissolve to extend their action ". . . perturbadora a la totalidad del espacio peninsular" (p. 317). All of these fantasies relate to futile attempts to free oneself from parental authority, a further mask to obscure longing for one's parents. Goytisolo's man without a country utilizes the ephemeral, sodomizing affairs, which serve as travesties of parental relationships, as obsessive mechanisms to deal with unwelcome psychological facts, and as anagogic techniques for the evocation of moods and feelings to provide visual and symbolic representations. Through his sadistic-anal ambivalent object relationships, he manifests an unconscious hostility to his father. In the novel, the primal scene evokes a terrible anger, and the child visualizes aggressive tribes who will fall upon his surrogate parents, behead them, suck their blood, and profane them. When they discover his betrayal, he will also partake of their brutalization and sodomization: "sorprendí siendo niño (a los cinco, seis años de edad?) . . . la intimidad conyugal de mis padres . . . espectáculo cuya vil sordidez . . . me hizo concebir un odio violento, insaciable . . . hacia la ordenada reproducción que sancionan las leyes y sus grotescos y ruines comparsas" (p. 155). The narrator then decides to outlaw orthodox and approved sex and to destroy all children produced by such relationships except those bastards who will be worthy to take part in his own revolution.

The author in this novel seems to engage in a hallucinatory weaving in and out of childhood, real and imagined, which he concretizes together with his freedom from society's sexual conventions: "desprenderse sucesivamente de sus tabúes políticos, patrióticos, sociales, sexuales. . . ."[11] The attainment of sexual security assumes, for him, an importance equal, in his formation, to the death of his mother. The perhaps subconscious hatred for most women, so apparent in La isla and other works, is reaffirmed in his latest novel. Goytisolo attributes to them all the sexual desires and clichés held dear by male chauvinists, epitomized in the ladies' lascivious reaction to King Kong and his masculine attributes and adornments, which the author later metamorphoses into a parallel Queen Kong. This novel smacks of one long hallucinatory or subconscious process with apparitions, happenings, fantasies, avenging serpent, Wandering Jew, and son of Hagar, but the bitter reality is everywhere apparent. His incongruous crocodiles are meant to come up through real sewers into real toilets to frighten human derrières, and he makes his Freudian ophidians terrifyingly real.

The narrator, as in previous novels, continues to attack religion in general and Catholicism in particular. Indulging in the same kind of hallucinatory syzygy previously seen, he recalls himself as a child brought up in the most religious of environments. Achieving saintly, missionary qualities, he becomes the spiritual father of a vast number of Africans through the power of his pen. As he sits at his desk, his genesic organ temporarily at rest, he knows it possesses as much phallic power to create authentic existences and souls as those produced by what he terms " la cópula fructuosa del tálamo . . ." (p. 279). He gives a novel explanation of the Holy Trinity, in human terms, and reveals his own elevation, as Alvarito, to a Christ figure who will be born "para redimir del pecado a todos los parias de la tierra" (p. 53). Identifying with the santería, fused pagan-Christian beliefs of the Cuban slaves, he paints a scene of the sugar mill chaplain kneeling and entoning the verses of the Magnificat to proclaim as a miracle the difference between the excretory process of animal and human, black slave and white aristocrat. To be sure, Jesus and the Virgin Mary and the saints of heaven do not defecate (nor did they during their earthly life) in a common ditch.

Goytisolo contrasts the eye of God which sheds light and whiteness with "el ano bestial, el ojo del diablo . . . infección, hediondez, suciedad y pecado . . . lo que se corrompe en parte es corruptible en su totalidad . . . eso está claro y bien claro: ni el Redentor ni la Virgen expelieron materias fecales" (p. 21).

Goytisolo (perhaps the narrator) invites the reader to divide this imaginary scene into word pictures, a white clarity for virtue on the one hand and blackness for sin on the other. The chaplain explains that the Church promises heavenly happiness to the slaves in return for their bodily labors for the master race. God, a kind of Chief Accountant, keeps daily track of their efforts, rewarding the good with Paradise and punishing the evil with Hell. The products of divinity, if they had existed, being privileged and immortal, would have been devoutly conserved by pious souls as precious relics and so described in Holy Writ and patristic documents. And for unbelievers, the narrator informs us though the chaplain that the digestive process of the Holy Family (who of course ate) was undoubtedly different. Few can ascend to the celestial state, but God, in his wisdom, has created an inferior black anus to contrast with that of the masters who represent a halfway stage to the blessed in Paradise. Goytisolo here calls to mind the imagery in León Felipe's description of his defecating deity: "Este orgulloso capitán de la historia--que nos defeca un Dios . . . El excremento de un Dios. . ."[12]

Continuing his diatribe against all aspects of Spanish Catholicism, he comments in parodic fashion on a Spanish <u>auto de fe</u>. If one does not like Bach it is not necessarily the fault of that great musician. By the same token, a visitor to Spain, without the requisite musical ear, cannot appreciate the positive features of the Inquisition. The thrust of Goytisolo's vision of suffering, dying, and exhortations by the noble burners, who think only of their victim's salvation, is against the Catholic Church which he has found blemished in all his novels. He parodies the Inquisition as a Spanish necessity to maintain the moral and spiritual health of the country against germ-bearing provocateurs in the same way that the contemporary government censures literary works which it feels contain pernicious sexual material (his own). The real villains are those who do not understand the charity and mercy of Spain in burning for brief periods to provide eternal salvation.

Whatever their continuing perverse personality traits, the narrator(s) concern themselves with the context of class structures, evincing an interest in the dynamics of society as they continue to show that the world's hypocrisy is a façade which in effect is totality, for only emptiness lies within. In his attack on the meretricious and on the cacodemons of the capitalistic world, and in his denunciations and protests of dehumanization brought about by socioeconomic problems, Goytisolo, beyond juxtaposing the moral dichotomies of good and evil, seems to say that only violence, however much disguised as play acting, is the veritable reality of the materialistic world. Decency is dead, and so he is dead to decency. Yet his bitterness is buttressed by his concept of human anguish which negates his parodic examination of human aberrant conduct as he satirizes the conventions of civilization and compares them with the realities of sexual and political life. He concludes that the primitive, religious, political, and sexual mode, given the total absurdity of society, is the more meaningful.

Goytisolo begins his examination of society in Cuba, and then travels to New York. Tangiers, Turkey, Paris, Istanbul, the Nile, and the desert. He engages in an aerial, geographical, and temporal excursion through Arab and Turkish history as part of his visited or noted world geography, embracing the continents of both Americas, Europe, Asia, and Africa. Unable to accept the conformity of any society or the rigid codes of government, the moment he feels even the slightest weight of authority he must reject all ties and flee. Goytisolo, realizing that his debt is not paid in full, rechannels his personal rancor and rekindles a remembered empathy for the poor and the outcast, so prevalent in his early fiction. Having rejected both God and his homeland, he becomes a pariah. The geographical shifts have changed not the essence but only the symbols of his need for expiation of real and fancied sins, as he reincarnates as a German munitions maker or the offspring of a Negro slave.

In addition to the sins of humanity, he resurrects his guilt feelings (much like those which caused the Rockefellers and the Fords to set up their foundations) about his ancestors in Cuba and their responsibility for the continuing degradation of human slaves. Their efforts in the sugar mills resulted in benefits for their masters, whose posterity Goytisolo represents. The narrator recalls the incredible tortures suffered by the blacks (including burying a wounded one, still alive) and admits: "resuscitando . . . tu odio hacia la estirpe que te dió el ser: pecado original que tenazmente te acosa con su indeleble estigma a pesar de tus viejos, denodados esfuerzos por liberarte de él" (p. 51).

While his ancestors, enriched by slave labor, spend their time on the ski slopes of Switzerland, the slaves suffer, endure, and die. But the chaplain believes they should be satisfied with hard work, inferior food, and little sleep, for God has planned it thus. By demanding food and avoiding torture, they reject salvation. Goytisolo resurrects, to demolish with parody, the ancient myths about blacks. How noble it would have been to see purity beneath the unworthy black skins, for they had the possibility of triumphing over their imperfections. Black women have a weakness for fornication and other sexual and physical activities--"la hembra que se abre y defeca, la negra que orina, las nalgas al aire" (p. 27);--but the upper class whites, in contrast, avoid all such activities, playing the violin, reciting poetry by Lamartine, or practicing embroidery and prayer for their edification. Goytisolo evokes the witchcraft practices of the slaves, prepares his camera shots and frozen close-ups, and examines the passage into womanhood of girls. Their bodily emanations and their menstrual flow show them to be all too human and thus identical with the slaves they torture. Similarly, the common ditch differs in no real detail from the overflowing holy watercloset.

Goytisolo rejects Spanish history from Pelayo on and twists it to turn his world upside down: hermit means sybarite; love means hate; heterosexual means homosexual; and man means woman. In short, he uses his words to destroy, to dissect and to recreate his own Spain, a soiled and sorry place.

The author in his diatribe against all social classes, and through his parodies, hopes to wipe out his demons, beginning with a lampoon of the Spanish monarchy whose "primoroso sistema digestivo . . . excluye ab initio cualquier emisión visceral hedionda o abyecta evacuación de sentina. . ." (p. 208). Goytisolo dwells on the digestion of Spanish rulers and their concomitant bottling of their special essence to compete with French perfume (and incidentally to attract the tourists who come for the wonderful Spanish auto de fe). Classifying social rank by the elegance of the toilet facilities: "dime como hueles y te diré quien eres" (p. 211), he rejects his own sickly, middle class which reinforces stultification--"atrofiada, extemporánea burguesía" (p. 182)--sexual neuroses, machismo. His suggested cure is subversion and anarchy. But the pueblo also is ignorant and stupid. Spain never benefited from the Enlightenment, from social revolutions, or from its flirtation with the capitalistic system, a "utopia sin culo" (p. 233).

Goytisolo, in his attack on the materialistic societies of the capitalistic world, dissects their symbols from Coca Cola to credit cards and computers, mangles their marriage manuals and sexual myths, and reveals the phony fantasy world of American film and society. Wanting to destroy the established hierarchy of values and couples who are the product of centuries of order, the narrator finds those who have blind faith in law and order more disgusting than society's dirtiest outcasts. He proposes a return to raids, robbery and pillage and orgiastic parties as a substitute for economic systems, which simply hide the specific form of governmental exploitation. Demolishing famous cathedrals like Canterbury and Notre Dame, museums like the Louvre and the Prado, national symbols like the Arc de Triomphe and the Statue of Liberty, he will also destroy the ashes of past great men from Manzoni to Kipling and exhalt the execrated members, especially serpents, of the animal kingdom who will take their rightful place, even in the conjugal bed. Goytisolo's savage parodies spare no society. Among others he damns the Castro Revolution by an examination of the equal and interchangeable defecatory processes demanded now that the pueblo has taken charge of its own destiny. Symbols are no longer needed. Instead of flags, soiled shorts or even Kotex will do, for one must replace the depersonalizing deodorants of modern existence and create a new one which will bridge the gap between the visible acceptable world and an invisible unmentionable one.

In this novel, Goytisolo is again a witness and participant in the cultural, social, and political history he describes. His technique and content seem almost indistinguishable, for he alters illusion and perception to create superimposed layers of simultaneously existing states of consciousness. Aside from his person shifts and obscuring of the functions of narrator, observer, and reader, he, like the producer of a movie, has his director move his characters around in conformity with a pre-conceived set design or photograph to establish an imaginary setting. As in Señas de identidad, his point of departure is from real, if faded, photographs from his Spanish childhood and ancestral memoribilia, and he feels himself drawn to the sexual emanations and rhythms of his ancestral Cuba. The funny stereotypes, structural ironies, and linguistic codes, however bewildering their hallucinatory, kaleidoscopic shifts may be, prove aesthetically effective. His humor, recalling Goya's black paintings, Bosch's monstrosities of life, and the Marquis de Sade's writings, offers a caricature of the social conventions and conformity he finds so nauseating. Goytisolo's grotesque characters (for example, an Arab beggar) become positive symbols of his rejection through their incarnation in Vosk, his created alter ego whom he also finally destroys.

His characters become equal directing partners in his fiction; he writes literary criticism of his own novel within it and defends himself against previous and current critics of that work. Poking fun at those who would have him win fame and popularity by retaining old genre distinctions and the realistic creation of character, he comments perceptively on his own creative process, his languages, characters, and series of games and oppositions. Writing causes him to find himself in an insane asylum, interviewed by psychiatrists, one of the many Vosk incarnations. After treatment most of the inhabitants tear up their old manuscripts and write feverishly about their new experiences; freed from obsessions and masturbatory writing, they wish to fecundate an attentive public. Goytisolo compares writing to a consuming orgasm allowing "su licor filiforme en la página en blanco" (p. 298). He attacks the religious, social, realistic, or psychiatric critics of his novels for taking him to task for his crime of writing "sin provecho del público y sus múltiples y urgentes necesidades. . ." (pp. 298-99), but in reality he does exactly what he is denying in the process. In writing and creating characters who live their fictional plane of reality which becomes identified with and superimposed on the author's own, Goytisolo reviews the manuscript actually being written (Juan sin tierra itself). Thus he incorporates the negative criticism, which he had suffered in the real world, that is, concerning his pessimism, resentment, psychiatric factors, and fantasy, into his creative process. Goytisolo, affected by the negative criticism, debates with his temporary alter-ego about his eccentric creations, the fantastic situations, his morbid obsessions, and the lack of critical acclaim he has received in his own country. Yet he finally breaks free from the deadly fragrance of his socially revered self (saintly child to spiritiual father) to declaim to his dream creations on his sinful nature.[13]

His typewriter becomes fecal material which he is able to excrete, to identify with the I-you of his childhood urinal, with sin, dirt, and corruption. He reserves his ultimate degradation for language, for by destroying pronouns and gender, together with the certainty of any verbal structures, by inverting King into Queen Kong and converting unnatural acts into accepted ones, and by using his prodigious imagination, he will shape and remake the world in his own image. Playing with the concept of God, the writer becomes God, not an uncommon occurrence, but at times, even given self-mockery, a manifestation of serious neurotic problems. By including references from everything from Inés de Castro to modern films, rock music, and current events, "extraviarás al futuro lector en los meandros y trampas de tu escritura" (p. 145).

Goytisolo's linguistic experiments in Juan sin tierra finally achieve what he was unable to accomplish in previous works: the destruction of his native tongue. In his latest novel he destroys not only syntax and gender but also personal pronouns as irrelevant, for everybody is "I." Through his use of yo-tu as a personal pronoun for the writer, he can make it turn out to be anyone and thus control the contradictory impulses which govern human behavior. Using his language as a weapon, he deprecates and destroys the printed word and yet paradoxically uses it, not only for self-destruction but also as an instrument of attack. It reflects like a deforming mirror held before the world of literature, film, and the real but yet make-believe world of sexual fantasy which for him symptomizes both society and self, perverted sado-masochistic entities, which he hypostatizes as the normal values of the capitalistic world. He uses a free operation of linguistic opposites to destroy language for its own sake because it is an independently important entity, whatever its relationship to the sociological, psychological, and religious motivations of the text. At the same time he makes of his weapon a magic instrument to captivate and mystify, creating elusive verbal constructions which will make him doubt any future truth expressed in language. Through the power of words he will obtain "el desmesurado placer de lo caprichoso e inverosímil: universo infinito de lo improbable en donde la sinrazón florezca y el fascinante caos emborrone la blancura del papel de una enigmática, liberadora proliferación de signos" (p. 312). And, through these signs made by his pen, he will obtain power: "ambiguo vaivén de la pluma, cifra de tu asombroso poder" (p. 154). The author, consequently, controls his environment to achieve what reason, enlightenment and progress never achieved in Spain: "paraíso el tuyo, con culo y con falo, donde un lenguaje-metáfora subyugue el objeto al verbo, y liberadas de sus mazmorras y grillos, las palabras al fin, las traidoras, esquivas palabras, vibren, dancen, copulen, se encierren y cobren cuerpo" (p. 234).

The words which have finally betrayed Spain also serve as his vehicle for freedom: "la liberación del instrumento y vehículo de tu (su) propia ruptura . . . progenitura infame, su (tu) subversion (ideológica, narrativa, semántica). . ." (pp. 319-20). Mocking the role of the written word as an instrument of colonization and tyranny, he reproduces oral combinations and new variant forms of slave language, which he combines with German, Italian, English, French, Latin, and finally, in an accelerating dismantling of Spanish into an approximation of Arabic, his final destruction and final vengeance. Parodying medieval and modern language, reproducing Afro-Cuban dialect, mimicking beautifully the very language of the sugar field in the imaginary sermon preached by the chaplain, Goytisolo, whether in specialized slang or in rhetorical speeches, reveals a sensitivity to the nuances which accurately reflect a narrative transcription from an oral source.

He indulges in a long series of barbs at idiomatic usages: "Oiga, joven! dirá: ¿se ha propuesto usted tomarme el pelo? aunque me lo propusiera no lo conseguiría, responderás tú: es usted absolutamente calvo. . ." (pp. 302 ff.). Goytisolo makes veiled and obvious jokes and plays on words (faro for falo), and he changes proverbs such as "mejor un pájaro en mano que cien volando," to a sexual organ ready to be launched, arrow-like, by the bow of his laughter to pierce the phony linguistic mask: "pájaro en mano pero sin desdeñar los cien que vuelan . . ." (p. 88). Goytisolo's outpouring of words (as he himself relates) constitutes an orgasm or anal relief. He concentrates on the sound of a word, its rhyme, and puns, as though through the superficial or the verbal, he might achieve peace and tranquility.

Kept out of the mainstream of Spanish literature, and thus a denaturalized don Julián, Goytisolo now prays: "Ayúdame a vivir sin suelo y sin raíces: móvil. . ."(pp. 124-25). Reaffirming his own private mythology also necessitates the complete annihilation of Spanish literary values, which he attacks, sparing neither the Middle Ages, Don Quijote, or realism, as represented by Benito Pérez Galdós. Although he dwells on the nugatory creations of Menéndez y Pelayo, it is the Generation of '98, especially Unamuno, and their view of the classics, which produces indigestible, constipating foodstuffs, creating in turn the delicious miraculous perfume of the Gods. Goytisolo literally considers Spain a nation of excrement and excretors, projected through its painting and literature. Sadly, in the final analysis, the Generation of '98, by preaching a return to old eternal Spanish traditions, is simply avoiding newfangled waterclosets in favor of a return to "los viejos entrañables placeres de la emisión de la zanja pública" (p. 225).

The National Tree of Letters, which he catigates in the manner in which Biblical references lament the damage caused by the tree of knowledge, will be accursed, will not flourish, and will eventually become (Arabic vengeance) one with the timeless desert. Goytisolo's triumphant rejection of Spanish language and literature, consciously or unconsciously, reproduces almost a schizophrenic state, with many parallels in psychoanalytic literature;[14] thus he relates most positively to non-Hispanic marginal figures of the Arab world like Fra Turmeda, a renegade Mallorcan, or Père de Foucauld.

As Goytisolo himself has pointed out, Juan sin tierra, lacking a unity of time, place, or character, must be penetrated by the reader "as if it were a dream, confronting a slippery and ever-changing world, one which appears and disappears incessantly before his eyes. The personal pronouns which appear . . . do not express an individual voice, but rather all voices or none at all . . . and at no time does the reader really know who is the actor and who is the recipient . . . In

Juan sin tierra logic and time are systematically destroyed and the structure of the work, like that of the poem, develops on a spatial plane."[15]

Juan sin tierra may be the final cathartic chapter of Goytisolo's aesthetic, psychological, and sociological search for meaning to his existence. More than an aesthetic enterprise, it reinforces once more his interest in and moral commitment to society, however negatively he symbolizes it, and reflects a return, in this sense, to earlier modalities. Nothing has changed in his political and social philosophy, whatever he may say in interviews about the subject, but the author, a highly cultured individual, with more insight and added exposure, has been able to refine his individual, frustrated, and guilt-ridden communication. A disoriented victim of his own idealism (which he pretends not to possess), he denounces with nightmarish intensity the system which falls so much short of the impossible paradise he once visualized for himself and for humanity.

He weaves his world of fantasy, his linguistic and literary creativity, and reality into an old mosaic with sharper colors and designs, continuing his use of geographical shifts and spatial transpositions. He emphasizes the phonic and emotional rather than the semantic value of words, which, ironically, with his multiple and complicated points of view, convey the very meaning he pretends to deny. Juan Goytisolo continues to want to belong, desperate for the very love he cannot consider because of his fear of rejection. He thus makes it almost impossible for himself to be accepted because he degrades all components of life which might afford him that possibility. Finally having eliminated the bitterness, purified, he may be able to discover positive aspects of the process of living in an imperfect world, employing his passionate concern for truth, not to refute and reject but rather to rectify and illuminate, transcending his self-imposed emotional shackles to assume his pre-eminent position as Spain's greatest living novelist.

Notes

[1] See Kessel Schwartz, "Sytlistic and Psychosexual Constants in the Work of Juan Goytisolo," Norte, 13, Nos. 4-6 (July-December 1972), 119-28.

[2] Juan Goytisolo, Juan sin tierra (Barcelona: Editorial Seix Barral, 1975). p. 179. Further citations in the text are from this edition.

[3] Kessel Schwartz, "Stylistic and Psychosexual Constants," p. 123.

[4] Bertram D. Lewin. "The Compulsive Character," Selected Writings, edited by Jacob A. Arlow (New York: The Psychoanalytic Quarterly, Inc., 1973). p. 5.

[5] See A. A. Brill. "Sexuality and its Role in the Neuroses," in Psychoanalysis Today (New York: International University Press. 1944), p. 185.

[6] Paul Schilder, "Neuroses and Psychoses," Psychoanalysis Today, p. 268. See also Melanie Klein, "Early Development of Conscience," Psychoanalysis Today, p. 69.

[7] Bertram D. Lewin "Anal Erotism and the Mechanism of Undoing," Selected Writings, p. 27.

[8] Ibid., p. 44.

[9] Karl Abraham, Character and Libido Development (New York: W.W. Norton, 1966), pp. 74-75.

[10] Ibid., p. 75.

[11] Julián Ríos, ed., Juan Goytisolo (Caracas: Editorial Fundamentos, 1975), p. 16.

[12] León Felipe. Oh! este viejo y roto violín (Mexico: Colección Málaga, 1968), p. 41.

[13] Goytisolo has commented that the Cervantine tradition involves destroying narrative material, which creates and recreates itself with corresponding self-commentary. See Juan Goytisolo, "Declaración de Juan Goytisolo de la mesa redonda celebrada en la Universidad de Wisconsin-Parkside," Norte, 13, Nos. 4-6 (July-December 1972), 94-95.

[14] See Bertram D. Lewin, "Metaphor, Mind, and Manikin," Selected Writings, pp. 435-41.

[15] Julio Ortega, "An Interview with Juan Goytisolo," *Texas Quarterly*, 18 (Spring 1975), 72-73.

LANGUAGE AND LITERATURE: RICARDO PALMA AND JUAN GOYTISOLO

Andrés Bello, José Martí, Manuel González Prada, Rufino Blanco Fombona and many other Spanish Americans have written cogently about the Spanish language. José Martí believed that American writers who used new words to augment the American scene could justify each new linguistic innovation only through a complete knowledge of the language in order to "separate themselves from rules promulgated by the orthodox academies of language, art, and literature."[1]

From the 1960's on, the question of language in literature has taken on added importance, especially in the development of what some critics term "novels of language" by novelists concerned with the transformation of narrative linguistic reality itself.[2] In this attempt to create a new language with a quality and form corresponding to its interior mystery, they create puns, neologisms, non-sentences and non-paragraphs. The same evolution may be seen in the works of Spain's leading novelist, Juan Goytisolo, vitally interested in language, as his collections of essays and novels and his many interviews reveal.

Guilllermo Cabrera Infante states: "In the speech of Cubans, Spanish is being converted every day into something different not only in its phonetics . . . but also in its syntax."[3] Essentially, Cabrera's well known Tres tristes tigres may be viewed as an attack on literature and a defense of language through its negation of the established lexicon, use of ambiguity and allusions, and parody of conventional language.

No doubt Cabrera Infante's novel influenced the language of Juan Goytisolo's own masterpiece, Reivindicación del Conde don Julián, which contains sarcastic references to well-known literary figures, a scathing and inconoclastic attitude toward literature, and a disassembling and reassembling of words in a syllabic, semantic game, much in the manner employed by Bustrófedon, Cabrera Infante's linguistic protagonist. Indeed, Goytisolo acknowledges the influence of Cabrera Infante in the foreword to his own novel.

These experiments have been accepted as something totally new and refreshing, perhaps akin to the poetic reformation a half century earlier by Vicente Huidobro and others. Yet except in degree and the inclusion of syntax as part of the focus of Goytisolo's irreverent attitude, one may find what at first glance seems to be a rather improbable ancestor of Goytisolo in Ricardo Palma, fascinated by language, Peruvianisms, proverbs, folkloric expressions, epigrams, Indian words, and neologisms. In his studies such as Neologismos y americanismos (1896) and Papeletas lexicográficas (1903), which includes about 2,700 words missing from the Royal Academy Dictionary, as well as in works such as Recuerdos de España (1899) and in his correspondence, he constantly attacked what he considered to be a moribund Royal Academy while at the same time professing his love of language: "a devotee, as I am, of linguistic studies. . ."[4]

Palma, while ostensibly digging into archaic linguistic forms, was rejecting artificial and stilted Castilian for a special mixture of neologisms and Peruvianisms, a combination of the castizo and the americano through which he managed to emphasize "curious and personal idiomatic creations."[5] He proposed fitting the language to multiple views, gave it meaning on many levels of abstraction, much in the fashion of contemporary writers, and created variants and curious turns and twists of language to meet his artistic purposes. His blend of "words, phrases, and turns, taken alternatively from the mouth of the common people, who swarm in markets and taverns, and from the books and other ancient writings of the sixteenth and seventeenth centuries,"[6] reveals that like Goytisolo, who professes to profane classical texts, he had to have a great knowledge of classical language and popular speech in order to be able to reproduce the living document and to restore the original force of words.

Palma offers us the same kind of burlesque of official Peru found in Goytisolo's mockery of a static Spain. He uses the equivalent of associative chains, irony, and malicious portraits in satirizing literary and linguistic intransigence, although the contemporary writer's devotion to lavatory graffiti is matched, in Palma's case, only by his insistence on new and funny words. A master of locutions, Palma delights us, as does Goytisolo, with his semantic and phonetic implications. He believed that an author, in order to convey humor, had to know the very nature of language and "to make a serious study of the structure of sentences, of the euphony and rhythm of words. . ."[7] His tolerant contempt for some figures of the past matches that of Goytisolo for the giants of his country's literature, and he also uses irony, tongue in cheek puns, and words with double meanings. His attacks on what he calls "the impropriety, unsuitability, and vulgarity in the form of our bureaucratic communications" (TPC, pp. 1510-16) reflect, in a more traditional way, Goytisolo's reproduction of Don Alvaro's discourse in Reivindicación del Conde don Julián.[8] Goytisolo differs in the intensity, to the point of irrationality, in his persecution of the "marvelous language of the Poet, vehicle necessary for betrayal, your beautiful language,"[9] and in his insistence on the need for multilevel and ambiguous expressions through which to launch an attack on the social and political status quo. Goytisolo feels the need to destroy linguistic myths as part of his forays against cultural and historical values and that his duty, as a modern writer, is "that of being myth destroyer."[10] Palma also saw the need for change and realized that the younger generation in his country "neither loves nor hates Spain; it is indifferent to her."[11] Both writers picked up the sound of the adolescent of the street and the unique verbal contours of living Spanish, but Goytisolo is aggressively ideological and Palma is not.

Ricardo Palma, at various times in his speeches and writings, mentions his efforts to preserve the purity of the language in spite of giving it a contemporary flavor through his use of current dialect, but his love for linguistic purity seems reserved almost exclusively for Spanish syntax: "The spirit, the soul of languages, lies in its syntax more than in its vocabulary. Enrich the latter, revere the former, that is our doctrine" (TPC, p. 1380). He repeats this refrain a number of times: "For me, purity must not be sought through vocabulary but rather through correct syntax, for syntax is the soul, the characteristic spirit of all tongues."[12]

Juan Goytisolo also believes in being true to language: "The oscillation of the writer between ideal and effective language is not a secondary and circumstantial phenomenon; probing more throughly we can affirm, on the contrary . . . that it is situated in the very center of artistic creation."[13] Goytisolo sees more clearly than Palma that questioning so-called sacred linguistic cows must also undermine the very foundations of Spanish, neither excluding syntax nor any other aspect of language in his "implacable criticism of that stale Castilian prose which is, at the same time, a sanctuary and bank of sublime values of Classic Style."[14]

And Palma, too, in spite of professing love for the syntactical integrity of his native tongue, chides those who strive for a virginal Castilian, for languages, he claims, "are not virgins: they are mothers, and fecund mothers who are always providing from the claustrum of their brain through the opening of their lips new children to the world of love and human relations" (TPC, p. 1380). He rejects the "anemic lexicon of Castile" (TPC, p. 1541) and reiterates that one must be prepared to sacrifice the purity of Castilian to be truthful to a living Spanish.[15] He argues that one should have the right to create any word necessary to convey an expression and to realize the peculiar potentialities of his native speech, that Peruvian is not Castilian, and that new flexibility and meanings are needed to have a living and not a dead language. This revolution in language, "an irresistible imposition of the twentieth century" (TPC, p. 1506), is imperative because a "liturgical language is a language condemned to die" (TPC, p. 1540).

Goytisolo, for his part, states that one can talk of the occupation of a language as well as the occupation of countries by an enemy force: ". . . a language controlled by an all embracing caste which mutilates its expressive possibilities by exercising a violence, concealed beyond its virtual significance."[16] He believes with Palma that Spanish intransigence may well have created two languages, an American one and a Spanish one, and that a language which reveals neither evolution nor adaptability to new forms, "is on the road to becoming a liturgical language or dead one" (TPC p. 1507). Goytisolo finds modern Spanish a refined and anemic language, an imprisoned entity, "language incapable of capturing and expressing the novelty and complexity of the modern world and condemned therefore, to a dead end and to the cementery of finished styles. . ."[17]

The Royal Academy is a favorite target for both Goytisolo and Palma. In Neologismos y americanismos, Recuerdos de España, and in a series of letters, Palma complains about Academy intransigence to changes in language or the acceptance of Americanisms. He laments the fact that the only potential tie between Spain and the New World is language, a fact the Royal Academy refuses to recognize, to its sorrow; for new expressions and forms will prevail because "to exclude or condemn them there exists no institution sufficiently powerful or authorized . . ."[18] He praises the American spirit of Castelar for accepting new modes of expression in spite of an "intransigent academy majority" (TPC, p. 1352); contends that language, independent of all rules, will survive, "in spite of the Academicians. . ." (TPC, p. 1381); rejects the Academy dictionary as "a cordon sanitaire between Spain and America (TPC, p. 1383) and as a "restrictive measuring stick" (TPC, p. 1509); and states that usage and not "the doctors . . . those who impose such and such a word" will prevail (TPC, p. 1507). He rejects the Academy view that languages are vestal virgins whose purity they are charged to preserve as ridiculous as the Academy itself, for him "of slight importance" (TPC, p. 1542). He reiterates that Academy authority simply turns writers and young Americans away from the study of language and literature (TPC, p. 1548). Fifty million Spanish Americans are the true owners of the language because, in truth, Castilian has become, even in Spain, little more than a regional tongue (TPC, p. 1539).

Juan Goytisolo also believes that the domination of Castilian over other Spanish-speaking countries is an unjust, anachronistic, prejudicial, and false condition. The Academy, he maintains, is not "the temple . . . of Classic Style and the musty, chaste prose . . . with which it cradles its ears . . . can in no way serve as a model for anybody . . . society and not grammarians create language . . . Frequently what they call incorrect . . . is but the expression of a new way of looking at things. . ."[19]

Ricardo Palma's ironic tone in his attacks on the Academy differs only in degree from that of Goytisolo. Palma says: "Rather let the celestial dome collapse on the Academy, and the language and all of us perish than to allow entrance into the Dictionary the word 'gubernamental'. . ."; "do not boast of being a greater hairsplitter than an academic flea" (TPC, pp. 1507-08; 1510). His lexical congeries lacks the sometimes coarse implications of his twentieth century counterpart, but he utilizes what some might consider deliberately solecistic transcriptions. Even though Goytisolo lacks the at times respectful reverence of Palma for Spanish syntax, he, too, metamorphosing his language, is unable to destroy it. He vents his wrath, instead, on the Royal Academy and its stuffiness through a burlesque of its entrance speeches. Don Alvaro's death rattle of cu-cu-cu after his fiery speech filled with hyperbole, antithesis, transitions, and metaphors,[20] is but a part of the equation. Count Julian and Goytisolo cannot use their language, for Spanish authorities proclaim it to be their private property: ". . . from pulpits, from academic chairs, from speakers' platforms the Hispanos proudly proclaim their property rights over language it is ours, ours, ours, they say . . . we transported it to eighteen nations who today speak and think, pray, sing, write as we do daughter nations and their children our grandchildren are also Castilians . . . we still have the Word . . . you must rescue your lexicon: dismantle the age-old linguistic fortress: . . . paralyze the circulation of language: suck dry its sap. . ."[21]

The new writers of Spain and Spanish America boast of their freedom from linguistic restraints and from what they believe to be an institutionalized, petrified language. Without denigrating their efforts to create and to use a new language, or denying the emergence of what may be a new spirit of linguistic concern to match the other twentieth century technical innovations of interior monologue, flashbacks, temporal experimentation, simultaneous dialogue, and a new sensibility in a world without apparent values, one concludes that they offer us only relatively old wine in somewhat new bottles. Language, of necessity, reflects the disintegration of human and social relationships, and, in a demythified world of drugs, disillusion, and dehumanization, writers need equivalent expressions to match their often-times grotesque visions of life.

Carlos Fuentes sees the search for language as "a temporal return to the fount of language . . . to encounter a language which is at long last the answer of the writer as much to the exigencies of his art as to the needs of his society, and I believe that herein lies the possibility of contemporaneity."[22] One may accept the anticultural aspects of Goytisolo's fiction and the contention of critics like Rodríguez Monegal about the creation of new relationships between the modifications of the individual and his reality while at the same time insisting that, linguistically speaking, the search for artistic authenticity among contemporary writers differs only in degree from that of other generations. Palma was responding in the nineteenth century to invariable artistic exigencies through his language and unusual connotations, much as Goytisolo, in his experimentation with new form, was reacting to what he termed linguistic myths. In the final analysis, both, true artists, rejected the concept of language as something inherited or definitive, adapted words and sentences to each nuance of content, and created a highly original, metaphorically informative, and authentic language, as they explored their transmuted realities in compelling and stylistic interpretations of society and history.

Notes

[1] Roberto Agramonte, Martí y su concepción del mundo (Barcelona: Editorial Universitaria, Universidad de Puerto Rico, 1971), p. 50.

[2] Emir Rodríguez Monegal, "Diario de Caracas." Mundo Nuevo, No. 17 (1967), pp. 22-23. In El arte de narrar (Caracas: Monte Avila, Editores, 1968), pp. 269-292, he discusses language strata and the correspondence of linguistic levels to ontological and ethnic realities.

[3] J. Corrales Egea, "Escritores hispanoamericanos en París, I. Con Guillermo Cabrera Infante," Insula, No. 195 (1963), p. 7.

[4] See letter to Daniel Granada in Ricardo Palma, Tradiciones peruanas completas (Madrid: Aguilar, 1961). p. 1534. Futher citations in the text are to this edition, hereafter cited as TPC.

[5] Raimundo Lazo, Vigil, Palma, González Prada (Havana: Cultural S.A. 1943), pp. 20-21.

[6] Ricardo Palma, Tradiciones peruanas, (Madrid: Espasa-Calpe, 1939), II, p. 7.

[7] José Miguel Oviedo, Genio y figura de Ricardo Palma (Buenos Aires: Editorial Universitaria, 1965), p. 165.

[8] Juan Goytisolo, Reivindicación del Conde don Julián (Mexico: Joaquin Mortiz, 1970), pp. 177-181.

[9] Reivindicación . . ., p. 70.

[10] Declaración de Juan Goytisolo, Norte, No. 4-6 (1972), p. 91.

[11] Guillermo Feliu Cruz, En torno de Ricardo Palma (Santiago de Chile: Prensas de la Universidad de Chile, 1933), II, 190.

[12] En torno . . ., p. 212. See also, José Miguel Oviedo, p. 164: "What I don't want, friend, is linguistic anarchy."

[13] Juan Goytisolo, El furgón de cola (París: Ruedo Iberico, 1967). p. 136.

[14] El furgón. . .p. 183. f.n. 4.

[15] Ricardo Palma, Tradiciones peruanas (Madrid: Espasa-Calpe, 1939), V., p. 369.

[16] Juan Goytisolo, Obra inglesa de D. José María Blanco White (Buenos Aires: Edicones Formerntor, 1972), p. 72.

[17] Juan Goytisolo, El furgón de cola, p. 48.

[18] Guillermo Feliu Cruz, p. 213.

[19] Juan Goytisolo, El furgón de cola, p. 135.

[20] Juan Goytisolo, Reivindicación del Conde don Julián, p. 181.

[21] Reivindicación. . ., pp. 192-196.

[22] Carlos Fuentes, "Situación del escritor en América Latina," Mundo Nuevo, No. 1 (1960), 17.

EROS AND THANATOS: THE POETRY OF VICENTE ALEIXANDRE--SURREALISM OR FREUDIANISM?

Dámaso Alonso states that Vicente Aleixandre may have helped initiate surrealism in Spain without any intention of doing so. He denies that Aleixandre had any knowledge of the French school.[1] Other critics qualify their statements with limiting adjectives such as "telluric" or "existential" in order to define Aleixandre's surrealism and to make a connection between what is obviously a personal spiritual and psychological projection and broader literary manifestations. Ricardo Gullón believes that Aleixandre's surrealism is neither French nor complete.[2] Carlos Bousoño also agrees that Aleixandre's surrealism "no fue nunca puro--ni aun en Pasión de la tierra--cada vez lo había de ser menos."[3] José Luis Cano also points out that Pasión de la tierra, written in 1928-1929, which seems to resemble the French school, was partly composed before the Spanish poet's contact with French writers.[4] Even among those accepting Aleixandre's complete surrealism, no agreement exists as to its beginning or end in his poetic works. Villena believes that Pasión de la tierra marked "su inicio en el superrealismo"[5] and that it continued at least through Mundo a solas.[6] Guillermo Carnero, on the other hand, contends that even in Ambito an attitude "afín a la del superrealismo europeo debe ser admitida."[7] Angel del Río labels La destrucción o el amor as specific and frank surrealist poetry.[8] For others Aleixandre was "el maestro indiscutible de esta corriente literaria",[9] "uno de sus [surrealism's] más grandes poetas en cualquier idioma";[10] "the most fervent and definitely surrealistic Spanish poet,"[11] and the one who remained faithful to surrealism as a form of expression for the longest time.[12]

But the position of Aleixandre himself remains unclear. André Breton in his first manifesto defined surrealism as a psychic automatism through which he proposed to express the real functioning of thought without control by reason, revealing the narrow relationship between the real and the imaginary. He talked about pure psychic automatism, the suspension of consciousness in order to express subconscious ideas and feelings.[13] Aleixandre states that he never believed "en lo estrictamente onírico, la escritura automática, ni en la consiguiente abolición de la conciencia artística."[14] Furthermore, in a letter to Fernando Charry Lara he writes: "dice usted bien: Yo no soy un poeta superrealista."[15] Yet Aleixandre, in a poem dedicated to Breton's death in 1966, apparently acknowledges that La destrucción o el amor is surrealistic:

> Oh desvarío: tierra, tú en tu voz
> Poetas. Si Poeta en Nueva York.
> También, corriendo fiel, Un río, un amor.
> Allá Sobre los ángeles sonó
> el trueno. No; la luz. La destrucción.[16]

In 1971 Aleixandre published Poesía surrealista which contains, among other poems, "Quien baila se consuma," of Diálogos del conocimiento, his latest volume of poetry. He also concedes that his total poetry contains irrational sequences, even though Pasión de la tierra was "el libro mío más próximo al superrealismo."[17] In his evaluation of that volume the poet speaks of a violent rupture with the poetry of the age and of subconscious elements: "Un mundo de movimientos casi subterráneos, donde los elementos subconscientes servían a la visión del caos original allí contemplado."[18] As for the poems themselves, a chaotic vision prevails, and Aleixandre proceeds by association of ideas without selection, although he also views this volume as a struggle toward light and a book in which "todavía me reconozco."[19] His next collection, Espadas como labios (1932), also seems to reject history and anecdote. The subconscious association, freedom from spatial and temporal laws, and the apparent destruction of logic in a world where real things disintegrate might lead one to conclude that his subjective imagery reflects his surrealism.

Yet an examination of Aleixandre's poetry reveals the possibility of another explanation that gives coherence and a kind of logic to these supposedly incomprehensible early poems concerning the encounter of the self with the reality that surrounds and defines it. Aleixandre, unable to escape the personal limits imposed by illness and a feeling of impotence, cannot help but include overtones expressive of the special circumstances under which the poems were written; without negating the imaginative elements, we can better understand them if we apprehend the circumstantial ingredients. In April of 1925 a serious illness caused Aleixandre to retire to the countryside for two years. This illness left an idelible impression on his poetry which, while apparently evasive, also revealed a profound preoccupation with the poet's own physical necessities. Juan José Domenchina, commenting on this illness and withdrawal, labels his poetry "biological."[20] Max Aub believes that Aleixandre's illness left a mark on his poems, "desperate songs of unsatisfied love".[21] Dámaso Alonso saw in him a poet whom God touched with physical pain that left a mark on his body and soul.[22] Aleixandre refers to his own illness and its effect on his career, emphasizing that his poetic consciousness "afloró con el cambio que años después una enfermedad larga y grave imprimió al rumbo de mi existencia.

Edad: veintitantos años. Campo y soledad . . . Este cambio total decidió mi vida."²³

Aleixandre consciously admits to another great influence: "Pero he de confesar la profunda impresión que la lectura de un psicólogo de incisiva influencia me produjo en 1928, y el cambio de raíz que en mi modesta obra se produjo."²⁴ Whatever the unconscious fantasies and their intensification through Aleixandre's illness, he also accepted the direct influence of Freud's works and admits: "Hace tiempo que sé, aunque entonces no tuviera conciencia de ello, lo que este libro [Pasión de la tierra] debe a la lectura de un psicólogo (Freud] de vasta repercusión literaria, que yo acabara de realizar justamente por aquellos años."²⁵ A further serious illness in 1932 reinforced his reliance on a dream world of the unconscious where one might escape the reality of impotence. Freud's work appeared in Spanish in 1923. Though it is difficult to pinpoint the superficial knowledge of Freudian theories by Aleixandre as opposed to later direct study, in all of his poetry Dionysian efforts to recreate a reality through imagery struggle with Apollonian tendencies to control his subconscious fantasy world. Robert Bly, in a review in the New York Times (October, 1977) comments: "In his work you can see more clearly than in any poet in English the impact of Freud. He evokes what it was like for a Westerner to read Freud's testimony of the immense and persistent sexual energy trying to rise into every vein and capillary of life." Aleixandre was never able to give an adequate explanation of his poetry, but he recognized it as based on subconscious desires and the need to relieve certain pressures. In En un vasto dominio (1962) he claims that he writes for everybody: "Para todos escribo . . Para ti y todo lo que en ti vive, / yo estoy escribiendo."²⁶ Yet in Diálogos del conocimiento (1974) we see a continuing dichotomy as in "Dos Vidas " he distinguishes between the poet who writes only "testimonio de mí" and the other who "entre los hombres eche a andar."²⁷ Although in their glorification of instinct and sexual expression surrealists bear a superficial resemblance to the Spanish poet, in reality Aleixandre does not share their radical transformation of values through total liberation of the unconscious, nor do his stylistic resources sever his poetry from the moral or human. Yet he conveys the feeling of Breton's second manifesto of having reached a point where opposites such as life and death are no longer perceived as contradictory. In surrealist poetry, metaphysical in nature, one should avoid equating techniques, such as automatic writing or collage, with the movement itself, though technique might be used to trigger the liberating mechanism of total love, beauty, and liberty. Breton himself later admitted that automatic writing was not the key.²⁸ The function of the "juxtaposition of incongruities" is to express receptivity to a modified

187

sensibility and to testify to the actualization of this change in a momentary vision of union. The major forces for union and vehicles for expressing awareness might be total love, liberty, contradiction of social constraints and exposure to free chance, and the perception of the marvelous in the universe. Surrealism does not translate symbols or deal in neuroses or personal exorcism. The imagery and concepts of Freudian psychoanalysis were used in varying degrees by the surrealists. But psychoanalysis assumes that neuroses result from the rejection by the conscious mind of factors which stay in the unconscious as dynamic repressions, causing conflicts which may then be resolved by analyzing these repressions through free association and dream interpretation. Aleixandre's poetry is often irrational, not by any means the same as surrealistic. He uses unexpected juxtapositions, but he does not really exploit chance effects.

Aleixandre reveals a total absorption in the material of his created world which comes, not from contrivance, but from deep necessity. The apparent rejected vision of the normal exterior eye cannot disguise the poet's participation in a reality which cannot exclude self. Indeed, many of Aleixandre's early poems seem analogues of the poet's psychological journey from annihilation, evasion, despair, and death to an affirmation of life and love and a striving toward light, even though his self-contained pattern of harmonies and disharmonies seems at times the paradigm of the dark forces at the very center of existence. In other words, his poetic vision seems to reject the material world, reality's affirmation in which the poet for a time felt he could not participate but which existed nonetheless for his subconscious experience in disguised form.[29] The poet shared in this way the thirst for love and life. His is a poetry of thematic unity of death and love, employing a pattern of unusual images.

As Paul Ilie points out, each poem in itself may be incomprehensible, but as a group they reveal certain motifs and patterns.[30] Let us, briefly, examine the story line. Ambito (1928), written during an illness, sensually examines fleeting aspects of time, and the poet, within his own boundary--the limits of his sickroom--creates poetry which contains "fuerzas que luego harían ostentación"[31] and which also "ensancha en mi memoria y queda."[32] A recurring archetype which integrates all of Aleixandre's poetry--the sea--appears, and morning light, especially the interplay of light and darkness--the former phallic, the latter feminine--also fascinates the poet as he longs to possess the night.

In Pasión de la tierra the poet joins passion in its human existential force and earth. One sees here Aleixandre's anguish in his relationship to the material universe, which lacks order and offers no clear-cut solution for man, a victim of the world and civilization much as Aleixandre, sick and solitary, was a victim. The poet rejects death for life, discovering nonetheless that love offers no relief, for it is an empty gesture in the face of threatening night or death which offers pain together with its suggested joy. To be with the night brings the pleasure of maternal union, but to sleep at that breast is to lose consciosuness, a kind of death. Aleixandre seeks to become one with basic elements by breaking the limits of form. Lost on the ocean of life, he recognizes that he cannot escape destiny, symbolized as a great serpent.

Espadas como labios again concerns the central themes of life, death and love. The poet petrifies and immobilizes the moment as he peruses dead roses and "coals of silence" (because they lack life-giving flame) and a series of other death representations. Here one encounters the poet's constant longing to be combined with a fear of not being. Though he continues to seek love and light as opposed to death and darkness, he also sees death as a rebirth, a kind of joy and awakening that wants to break the limits that prevent things from returning to earth. He recognizes that death may be a prolongation of life and that love takes many forms. The poet may seek in vain for truth and beauty in a hypocritical world where dreams are not fulfilled and may find true sexual and erotic expression in the more primitive and even threatening natural forces. Finally, the fusion with nature in flux, where a human arm can weigh more than a star, takes on new dimensions. Aleixandre momentarily becomes the universe, but he is constantly reminded of his tangible limits in an immobilized world.

So as we can see, the poet clearly conveys a connected narrative. His symbols represent a variety of sensual, erotic states involving a repressed sexuality, and a psychoanalytic examination of that symbolism reveals the poet's motivation behind, and preoccupation with the equation that love equals death.[33] Pathognomic in their psychological connotations, anxieties and fantasies, these symbols are rooted in the painful dynamic of Aleixandre's own life. These early collections, especially, seem to have offered him the opportunity to sublimate various thinly disguised impulses, and his selection of relevant imagery reinforces the belief that in his case the unconscious influences were so overwhelming that his creative process was simply a transmutation of his fantasies into an artistically and socially acceptable form. Frederick Prescott has pointed out in The Poetic Mind that poetry may serve as a catharsis: "the catharsis is accomplished by a psychological analysis to which Stekel likens poetry, except that in poetry the patient ministers to himself."[34] Without accepting the absolute validity of psychoanalytic principles we may understand the unconscious motivations of which the poet himself may not have been aware, which when analyzed clarify certain distortions dwelling in the dark corners of the human mind and provide flashes of recognition of symbols that one knows or almost knows as his own.

As Freud points out, love and death instincts fuse and blend with one another and reveal themselves in an ambivalent attitude toward various objects, "for [in] the opposition between the two classes of instincts we may put the polarity of love and hate. There is no difficulty in finding a representative of Eros, but we must be grateful that we can find a representative of the elusive death instinct in the destruction to which hate points the way."[35] Imagination, according to Freud, is a refuge which provides a substitute pleasure for narcissistic wishes that the artist had to abandon in real life. He states:

> An artist is originally a man who turns away from reality because he cannot come to terms without the renunciation of instinctual satisfaction which it at first demands, and he allows his erotic and ambitious wishes full play in the life of fantasy. He finds his way back to reality from this world of fantasy by making use of special gifts to mold his fantasies into truths of a new kind, which are valued by men as precious reflections of reality.[36]

"El amor no es relieve" of <u>Pasión de la tierra</u> may, in two lines, reveal clearly a technique which seems surrealistic[37] but with a Freudian explanation: "En tu cintura no hay más que mi tacto quieto. Se te saldrá el corazón por la boca mientras la tormenta se hace morada" (PC, 151). The first sentence seems to bear no relationship to the second. Yet, if we substitute for calm touch not the meaning of amorous caress which the conscious mind translates but rather the sense of mortal pressure or squeezing, we can easily understand the frightening second image. We often hear expressions such as "I could squeeze you to pieces," quite indicative of ambivalent emotions. It has been said that even cannibals have a devouring affection for their enemies. Emotionally then, squeezing fatally would cause the heart to leave through the throat. Obviously, if one has one's heart in the throat one is choking. So the image would come to mind of a purple face or a purple reality, hence a purple torment. Once again we see that Eros and Thanatos are identical, that love equals death. And so a caress becomes a purple torment because both are the same and both are death.

In *Ambito* Aleixandre sets the stage for the sea as a battleground between Eros and Thanatos. "Mar y aurora" shows us a living entity whose timid waves and passive foam awaken with the dawn. Gradually the sun's rays disperse the shadows and the sea becomes more active; the sunlight and the sea renew their daily symbolic relationship as the former indulges in its daily drinking of the waves. According to Jung, primitive belief held that the sea previously swallowed the old sun, and like a woman gave birth the following day to a new sun.[38] But in "Mar y noche" Aleixandre reveals a dark and threatening sea, viewed as a mouth, throat and gullet waiting eagerly to devour the night: "Boca-mar-toda ella, pide noche/ . . . para sus fauces hórridas, y enseña / todos sus blancos dientes de espuma" (PC, 101-02). Seeking to swallow its enemy, the sea, chained to its black bed, vainly strains to free itself. The moment before falling asleep, when the sense of being engulfed is strongest, a dreamer may at times be threatened by the jaws of death; in these two poems Aleixandre produces a kind of primal relationship and reciprocal cannibalism, as the day drinks the sea and the sea devours the night with which Aleixandre identifies, again implying that the drive for life and the impulse to destruction may be mutually dependent. Death may be both good and bad, for the sea may represent, too, a timeless afterlife which blurs the distinction between annihilation and immortality.

Throughout, Alexandre's works give us two basic images, one of tongue, teeth, warmth, dryness, wetness, ecstasy, and a host of maternal breast images, and the other of phallic impotence, a dark bewilderment of an enchained subjective self striving for expression in a world of frigidity and destruction. The fears of death and castration, as Ernest Jones shows, are extremely closely associated, and anxiety concerning indefinite survival of the personality constantly expresses the fear of a punitive impotence, a kind of death.[39] Aleixandre's youth in Málaga impressed the sea on his consciousness so that it became for him the symbol of his mother. In psychoanalytic literature the sea quite usually has this meaning. His desire to return and merge with that happiness and all it represents implies his death as an individual, for he will be absorbed by a larger unit. But this absorption is to be resisted. In "No existe el hombre," from *Mundo a solas*, Aleixandre specifies that the sea is not a bed where the body of a man can stretch out alone: "un mar no es un sudario para una muerte lucida" (PC, 423). The sea is not a bed, a shroud. The regressively attractive mother symbol, the sea, is said not to be the very thing he holds it to be, a mechanism of denial or negation. Intra-uterine life, being held pre-mortal except by the Church, is easily equated with post-mortal life, so that life before birth equals in fantasy life after death, both longed-for and feared.

Pasión de la tierra continues the personal combination of death and sexuality. In "El amor no es relieve" the poet exclaims: "Te amo, te amo, no te amo. / Tierra y fuego en tus labios saben a muerte perdida" (PC, 152). In "Ser de esperanza y lluvia" a dying poet does not know whether life can be found in the sea, both love and death. In his hand he holds a breathing (life-giving) lung, but also "una cabeza rota ha dado a luz a dos serpientes vivas" (PC, 159), an obvious castration implication.[40] "El amor padecido" again juxtaposes phallic symbolism, "para amar la forma perpendicular de uno mismo," (PC, 211) with death imagery, a wounding love, oedipal concerns and a sea with jaws. Throughout, this collection relates the sensual to death and decay and shows the sea as both love and death, involving a continuing symbolism of round mouths, throats, teeth, rotten fish, and a passion of water and death.

Espadas como labios through its very title combines the erotic with the deadly lips which kiss and love and swords which maim and kill, an erotic interplay with death which is "el tema principal de toda la poesía aleixandrina de la primera época: desde Ambito . . . a Nacimiento último. Se trata, como certera e insistentemente se ha dado en afirmar, del amor-pasión como impulso destructor."[41] A number of poems offer us a juxtaposition of love and death. In "El vals," though the world may ignore "el vello de los pubis," the "labios obscenos" convert into a kiss which "se convertirá en una espina que dispensará la muerte diciendo: Yo os amo" (PC, 236). In "En el fondo del pozo," contemplation of the beloved's long hair lasts all too briefly as we see "la música cuajada en hielo súbito" and "un corazón, un juguete olvidado" (PC, 238-39). "El más bello amor" offers one of the poet's most powerful sexual fantasies. Here Aleixandre, rejecting the unsatisfying love of women, finds himself a beloved shark:

> Así sin acabarse mudo ese acoplamiento sangriento
> respirando sobre todo una tinta espesa
> los besos son las manchas las extensibles manchas
> Una boca imponente como una fruta bestial
> como un puñal que de la arena amenaza el amor (PC, 243-44).

The fish inhabiting the life-giving seas represent a vital sexual destructive capacity. Aleixandre views the instinctive attack here and elsewhere of primitive animals as a form of love, but the implied sexual force may also represent a passive masochistic gratification, for these symbols of virility are both loved and feared. Similarly in "Con todo respeto," "el beso ardentísimo . . . nos quebranta los huesos" (PC, 81). Corresponding themes may be found in "Circuito" (224), where he seeks the love of "sirens of the sea"; in "Nacimiento último"

(230-31), where he views the sea as eternal life and death; and in "Muñecas" (247-48), where he relates the pleasant-unpleasant aspects of physical love. Indeed, in almost all of the poems he dwells on destructive death imagery and the pleasure-pain involved in love.

To wish to be eaten or possessed by menacing animals often represents a death fantasy equivalent to a fear of castration;[42] the neurotic dread of death is also primarily related to the fear of being devoured.[43] The poet both seeks and rejects love and death, ambivalently revealing that through dying symbols of detumescence a life may ensue. Everywhere we find rotten fish, drowning fish, fish like stone, and, less frequently, fish colored with the flush of living. Water, sea and ocean may mean "mother" in association with youthful innocence, happiness, the breast, absorption and death. The poet constantly juxtaposes sea, beach, moon, teeth, tongue, throat, and breast. In many of these poems he uses the sea as a surface on which to project his images in a manner analogous to the Isakower Phenomenon and the dream screen. According to Otto Isakower, a person falling asleep who sees dark masses approach and is unable to ascertain the division between the body and the masses reproduces a little baby's sensations of falling asleep at the breast. This phenomenon, also associated with well-known hypnagogic manifestations of an auditory and tactile nature, involves mouth sensations and especially bodilessness, floating, and sinking. The drowser feels small in the presence of something large or heavy and may vaguely perceive something indefinite or shadowy and of vast size.[44] Bertram D. Lewin, complementing this concept, postulates a dream screen as the blank background present in the dream, and the visually perceived action in ordinary manifest dream content takes place on it or before it.[45] The representation of the mother's breast during nursing (the dream screen) may involve various solid or convex shapes or fluid objects which serve as screen equivalents and the imaginary fulfillment of a wish to sleep and a breast to sleep at. Later events and situations are projected onto the original blankness (an image of the breast during the infant's sleep, as if it were a cinematic screen). In other words, the dream screen forms the background or projection drop for the dream picture.[46] These phenomena are often accompanied by loss of ego boundaries, visions of white clouds, receding waves, vaporous mists, roses or pinkish color (the aureole of the breast), white and blue contrasts (the breast and the veins), and the constant implication of thirst related at the same time to concepts of dry, sandy desert wastes. A casual examination of Aleixandre's poetry reveals the presence of the above elements to an intrusive degree even in Ambito, which is replete with blue and white interspersed with dust, mouth, dream, limitless forms, and especially the moon (a standard mother symbol), which through its curved surface is homologous to a dream screen. The breast symbolism, mouth sensations, and ecstatic states often seem to relate to the withdrawn aspects and dry-thirst tongue and mouth sensation. In "Vida," from Pasión de la tierra, a moon-colored mermaid, her breast like a mouth, divided in two "me quiso besar sobre la sombra muerta. Le faltaba otro seno (PC, 149). The poet relates his death to the mermaid who gasps for breath on the surface of the sea. The idea of eating and being eaten by an object is of course also a way of becoming united with it. Mermaids quite often represent the primal mother, and as Géza Roheim points out in Gates of the Dream these water beings devour their victims, a kind of oral aggression in talion form, that is, the punishment is identical to the offense.[47] Paradoxically, sleep which brings pleasure also involves the anxiety of being eaten and dying. The young baby projects its self-aggression onto the breast, which it then fears as destructive. In "Ansiedad para el día" (PC, 200-01) the poet, on the surface of a bubble, cannot find the flesh destined for him. Lost against the background of a wave composed of a handful of umbrellas, he wets his tongue in "the subheaven, the ecstatic blue," a projection of the image of the breast onto the sky. As he fuses with the ocean he views the potential threat of "las gargantas de las sirenas húmedas," and, merging with the larger whole, finds "una orilla es mi mano. Otra mi pierna." The most striking aspect of what Isakower observed involves the blurring of the distinction between different regions of the body, between what is internal and external, and the amorphous character of the impressions conveyed by the sense organs. "Part of the perceptual apparatus," says Isakower, "observes the body ego as its boundaries become blurred and fused with the external world, and perceptions become localized as sensations in a particular body region.[48] Aleixandre misses a finger of his hand and is threatened by an earless monster who carried "en lugar de sus palabras una tijera breve, la justa para cortar la explicación abierta." The poet surrenders to the threatening shears, possibly the manifest element of a frightening dream, a true disturber relating to repressed impulses that may break through as projections.[49] Aleixandre indulges in a kind of autocannibalism: "Lloro la cabeza entera. Me rueda por el pecho y río con las uñas, con los dos pies que me abanican." Sinking and smothering sensations or the loss of consciousness are also found in fantasies of oral incorporation or being eaten. A baby treats the breast as it does its own fingers or others which it stuffs into its mouth, indulging in the identical autocannibalism of the poem. This type of anxiety (recall the title of the poem) is related to childhood fantasies about the prenatal state, an aspect of which is the child's imagining it entered into the mother by being swallowed. The concept of mother earth in the total collection, indeed

Aleixandre's fusion with the earth in a final death as an ultimate kind of love and possession, combines with Freudian preoccupations, especially those involving the sea and breast symbolism. The poet is supported by the waves and yet is threatened, a typical reaction of anxiety dreams about merging with a larger whole and perishing as an individual and one of the constants not only in Aleixandre's early poetry but throughout his work.

These images and the dream screen continue in Aleixandre's later poetry. In addition to the human ego overwhelmed by elemental forces, repeating the anxious transmutation of the original pleasure of falling asleep, not only the active eating process but (through fierce animal attacks with swords and teeth) the passive idea of being eaten also becomes a part of the nursing situation. Throughout the collection we see concepts involving seas that steal from breasts, tongues connected with "sweet savor," and breasts in the form of harps, as Aleixandre constantly emphasizes feeding and breast imagery. One poem, among many, "Mar en la tierra," from his masterpiece <u>La destrucción o el amor</u> shows clearly his continuing maternal and dream screen symbolism:

> El resonante mar convertido en una lanza
> yace en lo seco como un pez que se ahoga,
> clama por esa agua que puede ser el beso,
> que puede ser un pecho que se rasgue y anegue.
> Pero, la seca luna no responde al reflejo de
>   las escamas pálidas. . .
>
> Entonces la dicha, la oscura dicha de morir
> de comprender que el mundo es un grano que
>   se deshará,
> el que nació para un agua divina,
> para ese mar inmenso que yace sobre el polvo.
> La dicha consistirá en deshacerse como lo minísculo,
> en transformarse en la severa espina,
> resto de un océano que como la luz se marchó
> gota de arena que fue un pecho gigante
> y que salida por la garganta como un sollozo
>   aquí yace (PC, 379-80).

The state of sleep bears a marked resemblance to the prenatal state and uterine regression, which explains the dark joy of fusing with the sea, of returning to the womb. The "gigantic breast" gives the theoretical genetic origin of the screen, that is, the way it would look to a baby. The gigantic breast which comes out of the throat may be viewed as a withdrawal from the breast. It seems gigantic to the tiny observer, for the adult sees the hallucinated mass to be of extraordinary magnitude, as a baby would view it. The dry, frustrating breast explains the "dry" ocean. A desert (camels are called ships of the desert) is a kind of dry ocean, and a dry moon equally symbolizes a dry breast. Strikingly, the dream screen frequently represents something inedible, "tasteless or even disagreeable to the mouth such as a desert, or other wastes and barren tracts."[50] Through this poem, Aleixandre stresses the relationship of the sea and dryness, as the dry moon fails to respond and the immense sea lies on the dust. The dryness and sand typify thirst sensations, much as a gritty mouth would be projected onto the breast symbol.

Often, in fusing with mother earth, Aleixandre experiences both a pure and holy joy. In "No basta, " from Sombra del paraíso (1944), in which the poet associates the cloud's (breast's) withdrawal with a lost happiness, he tells Mother that only in her bosom "rindo mi bulto, solo en ti me deshago" (PC, 578). The poet's use of deshacer (to vanish or be consumed) in connection with his mother's breast combines pleasant and unhappy memories related in the primitive wish to sleep and join Mother, to be one with her at the breast and in sleep, to lose individual consciousness or ego and thus, in a sense, to die.

La destrucción o el amor (1935) examines more closely a world of mystery and darkness whose basic fabric is erotic love in a universe of unchained telluric forces that may prove fatal to man, absorbing and destroying him. Human love is fleeting and only a final fusion with the earth will prove to be enduring. But one must accept the virgin forests and ferocious beasts and seek salvation in an identification with nature in all its forms, thus affirming rather than denying love for all creation. The limits between flora and fauna disappear in a new unity; the sea's fish appear to be birds; foam is hair; body is ocean; a heart is a mountain. This amorous unity includes poems like "La selva y el mar" (PC, 299-300), involving powerful destructive forces in a formless world in flux where each being wishes existentially to be the other. Through an erotic act they partially discover real essence; for these creatures--tigers, lions, eagles--represent a form of love: "al descubierto en los cuellos allá donde la arteria golpea,/ donde no se sabe si es el amor o el odio / lo que reluce en los blancos colmillos / . . . la cobra que se parece al amor más ardiente."

In other poems Aleixandre suggests that human love and the erotic force of nature are fragments of the same unity, as the poet dissolves in living flesh against a cosmic background where nature is both destroyed and engendered. In "Unidad en ella" Aleixandre clearly states:

> Quiero amor o la muerte, quiero morir del todo,
> ....
> Este beso en tus labios como una lenta espina
> ....
> luz o espada mortal que sobre mi cuello amenaza (PC, 308).

In "Ven siempre, ven" the poet also longs for love or death: "Ven, ven, muerte, amor; ven pronto, te destruyo;/ven, que quiero matar o amar o morir o darte todo" (PC, 316). In "Soy el destino" the poet continues: "Si, te he querido como nunca./ ¿Por qué besar tus labios, si se sabe que la muerte está próxima,/ si se sabe que amar es sólo olvidar la vida?" (PC, 375). In "Sólo morir de día" he again talks of "un amor que destruye" (PC, 386). The poet unifies light, water, and vegetation in a totality of testimony and experience, recreating emotional contexts on a level far beyond poetic reality, an intuition of his moment of creation but originating from ecstatic elements and profound fears of his subconscious.

From his earliest poetry Aleixandre has stressed the concept of limits or boundaries. Perhaps love can save one from society's mask, but to achieve fusion with the earth one must give up limiting structures. A hunger of being in everything impels to that autodestruction; in order to be everything or something one stops being what one really is. Thus Aleixandre sees nature as a physical whole in which violence and love are but two parts of the total picture of the primary forces of life. The poet contemplates the need for fusion and integration in the cosmic scheme of things for a final birth or death; everything attacks, destroys, for life is death.

<u>Mundo a solas</u> (1950) provides us still with tormented love as Aleixandre strives towards a virginal existence of light and purity in the face of an inevitable death which impedes progress to Paradise. In "Bulto sin amor" the poet loves intensely but when he attempts to embrace his loved one it becomes rock, hard, death. "Te amé . . . No sé. No sé que es el amor./ Te padecí gloriosamente como a la sangre misma,/ como el doloroso martillo que hace vivir y mata" (PC, 427). In "Humano ardor," he states that "Morir, morir es tener en los brazos un cuerpo / del que nunca salir se podrá como hombre" (PC, 434).

In <u>Sombra del paraíso</u> the poet continues to explore his limits. He evokes a Paradise where he may find lost happiness, but he must also be conscious of the darkness in his universe of light and beauty. As he recreates his love he achieves only a momentary glimpse of Paradise, not its substance—hence the title. This shadow world clothed in living and beautiful flesh may be an illusion, for purity implies the existence of a less innocent reality. Aleixandre discovers a fleeting virginal beauty in the ephemeral and transient qualities of nature, but he seeks relief from his human condition through love, a familiar human emotion. He communicates thus a poetic double vision, the instinctive one of innocence and the experienced one of adult knowledge, for he knows that his dawn creatures will become human ones for whom fate and death exist. In "El poeta" we learn that sexual energy has not abated, for the poet must still ward off the brutal attack of heavenly birds and face the loss of phallic power: "como se ve brillar el lomo de los calientes peces sin sonido" (PC, 463). Similarly, in "Destino trágico," in an act of love his body falls "espumante en los senos del agua;/vi dos brazos largos surtir de la negra presencia/ y vi vuestra blancura, oí el último grito." In "Poderío de la noche" we see: "Unos labios inmensos cesaron de latir, y en sus bordes aun se ve deshacerse un aliento, una espuma" (PC, 483), as sexual energy leads to dissolution. "Cabellera negra" offers us "Cabello negro, luto donde entierro mi boca,/ oleaje doloroso donde mueren mis besos" (PC, 549); in "Ultimo amor" Aleixandre exclaims: "Amor, amor, tu ciega pesadumbre,/ tu fulgurante gloria me destruye" (PC, 568). Finally, in "Sierpe de amor" (PC, 473-74)[51] the poet, a serpent in Eden, longs to possess the naked, beautiful goddess, but the menace of light from her brow impedes his sliding like a tongue between her living breasts. Yet he penetrates her, bathing in her blood, a celestial destroying fire which will consume him. The serpent, usually associated with negative symbols, here becomes a symbol of both liberating love and death, surrendering to nature, the ultimate reality of the world. The serpent, a shadow, desires to die, that is to become light. To do so he kisses his beloved, mortally biting her, and so both at the same time are victims and vanquished: "Boca con boca muero,/ respirando tu llama que me destruye."

In Nacimiento último (1953) Aleixandre broadens and humanizes his perspectives of love and death. As the title shows, in the mind of the poet death is a final birth, for when man dies he finds his destiny. In a sense the volume marks a natural close to Aleixandre's cosmic cycle, for the only complete love lies in the final act of death, as he continues to seek love and find death: "decía un gemido y enmudecían los labios, / mientras las letras teñidas de un carmín en su boca / destellaban muy débiles, hasta que al fin cesaban" ("El moribundo," PC, 591). Aleixandre himself states: "Si bajo tal mirada la muerte es amorosa destrucción y reintegración unitaria, a ese término, verdadero 'nacimiento último,' está dedicada esta sucesión de poemas finales."[52] The very titles convey the tone; in "Los amantes enterrados" (PC, 596), he reiterates "Siempre atados de amor, sin amor, muertos"; in

"Acabó el amor" (PC, 600) "el amor, si fué puñal instantáneo que desangró mi pecho."

In Historia del corazón (1954) Aleixandre, as he describes historical and existential man, also portrays his own life, desperate and lonely. The poet knows it is the only life he has and he must live it with joy. The collection explores human solidarity, and the poet alleviates his solitude by identifying with the life of the world, finally realizing that he may achieve authenticity through love. Increasingly he also becomes aware of death but faces it stoically. In spite of the more optimistic note, one still encounters a continuing association between Thanatos and Eros. In "Como el vilano" Aleixandre clutches for love but finds it only a shadow of reality; in "Sombra final" (PC, 697) he associates love, "beso / Alma o bulto sin luz, o letal hueso," with death. In "La explosión" love is limited by the experience of one unique afternoon of infinite duration, but as the light dies it is as though life itself is ending: "Y luego en la oscuridad se pierden, y nunca ya se verán" (PC, 764). Finally, in "Mirada final" (PC, 782) Aleixandre recognizes his solitude and death, but he knows that to live, one must die.

In En un vasto dominio (1962) he also sorrows at the thought of man's finality; he views him as a spatial being within a temporal framework but still material of the cosmos in flux. The poet seeks the answer in the vastest of dominions, that of man and his spirit, understood as the condensation and expression of a single material in which everything is integrated irrevocably. As he explores life from birth to death he discovers that reality cannot exist without limits,[53] that "hesitant truth without borders is like a sad stain" (EVD, 48). Aleixandre sees himself in the parts of the body, in man's created objects, but we can also see his desire for youth and love through his recapitulation of those parts. It is now the human protagonist who has assumed a central role in the process of transformation and unification of matter.[54]

Poemas de la consumación (1968) reflects the serene reencounter with Aleixandre's existence, as he returns to the primary and ultimate theme of his entire poetic output, the interrelationship of love, life, and death. Indeed, as one critic has noted, there are "notables puntos de semejanza . . . de algunos poemas . . . de Ambito con otros del último libro de Aleixandre (Poemas de la consumación)."[55] He also reverts to one theme of Historia del corazón, that of old men from whom we can learn as they wait for death and dream of life, of which they are almost no longer a part. Aleixandre continues an inner-directed contemplation of old age and wisdom, seen as sterile and useless because he can only remember and not act;

the poet expresses his sadness for something forever lost and now only half-remembered, the culminating reality of what was hope and a dream of innocence. Wisdom is useless in this confrontation, for youth, exulting in its transitory life, knows that to exist is enough. The poet's wisdom brings not life but death, the only truth. The sea for him is now a symbol of death, dryness, and defeat, but he has not surrendered completely to solitude and separation. Life is time, and man lives within this framework from birth to death. Old men know. The child strives to know. But Aleixandre realizes that words are not enough. They are pretty, but they do not last. In "El poeta se acuerda de su vida" he realizes that words die like the beautiful night or dreams of yore.[56] Once again death, both in the form of knowledge and love, is omnipresent. Aleixandre, presaging the dialogues of his last work, indulges in a continuous conflict, realizing once again the unhappy synergy; as in his earliest works he feels limited, by age now rather than the sick room. His repressions still pass in review, for he thinks of his life as wasted. Consciously he resists these ideas, but they enter in disguised form.

Thanatos and Eros continue to play a significant role. As Leopoldo de Luis states: "La carne es sueño si se la mira . . . pesadilla si se la siente . . . visión si se la huye . . . piedra si se la sueña (consumación y muerte)".[57] In "Como la mar, los besos" Aleixandre notes: "Como un alga tus besos./ Mágicos en la luz, pues muertos tornan" (PdC, 30); in "Visión juvenil desde otros años" he writes: "el mundo rodando,/ . . . es cual un beso, /aun después que aquel muere" (PdC, 32). Old age finds it difficult to accept love and life; living is loving and being loved. In "Supremo fondo" we see the sea "muy seca, cual su seno, y volada./ Su recuerdo son peces putrefactos al fondo/ . . . miramos a los que aman ya muertos" (PdC, 50); in "Cueva de noche" a kiss becomes "oscuridad final que cubre en noche definitiva / tu luminosa aurora/ . . . mi aurora funeral que en noche se abre" (PdC, 83). In this collection then, filled with mouth, lips, kisses, and love--a love vanished with the fires of youth--death and love combine, for "Soy quien finó, quien pronunció tu nombre / como forma / mientras moría" ("Presente, después," PdC, 103).

Aleixandre's Diálogos del conocimiento consists of 14 poems in which two people talk, without listening to one another, in a kind of free association on the conflict between living and thought. Love and death form part of the knowledge the poet had from the beginning, and he continues to connect sensuality, love and death. For Guillermo Carnero, "El amor es, para Aleixandre, junto a las manifestaciones de los sentidos, una necesidad, desde la ignorancia de conocer."[58] Also, says José Olivio Jiménez, in this collection Aleixandre continues the "irracionalismo expresivo que conociamos en Aleixandre desde sus años de juventud."[59] Aleixandre again postulates a kind of destruction or love in these dialogues. One speaker always talks of hope and liberty, struggle and doubt; the other of fatality, desolation, and renunciation. Aleixandre wants to know the meaning of life and living, but his speakers, unable to communicate, speak only to themselves. These dialogues resemble the manic-depressive state; on the one hand libidinal impulses have access to consciousness; on the other, everything tends to the negation of life.

Aleixandre calls dynamic knowledge <u>conocer</u>, 'to become acquainted with,' and static knowledge is <u>saber</u>, but sometimes, as in the first dialogue, even <u>conocer</u> means death. Conocer involves sensation and seeking, difficult for those possessing knowledge. Yet to know, <u>saber</u>, is to die.[60] Thus, to recall the fixed and limited past is to die. Again we see the paradox that one looks backward (toward death) while looking forward to life, reaffirming once more the central role of Eros (life), identical to Thanatos (death), a conclusion which is also a beginning.

<u>Diálogos del conocimiento</u> offers a refinement and restatement of previous collections. In <u>En un vasto dominio</u> Aleixandre commented: "Boca que acaso supo / y conoció, o no sabe, porque no conocer es saber último: ("Amarga boca," EVD), 58). In these dialogues he also reemphasizes his previous identification with the cosmos, associating real objects with a strange reality of size or dimension in order to escape the circumscribing and imprisoning knowledge, his own preoccupations with a reality he would rather not face. In "Sonido de la guerra" Aleixandre mentions "my mineral body"; in "Después de la guerra" he stresses that the stars' light "is flesh like mine"; in "Misterio de la muerte del toro" he perceives in his hand "the order of some star." He also reviews his concept of death as a force attracting life. In "Sonido de la guerra" blood lives only when it struggles to flow forth, but if it does, it dies: "Sólo sobre unos labios coloridos,/ . . . se adivina / el bulto de la sangre. Y el amante puede besar y presentir, sin verla!" (DC, 13). For the old lovers in the dialogue by that name, "Conocer es amar. Saber, morir. Dudé. Nunca el amor es vida" (DC, 26). The inquisitor in "El inquisidor, ante el espejo" associates Eros and Thanatos, "Luto de amor o muerte" (DC, 56), as does the dandy in "Diálogo de los enajenados," who exclaims: ". . . amar desnudo es bello, . . . como los huesos conjugados de los amantes. Muertos. / Muertos, pues, que se estrechan. Lo que suena es el hueso" (DC, 65). "Los amantes jóvenes" reinforces the idea: "donde mis labios tocan, no su verdad, su muerte" (DC, 85). Finally in "Quien

baila se consuma" we discover "Un montón de lujuria, pero extinto, en la sombra" (DC, 146).

"Después de la guerra" contemplates the end of the planet, again an earth without human beings except, temporarily, two survivors, an old man and a girl. He knows that even "el alba ha muerto" (DC, 77); she exclaims: "Cómo germina el día entre mis senos" (DC, 78). She believes in the future; he knows that tomorrow has already past. In "La sombra" Aleixandre contemplates solitude as pleasure and man as a dream who creates nothing but the dream within which he is consumed. In the poem the boy once more returns to Mother earth: "A ti vuelvo, y a solas, y me entierro en tu seno" (DC, 131). Aleixandre continues to play with the concept of love and life, claiming that he who lives loves, but he who knows has already lived. To be young is to live, but one who never loved was never even born. Even the destroyers of life grow old. The soldier was young but now is old. The magician who once put the poison of not being in his brews is himself now alone in a world where nature itself has fled.

In his pursuit of ultimate knowledge of reality Aleixandre juxtaposes stubborn existential awareness with a vague transcendental intuition, visualizing love and death as coordinating elements of the universe, although love is still a metaphor of self-destruction. The poet knows that he cannot conquer death but nonetheless wants to live life to the full, for loving is an endless process in a fleeting world which leads to personal death; thus he continues to seek for love, for knowledge, for truth, and for hope. One finds, therefore, a continuing juxtaposition of incongruities in a vast dominion, an ambivalent psychological universe in which, essentially, the early anguish at limits imposed upon activity and creativity is once more reinforced in a continuing interplay of renovation and conservation. Aleixandre, inspired by the same enigmas that beset us all, through his irrational imagery imaginatively challenges his readers' established preconceptions as he seeks to recapture an unconscious knowledge and create a unity of perception. In the final analysis we may read into his personal vision of experience and inner emotions a communication of deeper significance, seeking those moral and psychological imperatives which constitute their human quality.

Notes

[1] Dámaso Alonso, *Poetas españoles contemporáneos* (Madrid: Gredos, 1952), p. 287.

[2] Ricardo Gullón, "Itinerario poético de Vicente Aleixandre," *Papeles de Son Armadans*, XI, Nos. 32-33 (1958), 197.

[3] Carlos Bousoño, *La poesía de Vicente Aleixandre* (Madrid: Gredos, 1968), p. 208.

[4] José Luis Cano, in Vicente Aleixandre, *Espadas como labios-La destrucción o el amor* (Madrid: Ed. Castalia, 1972), p. 20.

[5] Luis Antonio de Villena, in Vicente Aleixandre, *Pasión de la tierra* (Madrid: Narcea, 1976), p. 32.

[6] Luis Antonio de Villena, *Insula*, Nos. 368-69 (1977), 8.

[7] Guillermo Carnero, "Ambito como proyecto del surrealismo aleixandrino," *Insula*, No. 337 (1974), 12.

[8] Angel del Río, "La poesía surrealista de Aleixandre," *Revista Hispánica Moderna*, II (1935), 21.

[9] Francisco Carenas and Alfredo Gómez Gil, "En torno a Vicente Aleixandre," *Cuadernos Hispanoamericanos*, No. 270 (1972), 566.

[10] Leopoldo de Luis, "Vicente Aleixandre: Antología total," *Cuadernos Hispanoamericanos*, No. 310 (1976), 218.

[11] Alberto Monterde, *La poesía pura en la lírica española* (Mexico: Impta. Universitaria, 1953), p. 105.

[12] Luis Cernuda, *Estudios sobre poesía española contemporanea* (Madrid: Ediciones Guadarrama, 1957), pp. 195-96.

[13] André Breton, *Manifestes du surrealisme* (Paris: Pauvert, 1962), p. 40.

[14] Vicente Aleixandre, *Mis poemas mejores* (Madrid: Gredos, 1961), p. 11.

[15] Fernando Charry Lara, *Cuatro poetas del siglo veinte* (Bogotá: Universidad Nacional de Colombia, 1947), p. 31.

[16] Vicente Aleixandre, "Funeral," in *Antología total* (Barcelona: Seix Barral, 1975), p. 348.

[17] Vicente Aleixandre, Mis poemas mejores, p. 11.

[18] Ibid., p. 10.

[19] Ibid., p. 31.

[20] Juan José Domenchina, Antología de la poesía española contemporánea (Mexico: UTEHA, 1947), p. 391.

[21] Max Aub, La poesía española contemporánea (Mexico: Impta. Universitaria, 1954), pp. 156-59.

[22] Dámaso Alonso, Poetas españoles contemporáneos, p. 323.

[23] Vicente Aleixandre, La destrucción o el amor (Madrid: Alhambra, 1945), p. 17.

[24] Ibid., pp. 17-18.

[25] Vicente Aleixandre, Mis poemas mejores, p. 31.

[26] Vicente Aleixandre, En un vasto dominio (Madrid: Revista de Occidente, 1962), pp. 13-16. Further citations in the text are to this edition, hereafter referred to as EVD.

[27] Vicente Aleixandre, Diálogos del conocimiento (Barcelona: Plaza y Janes, 1967), p. 97. Further references in the text are to this edition, hereafter cited as DC.

[28] André Breton, Manifestes du surrealisme, pp. 15ff.

[29] Paul Ilie, The Surrealist Mode in Spanish Literature (Ann Arbor: The University of Michigan Press, 1968), pp. 43-44 concurs that Aleixandre is "concerned only with his own reality which consists of the way he articulates his feelings with the raw material of the outer world."

[30] Ibid., p. 45.

[31] Vicente Aleixandre, Mis poemas mejores, p. 10.

[32] Vicente Aleixandre, Poesías completas (Madrid: Aguilar, 1960), p. 91. Further references in the text are to this edition, hereafter cited as PC.

[33] As Carlos Bousoño states: "Si amor es destrucción, amor, cólera y odio pueden confundirse en la mentalidad aleixandrina." See La poesia de Vicente Aleixandre, p. 70.

[34] Frederick Clark Prescott, The Poetic Mind (New York: Macmillan, 1926), p. 276.

[35] Sigmund Freud, *The Standard Edition of the Complete Works of Freud* (London: Hogarth Press, 1961), XIX, 42.

[36] Sigmund Freud, "Formulations of the Two Principles of Mental Functioning," in *The Standard Edition* (London: Hogarth, 1958), XII, 224.

[37] These lines were used by Carlos Bousoño in a lecture on Aleixandre's technique sponsored by the Spanish Institute (New York, Nov. 19, 1977).

[38] Carl Jung, *Psychology of the Unconscious* (New York: Dodd, Mead & Co., 1944), p. 237.

[39] Ernest Jones, "The Psychology of Religion," in *Psychoanalysis Today*, ed. Sandor Lorenz (New York: International Univ. Press, 1944), p. 317.

[40] Paul Ilie, pp. 40-56, devotes an entire chapter to this aspect of Aleixandre's imagery.

[41] Alejandro Amusco, "El motivo erótico en *Espadas como labios* de Vicente Aleixandre," *Insula*, No. 361 (1976), 11.

[42] See Bertram D. Lewin, *The Psychoanalysis of Elation* (New York: Norton, 1950), p. 104.

[43] Ibid., p. 48.

[44] Otto Isakower, "A Contribution to the Patho-Psychology of Phenomena Associated with Falling Asleep," *International Journal of Psychoanalysis*, XIX (1938), 331-45.

[45] Bertram D. Lewin, "Sleep, the Mouth, and the Dream Screen," *The Psychoanalytic Quarterly*, XI (1946), 420.

[46] Bertram D. Lewin, "Reconsiderations of the Dream Screen," *The Psychoanalytic Quarterly*, XXII (1953), 174-99.

[47] Géza Roheim, *Gates of the Dream* (New York: International University Press, 1952), p. 347.

[48] Isakower, p. 340.

[49] Lewin, *Psychoanalysis of Elation*, p. 112.

[50] Lewin, "Reconsiderations," p. 187.

[51] Vicente Cabrera, Tres poetas a la luz de la metáfora (Madrid: Gredos, 1975), pp. 120-22 has a good discussion of this poem.

[52] Vicente Aleixandre, Mis poemas mejores, p. 153.

[53] For a good discussion of this collection see José Olivio Jiménez, Cinco poetas del tiempo (Madrid: Insula, 1964).

[54] For an elucidation of this point see José Angel Valente, "Vicente Aleixandre: la visión de la totalidad," Indice de Artes y Letras, XVII (1963), 29-30.

[55] Vicente Molina-Foix, "Vicente Aleixandre: 1924-1969," Cuadernos Hispanoamericanos, No. 242 (1970), 282.

[56] Vicente Aleixandre, Poemas de la consumación, (Barcelona: Plaza y Janés, 1974), p. 82. Further citations in the text are to this edition, hereafter referred to as PdC.

[57] Leopoldo de Luis, "Poemas de la consumación," Cuadernos Hispanoamericanos, No. 231 (1969), 718.

[58] Guillermo Carnero, "Conocer y saber en Poemas de la consumación y Diálogos del conocimiento de Vicente Aleixandre," Cuadernos Hispanoamericanos, No. 276 (1973), 574.

[59] José Olivio Jiménez, "Aleixandre y sus Diálogos del conocimiento," Insula, No. 331 (1974), 1.

[60] For a good study of conocer-saber see Guillermo Carnero, Cuadernos Hispanoamericanos, No. 276, 571-79.

SYMBOLIC LIPS IN THE EARLY POETRY OF
VICENTE ALEIXANDRE

In Aleixandre's poetry the process of cosmic fusion, love, light, and death involves his senses and his body in an intimate union, for he feels the night and the light in his mouth and on his lips. Through his constant reflection of the physical, involving many components of the human body, he expresses his evasion or confrontation, despair or affirmation, life and death, or light and darkness.[1]

In Aleixandre's system of symbols, the lips seem to be his particular preoccupation and his most poetically persuasive multivalent representation. They are, I believe, the key to understanding the poet's continuing battle against reality, his contradictions, and his cosmic love affair because they involve the projection of pure feeling and communication. Many poets use physical imagery to convey non-physical concerns, but few, if any, have made it such an overwhelming presence, both in its metaphysical expression and as a reflection of poetic communication.

In Aleixandre's poetry negation becomes affirmation as he acknowledges the ambivalences of existence which divide us while at the same time recognizing their communion as part of a totality, the unity of love as an approach to the absolute. In his Royal Academy entrance speech on love and poetry he stated: "A veces pensamos que el amor existe, pero fuera del hombre, como existe la luz que lo manifiesta, y que el hombre penosamente lo imita como un remedo, como una sombra en medio de la radiante, de la misteriosa Creación revelada . . . Más vale dejar de amar, muriendo, que vivir muerto por el sufrimiento de amor . . . Cada amador oscuramente lo incorpora, cuando no luminosamente lo intuye."[2] Aleixandre elsewhere comments on words as building bricks in poetic composition, defining the best poetry as emotion rather than beauty, and poetry itself as "una forma del conocimiento amoroso" (OC, II, pp. 667-69). The dichotomy between feeling and communication can be seen in Aleixandre's associations which reflect a disharmony between the conscious and the unconscious, the Apollonian and the Dionysian, as opposing elements which remain unresolved, swords like lips, destruction or love, old age and youth, love and hate, good and evil, life and death.

Lips, by definition part of an erotic anatomy and a channel for childhood pleasures, as used in Aleixandre's images quite often seem to involve memory traces of a remote preverbal period. The poet strives for visual forms, involving light and shadow, to express a stage of consciousness involving pure feeling. Difficult to put into words, they are, perhaps, menemonic traces of an infancy when these sensations fused with visual images which, in his poetry, he seems to transform into metaphorical or hypnagogic ones.³ Lips provide the instrument for this combination of love, the pre-verbal, non-linguistic feeling, and communication, specifically linguistic and involving the use of language to convey poetic imagery. One of the constant behavior patterns of children involves their sucking habits, an auto-erotic phenomenon according to Freud, and a function important for the preservation of life. This sucking for nourishment is associated with "an erotogenic zone, the mucous membrane of the lips . . . The . . . lips must, moreover, possess an erotogenic quality, which fluctuates in intensity . . ."[4]

Also, as René A. Spitz has shown, "the oral cavity with its equipment of tongue, lips . . . is the first surface in life to be used for tactile perception and exploration. It is well suited for this purpose, for in it are represented the sense of touch, of taste, of temperature, of smell, of pain, and even of deep sensitivity, as the latter will be involved in the act of swallowing."[5] Aleixandre in his poetic creativity and introspection seems, at times, to combine imagery of an early sensuousness which stresses modalities of sight and touch with pictorial images which reflect later experiences. This may account for his almost obsessive interest in limits and the difficulty of poetic communication. Many authors experience a dichotomy between feeling and language. For Aleixandre, a poetry without polarity may be impossible because his poetry depends on a primitive affect which precedes all abstraction and which may account for his emphasis on intuition, half-glimpsed reality, and chiaroscuro.

In Ambito, drained of life, he is unable to identify his poetry with his love but still wants to convey the former, even if he cannot give the latter. Indeed, the very act of communication is the reflection of love rather than love itself, and the attempt to describe it changes and kills it:

> Obra de amor tejida sin ensueño:
> sombra fresca, no verde, que hace a gusto
> siesta a los ojos, blancos más los dientes.
> Paréntesis oprimen las palabras.
> Rojos de vida en carne suavemente
> meta, carmín, jugosos les openen:
> palabras que se tocan con los labios,
> desfallecen y mueren, besos lisos
> dando al pasar cayendo sin sonido. (OC, "Cabeza, en el recuerdo," p. 120)

Aleixandre has always been intrigued by the ideas of limiting forces. In Pasión de la tierra, hoping to break the limits of form, he explores, in a final kiss, "los límites con mis labios, repasando las solas fronteras a que puedo alargarme . . ." (OC, p. 227), an image he repeats in Espadas como labios where he wants to dissolve the limits:

> Esa senda hecha para la planta de oro,
> también para los labios,
> para recorrerla despacio,
> para ir diciendo los nombres a los horizontes,
> para que todo lo más en un momento de desfalle-
> cimiento se pueda uno convertir en río.   (OC, "Libertad,:
> p. 304)

Although a meaningful communication may transcend limits, it is difficult to achieve. Aleixandre's ambivalence affects his ability to communicate meaningfully in human terms,[6] but he wants the warmth of love and life, to distinguish the loving kiss given by lips from the effort to pronounce the name of things. Converted into a snail, he warns:

> que sepas . . . que mi voz no es la tuya
> y que cuando solloces tu garganta
> sepa distinguir todavía
> mi beso de tu esfuerzo
> por pronunciar los nombres con mi lengua.
> Porque yo voy a decirte todavía,
> porque tú pisas caracoles
> que aguardaban oyendo mis dos labios.   (OC, "La palabra",
> pp. 248-49)

Aleixandre does not divorce words from their meaning, but no words exist to express pure affect. In any event, however significant, they can recall only the memory and not the real passion involved; thus Aleixandre is restricted in communicating by the limits words impose. Once love is gone, it cannot be repeated, nor can human tongue depict reality, any more than a raging storm above can reflect the calm and repose below, "palabra entre dos labios" (OC, "Tempestad arriba," p. 293). The poet tries to shut out conflicting stimuli created by a magical world of strange forces in constant flux and involving human changes, hoping he can bring order: "Cada cosa debe estar en su sitio . . . si sello mis labios y me hago impenetrable a las preguntas de peces fríos" (OC, "Cada cosa, cada cosa," pp. 311-13). By doing so, he achieves a kind of truth and reality:

> Todo está bien. Pero está mejor ser de verdad
> Ser de verdad lo que es, lo que es solo.

> Por ejemplo, "esperanza".
> Por ejemplo, "estepario".
> Todo lo que realmente tiene un sentido. (OC, p. 313)

In <u>Mundo a solas</u> Aleixandre rejects the dream for reality, which may involve a love beyond the physical but which needs lips to utter words and to give a kiss of love, words which may construct an illusion, lips which may create images which blur the distinction between the natural world of beauty and the daily dying of man in a socially indifferent world. In seeking to define his human love affair with nature, the poet can use only his poor human mouth and acknowledges that his lips convey not words but only their dream image:

> A veces me pregunto si tu cuerpo es un ave.
> . . .
>
> pero siempre te estrecho como voz entre labios.
> Besarte es pronunciarte, oh dicha, oh dulce fuego dicho.
> Besarte es pronunciarte como un calor que del pecho surtiera,
> una dulce palabra que en la noche relumbra
> . . .
>
> Tus labios son esa suave tristeza que ciega cuando alguien pone su pobre boca humana;
> eran, no una palabra,
> sino su sueño mismo,
> su imperioso mandato que castiga con beso
> . . .
>
> Pero yo te acaricio sabiendo que la vida resiste
> más que el fuego
> que unos dientes se besan, se besan aun sin labios
> y que, hermosa o terrible, aves enfurecidas
> entre pestañas vuelan, y cantan, o aún me llaman. (OC, "Humano Ardor," pp. 451-52)

Aleixandre projects a torment of emotion, expressing, through mouth and lips, a love for woman, human and mortal, but also for a larger entity, even in its destructive aspects, but he suffers a sense of his own impotence as he sings, "tus dientes feroces sin palabras" (OC, "Tormento de amor," p. 469).

The poet realizes the difficulty of orientation in a world where a breast, a heart, or a tree may seem identical, a universe of:

> labios mudos, extremos, veleidades de la sangre,
> corazones marchitos como mujeres sucias,
> como laberintos donde nadie encuentra su postrer ilusión
> su volada palabra
> . . .
> rompiendo con la frente los ramajes nervudos,
> la prohibición de seguir en nombre de la ley,
> los torrentes de risa, de dientes o de ramos de cieno,
> de palabras machacadas por unas muelas rotas;
> limando con el cuerpo el límite del aire,
> sintiendo sobre la carne las ramas tropicales,
> los abrazos, las yedras, los millones de labios,
> esas ventosas últimas que hace el mundo besando.   (OC, "Nadie," pp. 476-77)

Part of Aleixandre's attempts to communicate involves light, one of the most important components of his poetry. It expresses his spiritual resurrection, his cosmic love affair, happiness, and occurs in his works in a variety of combinations. Often, he feels the final kiss of the setting sun, which obviously sustains life on earth with its life-giving rays, but also implies its negative characteristics. Since nature is the context for Aleixandre's poetic truth, part of which involves the search for life and happiness, the relationship between avid lips which kiss and love and the light which kisses the earth seems clear enough. As day fades into night, lips become more anxious than ever to possess the light, to create their own life:

> La inocencia reclama su candor
> (bajo un monte una luna o lo esperado)
> la inocencia está muda . . .
> aquí en esta muralla están las letras.   (OC, "El frío," p. 294)

We see that Aleixandre, a solitary being, contemplates a nature with which he cannot truly communicate, a loving world, weighing on his lips, which nonetheless rejects his poetry as words mashed by broken molars, for poetry and communication may be mutually exclusive. In any event, the poet's act of communication, involving heterogeneous and apparently contradictory elements, must come from his lips:

> Acariciar unos senos de nácar,
> una caja respira y duele todo,
> acariciar esta oculta ceniza,
> bajo carmín tus labios suspirando
> . . .
> cuando la luz escape sin notarse.   (Ibidem)

Night, naturally, implies the presence of the moon but paradoxically also hints at an impatient dawn to come later. In La destrucción o el amor the moon may, of course, unjustly close the eyes of one fatigued with life but may also be a sign of the glory of the human body and of continuing love: "Unos labios lucientes, labios de luna pálida,/ labios hermanos . . . signo de amor en la vida vacía . . . Es la luz o su gema fulgurante: los labios" (OC, "Triunfo del amor," pp. 385-86). In this poem love conquers night, and in other poems in this volume night light becomes an amorous breathing form, desired by a living poet. Moonlight reflects the amorous being, the other face of a virginal daily renewed sunlight; it also recalls nights of love when the poet's lips drank the pure light. Since the world is in a constant flux, chiaroscuro best reflects the transformations, the constant interchange and relationships between light and darkness which interact as they mutually modify one another.

Aleixandre quite often uses this association of the light of love on his lips with the grace and airiness, the feeling of happiness conveyed by the winged flight of birds, to be enjoyed and not explained. In Espadas como labios the thought of being and not being, a prophecy of kisses, and a smiling countryside relate to a dreamless hand, the size of "un ave, unos labios" (OC, "Silencio," p. 255). In La destrucción o el amor, he relates a happy kiss to a dove, a whiteness in his hand; the heat of the day to "el ala peinada por los labios ya vivos;" and the love in his mouth, an indestructible kiss, to wings, for his love of warmth and light is like the last bird (OC, "Hay más," p. 428). The world may reflect a love of shining kisses like a wake of light in the air or the passion of a star-filled night. In Ambito Aleixandre views the night as a piece of fruit ready to burst as he sinks his red lips in it: "Mis rojos labios la sorben./ Hundo en su yema mis dientes. Toda mi boca se llena de amor . . ." (OC, "Posesión," p. 172). The light on his tongue identifies both the burning pulp of night with which he achieves union and the growing taste of dawn, a continuation of the poet's eternal vacillation between the polarities of hope and despair, as the light plays on his beloved's body.[8] Aleixandre fuses with the erotic feminine night, necessarily human and sensual, but which may be both protective and threatening.

Pasión de la tierra is filled with the contrast between light and darkness, conveyed through the lips. In "El silencio" the moon awakens a desire for love difficult to fulfill: "No quiero saber si los labios son una larga línea blanca" (OC, p. 194), as the poet awaits a radiant dawn; in "La forma y no el infinito" white roses welcome the arrival of night, and light and darkness intermingle. The poet is the night, "sombra que no tiene labios," and, limited by it, "labios . . . soledades que aguardan," continues to search for life and love (OC, p. 198). In "Sobre tu pecho unas letras," since the time for kisses has not arrived, "dejando mis dos labios insensibles," he awakens each morning with blue lips, aspiring to a happiness found in the loving light of day but prepared by the non-amorous light of night (OC, pp. 212-213). In La destrucción o el amor Aleixandre contrasts the silence where the blood of life is never seen with the heat which "por los labios se bebe" (OC, "No busques, no," pp. 325-26). The poet contrasts the blue of the night with the loving light of day. Moon and night have made little impression on his senses, but the poet fuses the amorous unity of a physical presence with the night to achieve sensation. In "Sobre la misma tierra" we find:

> Esa subida lenta del crepúsculo más rosado,
> crecimiento de escamas en que la frialdad es viscosa
> es el roce de un labio independiente
> sobre la tierra húmeda
> . . .
>
> La noche solo es un traje.
> No sirve rechazar juncos alegando que se trata de dientes
> . . .
>
> o que el fango son palabras deshechas,
> masticadas después de amor
> . . .
>
> Mejor sería entonces
> . . .
>
> ver si allá se comprueba lo que ya es tan sabido que la
> noche y el
> día no son lo negro o lo blanco
> sino la boca misma que duerme entre las rocas
> cuyo alterno respiro
> no es el beso o el no beso,
> sino el polvo que llueve sobre la tierra mísera. (OC, pp. 387-89)

Aleixandre may rationalize, but reality thrusts itself upon him in the guise of life and death, light and darkness, fruition and sterility. In truth, night is not necessarily a time of sadness after the suffused yellow light of day. Silence loses its opacity but acquires its own special vibrations. In a continuous process, matter struggles to take human form.

One of the primary associations of chiaroscuro (again seen in conjunction with lips) concerns Aleixandre's constant longing to be, combined with a fear of not being. Although seeking love and light, as opposed to death and darkness, he admits that death can also be a rebirth, a force which attracts life, a joy and awakening. Death may take many forms but the poet relates it to liberty, doubt, life and the reality of the world. In the struggle between light and darkness, the latter often triumphs. In Pasión de la tierra, in "Del color de la nada," the sun sings in a high register and lips turn to gold; the sun of summer gives light and life in a night of scattered mannequins, symbolizing the sterility of existence, which offer their nakedness in a world of inevitable death. Darkness gives a thematic coloration to his cosmos, but, as he says in "El crimen o imposible," he cannot remember whether day comes before night or its light from his own body. Blood does not flow as it should, its light like a torrent leaving spent lips, but Aleixandre will not shed tears at a lack of true perception if "ese halo por los labios, ese resplandor que todos esperabais . . . al cabo me consumiera, dejándome convertido en un proyecto abandonado." One's ending cannot be discovered no matter how one strives for life and love, and in the fusion of day and night, not mutually incompatible, he seeks to earn back the world of innocence which, on that dark winter day, remains indecipherable (OC, pp. 208-09). Within the opaque labyrinth of night, with the natural changes from light to darkness and back to light, the original outlines of objective reality lose distinguishing features. Night, a transitory phase of a hallucinatory universe, may be dangerous. Aleixandre, beneath the moon, plays at life and love, as a death-dealing wind, in "El solitario," sweeps away the cards. Night gives way to day and the kisses of light; the ace of clubs, falsely conveying youth and love, cannot bring life any more than the final card, but lips may bring one to death: "Acaso yo pondré los labios sin miedo a la espina más honda" (OC, pp. 218-20). Lips, nonetheless, convey the possibility of renewed life, of non-permanent goodbyes, of hope and solace: "¡Qué espejo cóncavo recogió el corazón como los labios y dejó su sonrisa en la esquina difícil, allí donde la flor dejada anteanoche era del color de la espera . . . Quiero dormir cansado. Quiero encontrar aquí, en el hueco apercibido, ese caparazón liso donde cantar apoyando mis dos labios" (OC, "Ser de esperanza y lluvia," pp. 187-88). Lips may also offer salvation. The poet seeks fusion with the life-giving sun which gives flame to what was ash, and spiritual union with the light of eternal life, also death, through the kiss of God's lips: "Labios de dios besadme, salvadme de . . . mi ceniza desmoronándose" (OC, p. 238).

In La destrucción o el amor the poet continues his search for the reality of love, again involving lip symbolism:

> Todo pasa.
> La realidad transcurre
> como un pájaro alegre.
> Me lleva entre sus alas
> como pluma ligera.
> Me arrebata a la sombra, a la luz, al divino contagio.
> Me hace pluma ilusoria
> que cuando pasa ignora el mar que al fin ha podido:
> esas aguas espesas que como labios negros ya borran lo distinto
> (OC, "Después de la muerte," p. 328)

Hemmed in by the limits of life and the reality of nature, Aleixandre must contend with light and shadow in seeking truth and certainty. He seeks love in a risky temporal and spatial framework: "Así besándote despacio ahogo un pájaro . . . batiendo mientras me olvido de los dientes bajo tus labios" (OC, "Mañana no viviré," p. 346). In "A la muerte" he links the memory of the escaping night with the noise of day about to be born between his lips, a light which smilingly arrives, in "La luz," "como unos labios de arriba . . . que brillan . . . luz que llegas todavía como dicha por unos labios" (OC, pp. 365-66). Light also gives pain; in its reflection of the duality of life and death it speaks to Aleixandre: "Duele la cicatriz de la luz,/ duele en el suelo la misma sombra de los dientes./ . . . donde palomas blancas como sangre/ pasan bajo la piel sin pararse en los labios/ a hundirse en las entrañas con sus alas cerradas" ("Humana voz," OC, p. 367). In a number of poems he continues to stress that death is necessary for complete love, associating the thought with both lips and chiaroscuro.[9] Heaven and earth exchange a radiance which the poet feels on his real lips as real love, though he senses the radiance may also enclose a dark message of death as it withdraws. In "Se querían" the lovers:

> Sufrían por la luz, labios azules en la madrugada
> labios saliendo de la noche dura
> labios partidos, sangre, ¿sangre donde?
> Se querían en un lecho navío, mitad noche, mitad luz
> . . .
>
> entre las duras piedras. . .
> duras como los besos de diente a diente solo. (OC, p. 424)

Loving lips cloud the inevitable fatality of a closed system, of a harsh night or death, as Aleixandre interlaces textures of light and shadow, combining material and spiritual landscapes of "Día, noche, ponientes, madrugadas, espacios /. . . metal, música, labio, silencio, vegetal, / mundo, quietud, su forma . . ." (OC, pp. 424-25). Intense light contrasts with the foreboding darkness, part of a vast equation of terrestrial and metaphysical reality.

Mundo a solas contributes a number of variations to the thematic development of the life-death concept. In "Ya no es posible" the tragic moon casts its shadw on a loveless world where kisses break against harsh walls as the poet tries to grasp a rose of fire "y acercarla a unos labios de carne que abrasen" (OC, pp. 456-57); similarly the hot harsh sun of "El sol victorioso" "atiranta los labios," conquering night with its destructive clarifying ray. In "Filo del amor" the poet identifies light with love "como dos labios reales que en el cielo se extienden," again seeing the reality of nature as encompassing an act of love. His beloved's nubile form fuses with that nature which may bring happiness with its light, also a knife which divides and destroys (OC, pp. 463-64).[10] The light in these poems, a metaphor of purely erotic physical pleasure, also relates to metaphysical implications. Aleixandre's ambivalence, his alternation between pleasure and pain, rises from his exposure to temporal and libidinal forces, the fear and foreboding of an impending death. Light may signify a world of illusion and life; darkness an eternal reality. Chiaroscuro bridges these metaphysical considerations and together with lip symbolism allows the poet to project both a positive and disillusioned world view. Although light offers life and darkness death, the poet feels both on his lips, reflective not of a despairing cosmos but rather of a universe whose motivating force is love. The poet's quest for clarity and light and its association with the shadows of night relate to the amorous relationship so much as part of him and whose totality includes life and death, doubt and despair, hope and salvation.

Love for Aleixandre turns out to be a self-transcending force. His trembling lips touch those of his beloved; he feels her body close to his; he sees her smile. Quite often the fusion between the human presence and the natural one is so seamless that we are not aware whether he is embracing nature or his loved one. His love may occasionally be narcissistic, but he accepts it as an aspect of an interwoven mosaic, never defined or fixed but always an eternal becoming. Whether one wishes to interpret the related emphasis on lips as stemming from pregenital and autoerotic factors, including the all-important alimentary orifice, or more conscious considerations, one may conclude that his displacement and distancing of that love represent a subconscious evasion from the physical to the safer cosmic. Love may arouse anxiety and be threatening, but the poet cannot survive without it, beyond the sensory contact, and he searches always for a future unfulfilled. In Espadas como labios the poet flees from the ordinary world of limits. In "Cada cosa, cada cosa" a cousin might reveal her thighs to his lips, but in "El más bello amor" his love assumes a more unusual, passionate and threatening coloration. His possessive anxiety, beyond life and death, is for a love which resembles a shark's voracity, a mouth, akin to a bestial fruit which involves "todo lo que musitan unos labios que adoro" (OC, p. 270). Apparently, Aleixandre's attempt at intellectual self-protection surrenders, here, to a contradictory emotional representation. La destrucción o el amor, of course, is his declaration to the world of his cosmic love affair, not all of whose elements involve the association of eros and thanatos. In "Noche sinfónica" breasts in the form of a harp hide their kiss, and lips perform an arpeggio of water; in "Ven, ven tú" nature accepts and rejects the ebb and flow of love: "Un pájaro dorado por la luz que no acaba / busca siempre unos labios por donde huir de su cárcel / . . . este aliento que sale de unos labios entreabiertos / . . . esta carne que amo con mis besos de aire" (OC, pp. 347-48). The poet loves all nature, its soft caresses like a yellow bird asleep between his lips, because the world, composed of many elements, is one material in which light, moon, and rain accept the poet's loving lips in his exploration of the limits and meaning of his universe. Thus in "Verbena" he unites a "muchacha conocida" with all aspects of nature, singing of "un beso silencioso que se enreda / . . . de los labios se escapan flores verdes / . . . ese clamor caliente ciñe faldas / del tamaño de labios apretados" (OC, pp. 397-98). And so Aleixandre continues his equation of human and cosmic love whose kisses reside in secret breasts and eternal lips.

Aleixandre's poems may be viewed as analogues of his psychological journey from repressed sexuality, annihilation, evasion, despair, and death to an affirmation of life and love, a striving toward light in order to escape from the dark forces at the center of existence. Aleixandre contrasts and coalesces this longing for life and yearning for eternity in a cosmic love affair. He expresses himself through all living things in the world as a kind of blind impelling force which leads to the recognition of the will to live and resisting forces which have as their essence a never-satisfied want. The drive for love (and by implication, life) and the impulse to destruction and darkness seem mutually dependent in his poetry. Thus, from the beginning, Aleixandre seeks to light up his world and reinforce life with his love, even though it may involve "unos labios que irritan" in a world dead to his pleas (OC, Espadas como labios, "Suicidio," p. 301). One can feel the force of love and life as one awakens in the morning," una rosa en los labios . . . unos labios pegados mientras los muslos cantan" (OC, La destrucción o el amor, "Juventud," p. 353). So love, a part of life, inevitably forms part of death, undoubtedly Aleixandre's most persistent equation, previously mentioned, since both are aspects of a cosmic unity or totality and an aspect of his transcendental goals. Eros then is simply another facet of thanatos or death against which it is constantly juxtaposed. Louis M. Bourne sees the erotic transmutation as a spiritualization and admits: "On a metaphysical level, Aleixandre's imagined union with some aspect of nature can lead to moments when death and life are equally appreciated and the dichotomy between them is resolved."[11] From first volume to last Aleixandre equates love and death, bestowing a central role to the lips. Pasión de la tierra concentrates on love's destructive force as part of earth and fire. The taste of death on his beloved's lips clouds with thoughts of death the otherwise passionate arousal offered by her charms. Thus, in poems like "La muerte o antesala de consulta," death becomes the words of love themselves on the lips of the poet, and he openly embraces it as an aspect of the anteroom of salvation, the antidote for despair. In "El amor no es relieve," an amorous caress turns into the frightening clutch of death, and a sea of blood becomes "este beso estrellado sobre tus labios." Blood, of course, may be an integral part of both life and death, a dichotomy he senses as he kisses her, "Te amo, te amo, no te amo. Tierra y fuego en tus labios saben a muerte perdida" (OC, pp. 179-80).

As previously stated, Aleixandre, in his anatomic conglomerate, affirms his entelechy primarily though the lips in their double aspect of expressing love and poetic communication. Eschatology, but one more aspect of existence, relates final things to the poet's total creation. Aleixandre chooses not to waste precious moments as he strives for order in his life: "Si yo quiero la vida no es para repartirla. Ni para malgastarla. Es solo para tener en orden los labios" (OC, "Víspera de mí," p. 191). Illness, sterility, and solitude may prevail, but he wets his lips, "humedeciendo los labios," in the hope that in a world filled with sound, music, and song, he may put off his fate (OC, "El mar no es una hoja de papel," pp. 210-11). Aleixandre is always just too late," que un labio velase sin oírse" (OC, "Hacia el mar sin destino," p. 221), as fleeting life vanishes. The poet finally realizes that lips symbolize life and love but also death: "Una bella palabra, un árbol . . . todas las incidencias de los besos, se repartían mintiendo . . . No era la buena voz, mentira idiota, sino la cerrazón de los fríos, las dos violetas pálidas de ansia, ese instante de los labios en que se adivina que la sangre no existe" (OC "El amor padecido,"p. 240).

Espadas como labios might as easily have been called "labios como espadas," for love and death are interchangeable. Love, a cosmic force, recalls the touch of lips, not necessarily in human form, as a river, a mountain, or even a star. Yet human life and sexuality cannot be avoided in the contrasts and coalescing of the longing for life and the yearning for death. The world ignores, in "El vals," the "vello de los pubis," but "labios obscenos" will convert into a kiss, "una espina que dispensará la muerte diciendo: Yo os amo" (OC, p. 262). In other poems death, the only reality, may be a prolongation of life. Lips form the end product of the blood flow, and a buried one, unaware of some signs of life, "la íntima onda que se anega sobre los labios" (OC, p. 264), feels others above him as a memory of life. The dead have their own reality and love that death as a continuing life. Death offers a non-life memory as world and time pass like a sea dislodged by kisses, "como los dos labios a plomo / tristes a luces o nácar bajo esteras" (OC, p. 318).

Destructive swords or loving lips equal the destruction or death of Aleixandre's next collection where lips may be teeth or flowers, life or death. As Bousoño states: "Si amor es destrucción, amor, cólera, y odio pueden confundirse en la mentalidad aleixandrina."[12] In "Unidad en ella" the poet dies because he wants to die by living in the exterior air which with its hot breath "quema y dora mis labios desde un fondo." His erotic feeling, part of the total unity, must involve the destruction of passion, for to feel life one must experience death, the only state which can, in any event, offer a final total mutual destruction and fusion:

Este beso en tus labios como una lenta espina,
como un mar que voló hecho un espejo,
como el brillo de una ala,
es todavía unas manos, un repasar de tu crujiente pelo,
un crepitar de la luz vengadora,
luz o espada mortal que sobre mi cuello amenaza,
pero que nunca podrá destruir la unidad de este mundo.
                                        (OC., pp. 331-32)

Aleixandre, with his lips, seeks the uncertain music of youth, the ardor of the green earth, both parts of eternity:

Cuando acerco mis labios a esa música incierta,

a ese rumor de lo siempre juvenil,
. . .

Siento el mundo rodar bajo mis pies
. . .

Mirar tu cuerpo sin más luz que la tuya,
que esa cercana música que concierta a las aves,

                a las aguas, al bosque, a ese ligado latido
                de este mundo absoluto que siento ahora en los labios.
                            (OC, "A ti, viva" pp. 354-55)

The theme is constant.[13] Lips may signify life and death: "Por qué besar tus labios, si se sabe que la muerte está próxima," he asks in "Soy el destino," (OC, p. 395). His heart is an earthbound bird, "como dos labios solos que ayer se sonreían;" but earth or moon, its dryness thirsts for a passionate and even destructive love not to be his: "¡Oh corazón o luna, oh tierra seca a todo, / . . . linfa que goteando sobre la frente fría / finge pronto unos labios o una muerte escuchada!" (OC, "Sólo morir del día," pp. 405-06).

In Mundo a solas the images intensify as the beloved earth becomes a surrendering body which bleeds itself dry, "mientras se besan labios o burbujas de muerte." The lips clearly here represent the death which bestows upon the earth a fatal kiss, an inexorable answer also repeated by the heavens (OC, "Libertad celeste," p. 461). So Aleixandre, searching for life in the heavens and the sea, discovers that nothing smiles at him: "Son besos con sus labios, o pozos beso a beso . . . Pero los dulces vidrios que otros labios repasan / dan su frío de vida, de muerte entre los soles" (OC, "Los cielos," pp. 478-79). Aleixandre reinforces the reality of love and death; libidinal impulses assail his consciousness, but nature also negates life. Thus we see once more the paradox that one looks backward (toward death) while looking forward to life, as Aleixandre reaffirms the central role of love and death, a conclusion which is also a beginning. Death may offer a perfect love, but lips which kiss and love may also devour, masking the background of teeth and throat. Cosmic and human love may not be easily separated; to fuse with the cosmos may be difficult, but life without love is another kind of death.

The ambiguities in Aleixandre's vision overwhelm the vehicle provided by the inadequate words of even a most powerful poet. Indeed, a metaphorical person or persons and not the poet himself seems, at times, to carry on the poetic discourse, visualizing love and death as the coordinating elements of the universe. Love may be a metaphor of self-destruction, but Aleixandre also relates it closely to the life force within him even as he faces the truth that he moves though time toward death. Love is momentary, death eternal. He cannot conquer that spectre, but he wants to live life to the full in an ambivalent universe of imposed heterogeneous limits in which one strives to transcend the duality of life and death. Aleixandre seeks to communicate, through visual imagery, indefinite feelings, mnemonic traces of a preverbal period of sensations, unhappy memories related to pleasurable ones involving the loss of individual consciousness or ego and thus, in a sense, death.[14] The loss of bodily boundaries, destruction, a fusion with the cosmos implies oral action, for "the absence of ego boundaries implies an antecedent oral event."[15] Renovation and conservation present us with the contrapuntal perceptions, combinations, and permutations which seem incomprehensible but which, nonetheless, imprint emotion and conviction through a kind of poetic osmosis. Love, life, and death find their expression on Aleixandre's lips, human lips which seek to elucidate the same enigmas which beset us all.

Notes

[1] Gabriele Morelli has analyzed the presence of the human body in Pasión de la tierra: "In particolare, la figura del corpo colta nella sua materia elementare balza in tutta evidenza determinando momenti di trepida commozione . . ." "Il corpo umano, insomma, divente l'oggetto di un'attenzione che oseremo dire nuova per l'interesse che viene dato alla splendida forma dei suoi sensi pronti a mostrarsi nella loro prorompente vitalità, a testimonianza di un anelito umano verso la luce e lo spazio celeste." See Gabriele Morelli, "La presenza del corpo umano in Pasión de la Tierra," Revista de Letras (Mayagüez, P.R.), 6 (1974), 227; 230.

[2] Vicente Aleixandre, Obras completas (Madrid, 1977), II, pp. 402, 411, 422. Further references in the text are to this edition hereafter cited as OC.

[3] See Bertram D Lewin, "Remarks on Creativity, Imagery, and the Dream." The Journal of Nervous and Mental Disease, 140 (1969), 115-121 for a discussion of this kind of visual image.

[4] See Karl Abraham, On Character and Libido Development, ed. Bertram D. Lewin (New York, 1966), pp. 36-37.

[5] René A. Spitz, On the First Year of Life (New York, 1965), p. 64.

[6] Aleixandre had posed this problem in Ambito, his earliest work: "Lo que yo no quiero/ es darte palabras de ensueño, / ni propagar imagen con mis labios en tu frente" (OC, p. 108).

[7] The virgin sirens of "Circuito" in Espadas como labios edge the world with kisses "secos al sol que borra labios húmedos" (OC, p. 252); the setting sun in "Lenta húmedad" of La destrucción o el amor brings "Frío, humedad, tierra a los labios" (OC, p. 377).

[8] Erich Neumann, Art and the Creative Unconscious, tr. Ralph Manheim (New York, 1959), pp. 55-56 states: "The favored spiritual symbol of the matriarchal sphere is the moon in its relation to the night and the Great Mother of the night sky. The moon, as the luminous aspect of the night, belongs to her; it is her fruit, her sublimation as light, as expression of her essential spirit."

[9] Among the numerous examples we find: "Canción a una muchacha muerta," who keeps the "color de beso o labio," and "Que asi invade" where he hopes his thrust for life will avoid

destruction, "ni mis labios que no se purifican con su lumbre profunda" (OC., p. 369; p. 410).

[10] Emil Arthur Gutheil, The Language of the Dream (New York, 1939), p. 51. stresses that lips convey the idea of the female organ as well as other openings of the body such as mouth and eyes. Some of Aleixandre's imagery, the kisses which break against harsh walls or light which divides, conveys this connotation. By the same token light often serves as an archetype of the masculine sexual principle. See Jacquetta Hawkes, Man and the Sun (New York, 1962), pp. 60-61. Aleixandre's imagery also stresses the sexual implications of love, life, and death to be found in chiaroscuro.

[11] Louis M. Bourne, "The Spiritualization of Matter in the Poetry of Vicente Aleixandre," Revista de Letras, 6 (1974), 171.

[12] Carlos Bousoño, La poesía de Vicente Aleixandre (Madrid, 1968), p. 20.

[13] The cutting edge of a bird's beak "en algún labio cortó unas flores . . . polen luna / de una luna o una sangre o un beso al cabo"; life's sadness perches like a bird on his shoulders "como unos labios salobres que se llagan"; the earth, unpleasant to his lips, is a "palabra que pendiente de unos labios morados / ha colgado en la muerte putrefacta o el beso" (OC, "A ti viva," p. 355; "Corazón en suspenso," p. 360; "Tristeza a pájaro," p. 371; "La dicha," p. 383).

[14] For a further exploration of this idea see, Kessel Schwartz, "The Isakower Phenomenon and the Dream Screen in the Early Poetry of Vicente Aleixandre," Revista de Letras, 6 (1974), 210-218.

[15] See Bertram D. Lewin, "Sleep, the Mouth, and the Dream Screen," in Selected Writings of Bertram D. Lewin (New York, 1975), p. 94.

POSIBILISMO AND IMPOSIBILISMO:
THE BUERO VALLEJO-SASTRE POLEMIC

Antonio Buero Vallejo and Alfonso Sastre, probably the two most important living contemporary Spanish dramatists, contributed moving tragedies of modern man. Yet, with apparently diametrically opposed concepts of theater, they engaged in a fifteen-year polemic, perhaps not surprising in Spain, whose literature has been marked by a constant dualism.

The two theories concern the possibility of an open versus a closed situation, that is, a tragedy of hope (Buero's idea) as opposed to a tragedy of anguish (Sastre's existential position). The latter claimed that tragedy implies a situation in which human life cannot escape and is always defeated. For him the essence of tragedy, its metaphysical substance, "es la existencia humana en su modalidad (llamada por Heidegger) 'auténtica'."[1] Tragedy deals with existing beings who, living in a closed situation, seek a happiness which is denied to them and die or end badly. These unhappy beings reflect on their mundane and ultramundane destiny and on the unknown sin for which they are being punished: "Es una lucha en la que la vida humana es siempre derrotada en momentos que provocan horror (ante la magnitud de la catástrofe) y piedad (ante la nihilidad del ser humano)."[2] Sastre agrees with Aristotle's concept of horror and pity, but he bases it on what he calls the authentic human existence. That is, when existentially we face boundaries and limiting situations which we cannot overcome, when we come to grips with true human existence, when we face our true possibilities, when we are anguished at the thought of nothingness, when we have a clear representation of human existence, then we have a tragedy. A drama of social reform which involves an apparently open situation may still be a tragedy if the individual can find no solution or if he is unable to take advantage of it, for even without a tragic situation, "la tragicidad de la existencia humana en general" will not disappear.[3]

Buero, on the other hand, as early as 1950 postulated a theater freed from the usual "concepción del Destino a la manera clásica, externo en sus irrevocables decisiones a la voluntad de los personajes."[4] Although a clearer definition of his theory of tragedy can be found in later works, even Buero's Historia de una escalera may be an open tragedy, for there exists the possibility of another chance born from the very heart of the impossible situation: "La tragédie est toujours sous un certain aspect, tragédie de l'espoir. Notre condition d'humains, seul ressort en definitive de toute l'oeuvre que nous abordons, n'est pas autre chose que cette espérance pathétique."[5] In that same year Buero stated: "Y me atrevía a pensar que mi obra encerraba un sentido trágico positivo."[6]

Buero repeated his theory in April, 1952,[7] and also the following year: "Tragedia no es necesariamente catástrofe final, sino una especial manera de entender el final, sea feliz o amarga. Algún día, con mejores pertrechos que esta vez si me es posible, intentaré escribir una obra a la que podré subtitular rotundamente: Tragedia feliz."[8] Buero restated more fully his idea de "esperanza trágica" in 1956[9] and in 1957: "Esa fe última late tras las dudas y los fracasos que en la escena se muestran; esa esperanza mueve a las plumas que describen las situaciones más desesperadas. Se escribe porque se espera, pese a toda duda. Pese a toda duda, creo y espero en el hombre, como espero y creo en otras cosas."[10] In that same year he wrote his promised "happy tragedy," in which he attempted to sketch the tragic character of hope in the tragic age in which we live. For this Buero postulated a tragic mode to trigger adult reaction to and comprehension of the problem of our age, a vital mode, therefore, in no way pessimistic or filled with desolating negations: "Es más que probable que el meollo de toda tragedia esté formado por el problema de la esperanza. Incluso en la más aparentemente desesperanzada; también en la tragedia de la desesperación. Somos, querámoslo o no, animales esperanzados, y cuando se nos cierran todos los caminos vivimos una agonía que viene a ser como la cara negativa de la esperanza que se obstina en latir en nuestro corazón . . . Se espera. Se espera siempre. Se espera incluso sin creer en la realidad de lo que esperamos."[11] Even without a concrete answer, then, man will always hope for the future.

In 1958 Buero added that a final act of liberty or faith may resolve tragic destiny. Tragedy in the twentieth century cannot be pessimistic, even if its author maintains a pessimistic philosophy of life, for however disguised, the certainty or possibility of resurrection maintains its force. Pessimism is contrary to the spirit of tragedy which, far from being negative, proposes all kinds of values. This positive aspect may not always reveal itself explicitly, and the drama may even end without apparent solution, but even here "como caso particular de la gran afirmación vital que es el género a que pertenece, es positivo. Y su meollo es la esperanza."[12]

Buero reiterated his position through the years: "tragedia no significa negatividad o desesperación. La tragedia de más desesperada apariencia se basa en la esperanza y postula, explícita o implícitamente, ciertas 'Eumenides' finales que todo conflicto trágico, en su tensión, busca."[13] Buero states: "The meaning of tragedy is not, therefore, desperate and closed, even though it describes desperations and situations without exit, but the putting forth of a conflict between necessity and liberty, which is often terrible but which, in fact, may be resolved in favor of the latter."[14] "Yo creo que el fenómeno de lo trágico en el teatro, y en la literatura en general--fenómeno que a mí me parece de la mayor importancia porque es para mí el fenómeno fundamental del teatro--es un fenómeno en el fondo radicalmente esperanzado. Incluso cuando la obra parece que solamente describe desesperanzas."[15] In all his dramas Buero Vallejo carried out his theatrical theory proclaiming the hope which lies in the human soul and man's possibility of gaining victory over himself.

Alfonso Sastre rather consistently tried to refute Buero's theory. In commenting on <u>Waiting for Godot</u> by Beckett, Sastre referred to it as "un acta de defunción de la esperanza . . . Seguiremos esperando, pero nuestra espera será ya una espera sin esperanza; una espera desesperada."[16] Sastre's attacks continued through the years. In an article written for French consumption, he lamented what he terms Buero's abandonment of early principles found in <u>Historia de una escalera</u>: "Nous verrons plus loin combien il déçut nos espérances . . . Quel a été le rôle de Buero Vallejo dans notre vie théâtrale?. . . La tendance dominante est incontestablement la comédie bourgeoise inspirée de Benavente. . . .Cette comédie revet tous les aspects du répertoire benaventin. Elle va de la comédie légère (López Rubio) a la satire sociale (Calvo Sotelo), de la farce (derniers ouvrages de José M. Pemán) au drama historique (Buero Vallejo). Cet auteur qui promettait beaucoup (par exemple dans <u>Historia de una escalera</u>) subit inconsciemment l'influence de la tradition benaventine et semble vouloir se detacher de son naturalisme initial, son seul apport de réelle valeur."[17] Sastre, denying that social criticism might be read into Buero's historical theater, viewed it as a kind of bourgeois sequel to Benavente's plays.

One of Sastre's most ardent supporters, José María de Quinto, who had helped Sastre create the Teatro de Agitación Social in 1948 and the Grupo del Teatro Realista in 1961, claimed that playwrights (Buero Vallejo among others) ignoring the political, social and religious realities of the country were, in effect, perpetrating a fraud: "Este fraude, al que viene favoreciendo una crítica apática y confusa, ha impedido el desarrollo de la tragedia. Sin verdad--autenticidad última--no hay tragedia. La tragedia aparece cuando son reveladas, de algún modo, las zonas más auténticas y vivas de la existencia."[18]

Insisting that Buero Vallejo vacillated between naturalism and existential anguish, Quinto declared that the attempt to reconcile two distinct interpretations of theater had caused "como una requebrajadura del sentido homogéneo que debe informar toda obra de arte."[19] Alfonso Sastre, on the other hand, had found his path: "Su teatro--más o menos discutible--parece responder a una línea vertebrada y libre de impurezas . . . Alfonso Sastre ha adoptado una técnica, un modo de expresión, que se corresponde con una de las más vigorosas corrientes trágicas de nuestro tiempo: la profundización dentro del realismo . . . El teatro de Alfonso Sastre es un teatro social, deliberadamente social."[20]

Sastre continued to oppose historical drama as defined by Buero. One critic explains: "Buero ha econtrado un camino sólido y valiente, el de la parábola brechtiana."[21] It is not surprising, then, to discover that Sastre also attacked the theater of Bertolt Brecht, accusing him of treating tragedy as the past because he feared to present it as immutable and without remedy. The object of our struggle should be here and now, for:

. . .el optimismo histórico puede, en efecto, inhibir al espectador de la acción práctica: si el dolor se presenta como pasado es que pasará. Si el espectador al que se le presentaba todo dolor como irremediable no se movía porque era inútil intentar un cambio de las cosas, el espectador al que se le presenta la historia como un feliz desarrollo puede decidir no moverse en vista de que la historia ha de moverse por él. A la conformidad del otro corresponderia el conformismo de éste . . . la descarga de lo trágico a que procede Brecht [one might substitute Buero] se parece mucho a la catarsis aristotélica, entendida como aliviadero estético de lo que en realidad es insoportable.[22]

Since one of Sastre's principal themes is the social and revolutionary nature of tragedy, he finds the socially oriented theater the only one which has modern meaning. He carefully distinguishes his social art from that of the proletarian theater which, along with the bourgeois theater, mutilates true theater. The theater, in its social function, must not merely provoke esthetic emotions, for the theater is more than an art form. It must take a role in the struggle of our time, "recoger la angustia social de esta hora y denunciarla. El dramaturgo es dramaturgo porque le ha sido concedido hallar el 'drama' que hay en su mundo y formularlo."[23]

Francisco García Pavón, denying that Sastre was a social or revolutionary playwright, considered him overly intellectual and obscure: "De donde resulta . . . como otras obras de Sastre, [que] es casi un artístico y metafórico tratado de filosofía revolucionaria."[24] Sastre, recognizing the ambiguity, claimed he was willing to risk it in the hope that the true nature of his message would be visible.²⁵

Sastre asked various contemporary Spanish playwrights, including Buero Vallejo, whether they tried to give some deliberate social intent to their work. Buero's answer was that he did not deliberately attempt to incorporate such a message but that the problems of the day, even when they seemed to be of a metaphysical nature, "poseen una social transcendencia. La misma que posee siempre el verdadero teatro, que es por esencia el arte representativo de las sociedades humanas."²⁶ This answer did not satisfy Sastre, who defended his own position, which he termed an intermediate one: "Je cherche toujours à provoquer une double prise de conscience: celle du moment historique que nous vivons, et celle de notre situation en tant qu'hommes. Telle est ma métaphysique, telle est ma politique actuelle."²⁷ Through the years Sastre continued to champion similar positions, and as late as 1964 concluded: "nos parece que el escritor literario está obligado a 'contemplar su compromiso' por medio del trabajo científico y de la actividad propiamente política . . . Hacer literatura--concluiríamos--no es bastante."²⁸

Buero stated that he realized that the duty of the theater was to pose conflicts of man and the society in which he lives, and "despertar las conciencias frente a ellos, enfocarlos con autenticidad y verdad; combatir los errores y los males; abrir los ojos; denunciar las injusticias; mostrar lo que el hombre tiene de humano y de inhumano; y lo que tiene de ser histórico; y, siempre, lograr arte auténtico."²⁹ His supporters, such as Carlos Muñiz, felt strongly that, "De todos nuestros autores ha sido él quien más a la española ha abordado nuestros problemas españoles."³⁰ Jean-Paul Borel supported Buero's claim to a moral and ethical theater: "On voit ainsi que Buero Vallejo a hérité de toute cette tradition théâtrale dont l'aspect essentiel est de denoncer l'impossible de la vie, pour ensuite en tirer certaines affirmations de caractère éthique."³¹

Sastre, in spite of his ambiguities, apparently favored a closed situation of existential anguish, based on a realism which encourages social action. Buero favored a concept of tragedy based on faith and doubt, both of which, he deemed necessary for harmonious development of man's potentialities. Even in the blackest tragedy, ending in a catastrophe without apparent hope, we may ascertain the great dangers besetting man and perhaps find an implicit invitation to create conditions which will avoid future tragedies.

Sastre, attempting to redefine the battle lines between his theories and those of Buero, refocused the polemic on what he called "posibilismo" versus "imposibilismo."[32] He claimed that the theater was largely in the hands of the wealthy producers who systematically resisted "las grandes y arriesgadas empresas dramáticas que los manuscritos de los dramaturgos ofrecen."[33] In a world filled with hunger, misery, and war, the bourgeois public insisted on a theater of evasion.[34] Through the years Sastre maintained his position that the Spanish theater was a business strictly interested in making a profit and content to work within the limitation of government censorship. The national theaters, for much more complex reasons, he stated as late as 1964, did almost nothing to promote drama and were incapacitated "para ese trabajo profundo y arriesgado de revitalización, y más teniendo en cuenta el carácter inconformista del nuevo teatro."[35]

Sastre first brought up the matter of "posibilismo" and "imposibilismo" as definitions in 1960.[36] Of the two primary attitudes, that of Buero Vallejo, criticizing "imposibilismo" in the theater, contends that certain authors deliberately write theater whose staging is impossible, for private or official reasons, in order to achieve publicity and possible publication of their work abroad. What one needs is a "possible" theater in Spain, even at the cost of certain sacrifices such as accommodating oneself to those interests which are opposed to the dramatist's work. The second attitude, that of Alfonso Paso, recommends signing a social pact with the established interests. Afterwards, one one may betray the clauses thereof and indulge in progressive writing. Sastre rejects both points of view, and finds that Paso's is simply an offshoot of Buero's. Since no accurate criteria exist as to the impossibility of performance of a drama, since one cannot prognosticate the controlling interests' action, and since in some instances drama is being performed which formerly was rejected, one can only maintain a thesis about a momentary "imposibilismo": "Todo teatro debe ser considerado posible hasta que sea imposibilitado; y toda 'imposibilitación' debe ser acogida por nosotros como una sorpresa." Progress, says Sastre, is not made through accommodation but through contradiction and opposition. O'Neill and Pirandello wrote impossible theater, but their struggles turned it into a possible one. As for Paso's position, Sastre doubts that it is workable.

Buero saw some of the contradictions inherent in Sastre's position and in general viewed the article as a kind or unconfessed attack on his concept of "esperanza." He rejected the idea of "imposibilismo" as a smoke screen, and sought to answer Sastre in the next issue of *Primer Acto*.[37] Buero lamented the fact that Sastre had attacked him publicly on several occasions. He had never indulged in such activity, although he had had private disagreements with Sastre on dramatic theories. He read into Sastre's praise of Historia de una escalera a criticism of later dramas which followed theories not accepted by Sastre. Although readers might consider him in error for attacking through his theory, Buero stressed that he had been observing for some time that Sastre and his friends kept accusing him of writing "contaminated and insufficiently positive" works, that Sastre as early as August 15, 1951, had lumped his drama with that of dramatists like Calvo Sotelo, and that when he (Buero) had only published Historia de una escalera and En la ardiente oscuridad, the first of which Sastre had praised, the latter was already accusing Buero of "conformismo," veiling his criticism by a "magnánimo reconocimiento de que es el [the theatrical production] que más le interesa en España . . . después del suyo." Buero believed that Sastre, far from attacking a theory of theater, was directly attacking his works, for a criticism of the work is an inevitable parallel to opinions expressed, "y a las opiniones como consecuencia-- 'coartada'--inevitable de tal obra." Buero, therefore, felt compelled to examine Sastre's own position on "posibilismo" and "imposibilismo." To affirm, as Sastre does, that one must write with absolute interior freedom and liberty because in principle all theater is possible and to imply that he (Sastre) does so, is to formulate "un aserto no ya increíble, sino imposible." Such a position leads to an abstract and mechanical rather than dialectic conceptualization. A writer must live his situation; he may struggle successfully or otherwise with his environment, but he acts on the circumstances which he lives, even when he pretends to disdain them. Furthermore, the words "teatro posible" do not imply a theater of accommodation. One must write a theater, not only which

> . . .debe escribirse, sino estrenarse. Un teatro, pues, "en situación"; lo más arriesgado posible, pero no temerario. Recomiendo, en suma, y a sabiendas de que muchas veces no se logrará hacer posible un teatro "imposible". Llamo por consiguiente, "imposibilismo" a la actitud que se coloca, mecánica y antidialécticamente, "fuera de situación"; la actitud que busca hacer aun más imposible a un teatro "imposible" con temerarias elecciones de tema o expresión, con declaraciones provocadoras, con reclamas inquietantes y abundantes, y que puede llegar tristemente aun más lejos en su divorcio de la dialéctica de lo real: a hacer imposible un teatro . . . posible.

So, claimed Buero, "imposibilismo" is a tactic writers employ to create the impression that it was the only cause for the drama's rejection when, in truth, there might be many reasons why a play could not be performed.

If one speaks historically of an author and his work, a dialectical position is difficult to distinguish from accommodation. Not too long before 1960, the very attempt to give to the Spanish stage a true tragic dimension, whatever the theme, was in itself a kind of "oposición dialéctica" which many confused with accommodation. Given the dialectic contradiction of an artist with his society and the obfuscation involved in any kind of acting in certain circumstance, it is easy to make a mistake and write a theater of accommodation while sincerely believing that one is developing subtle dialectic differences. To insist that a defense of "imposibilismo" is the only allowable form of dialectic opposition is unjust and leads to obvious contradiction. Many of Sastre's own plays, instead of being "dialectic opposition," might easily be considered as "accommodations" and possible rather than impossible dramas. Sastre's own followers saw a lack of "inconformismo" in his later theater, and he admitted at the time that "sólo una pequeñísima parte del teatro que escribo llega a los espectadores." Thus Sastre implicitly admits that his published drama is not so centrally in the area of "inconformismo teórico." Buero commented also that Sastre, partly abandoning his concept of a closed, existential situation, finally came to realize that tragedy in general "debía ser, por revolucionaria e investigadora, 'abierta.'" Furthermore, although not all of Sastre's dramas are social or political, he seeks to justify them, for he considers himself the standard bearer of the Spanish theatrical revolution.

In the following issue of <u>Primer Acto</u> Sastre reaffirmed the dialectical sense of his position and the necessity for the exercise of social pressure. He clarified his statements about writing with absolute liberty, or "libertad irónica," and redefined it as a kind of Socratic ignorance which would lead one to seek answers to the self-imposed questions. Although this liberty may not exist, by acting as though it does, one may define the measure of its non-existence in order to struggle to obtain it, an awareness of the situation which operates at all times. If Buero's attack on "imposibilismo" was directed at what Sastre labels "los anarco-libertario-blasfematorios," he agrees wholeheartedly, but Sastre maintains that the so-called "posibilista" position might well be a disguised form of "actitudes conformistas." He does not believe that Buero belongs in this category, stating that he admires Buero's moral and intellectual virtues, and lamenting Buero's attacks on him. He refuses, however, to accept Buero's invitation to silence, for writers must always speak up. He denies that he is a revolutionary in speech but a conformist in his work or that he is a tactician who seeks publicity, and claims that in his evolutionary drama he has the support of the young writers.[38]

232

As the polemic continued, more indirectly, Sastre stressed the need for debate "en forma noble y elevada, rechazando los tristes, deprimentes combates 'cuerpo a cuerpo' en que aquí degeneran inmediatamente los encuentros polémicos que se producen."[39] He recalled that during the 1960-61 season, among a great number of "tomas de partido" in favor of or against certain aspects of theatrical development, some critics referred to his work En la red as "ardiente compromiso," a debate he considered a healthy development away from the masked relationships of previous years: "Están cayendo, por fin, algunas máscaras. Empezamos a ver, con alegría o con tristeza, algunos rostros. Esto--verse las caras--, que puede resultar doloroso, es una buena y saludable cosa."[40] This clear division of positions seems a good thing, even though it may prove attractive to perennial opportunists.[41] As for him, he feels very happy fighting for what he believes to be the truth, even if it has to be "en un teatro que está medio vacío, pero muy lleno de gente que me importa."[42] In 1965 Sastre claimed that he had been correct all along:[43] "El hecho, evidentemente real--pero también, creo yo, 'momentáneamente' real--de la desautorización de obras dramáticas por los organismos de Control de Estado y de no conseguir otras su 'publicación' como teatro, es decir, su representación dramática . . . ha sido explicado por algunos como una consecuencia de actitudes poco 'realistas' 'imposibilistas'." Realism, in this functional sense, would resemble a "posibilista" attitude, a somewhat idealistic concept of "posibilidad." A play falling into the impossible category at one time through special circumstances might become possible later, for no objective measure of what is possible exists. Furthermore, such concern might lead to self censorship. Recalling that since the debates in Primer Acto some of his works deemed "imposible" had been performed, he insists that it makes no sense to claim that someone cultivates "imposibilismo." By the same token it is fruitless to recommend "posibilismo" which runs the risk of leading to self censorship. He concludes: "El tema, en suma, que tiene sentido en lo social-político, no lo tiene en lo estético-poético. A esto puede reducirse mi posición desde un principio. . ."

Sastre continued to view tragic incidents as involving destruction, pain, and agony, both physical and mental, and praised the unhappy ending and the closed situation, but he recognized, nevertheless, the possibility of a tragedy of hope and salvation. He continued to attack Buero's theory, directly and indirectly, ". . . entiendo por esperanza la superación dialéctica del pesimismo (y el optimismo); para Brecht la tragedia no tiene sentido porque él encuentra y presenta las razones de un optimismo fundamental y fundamentante."[44] Yet he comes quite close to accepting Buero's theory as his own: "Si se cree, como yo lo creo, que la tragedia significa, en sus formas más perfectas, una superación dialéctica del pesimismo (casi siempre fijado en lo social)--y en este sentido propongo como fundamental determinación de lo trágico la esperanza. . ."[45] Sastre reaffirmed this position in 1965, stating that his work was neither optimistic nor pessimistic and that tragedy, when it fulfills that concept, "es una unidad dialéctica superior que quizás podamos llamar la esperanza, al margen--o sea, por encima--de cualquier optimismo o pesimismo excluyentes de sus contrarios."[46] Tragedy, nevertheless, as a literary mode of our time, must be profoundly realistic.

Although he had been attacking "posibilismo" since 1960, in 1966 he seemed to agree that it was something he had been practicing, too. Asked whether he had always written what he wanted, he answered: "He escrito todo lo que he 'querido-podido.'"[47]

In June, 1966, Buero Vallejo and Sastre, members of a special panel discussing contemporary Spanish theater, engaged once more in a defense of their theories of open versus closed tragedy and the criteria for the staging of Spanish theatrical works.[48] Buero believed the middle-class theater-going public would now support works which in essence are "antiburguesas": "El público . . . es capaz de aceptar, por lo menos en la escena, una crítica acerba hecha desde puntos de vista radicalmente opuestos a los suyos." As for Spanish theatrical producers, Buero pointed out that, as business men and rarely ideologists, if in their judgment a revolutionary work opposed to the bourgeois point of view might prove a financial success, they would stage the play.

It is true, however, that political factors, external to the theater, contribute largely to staging difficulties. Buero stated that he had always proclaimed the necessity of "posibilismo," because "el posibilismo es una realidad; es decir, no hay otra cosa que posibilismo; lo que sucede es que los márgenes de este posibilismo son muy diferentes en cada lugar . . . pero debemos tener muy presente que nuestra presencia como autores tiene que ser una presencia efectiva, no una esterilidad; tenemos que hacer un posibilismo dinámico, progresivo, combativo." Yet an author who contends he is veracious may be conforming to a conditioned reality. Years after producing a drama he may realize that "hemos enmascarado nuestro auténtico pensamiento o lo hemos deformado; y, sin embargo, lo hicimos con auténtica buena fe, sin creer que lo hacíamos." Although he acknowledges the need to be "engagé," his choices are to write plays and postpone their production for a happier day, or write plays in a masked manner in the hope of being understood. Even when one puts politics into the theater, however, "no debemos hacernos demasiadas ilusiones de que nuestra actividad sea resolutiva y directa."

Sastre, reiterating previous positions, stated that an author is a political being, that he must so function both in and out of the theater: "Creo que nuestro deber no como autores, sino como hombres que, además hacemos teatro, consiste en preparar las condiciones para que sea posible el teatro que en esos momentos está imposibilitado." Partly concurring with Buero, Sastre admitted: ". . . yo trato de defenderme contra el optimismo que en algún momento he tenido, y el cual consistía justamente en tener demasiada confianza en las consecuencias social-políticas del trabajo propiamente teatral." He insisted that he wanted to reject demagogic excesses in order to create "un teatro muy difícil, pero no imposible."

According to Pérez Minik, later dramatists combined the human stoicism of Buero with the dialectical investigation of Sastre to achieve Laín Entralgo's definition: "La esperanza sobrenatural más firme y robusto no excluye la posibilidad de sentir angustiosamente la instalación de la vida personal en el tiempo. Antes tenía que afirmarse el cristianismo como pura doctrina. Ahora, en cambio, la nueva sensibilidad histórica le invita a mostrarse como vida o existencia capaces de expresión doctrinal." Social or personal life put to the test as a counter example of absurd life may well be "una de las melodías más poderosas y significativas de todo este quehacer peligroso."[49]

It is unfortunate that Sastre and Buero felt compelled to involve themselves in a continuing polemic, especially since the former came to accept some of Buero's ideas and claim them as his own. Sastre, apparently arrogating to himself the title of the exclusive saviour of the Spanish theater, continued to attack Buero's theater. Buero, feeling himself the older and more experienced dramatist, reacted strongly to what he considered the unjust attacks of Sastre, "tanto él como sus corifeos. . . haciendo lo posible--si bien con cautelas--para descreditar mi labor".[50] Buero believed that he had adopted moral positions and fought the good fight in the ongoing Spanish tragedy, and he resented the implication of immorality implicit in Sastre's earlier definitions of "posibilismo". Finally, Buero stated that Sastre, too, had written "posibilismo" and that, in his judgment "ha hecho bien; porque hay dos clases de posibilismo y yo nunca he defendido la mala sino la otra, que es lo único que se hace cuando se hace algo."[51]

Both Buero and Sastre continued to write for the theater, although in the seventies the latter concentrated on other forms of literary expression. In the final analysis, Sastre's didactic and intellectual dramas and his view of tragedy as a social sin proved less successful than Buero's theater which stressed ethical and moral beliefs as well as the need for love and understanding and the possibility of spiritual if not physical survival, even in a sordid and unjust world.

Notes

[1] Alfonso Sastre. *Drama y sociedad*. Madrid, 1956, p. 20.

[2] Ibid., pp. 23-24.

[3] Ibid., p. 37.

[4] Antonio Buero Vallejo. "Palabra final", *Historia de una escalera*. Barcelona, 1950, p. 154.

[5] Jean Paul Borel. *Théâtre de l'Impossible*. Paris, 1963, pp. 158-159.

[6] Antonio Buero Vallejo. "Cuidado con la amargura", *Correo Literario*, June 15, 1950, p. 8.

[7] Antonio Buero Vallejo. "Lo trágico", in *Informaciones. Extraordinario Teatral del Sábado de Gloria*, Madrid, April 12, 1952.

[8] Antonio Buero Vallejo. *La señal que se espera*, Colección "Teatro", No. 21. Madrid, 1953, pp. 66-67.

[9] Juan Emilio Aragonés. "Buero Vallejo, autor del momento", *La Hora*, Madrid, November 1, 1956.

[10] Antonio Buero Vallejo. "El teatro de Buero Vallejo visto por Buero Vallejo", *Primer Acto*, Madrid, 1 (April, 1957), p. 6.

[11] Antonio Buero Vallejo. "Comentario", *Hoy es fiesta*, Colección "Teatro", No. 176. Madrid, 1957, pp. 99-100.

[12] Antonio Buero Vallejo. "La tragedia", in *El teatro, Enciclopedia del Arte Escénico*, ed. Guillermo Díaz Plaja. Barcelona, 1958, pp. 71-76.

[13] José R. Marra López. "Conversación con Buero Vallejo sobre el teatro español", *Cuadernos*, 42 (Mayo-Junio, 1960), p. 56.

[14] "Antonio Buero Vallejo Answers Seven Questions", *The Theater Annual*, XIX (1962), 5.

[15] Bernard Dulsey. "Entrevista a Buero Vallejo", *The Modern Language Journal*, L, 3 (1966), 153-154.

[16] Alfonso Sastre. "Siete notas sobre Esperando a Godot", *Primer Acto*, 1 (April, 1957), p. 49.

[17] Alfonso Sastre. "Le théâtre espagnol contemporain", Preuves, 124 (May, 1961), pp. 27-28.

[18] José María de Quinto. "El Teatro" in "Los cuatro ángeles de San Silvestre", Almanaque para el año 1958 de Son Armadans, pp. 333-334.

[19] Ibid., p. 338.

[20] Ibid., pp. 339-341.

[21] Ricardo Salvat. "Teatro en 1961", Primer Acto, 29-30 (December, 1961-January, 1962), p. 107.

[22] Alfonso Sastre. Anatomía del realismo. Barcelona, 1965, pp. 221-222.

[23] Alfonso Sastre. "Los autores españoles ante el teatro como 'arte social', Correo Literario, August 15, 1951, p. 5.

[24] Francisco García Pavón. El teatro social en España (1895-1962). Madrid, 1962, p. 177.

[25] Alfonso Sastre. Cuatro dramas de la revolución. Madrid, 1965, pp. 8-10.

[26] Alfonso Sastre. Correo Literario, August 15, 1951, p. 5.

[27] Preuves. Op. cit., p. 28.

[28] Anatomía del realismo, p. 256.

[29] Primer Acto, 29-30 (Dec., 1961-Jan., 1962), pp. 5-6.

[30] Carlos Muñiz. "Antonio Buero Vallejo, ese hombre comprometido", Primer Acto, 38 (1962), p. 10.

[31] Borel, p. 154.

[32] The terms posibilismo and imposibilismo have been applied to the concepts of tragedy of Buero Vallejo and Sastre. One continuing aspect of their polemic to which these terms also apply is that of the possibility of staging the plays which promote their point of view, because of political and economic conditions in Spain. For the playwrights and their supporters the two aspects have become fused into one. Through Sastre's insistence on defining the polemic partly in these terms, the words have come to include their divergent philosophies of reality, tragedy, theater, and staging.

[33] *Drama y sociedad*, pp. 146-147.

[34] Ibid., p. 155.

[35] Alfonso Sastre. "Lo nuevo y lo viejo en el teatro español", *Primer Acto*, 51 (March, 1964), p. 14.

[36] Alfonso Sastre. "Teatro imposible y pacto social", *Primer Acto*, 14 (May-June, 1960), pp. 1-2.

[37] Antonio Buero Vallejo. "Obligada precisión acerca del 'imposibilismo'", *Primer Acto*, 15 (July-August, 1960), pp. 1-6.

[38] Alfonso Sastre. "A modo de respuesta", *Primer Acto*, 16 (Sept.-October, 1960), pp. 1-2.

[39] Alfonso Sastre. *Primer Acto*, 29-30 (Dec., 1961-Jan., 1962), pp. 26-27.

[40] *Anatomía del realismo*, p. 150, note.

[41] Ibid., p. 170.

[42] Ibid., p. 152.

[43] Ibid., pp. 76-77, note 3, "En torno al 'posibilismo' literario".

[44] Alfonso Sastre. "Tragedia y esperpento", *Primer Acto*, 18 (November, 1961), p. 16.

[45] Ibid.

[46] *Anatomía del realismo*, p. 129.

[47] Alberto Miralles. "Hombres de teatro: Alfonso Sastre", *Yorick* (Barcelona), 11 (January, 1966).

[48] *Cuadernos para el diálogo. Extraordinario dedicado al teatro* (Madrid), June, 1966, pp. 43-46.

[49] Domingo Pérez Minik. *Teatro europeo contemporáneo*. Madrid, 1961, pp. 467-468.

[50] In a letter from Buero to the author, dated June 23, 1966.

[51] In a letter from Buero to the author, dated Oct. 12, 1966.

VERBUM AND SPANISH CULTURE

Although only three issues (June-November, 1937) of Verbum, the "órgano oficial de la Asociación Nacional de Estudiantes de Derecho" of the University of Havana, were published, this apparently unimportant little journal signaled the birth of a new intellectual group. Founded by Lezama Lima, who served as secretary under the direccion of René Villarnovo, it elicited from Gastón Baquero the claim that "la tendencia de rigorismo cultural, de inalterable servicio a muy puros ideales religiosos y de creación . . . aparecieron con tales caracteres, acaso por primera vez en la historia literaria cubana, en la revista Verbum."[1]

The journal contains some notes on Cuban painters, a few general essays, and some original poems by Cuban poets of the stature of Emilio Ballagas, Angel Gaztelu, Eugenio Florit, and José Lezama Lima. The writers wanted to renovate what they saw as the University's decadence and hoped to guide it to a position "una equidistancia de la irresponsabilidad multitudinaria como del pragmatismo del especialista, incapaz de brindarnos una decisiva conclusión de unidad y de fervor."[2] José Antonio Portuondo, in speaking of the Second Republican Generation, believes that its "participación activa en las luchas políticas ha contribuido a dividirla profundamente, y sólo han mantenido vida más continuada aunque precaria aquellas revistas como Verbum . . . que, desasidas de lo político, han consagrado sus esfuerzos a lo artístico, alcanzando resultados de encomiable calidad estética."[3] Yet in spite of their stated objective of reforming the University of Havana and the praise of critics like Portuondo about their role in Cuba, the contributors evinced more concern for Spanish culture than for Cuban intellectual life.

The journal, written during the Spanish Civil War, mentions the political situation only in passing, for the writers were interested principally in a new aesthetic effort. Believing that the public would reject their new art, they defended themselves from implied though non-existent attacks. In the one article written about a Cuban literary work, Lezama Lima's "Muerte de Narciso," Angel Gaztelu calls it ". . . tal vez . . . en Cuba el más alto y atrevido intento de llevar la poesía a su desligamiento y región sustantiva y absoluta en virtud y gracia de esa esencial y mágica deidad de la metáfora. . ."[4] No special attempt was made to fit Spanish works into a single artistic or conceptual framework, but the bias of the group in favor of the aesthetic and artistic viewpoint of Hispanic capabilities or their conception thereof is quite clear. Lezama Lima, especially, shows sophisticated control as he scrutinizes the subtleties and shadings in the poetry of Garcilaso or Juan Ramón Jiménez.

Lezama's study of Garcilaso's poetic world, "El secreto de Garcilaso," shows great familiarity with his source material and with Spanish literature in general. He mentions Jorge Manrique, the Marqués de Santillana, Salvador Jacinto Polo de Medina, a follower of Luis de Góngora, and Gregorio Silvestre, a member of the traditionalist school of Cristóbal de Castillejo. Much of Lezama's essay concentrates on the baroque aspects of Spanish literature and the relationship of Garcilaso's poetry to that of Góngora: ". . . la polarización sensorial de Garcilaso . . . su espectralización ambiental, surge clareadora contrastándola con la unidad orgánica-sintética de Góngora . . . Mientras Góngora ofrece la textura de tensa nerviosidad y exterior hialino, en su intimidad reducida es frutado y goloso; Garcilaso, arquitectonicamente fluyente, de adamado discurso, reserva su almendra presentida, desaparecida, punto que vuela, al fácil alcance de la mano y a la imposibilidad de su total asimiento."[5] Lezama had always been fascinated by Luis de Góngora for whom he had great affinity "por la desligada y lujosa . . . ornamentación de la metáfora, por esa constante y dulce huida del nombre, reduciendo a veces las cosas a una pura ecuación de color y acento. . ."[6]

Twentieth century Spain is represented by the inclusion of two García Lorca poems,[7] by two contributions from Juan Ramón Jiménez, to whom Lezama had dedicated his Garcilaso article, and by an essay on the contribution of Juan Ramón to Cuban poetry. Juan Ramón Jiménez, in "Brazo español," discusses Eduardo Rosales, José Gutiérrez Solana, Juan de Echevarría, and Eduardo Vicente, Spanish painters.[8] In another brief essay written in la Habana, "Límite del Progreso," the poet tells of his arrival from Spain to New York, a "cárcel laberíntica del hombre estraviado por los salientes, los picos del injenio." He sees New York as "Babel de la melancolía progresista, no es ya sino una sola desmedida máquina que su hombre ve desde dentro."[9] His words recall almost the same description given by García Lorca of New York as "esta babilónica cruel y violenta ciudad,"[10] The New York "machine" upsets the natural harmony and relationship which man must maintain with nature. To live there is to give up liberty, one's greatest gift, and thus, in a sense, to die.

José Lezama Lima's "Gracia Eficaz de Juan Ramón y Su Visita a Nuestra Poesía" touches on a fundamental component of Cuban literary history and development. Juan Ramón, while he was living in Havana in 1937, brought out an anthology of Cuban poets, both young and old, known and unknown, analyzing in the prologue the position of Cuban poetry at that time. Lezama views Jiménez's poetry as "una invocación al mar del sur en abril," talks of "la naturaleza naturalizada de su obra," and defines his role as poetic mentor of Cuban poets as that of a "poeta de cuidada madurez que va a tropezar con una lírica incipiente."[11] Juan Ramón's task was doubly hard because of the lack of previous worthwhile Cuban criticism, but contact with him was of inestimable symbolic value for the development of contemporary Cuban poetry.

The Verbum writers, in their attempt to revitalize the intellectual life of the university and their own literature, exhibited some artistic prejudices, something one would expect from a group of young law students. Eager to reform their own culture and believing that national culture depended on creative imagination rather than on morality, they sought their inspiration both in Spanish classics and in the poetry of Juan Ramón Jiménez, himself a symbol of poetic renovation and one who had always lived almost exclusively for his art. What one misses in Verbum is a faith in human values and at least a psychological awareness of the dehumanizing experience through which their Spanish cousins, as well as art, were passing, as though it were possible for them to divorce the agony of a people and their historical crisis from their culture, identifying with the one and ignoring the existence of the other.

Notes

[1] Gastón Baquero, "Tendencias de Nuestra Literatura", Anuario Cultural de Cuba (Havana, 1943), p. 269.

[2] Verbum, no. 1 (June, 1937), p. 2.

[3] José Antonio Portuondo, "Tarjetero: Cuba Literaria (1941)", Revista Bimestre Cubana, L (1942), p. 100.

[4] Verbum, no. 3, pp. 49-52.

[5] Verbum, no. 1, pp. 37;40.

[6] Angel Gaztelu, "Muerte de Narciso, Rauda Cetrería de Metáforas", Verbum, no. 3. p. 51.

[7] Gastón Baquero, "Los Poemas Póstumos de Federico García Lorca", Verbum, no. 3. pp. 53-56.

[8] Verbum, no. 1, pp. 3-8.

[9] Verbum, no. 2, p. 4.

[10] Letter written to Philip Cummings of Woodstock, Vermont, July, 1929.

[11] Verbum, no. 3, pp. 58, 60, 62.

CICLÓN AND CUBAN CULTURE

When José Lezama Lima, the director of Orígenes, included an article on Vicente Aleixandre, José Rodríguez Feo, the co-director, because he had not been consulted, decided to start a rival Orígenes. Lezama threatened to sue over the use of the name, and as a result Rodríguez brought out Ciclón, a new journal. The dedication page of the first number (January, 1955) proudly states: "With it, we erase Orígenes which, as everybody knows, after ten years of efficient services to Cuban culture, is at the present time only a dead weight . . . one might say that Orígenes had already lived out its life." Just as Lezama had supplanted Espuela de Plata with his journal, so Rodríguez hoped to replace Orígenes with Ciclón.

The title, deliberately chosen for its suggestion of tropical violence, mirrors the aggressive tones many of Ciclón's contributors used in their conjectures concerning contemporary Cuban culture. The journal, a bimonthly devoted to both translations and original works, became a quarterly in 1957 and, with the exception of one special number published in 1959, ceased formal publication with the April-June issue. Aside from original poetry, theater, short stories, and essays on a variety of Cuban topics, the contributors also concentrated on foreign culture, examining subject matter as disparate as the Marquis de Sade's view of the darker aspects of man's sexual behaviour, Marx as an existentialist, and the theater of the absurd. Edith Sitwell, Henri de Montherlant, Raymond Queneau, Alfred Jarry, Lionel Trilling, and W.H. Auden are among the many non-Hispanic writers treated in the journal. Spanish and Spanish American authors who also receive attention include Julián Marías, Francisco Ayala, Carlos Bousoño, Dámaso Alonso, Emilio Prados, Luis Cernuda, Vicente Aleixandre, Guillermo de Torre, Ernesto Sábato, Alfonso Reyes, Victoria Ocampo, Julio Cortázar, José Bianco, Miguel Angel Asturias, and Octavio Paz.

THE CONTRIBUTORS

The Ciclón collaborators, some of them obscure, comprised Anton Arrufat, Niso Malaret, Ramón Ferreira, Ambrosio Fornet, René Jordán, Luis Lastra, Luis Marré, Rine Leal, Fayad Jamis, born in Mexico but a Cuban by culture, José Antonio Portuondo, and Virgilio Piñera, Rodríguez Feo's co-director. Ciclón writers, whatever their interest in foreign literatures, sought principally to define Cuban culture. Virgilio Piñera gave the first of a series of lectures sponsored by the journal in the Lyceum on February 27, 1955. In its reproduction in Ciclón as "Cuba y la literatura," he starts off by questioning the very existence of Cuban letters. His countrymen take pride in their swollen histories which seem to reveal an almost superhuman production, but their literature exists only in belletristic manuals. Cubans lack the literary tradition and the necessary language. José María Heredia, far superior to his French cousin, is less well known because he did not express himself in "the language of a great literature." Even a reform generation, such as the Avance group, produced politicians, professors and newspapermen rather than artists. Their mistake lay in believing that by rebelling against the previous generation they could supply a renovating force, but they soon became as decadent as those belonging to the cultural matrix they hoped to replace. Furthermore, most of the writers wrote not for Cuba but for a mutually admiring closed circle of intellectual snobs (March, 1955).

Some of the Ciclón writers seemed unaware of the dangers of overinterpreting; others offered more commentary than cultural insight, at times heavily interlarded with political catch phrases; still others seemed unaware that by counterposing their particular vision of art under the aegis of investigating Cuba's literary heritage, they would not receive unquestioning critical acceptance or popular acclaim. Yet in spite of the attempt by some to fit Cuban works into a single artistic and conceptual framework, these writers, beyond the literary content of their productions and their particular vision of Cuban culture and social reality, proved relevant. Their passion, as well as their own peculiar moral commitment and occasional capacity for self-transcendence, enables the reader to receive a critically coherent picture of the interplay of the rational and irrational in Cuban culture in the pre-Castro years.

ORIGINAL CREATIVE WORKS

Short Stories

Fayad Jamís, Luis Marré, Antón Arrufat, Luis Lastra, and many others, in addition to costumbrista contributions in their original short stories, provide parodies and grotesque, surrealistic, almost ultrarational themes. We meet a dead man turned into a toad, a man who must eat part of a mountain daily, knowing that nobody will acknowledge the changing geological configuration, a girl who returns to her mother's womb to be born again, a man who dances to music played by unknown hands, and many more. Some of the stories concentrate on more understandable vignettes of childhood, passion, pain, low life, love, and death.

Virgilio Piñera's stories are probably the most significant. In "El gran Baro" he writes about a clown of revolutionary technique who influences the spectators to clothe every act of their life in a jester's disguise. He succeeds in the creation of a society of clowns without himself being able even to titter until he dies laughing at their futile attempts to make him a member of their risible fraternity. After Baro's death, the people, normal again, use fragments from their statue to Saint Baro for children's games. Since Piñera accepts the absurd and irrational as symbols of the world's moral dilemma, it is not accidental that the central character is a clown (January, 1955).

In another Piñera story about the ambiguity and absurdity of life, "El Muñeco," an ironic attack on the Communist Party, the protagonist wants to create a double for the president to save him from the burden of ceremonial duties. Learning from an old Communist friend that he has touched the president, he becomes a Party member in order to contact the ruler. After a series of mishaps he meets the president and convinces him that he should allow perfectly reproduced dolls to perform his public functions. The idea spreads like wildfire among other officials, and finally, everybody waits in toy factory rooms for a child with innocent hands to provide salvation. In reality a fantasy of the absurd, his enigmatic story shows us man in an alienated world which prefers papier maché figures to those of flesh and blood (March, 1956).

Other stories in Ciclón include "Mi amigo Osia" by Ambrosio Fornet, about a lonely silent protagonist who hallucinates a week in his life before he dies; "Mumson" by Leslie Fajardo, a fantasy about weak-chinned Inferiors who rebel and take power from the strong-chinned Superiors; "Un día de Fiesta" by Luis Lastra, about envious Siamese twins; "Juan de Dios" by Ramón Ferreira, a pathetic story of a crippled boy sent to an orphanage; the ever-popular "Josefina, atiende a los señores" by Guillermo Cabrera, which presents us with an unfortunate prostitute and an old fraud of a Madame; "Hojas de un Diario" by Humberto Rodríguez Tomeu, concerning a voyeur of death who lives only through the agonies of the final moments of others; and "Visita de Cumplido" by René Jordán, about a sincere old lady who visits her old home, now a brothel, and temporarily evokes sparks of decency in one of the prostitutes.

Poetry

Original poetry, less abundant than short stories, appears in every issue. The July, 1955, number introduces "Cinco Poetas Jóvenes Cubanos." They are Ramón D. Miniet, who talks of faith, God, and death; José Triana, later known for his theatrical efforts, who discusses man's solitary anguish and search for himself through the experience of each cosmic moment; Severo Sarduy, better known as a novelist and Luis R. Moran and Joaquín Enrique Piedra who discuss man's journey through life together with themes of loneliness, God and death. In the same issue Aldo Menéndez contributes poems on national themes, human desires, and the horror of living. Later Ciclón volumes include poetry by Antón Arrufat about the brotherhood of man, the affirmation of love, the penetration of the unknown, and man's confrontation with himself; works by Rolando Escardó, who reveals his physical hunger, search for God and social justice; and poetry by Armando Blanco Furniel, Luis Lastra, Luis Marré, and many others about innocence, temporality, the historical trap, the future of Cuba, and death.

Theater

Contributors also published several short theatrical pieces. Virgilio Piñera's "Los siervos" (November, 1955) satirizes Russian Communism. A group wishes to stop Nikita from establishing Nikitism, which he defines as being the servant of the people. Afraid to do away with him, Party officials gain time by pretending not to understand his message. After a series of grotesque kicking scenes, participated in by a citizen who believes Nikita's proclamation, we discover that the characters are trapped by a vicious philosophical and political circle of servant and master, "based on the existing relationships between the foot of the declared master and the backside of the acknowledged servant." Another more realistic drama, "Donde está la luz" by Ramón Ferreira (March, 1956), deals with primitive passion. Adela, a jealous wife, kills her sister's boyfriend and then her husband when he confesses his love for the sister.

Ciclón also contains dramatic pieces which verge on caricature. Niso Malaret's "Anuncia Freud a María" (November, 1956) concerns a completely credulous character, María Duplassis, who for twenty years thought she could have a child by sending off to Paris for one or eating tomato seeds to become pregnant. After killing her unresponsive husband, she decides to fulfill her heart's desire with Abril, her servant. The work, filled with absurd scenes of ouija boards and Russian roulette, also presents us with a sword swallower and a crocodile woman. Antón Arrufat in "El caso se investiga" (April-June, 1957), first performed in the Lyceum on June 28, 1957, creates an absurd farce about a stuffy inspector who questions Eulalia about her husband's death. The play contains a sister who is deaf only in the morning and a library composed of one book read every four years. At the end it turns out that we are not even sure who it was that died.

CRITICISM OF CUBAN FICTION

The essays, book reviews, and analyses of Cuban sculpture, painting, and literature more precisely reflect "lo cubano," although several reviews such as José Rodríguez Feo's of La carne de René (1952) by Virgilio Piñera, impart a rather general moral, in this case that, imprisoned by our bodies, we are all men of flesh and bone (January, 1955).

Guillermo Cabrera Infante, in his review of Salvador Bueno's Antología del cuento en Cuba, criticizes the forced imagery and overly constructed plots of Hernández Catá and the carelessness and lack of creativity of Luis Felipe Rodríguez. Cabrera concludes that, in spite of an outstanding story of graphic horror and brutality by Carlos Fernández Cabrera, many works have been included because of their popularity rather than for their literary merit. He condemns the lack of discrimination and order in the anthology and the exclusion of fine writers like Silvano Suárez, Montes Huidobro, René Jordán, Lisandro Otero, and Julio Kouri (March, 1955). In the same issue José Rodríguez Feo reviews Aquellare (1954) by Ezequiel Vieta, whose stories of fantasy and dreams about the terrifying situation which confronts man he cites as among the finest of modern Cuban literature.

Julio Rodríguez Luis seeks the Cuban spirit in García Alzola's first short story collection, El paisaje interior (1956), but he concedes that many of the stories fail to come to grips with the true character of "lo cubano," even though they evoke successfully a particular character or environment (July, 1956).

Niso Malaret believes that Virgilio Piñera's Cuentos fríos (1956), clear and logical, offers spiritual guidelines for the recovery of pride in one's humanity. Man, rejecting his own hypocrisy in this attempted restoration, must replace his absurd values with sincere ones. Believing themselves to be creatures of sin, human beings strive for a sterile spiritual metamorphosis by shunning evil. They should, on the contrary, recognize their nature and impulses and realize that not all pleasurable things are the fruit of temptation. Many of the stories, which treat of love, hate, vanity, and death, exude an enigmatic mixture of the real and the absurd, which Malaret labels "aerialism" because one feels the same kind of pleasurable vertigo on reading them as that experienced by a trapeze artist (January-March, 1957).

Finally, in "Nueva trampa para la literatura cubana," Julio Rodríguez Luis admits that the atmosphere and dialogue of La Trampa (1956) by Enrique Serpa are authentically Cuban but laments that Serpa "instead of limiting himself to exposition, has slanted his work toward social doctrines and political theses, further complicated by his own quite dubious personal concepts." The author may have wanted to show the degeneration of a political system and the failure of revolution, but he has disfigured true Cuban history "by trying to idealize a wretched and sick criminal action and by attacking the intellectual who enters politics but who, in the final analysis, is an honorable man who responds in his own way to the attacks of his environment." The fine description of Havana life, the brilliantly handled interior monologues, and the few beautiful moments cannot disguise the contradictions, grammatical errors, carelessness, and surprising vulgarity. Rather than an existential fulfillment, the work is a simplistic journalistic report. After a few successful autographing sessions at cocktail parties by the author, it will be clear that Cuba "will have advanced a few more steps into the provincialism which overwhelms it and, of course, we shall be even further away from a national literature or from an effective contribution to Spanish American fiction" (April-June, 1957).

CRITICISM OF CUBAN POETRY

Virgilio Piñera, in a long essay on the poetry of Emilio Ballagas (1910-1954), deplores the attempts to transmute the poet, after death, into a good husband, father, and Catholic. Ballagas needs no purifying mythology to explain that his struggle was with himself. Furthermore, a real understanding of the Cuban poet must take into account his homosexuality (which he himself viewed as "abominable sin") as the decisive element even in poems such as the sonnet "El hijo," about a "father who has borne himself." His wife and son were indispensable in his fight against "sin." In "Psalmo," for example, he sees himself as a dark, weak failure, pursued by conscience. He searches constantly for peace and salvation through woman, but he cannot avoid a sense of horror at her carnality and breasts which aim at him like "two terrifying pistols."

Alluding to an unhappy homosexual affair in "Elegía sin Nombre," Ballagas, in his poetic volume Nocturno y Elegía (1938), struggles against his self-magnified sense of guilt. He seeks, almost obsessively, for expiation through self-immolation and humiliation in poems such as "Retrato," which reveals a poet who is condemned eternally to look at the mirror of himself. Later poems, psychic variants of Nocturno y Elegía, offer paradoxical views of real and sinful love. In Cielo en Rehenes, which won the 1951 national prize for poetry, Ballagas, accepting death as a kind of disinfectant spray, hopes for salvation through a new interpretation of his sinful nature. Piñera, citing his long friendship with Ballagas, says:

"although sensitive people may be scandalized . . . we decided to tell the true life of Ballagas and not the one which others, performing a dubious service, wished to give to him" (September, 1955).

José Antonio Portuondo wrote an extended essay on the poetry of Rubén Martínez Villena (1899-1934), stressing the poet's political and ideological bent. Portuondo divides his poetic production into three stages: 1917-1922, 1923-1927, and 1928-1934. In his first period the poet attempts the classical sonnet and amorous themes together with a few episodes from the struggle for Independence. Influenced by Boti, Acosta, and Poveda, he seeks a renewal of poetic themes in a personal and yet universal way. A victim together with other Cubans of the economic chaos and corruption which followed World War One, Martínez, along with other young poets, began to "seek in literature, in self-analysis, evasion as a common refuge." Along with others, Martínez belonged to the tertulia of the Café Martí. Experimenting from about 1920 on with a variety of musical rhythms and meters, the poet reveals his anguish and frustration at the gray mediocrity of his daily life. His best known poem, "Canción del sainete póstumo," filled with melancholy and irony, has remained as "the epitaph of that group of writers, nauseated by the crisis of their circumstances."

In his second stage, more interested in the ineffable, Martínez Villena augments his poetic thread of impotence, failure, and death with a note of hope for national redemption. According to Portuondo, the moral decay during Zayas's rule "which affected the great masses of Cubans, demanded an immediate and direct action to awaken the island from its dangerous stagnation. The beginning of that renovating action was produced, headed by Rubén, with "the protest of the Thirteen," the eighteenth of March of 1923." The first political literary battle in Republican Cuba (which Portuondo equates with that of the Parisian surrealists) marks the conscious entry of Cuban intellectuals into the ideological battles which "opened a new stage in our intellectual life."

Although Martínez Villena attacked sharply old sentimental topics, as the old Martí tertulia ceded to the Grupo Minorista, he continued to write formal love poetry and direct the literary pages of El Heraldo de Cuba while engaging in political activities. With the advent of Machado and ensuing struggles, he became a member of the Cuban Communist Party, and, as Portuondo rather subjectively notes, devoted his time to fighting "against governmental repression and terror and against the death which lay in ambush in his damaged lungs." Portuondo denies that the oft quoted "I am not a poet (although I have written verse). . . I destroy my verses, I despise them, I give them away, I forget them . . . " means that Martínez rejected poetry in favor of social action. That poet's passion for poetry and poetic form never abandoned him, even in his most ardent revolutionary struggles, for he fought for man's salvation with a wholehearted and "poetically heroic" dedication (January, 1956).

Antón Arrufat, in "Acerca de Eugenio Florit," disapproves of Doble acento (1937) as a "pretentious book." He concedes that in some of his poetry Florit manages to define "objects, signposts of the soul in its progression from childhood to the bittersweet juice of many years on our backs, or our thoughts and acts in the course of our lives. . ." Unfortunately, Florit seldom reaches perfection in his poems, because they evaporate in a flood of words which are lacking the precise "concrete adjective . . . manifest weakness of his poetic instrument . . . which becomes evident in his most pretentious poems." Florit, aside from occasional notes of freshness and grace, a poet of simple experiences, bourgeois emotional melancholy, and romantic nostalgia for the past, writes poetry quite inferior to that of Mariano Brull. Arrufat condemns Poema mío (1947) as a sample of what Cuban men of letters, conditioned by the lack of quality in Cuban literature, poverty of life, and lack of opportunity, find praiseworthy, and he concludes that Florit, reactionary and escapist, in reality is only a minor poet (July, 1956).

Among other poets treated are Angel Gaztelu, who though born in Spain is essentially Cuban, José A. Baragaño, Cintio Vitier, Mariano Brull, and Roberto Fernández Retamar. José Rodríguez Feo condemns Gradual de Laudes (1955) by Gaztelu as commonplace old-fashioned poetry unanimated by a single spark of genius. He believes that the laudatory prologue by Lezama Lima was an ironical one. Virgilio Piñera analyzes El amor original (1955) by Baragaño (1932-1962) in more flattering terms and hopes the poet will escape the trap of a ceremonial surrealism based on routine imitation of European sources and a repetition of old litanies (November, 1955). Piñera spoke somewhat prophetically, for Baragaño, abandoning the exoticism of Parisian bohemian life, later became a revolutionary poet. Antón Arrufat returns to the more common negative tone so much a part of Ciclón's criticism in his analysis of Cintio Vitier's Canto llano (1956), which he finds to be "banal, ineffective, and futile." Vitier, all method and system, writes artificial poetry filled with scandalous contradictions. As a professional man of letters, he should have evaluated his own productions more severely because "poems like those of Canto Llano may, perhaps, be written but never published" (May, 1956). Julio Rodríguez Luis in "Recuerdo de Mariano Brull (1891-1956)" eulogizes him as a man who lived every moment in search of "mysterious perfumes and most splendid vapors." Rodríguez also recalls Brull's membership in Amar, his friendship with Juana de Ibarbourou, and his generational activities (September, 1956). Finally, Luis Marré, himself a poet, discusses Alabanzas, conversaciones (1955), a poetry collection of Fernández Retamar. Marré praises him as a man who lacks the unrestrained ambition which has prevented successes for other young Cubans, and notes the change from an earlier poetry of delicate form to one which masterfully uses simple Cuban colloquialisms (July, 1956).

THEATER CRITICISM

Ciclón writers also reviewed several theatrical performances. Humberto Rodríguez Tomeu discusses "Las criadas," performed by the theatrical group Prometeo (January, 1955); Niso Malaret objects to the excessive length of development of the first act of Ramón Ferreira's "Donde está la luz" and condemns it as a short story given dramatic form (May, 1956). Rine Leal, along with Antón Arrufat and Calvert Casey, an important theater critic, disposes of "Falsa Alarma" by Piñera, a study of good and evil, as a farce in which nobody can really judge anything, and Arrufat's "El caso se investiga," another farce, as presenting "the absurd for the sake of the absurd" (April-June, 1957).

Humberto Rodríguez Tomeu contends that since the Cuban theater is "so flimsy and infantile, to be discrete is to begin to be something" (January, 1955), a viewpoint shared by all the theatrical critics who contributed to Ciclón. Rine Leal, even more destructive, declares: "In the first place we discovered that we have not had, throughout our history, a national theater, that we do not have one and, what is worse, that we are moving very slowly in search of one." Leal sketches the history of the Cuban theater, recalls the attempted renovations of Salvador Salazar and the various theater companies such as the Teatro La Cueva, Adad, Academia Municipal, Teatro Universitario, and Prometeo. He especially condemns Patronato del Teatro which he dismisses as an organization which presented performances in an elegant hall for elegant people who came to visit each other rather than to see theater. Even though a largely disinterested public has made the development of dramatic productions difficult, Leal sees some hope in the attempts by small theatrical groups to wean the Cuban public away from comedies of vulgarity, sex, and melodrama. He pleads for the restoration of theatrical contests and school dramatic performances. Contending that theatrical critics are trapped by a web of interlocking friendships, compromises, created interests, and gossip, he absolves them, for "if we do not have theater, how can we possess responsible critics. . ." He hopes that Cuba will some day come to a realization of the truth about itself and that "through seeing our own weaknesses, we shall be able to remedy them" (September 1955).

NON-FICTION WORKS

More foreign than native non-fiction works are analyzed in Ciclón. An exception is the lengthy review which José Rodríguez Feo gives to El heroismo intelectual (1955) by José Antonio Portuondo, whom he praises for facing squarely the crisis which confronts Cuba without hiding behind "obscure allusions or formalistic evasions." Admitting that a Marxist may be sincere in his deceitful portrayal of reality, he nonetheless rejects Portuondo's contention that revolution offers a solution to man's problems. Any Marxist critic, in trying to evaluate a literary work, cannot abandon the dogmatic prejudices implicit in a fanatical belief in a specific political doctrine. Claiming that Portuondo confuses the ethical with the esthetic because of his rigid political position, Feo concludes that Portuondo, unable to escape his divided loyalty between literature and Marxist thought, performs more easily the role of sociologist than that of literary artist (May, 1955).

Julio Rodríguez Luis, associating Loló de la Torriente with feminist and left wing activity in Cuba, concedes that her Mi casa en la tierra, written with an almost terrifying sincerity, presents us with writers, politicians, newspapermen, professors, and artists, alive and dead. In spite of her "complete vision of Cuban life during the Second Republic and accurate examination of revolutionary times," her book of memoirs, unorganized and without resolution, lacks a cogent analysis of the significance of related events and thus may be judged a failure (November, 1956).

José Rodríguez Feo in "Cultura y Moral" enumerates the dangers suffered by the artist from the anti-intellectual vendettas of the State. He states:

> In our country, where culture has always been tinged by improvisation and superficiality, the artist has lived on society's edges. Scorned and without the least stimulation by the government or its official organisms, he is the true pariah of the nation. To publish a book, sell a painting or a sculpture in these adverse circumstances is almost next to impossible. One reason is that in Cuba almost nobody reads and certainly not native works, sad to relate.

As a case in point he cites the Instituto Nacional de Cultura, composed, not of intellectuals, but of newspapermen of whom absolute conformity to orthodoxy is required. Their activities, pure entertainment, fail to inspire the true artist who, in order to publish his work, must leave Cuba or join the journalistic establishment. True culture, in opposition to the official one, is produced by a minority of artists in literary magazines and in works which, disregarding moral strictures, touch on the human condition. Morality in art, in any event, has nothing to do with an established cultural set, for only in the interchange of ideas and in the use of creative imagination can one speak of and achieve a true national culture (November, 1955).

Calvert Casey, in summing up the Cuban scene, declares that Cubans must admit their chauvinism, something which they had always criticized in others, and examine their "conviction that we were always ready to criticize ourselves, with the vague superiority which that certainty gave us." He laments the tendency of writers to forget their subject for a recitation of what they believe to be national virtues (July, 1956).

Ciclón writers, victims of their historical moment, filled their journal with satirical attacks on Marxism but allowed Communists like José Antonio Portuondo space in their pages. Throughout, the writers waver between conflicting philosophies, and one senses their political impotence at seeing their guidelines for a cultural revolution betrayed by a bureaucratic regime. They also oscillate between sympathy and repugnance, between human struggle for freedom and alienation from an older cultural matrix. Many of them offered soundly reasoned or intuitive insights; others, completely subjective and even aggressive, professed in shrill tones their exclusive ownership of artistic integrity. Since they possessed the truth, they were unable to be morally or culturally neutral. They rejected as myth and rhetorical exercise the grandeur and heroism of Cuba but had surprisingly little to say about language, a vehicle for the promulgation of those old myths and what they considered to be an outworn culture. They were deeply concerned about the role of the Cuban intellectual in society, but they lacked a structured theory of culture. Their common bond consisted of confronting rational and hierarchical forces with the irrational and anarchic.

In spite of its inconsistencies, Ciclón is a valuable document of the artistic attempts of the period to demythify Cuban culture in order to have a new beginning. The writers, frustrated, complained that the Cuban people were not aware that Ciclón was offering them the golden key to Heaven. As with all such groups, their sense of righteousness and their very dogmatism and slanted value judgments showed that they were, in reality, little different from the national cultural institutions against which they were supposedly fighting. Ciclón did not profoundly change Cuban culture, but it served as a bridge to more revolutionary journals, inevitably in some measure an extension of the past. Neither <u>Ciclón</u> nor its descendants have managed a radical metamorphosis or a destruction of "lo cubano," perhaps an elaborately constructed myth, but one with more strength and validity than reality itself.

CICLON AND THE CASTRO REVOLUTION

Ciclón, which sought to supplant Orígenes in order to contribute to the process of the demythification of Cuban culture, flourished between January, 1955 and June, 1957, when it ceased formal publication. During that period the journal's Cuban contributors confronted the rational and hierarchical forces with an irrational and anarchic counterattack but accepted both Marxist and anti-Marxist articles. After its apparent demise, Ciclón's director, José Rodríguez Feo, published one final number (Volume 4, No. 1, January-March 1959) of what was to have become a trimestral review. In theory, since many of this issue's writers were the same as before, one would have expected unrelenting attacks on chauvinistic interpretations of Cuban tradition and lo cubano and a continuing commitment to experimental and surrealistic literature. What one discovers, instead, is a sharply focused political orientation, clothed in a cultural cloak. In 1959 the writers no longer waver between conflicting philosophies or oscillate between sympathy and repugnance for certain cultural contributions. They still lay claim to the sole and exclusive possession of the "truth," but now, in addition to poetic and fictional thrusts against old literary traditions and cultural myths, the writers stress the new political revolutionary wave of the future.

In an editorial, "La neutralidad de los escritores," José Rodríguez Feo explains that Ciclón ceased publication in 1957 because during the fight against the tyranny of Batista, when people were dying in Havana streets and Oriente hills, he could not in good conscience offer simple literature to his journal's readers. Forbidden, he states, by a ferocious censorship from publishing any kind of political or social criticism, he had furthermore aroused the enmity of Dr. Guillermo de Zéndegui, the director of the Instituto de Cultura (which many had excoriated in earlier numbers of the magazine.) Now that Batista had fallen from power, it was time to judge both those writers who had lent themselves to the dictator's cause and those who had hidden under a mask of neutrality. He includes, among those whose integrity he attacks, former friends and some of the most famous Cuban writers such as Gastón Baquero, Franscisco Ichaso, Salvador Bueno, José María Chacón y Calvo, Medardo Vitier, Fernando Ortiz, Agustín Acosta, José Lezama Lima (always a favorite target because of their quarrel during Orígenes days), and Jorge Mañach. Rodríguez questions whether they can aspire to deserve "el respeto de nuestras juventudes revolucionarias cuando no tuvieron entonces el civismo de retirar su colaboración intelectual a la obra cultural del régimen depuesto. . . ."[1] All intellectuals, he claims, have a duty to censure those responsible for their intellectual collaboration with Batista and the cultural program he developed through the Instituto Nacional de Cultura.

The 1959 number of Ciclón contains short prose selections by Manuel Díaz Martínez, Ricardo Jordán, Calvert Casey, Luis Marré, and Frank Rivera, and poems by Severo Sarduy, Nivaria Tejera, R. D, Miniet, and R. T. Escardó. The stories, no longer in the surrealistic or experimental mode of earlier numbers, stress the Cuban reality of 1958 and the struggle against Batista. In "Relato de la Sierra" by Jorge Menéndez, the protagonist, a medical corpsman with the Batista forces, knows the pain and suffering of dying men. Himself wounded and captured by Castro partisans, he soon realizes that they are really simple people with the "necesidad de luchar y morir defendiendo lo que se considera justo . . ." (p.7). Because of their kindness to him and through his meeting with Fidel Castro, whom the men rightfully adore, he becomes convinced of the nobility of their cause and stays on to fight for the Cuban revolution.

The non-fiction contributions also reflect the tremendous revision of values suffered by the writers. Pedro de Oraá, acknowledging the "severa conmoción social que domina la isla" (p. 33), nonetheless believes that writers, even though they must abandon some established ideas, need Cuban tradition, which they can reinterpret and reintegrate (together with certain European esthetic developments) in order to reinforce the American aspects of Cuban culture. Virgilio Piñera, the most prolific contributor to earlier issues of Ciclón, recalls his own new hopes: "Grité fuerte al hacer mi brindis: ¡Viva la Revolucion! . . . en tal grito iban implícitas confianza y esperanza" (p. 10). Comparing Fidel Castro to Napoleon, he recalls positively the people's destruction of the symbols of tyranny. At the same time he attacks those writers, suddenly revolutionaries as of January first, now pouring forth noisy praise of the Revolution. He calls for creativity in the belief that good writers are as necessary for the Revolution as the soldier, worker, or farmer.

By far the longest contribution to the journal (some twenty of the seventy-one total pages), "Refutación a Vitier" by R. Fernández Bonilla, is a reply to an attack against him in El Mundo because of his adverse critical evaluation of Cintio Vitier's work. In that February 22, 1959, article Leonardo Acosta accused Fernández of launching a disguised attack on Orígenes and its supporters and of unfairly criticizing Cintio Vitier's book, Lo cubano en la poesía. Fernández, replying that these writers have "rehuido o han ignorado, simplemente, el sentido pleno de reivindicaciones de la Cuba contemporánea" (p. 52), feels that Vitier, in particular, has repeated old myths about Cuban indifference and lack of seriousness. He denies Vitier's contention that everything depends on a metaphysical solution and takes him to task for ignoring the superhuman sacrifices of Cuban youth in their fight for freedom.

For Vitier, liberty, without political overtones, is a poetic absolute, while patriotism is essentially the same everywhere. For him sacrifice is a poetic demand rather than dying for one's country. Vitier, constitutionally unable to "reconocer el sentido estelar que encarnaba el desembarco de Fidel . . ." (p. 60), together with Lezama Lima, has a peculiar idea of the function of poetry, one which "tuerce la esencia de una cultura, de una historia, y aun de los hechos que la sangre tutelar de la juventud dotó de sentido irreductible" (p. 60).

Vitier's categories or Cuban essences in Cuban poetry include arcadismo, nature, Indians, innocence; ingravidez, mystery, vagueness, delicacy; intrascendencia, games irresponsibility, anti-solemnity; lejanía, nostalgia, myth, culture as a dream; cariño, youthful beauty, criollo customs; despego, lack of stability, national sensibility; frío, resentment, absence of fate; vacío, oratory, politics, lack of goals, daily vulgarity; memoria, infancy as paradise lost, nostalgia for the past; and ornamento, the baroque and voluptuosness. Vitier does not know what criteria should guide Cubans in search of "lo cubano" but contends that the mere fact of being Cuban "nos dota de ciertas sospechas y vivencias que nos orienta" (p. 62).

Fernández, rejecting Vitier's attempt to categorize the Cuban through poetic testimony, claims it is absurd to try to create philosophy through the unreachable dimension of poetry. In any event, Vitier's book shows colossal ignorance of one of the most profound Cuban realities in its most brilliant moment. As for lo cubano, "es una simple abstracción que no tiene asiento real sino en la existencia del individuo nativo que se denomina cubano por accidentes históricos, geográficos y de nacimiento en un ámbito terrestre determinado" (p. 65). This does not mean it is indefinable but rather that one cannot use a unilateral and fleeting proof like poetry as an instrument for defining it. He scolds Vitier for his negative judgments of Cubans as weak and incapable of initiative or sacrifice for a new reality. Vitier, not a counter revolutionary because he does not have any political philosophy, reveals a complete ignorance of the meaning of the Cuban Revolution, an innocence which no real writer can profess.

As for Orígenes, though it represented at one time the best of an intellectual generation, it betrayed the hopes of the Cuban people by asserting that Cuba's problem was a metaphysical one at the very moment when the finest members of a new generation were being killed. For Fernández, the support its writers gave Batista, their self-denigration, their withdrawal from reality and indifference to national questions of moment, for which intellectuals must bear responsibility, makes them almost a grotesque and terrible joke. What Cuba needs, he concludes, is human poetry which will reflect historical human time and not the metaphysical and mythical reality of which Lezama speaks, not a metahistory but rather a reaffirmation and realization of human essence.

This last issue contains the same shrill tones of previous numbers, but the writers' idea of culture as a servant of a political and social cause rather than an intellectual one is quite new. Instead of fighting for their creative liberty as before, they propose, without being aware of the irony, literary straitjackets for themselves. Rather than reinforcing the cause of human aspiration or defending a new reality with their own literary emancipation, they seem to use words like "virtue" and "justice" to attack those with different political opinions, those who perhaps through a lack of personal bravery kept silent in the face of tyranny. Emotional and aggressive, they preach, as they protest their love for the Cuban people and their sacrifice, the very censorship against which they fought under Batista. Sadly, in the light of later events involving the intellectual castration of writers like Padilla and Arrufat (a constant contributor to Ciclón between 1955 and 1957) by the Castro government, one must conclude that sincerity of purpose is not enough, that charity, conciliation and love are virtues wisely to be followed, and that those who profess, however articulately, their exclusive possession of the truth and artistic integrity, are often discarded by history and by the ideological orthodoxy of the moment.

Note

[1] José Rodríguez Feo, *Ciclón*, 4, 1 (1959), 35. Further citations in the text are from this issue.

THEMES, TRENDS, AND TEXTURES:
THE 1960'S AND THE SPANISH AMERICAN NOVEL

In 1953 Luis Alberto Sánchez, revising an earlier opinion, contended that the Spanish American novelists had begun to "ponerse a tono con su realidad y, por consiguiente, a encontrar expresión cada vez más precisa y mejor adaptada a su sujeto."[1] As industrialization increased, the old themes of man against nature ceded to a quest for spiritual fulfillment in a computerized world where old traditions seemed to have little relevance. Some Spanish American novelists, following the creators of the "nouveau roman," rejected middle class reality for uncommitted description which was neither absurd nor significant. Others turned to the United States and especially William Faulkner for inspiration.[2]

In the 1960's some novelists combined their grotesque vision of the world with a continued interest in man as a universal being. Others, more interested in technique than meaning, conveyed reality through strange symbols and structures, preferring esthetics to life and superimposed and simultaneous structural levels to communication. Thematic parallelisms, interior monologue, free association, counterpoint, multi-dynamic approaches, the multiple view, interrelated symbologies, and the fusion of classic and modern myth proved effective. The use of circular and fragmented time, simultaneous narration, the avoidance of chronology to view events at the same moment, gave added mobility to the narration. As Mendilow had stated, "the time element in fiction . . . in large measure determines the author's choice of treatment of his subject."[3] The novelists fused poetry and prose, space and time, solitude, death, and despair into a central metaphysical framework, disintegrating novelistic structure and disregarding and deforming what might be termed reality. The extreme sample of this new kind of novel reflected a pre-verbal state which amounted to a kind of <u>babelismo idiomático</u>.[4]

Many novelists of the 1960's, through destruction of language in the classic mold, attempted to liberate prose by a return to the origins of language to find one in which the artist might utilize "tanto a las exigencias de su arte como a las exigencias de su sociedad . . ."[5] The novel's words transformed the narrative, a transformation which "es lo que la novela 'dice' y no lo que se suele discutir in extenso: trama personaje, anécdota, mensaje, denuncia."[6] Involving open, anti-cultural forms, this type of novel established "nuevas relaciones entre la modificación del invididuo y la modificación de la realidad."[7] The style became aphoristic and disjunctive as though metaphor no longer sufficed to carry the burden of violence and guilt of the modern world, and the novelists finally conceived of a language whose form corresponded to the mystery inhabiting it.

Existentialism and anguish at the world's absurdity carried as a concomitant element the inevitable relationships among all men in an insignificant corner of space and time. Surrounded by the infinite and death, as we seek our authenticity, "intentamos al menos comunicarnos con otros fragmentos semejantes a nosotros, pues la soledad de los espacios infinitos nos aterroriza."[8]

This anguished search for the meaning of human destiny assumed mythical proportions with ease, for to exist in a universe of Prometheus or Oedipus helped remove the inexorability of mortality, allowing man the possibility of a permanent existence. Sound, imagery, movement, magic, and temporal flights allowed the character's consciousness to deny normal reality in order to act in a dream world of fantasy and myth, a kind of magic realism to which there was a felicitous predisposition in Spanish America.[9] Timelessness and the avoidance of sentimentalism[10] as well as an insistence on thematic importance marked the magic realist who "exalta sus sentidos hasta un estado límite que le permite adivinar los inadvertidos matices del mundo externo, ese multiforme mundo en que vivimos."[11] Fable and fancy, beauty and terror, happiness and despair, hallucination and dream meld the visible and the tangible. Like the Indian the magic realist sees things not "so much as the events themselves but translated them into other dimensions, dimensions where reality disappears and dreams appear, where dreams transform themselves into tangible and visible forms."[12]

The new way of looking at time and space and the participation of the reader in the subjective world of the characters produced another kind of reality also, often shocking and aggressive in its exposure to violence and anguish. The social novel encouraged the reader to indulge in a unidimensional and emotive involvement, and often the novelistic exaggeration aborted the impact by an appeal to that facile emotional indulgence. The hopes of the thirties and forties that man might achieve a new political order and social justice (in many cases the new moral code was influenced by class hatreds) gave way to an increasing sense of futility. The novelists saw life as one absurdity among many in a cosmic nothingness and concluded gloomily that nothing could be accomplished. As Jean Franco states: "In the sixties . . . there is a growing feeling of impotence, of being caught between the Scylla of North America and the Charybdis of Russia. It is no accident that many contemporary novels are set in microcosmic communities and their characters are caught in situations as inflexible as those of Greek tragedy."[13]

The novelists of the sixties, searching for an explanation, almost an ontological exploration of the theme, felt just as committed politically as their predecessors, but they "make a clear distinction . . . between activism and literature. The first has to do with immediate issues, the second with invariables."[14] The new social novel examines the hearts of man "al igual que enfoca al cuadro social de conjunto. . . ."[15] In any event, the painted scene is no longer a stereotyped reality of a single truth but rather a transmuted reality, often a lyrical experience of meaning and a kind of "impermeable world." Mario Vargas Llosa constantly refers to the "insurrección permanente" of the artist, but the difficulty lies in giving artistic form to and extracting the esthetic possibilities from ordinary life.

The neo-realists view reality as conceptual as well as perceptual, and a novelist must be equipped to utilize three dimensional experience to communicate in an ever-shifting and changing world where realism and fantasy are no longer enemies. Characters incarnating various thematic parallelisms are at times prisoners of the very forces they seek to exorcise in the interplay of will and mechanical resignation to fate. Incomplete and lightly sketched, often for the reader to develop, they are incomplete and distorted entities struggling to become. The novelists view the fictional form as an esthetic experience in its relationship to man's role in the modern world, but for the most part they make no effort to "express a reality but rather to express their reality."[16] In almost all the novels of the sixties one finds a mysterious magic which transcends novelistic structures, what Conrad once termed "evocation of the unseen," but the unseen in human thought and passion, the identification of self, the relationship among men, and a reality within the façade of the temporal.

It is not always easy to separate and classify twentieth-century fictional mixtures, and attempts to do so are arbitrary exercises. In some novels magic realism, neo-realism, and existentialism are so intertwined as to form inseparable threads of a single fictional fabric. And even in the sixties, some novelists, both those belonging to older generations and those who from the first practiced the new techniques, often provided more traditional forms and at times combined the old and the new.

Novelists born before 1900

The Argentine, Manuel Gálvez (1882-1962), who published his first novel about fifty years earlier, wrote Me mataron entre todos (1962), a fantastic science fiction novel about a philosophy professor who could read minds. The Chilean, Manuel Rojas (1896-), used alternating life stories of a murderer and the man who receives his confession, to comment on man's moral failures in Punta de rieles (1960). Rojas' Sombra contra el muro (1964) completed the trilogy begun with Hijo de ladrón (1951). Of those born before the turn of the century and still writing novels in the 1960's the most progressive, undoubtedly, was the Guatemalan Miguel Angel Asturias (1899-1974).

Combining social themes and magic realism, Asturias affords us anthropological extrapolations of the Indian and his culture. Mulata de tal (1963) involves sorcery and Mayan and Catholic allegory. Celestino Yumí, after a series of transformations, arrives at Tierrapaulita, land of magic, where Caxtoc, the supreme Mayan devil, decides to destroy the earth invaded by the Christian demon. Asturias adapts archetypal symbols to convey his allegories, in a mythological layer of myths "making up a grand final myth . . . a fantastic land of Dali-esque optical distortions, a Coney Island of the unconscious. . ."[17] Maladrón (1969), subtitled "Epopeya de los Andes Verdes," shows the same mythic concerns as it emphasizes the confrontation of Spanish evil, energy, and civilization with Indian tropical magic.

Novelists born before 1910

By far the most prolific group of writers were Argentines. Jorge Luis Borges (1900-), even though he wrote no novels, had an incredible impact on the intellectual and technical development of the novel in his country with his labyrinths, discussion of the infinite, and mythic beliefs.[18] Leopoldo Marechal (1900-1970), with Borges the originator of the new novel in his country, wrote El banquete de Severo Arcángelo (1965), an allegorical, theological, paradoxical, and metaphysical examination of the meaning of good and evil. He mixes mystery, fantasy, and literature in the story of the metallurgist-magician who prepares his banquet for different guests representing various aspects of man's condition. Manuel Peyrou (1902-), a lesser member of the Sur group, wrote Acto y ceniza (1963), about a factory owner's search for honor during Perón days, and Se vuelven contra nosotros (1966). Eduardo Mallea (1903-), against whom so many of the younger novelist rebelled, continued his vast production about solitary protagonists and their existential boundaries in La barca de hielo (1967) and La penúltima puerta (1969).

Representing more traditional Argentine social and psychological themes, Leonidas Barletta (1902-) emphasized the problems of humble folk in De espaldas a la luna (1964). Juan Goyanarte (1900-) in Farsa (1961) created a grotesque vision of a Latin American dictatorship. Max Dickman (1902-) examined men and women trapped by abnormal feelings in Los atrapados (1962). Bernardo Verbitsky (1906-), a past master at discussions of slum life, voiced his fears of nuclear devastation in Un hombre de papel (1966).

El camino en la sombra (1963), by José Antonio Osorio Lizarazo (1900-64) of Colombia, a novel of the Indian as the white man's victim; Amasijo (1962), written by the Chilean Marta Brunet (1901-), about a rich homosexual who prefers death to a meaningless life; and the novels of Daniel Belmar (1906-), Los túneles morados (1961) and Detrás de las máscaras (1966), about life in Chile, seem strangely dated. Quite the contrary may be said about the Venezuelan novels of Ramón Díaz Sánchez (1903-68), Arturo Uslar Pietri (1906-), and Miguel Otero Silva (1908-), in spite of an occasionally tired theme and a traditional approach. Díaz's Borburatá (1961) examines life on a run-down cacao plantation. Uslar Pietri's Un retrato de la geografía (1962) handles the generation gap, political and sexual activities, and the role of the university. Estación de máscaras (1964) continues the story of Alvaro Collado, the protagonist of the previous novel, as he confronts corrupt Venezuelan politics. Otero Silva continues the story of Carmen Rosa, heroine of Casas muertas (1955), in Oficina No. 1 (1961). The characters, a cross section of the good and bad in Venezuelan humanity, form the nucleus for what the author hopes will be a stronger country. La muerte de Honorio (1963), set just prior to 1958, occurs on two temporal levels as five political prisoners, one of them a barber, live vicariously through the latter's fictitious son, Honorio.

The Cuban Alejo Carpentier (1904-1980) combined history, geography, time, violence, and sex in El siglo de las luces (1962), about the activities of the Frenchman Víctor Hugues in the Caribbean and the violent changes brought about by the French Revolution. He shows us the dichotomy between revolutionary idealism and practical politics, mixing mythology and magic, poetry and brutality in his neobaroque, geographic, and social panorama of the Antilles.

Born in the same year, the Mexican Agustín Yáñez analyzes Mexico City in Ojerosa y pintada (1960), concerning a twenty-four hour period in the life of a taxi driver and his passengers. La tierra pródiga (1960) examines the theme of tradition versus progress and the danger of depersonalization which a machine technology may bring. Las tierras flacas (1962) offers still another panorama of Mexican life and documents the disappearance of feudal power and the rise of a new individualism and way of thinking.

History and a continuing concern for human dignity mark the works of Enrique Laguerre (1906-) of Puerto Rico, Demetrio Aguilera Malta (1909-1981) and Alfredo Pareja y Diez Canseco (1908-) of Ecuador, and Gabriel Casaccia (1907-) of Paraguay. Laguerre's Cauce sin río (1962), in addition to his fears of man's depersonalization in a machine world, shows the dangers inherent in the capitalistic industrialization of his country. Aguilera's series of Episodios americanos in the 1960's seeks to give a fair perspective of American history. La caballeresa del sol (1964) treats of Bolívar's relationship with Manuela Sáenz; El Quijote de El Dorado: Orellano y el río de las Amazonas (1964) reveals that hero's reaction to the magic of the New World; Un nuevo mar para el rey: Balboa, Anayansi y el Océano Pacífico (1965) describes Balboa's love for an Indian girl and his betrayal by envious men. Pareja continues to write autobiographical novels under the general title of Los nuevos años, about his country from July 9, 1925 on. Los poderes omnímodos (1964) promotes the concept of universal brotherhood, as he fuses history and the imaginary, socialism and sex, in a telling analysis of his country and his people. Casaccia's La llaga (1964) is about an attempt to overthrow a dictator and an adolescent's suicide. Los exiliados (1966) treats of fraud, frustration and exiles in Argentina who dream impossible dreams of a return to their homeland.

Juan Carlos Onetti (1909-), whose El pozo (1939) reoriented the Uruguayan novel and influenced an entire generation of writers, presents fluctuating time values, animated objects, and isolated protagonists whose wish fulfillment fantasies represent ordinary human aspirations. They live alienated lives as victims of destiny and life's false values, unable to achieve fulfillment in their self-betraying shallow worlds. Onetti's setting is the village of Santa María, a microcosm of humanity. His lesser fiction of the 1960's includes La cara de la desgracia (1960), about a deaf girl's love affair, and Tan triste como ella (1963), about marital difficulties. El astillero (1961), a major novel, treats of Larsen, known as Juntacadáveres, a middle-aged ex-owner of a whorehouse who now works in a decaying shipyard in whose management he places his last hopes, one more absurdity in an absurd world. Juntacadáveres (1964) is the poetic story of the establishment of Larsen's whorehouse.

Novelists born before 1920

Colombian violence and sociological studies of sometimes sadistic social and political events provided much of the material of the contemporary Colombian novel. One critic mentions some forty such novels written between 1951 and 1965,[19] but another claims that from about 1961 on "se ha ido abandonando casi del todo el tema cansado y excesivamente apasionado de la violencia."[20] Violence is but one dimension in the work of Eduardo Caballero Calderón (1910-). Manuel Pacho (1962) presents the heroic possibilities of humble folk. Manuel, the half-mad protagonist, impelled by a half-understood ethical imperative, travels to Orocué so that a priest may give Christian burial to the half-decomposed corpse of his father. El buen salvaje (1966) tells of an abulic Latin American student in Paris who is smothered by the city and frustrated in his attempts to write a great American novel. Caín (1969) is a twentieth century exposition of the Cain and Abel story.

Augusto Morales Pino (1912-) and Gonzalo Canal Ramírez (1916-) also contributed to Colombian fiction. The former takes up the power of all-transcending love to free man from an existential world of anguish. La confesión (1961) involves incest and prostitution. Redoblan los tambores (1963) is about the Wars of Independence. Cielo y asfalto (1965) deals with the efforts of a painter to obtain spiritual tranquility and material success in the face of family tragedy. Canal Ramírez in Eramos doce (1963) and Contra la eternidad (1967) talks about the celibacy of priests, apostolic charity, and the meaning of Christ and maintains a surprising optimism in the face of his own rather bleak portraits of miserable peasants.

In Chile Francisco A. Coloane (1910-), Guillermo Atías (1917-) and Fernando Alegría (1918-) wrote excellent novels on themes as varied as the solitude of the sea, life aboard a whaling ship, and the life of a boxer from a poverty stricken district. The best novelist of this group is probably Carlos Droguett (1912-) whom Carlos Fuentes for some reason labeled "ese Luis Spota chileno."[21] Eloy (1960) is about a criminal who discovers life's values too late; Cien gotas de sangre y doscientas de sudor (1961) treats the Spanish conquest and its aftermath; Patas de perra (1965) tells us the life story of a cripple; El compadre (1967) concerns an unhappy alcoholic protagonist who reflects on his wife's adultery and seeks companionship from a religious statue. Droguett's other 1960's novels, Supay el cristiano (1967) and El hombre que había olvidado (1968), a kind of allegory of man's despair, are filled with the free association, dreams, and strange subconscious symbols common to his other fiction.

In Uruguay Clara Silva (1910-) wrote two novels of metaphysical and existential emphasis while Eliseo Salvador Porta (1912-), a social revolutionary, and Alfredo Dante Gravina (1913-), a confirmed Marxist, exploited social themes, Carlos Martínez Moreno (1917-), after Onetti probably the best Uruguayan novelist, pitilessly analyzes the vanity of contemporary man in an absurd world. El paredón (1963), "una eficaz integración entre el testimonio político y el conflicto humano, entre la visión documental y la trama novelesca . . .,"[22] depicts the evolution of revolutionary thought in a Uruguayan intellectual suffering from a generation gap in a society of middle-class values. Invited to witness an execution of a Batista policeman in Cuba, he draws a parallel with his own smug compatriots and through his exposure to another way of life may balance conflicting values and evaluate the moral and political future of his country. Con las primeras luces (1967) describes the decay and death of the Escudero family, its influence on the present, and its inability to abandon the old or accept the new. As the protagonist lies bleeding to death in a doorway, his interior monologues and associations reveal the sexual abnormalities and lack of human values in a society dying through loss of blood and energy. La otra mitad (1966) shows the attempt of a university professor, through his introspection, to recreate the reality of his mistress, killed by her husband. Unsuccessful, he realizes that even love holds no answer to man's desperate and despairing need to achieve a sense of his own authenticity. A master of circular time, Martínez analyzes an ambiguous world of indecision, one in which symbols play a large and impressive role.[23]

In Argentina Manuel Mujica Láinez (1910-) wrote a series of chronicles, mythical miscellanies of kings and vampires and demythifications of history. Among his novels, Bomarzo (1962) handles man's thirst for immortality and El unicornio (1965) is an ironic and elegant fictional autobiography of the Middle Ages narrated by the half-fairy Melusina. Silvina Bullrich (1915-) writes of the intimacies of a woman's soul and the feminine mystique. Un momento muy largo (1961) tells of the tortured love of a fifty-six year old man and a young girl. Los burgueses (1964), the first volume of a trilogy, treats of the hypocritical and trivial aristocrats about whom the author wishes to utter what she terms the "vomit of truth." Los salvadores de la patria (1965), the second volume, is about the intrigues, corruption, and empty lives of self-appointed saviors of Argentina. La creciente (1967) is a fantasy about the destruction of a Latin American capital, and yet another novel, Mañana digo basta (1968), concerns woman's role in modern society.

The two best known Argentine novelists born during these years are Ernesto Sábato (1911-) and Julio Cortázar (1914-). Sábato, constantly preoccupied with existentialism, in <u>Sobre héroes y tumbas</u> (1962) uses a retrospective historical episode to project the future, as he explores the strange relationship between Alejandra and her father. The patrician family lives through the memory of its "héroes y tumbas," but whatever good qualities their ancestors left have evaporated through the years. Alejandra, a victim of the callous and the corrupt, wipes out, with the death of her father and her own immolation, the final "héroe" and the "tumba" in which he lives. Cortázar treats all aspects of reality in paradoxical, absurd, and irrational combinations with fantasy. <u>Los premios</u> (1960) examines a group of people in the closed magic environment of a ship. The only member who insists on reaching the goal of knowing what is on the forbidden bridge dies for his pains. A polydimensional form beyond genre limits, the novel, through its soliloquies, offers us a nexus between the world and the interior reality of the work.[24] <u>Rayuela</u> (1963) is a philosophical, spiritual, burlesque mixture whose structure is so arbitrary that it may be read in different ways. The characters live in an ambiguous world of empty values. Horacio Oliveira, a frustrated writer, searches in vain for ultimate meaning as he indulges in apparently meaningless actions. Even when he attempts to play life's absurd game, a kind of hopscotch, he cannot win the final square and escape the loneliness of the real world, since life is a series of choices, all bad, in a world where only the laws of chance rule. <u>62. Modelo para armar</u> (1968), based on Chapter 62 of <u>Rayuela</u>, is a metaphysical search for rebirth. It continues the refined word play and offers the reader a kind of model kit to which he himself must give final shape. All the characters, bored by normal life, seek thrills, but all are parts of a game in which other players and their actions inevitably affect and modify ours.[25]

Magic realism and political events loomed large in the novels of many novelists born during the decade. Guillermo Meneses (1911-) of Venezuela, who had been writing haunting magical fiction since 1934, in <u>La misa de Arlequín</u> (1962), a satirical fantasy, described the evils of the military. The Ecuadorians Pedro Jorge Vera (1911-) and Adalberto Ortiz (1914-) combined poetry and political and social concerns in <u>La semilla estéril</u> (1965) and <u>El espejo y la ventana</u> (1967), respectively. Fernando Benítez (1911-) of México in <u>El agua envenenada</u> (1961), through the biography of a priest, told a tale of a revolt against an immoral <u>cacique</u>. The Costa Rican Fabián Dobles (1918-) wrote of the unjust political system in <u>Una burbuja en el limbo</u> (1962) and <u>En el San Juan hay tiburón</u> (1967). The Salvadoran Hugo Lindo (1917-) in <u>Justicia, señor gobernador</u>

271

(1960) examined the unfortunate consequences of a judge's passion for justice and in <u>Cada día tiene su afán</u> (1965) commented on the mystery of love and life.

In the Caribbean the Cuban José Lezama Lima (1912-) in <u>Paradiso</u> (1966) created ultra-rational material and a poetic language far outside the conventional as he sought the metaphor of time. He mixed erotic encounters, multiple fornications, and the history of homosexuality with a kind of autobiographical recall through José Cemí, his alter-ego, a combination of ordinary life with the author's metaphorical visions. José Soler Puig (1916-), on the contrary treated the Cuban Revolution, examining the struggle against Batista and defending the Castro cause in <u>Bertillon 166</u> (1960), <u>En el año de enero</u> (1963), and <u>El derrumbe</u> (1964). J. M. Sanz Lajara (1917-), a novelist with whom "entra la novela dominicana en la novelística universal,"[26] created characters for whom the telluric is still all-important. His <u>Viv</u> (1961), a first person narrative of a tragic love, and <u>Los rompidos</u> (1963) are his two best novels.

In Mexico, José Revueltas (1914-) in <u>Los errores</u> (1964) condemned the inhuman Stalinist purges. Olegario Chaves, a communist chosen to participate in a demonstration during which a Party member is marked for death, accepts the blame for a murder he did not commit. Juan José Arreola (1918-), in addition to new editions of his short story collections, published <u>La feria</u> (1963), a mosaic of biblical texts, sociology, and history, whose protagonist is the mythical town of Zapotlán whose multiple dwellers show us what is is to be sinful and anonymous human beings. Arreola is obsessed by man's inexplicable need to corrupt and destroy others and himself, a victim of his own rhetoric and inventions.

Many writers continued to emphasize the Indian in America. In Guatemala, Mario Monteforte Toledo (1911-) refined his tales of Indian-white relationships in his novel, <u>Llegaron del mar</u> (1966), a saga of Indian sacrifice and rebellion in defense of American culture and Indian gods. Doubtless the best of the Peruvian indigenista writers was José María Arguedas (1911-69) whose <u>El Sexto</u> (1961), nevertheless, tells about his own prison experiences. <u>Todas las sangres</u> (1964) describes Indian life in free communities, the continuing encroachments of <u>hacendados</u>, the capitalistic struggle for power, and an Indian rebellion and the ensuing reprisals. In spite of some metaphysical concerns, Arguedas, in this novel, recalls older treatments of the theme as opposed to the animistic, magic ones of some of his earlier novels. Bolivia's Raúl Botelho Gosálvez (1917-) elaborated one of his short stories into a novel. <u>El Tata Limachí</u> (1965) deals with a young priest in an isolated Indian parish who abandons his idealism to die unnoticed and unmourned by the Indians he was supposedly serving.

Finally, Paraguay produced its finest novelist in Augusto Roa Bastos (1917-). His Hijo de hombre (1960) contains a series of stories unified by the narrator Miguel Vera and a history of Paraguay from mid-nineteenth century to just after the Chaco War. Roa combines tortured imagery, allegory, fantasy, and myth to convey his basic concern for justice, freedom and brotherhood. The novel poses a fundamental dualism and theological query about the relationship of Jesus to the Church and to Christianity and may also be viewed as an allegory, a strange blend of Indian mythology, Christian legend, and poetic vision.27

Novelists born before 1930

The novelists born in the 1920's, often known as the "Generation of 1950," mixed Argentine politics and fantasy in their discussions of alienated people. Most were caught up in political events, but what they had in common, aside from their neo-realism, was a hatred for their literary forebears like Mallea and Borges. Frustrated in their desires to criticize the Perón regime, they battled, instead, on literary fronts, becoming what one perceptive critic calls a "generation of parricides."28 Argentina produced a large number of fine women novelists. Estela Canto (1920-) wrote of myth and fantasy and examined metaphysical states in novels like La noche y el barro (1961) and continued her interests in introspective psychological conditions in Isabel entre las plantas (1966), a defense of women's rights. Beatriz Guido (1924-) concentrated on the sexual aberrations and political foibles of her countrymen. El incendio y las vísperas (1964) recreates the burning of the Jockey Club in 1953 and the fight against Peronism. Marta Lynch (1929-) analyzes the quest for power and the political disillusion in the years immediately following Perón's fall in La alfombra roja (1962). Her Al vencedor (1965), through two young protagonists victimized by their society, tells, almost allegorically, about the general dissolution of the Argentine world. La señora Ordóñez (1968) details the decline of Peronism and explains a woman's erotic experience.

Hector A. Murena (1923-) explores modern myths and universal man. Los herederos de la promesa (1965), the third volume of a trilogy, recreates the intellectual circles of the Perón period, recalls the conformity of Argentine intellectuals, and describes the degenerate world of nymphomaniacs and demon-ridden individuals whose only possible escape from nothingness lies in the power of love. Epitalámica (1969), the first volume of a projected cycle of seven, pokes fun at his world through the protagonist, Ludovico, a twenty-five year old innocent who discovers the joys of sex with Africa and lives contentedly through her earnings as a high priced prostitute. It is not easy to discriminate between the honest and the meretricious, the sense and the nonsense, between artistic necessity and commercial exploitation, but Murena, at the very least, is a perspicacious and ironic observer of the absurdities of modern life.

David Viñas (1929-) deals with political and historical matters. Dar la cara (1962) is about youth's disillusionment and the politically disenfranchized; En la semana trágica (1966) recalls political and economic events of 1919. Los hombres de a caballo (1967) deals with the activities of an Argentine army unit sent to Peru to prevent a guerrilla revolt. Viñas traces the development of the military from a force fighting for the people into one against them, from defenders of freedom to defenders of imperialism. In 1969 Viñas published Cosas concretas.

Lesser members of the generation include Antonio di Benedetto (1920-) whose El silenciero (1964) examines city noise and modern man; Julio Ardiles Gray (1922-) whose El inocente (1964) is about migrant workers; Carlos Mazzanti (1926-), author of La cordillera del viento (1966); and Pedro G. Orgambide (1929-), who in Memorias de un hombre de bien (1964) exposes the hypocrisy of the "good old days," in El páramo (1965) documents the superstitions of Patagonia, and in Los inquisidores (1967) continues his criticims of the status quo.

In Chile there was also a "Generation of 1950." Its novelists tried to express a universal view-point in their politicial, social, ontological, metaphysical, and psychological themes, but they also attempted to link American myth to the new realities. Their protagonists, for the most part, are the "náufragos de la crisis contemporánea que se debaten en angustias psicológicas y morales."[29] José Donoso (1925-), Enrique Lafourcade (1927-), Jaime Valdivieso (1927-), Jaime Lazo (1927-), José Manuel Vergara (1928-), Guillermo Blanco (1926-), and Claudio Giaconi (1927-) are among the novelists of this group.

Donoso's El lugar sin límites (1966), a multi-level realistic view of Chileans victimized by their sexual and social environment, portrays the rape of a virginal whorehouse madam, herself the daughter of a homosexual. The novel, which is "naturalista, onírico, literal y simbólico, tradicional y renovador,"[30] shows the ambivalence of the human animal. Este

274

domingo (1966) analyzes the lonely men and women of a middle class Chilean family and their frustrations.

Enrique Lafourcade's El príncipe y las ovejas (1963) contains Satanism, sex and fatality and traces the downfall of a seminary student. Invención a dos voces (1963) presents a marvelous female robot whose inventors see her, the one as a daughter and the other as a materialistic investment. Lafourcade attacks United States materialism and the abandonment of Christian precepts, but he also examines the concepts of love and charity. Novela de navidad (1965) is about abandoned children in Santiago, and Frecuencia modulada (1968) treats of the circus, drugs, and youngsters.

Although Guillermo Blanco in Gracia y el forastero (1964) offers us a poetic story of pure and innocent love, most of his contemporaries write of sorry human beings, sexual aberrations, and man's alienation, themes common to contemporary novelists everywhere.[31]

In Colombia, Manuel Zapata Olivella (1920-), taught his novelistic techniques by Ciro Alegría, wrote Detrás del rostro (1963), about urchins and vandalism; En Chimá nace un santo (1964), a baroque novel about a town alienated by myth, witchcraft, and religious bigotry, and about miracles worked by an incurable paralytic; and Chambacú, corral de negros (1967), about the pueblo and its passions. Héctor Rojas Herazo (1921-), after the lyrical exaltation of Respirando el verano (1964), presented a mythical maritime village, Cedrón, in his second novel, En noviembre llega el arzobispo (1967). The town's monotony is broken only by chess games, incest, masturbation, and adultery. Rojas creates a mythical, astrological, zodiacal world of symbols, as mad prophets await the arrival of the Apocalypse and the Achillean ruler-hero, Leocadio Mendieta, searches in vain for a mother love he never had. A bewildering novel of good and evil, it reminds one of a Greek tragedy enclosed in a covering of scatology and hate.[32] Manuel Mejía Vallejo (1923-) combined a mixture of realism, symbolism, and alternating first and third person narration to tell us of a Colombian town "olvidado de Dios." In the village depicted in El día señalado (1964) violence, fear, and brutality reign. Some guerrillas, helped by the pueblo, destroy the government army, but after "the appointed day" the town is more desolate than before.

Gabriel García Márquez (1928-) is the Colombian novelist who has aroused the most critical and public interest. Always concerned with the thin line between the real and the fantastic, he sets all his action in the imaginary town of Macondo where one can obtain a metaphorical view of humanity and the absurd.

El coronel no tiene quien le escriba (1961) is about a vain fifty-year wait for a pension. *La mala hora* (1966), whose 1962 edition the author disavows, is about political rivalry, rumor, and terror. His acknowledged masterpiece, *Cien años de soledad* (1967), traces the history of the Buendía family through seven generations in Macondo, from its founding to its decay and destruction. The novel combines a retrospective future in a culture of myths, loneliness, and solitude, a world of phantoms and death. José Arcadio Buendía, the founder, receives a manuscript from strange old Melquíades about the family history, and Colonel Aureliano, adventurer and father of seventeen bastard children, continues the causal relationship between the town and the family. Another Aureliano (the same names repeat from generation to generation), the last of the male Buendía line, has an affair with his aunt, and she dies after giving birth to a monstrous child. Trapped by memory, and like all his lonely, incestuous family a victim of love and the inevitable death which awaits us all, Aureliano finally deciphers the manuscript written 100 years earlier and reads there of the family's doom.

Juan Arcocha (1927-) in *Los muertos andan solos* (1962) revealed the reaction of upper class Cubans to the Castro revolution. Humberto Arenal (1926-) talks of love and innocence in *Los animales sagrados* (1967). The best Cuban novelist born in the twenties, Guillermo Cabrera Infante (1929-), in *Tres tristes tigres* (1967) writes of Cuban night life, music, perversions, sexual fantasies, absurd creatures, and drunks. The three tigers, an actor, a photographer, and a writer, are less important than Bustrófedon, a kind of mythic creation and inventor of a fantastic language. The novel, a series of almost cabalistic word plays, tricks, and dialogues, contains also a series of parodies and burlesques in the style of Lezama Lima, Alejo Carpentier, and other Cuban novelists. A shuffler of similes and tongue twisters, Cabrera Infante combines, chaotically, geography and genealogy, politics and perversion, literature and lust in a parody of life verging on caricature but whose illusive mirrors of reality hide a profound underlying sadness.

Mexico's Rosario Castellanos (1925-) wrote magic tales of Indian life, and her *Oficio de tinieblas* (1962) deals with timeless Indian history, the destructive powers of the Church, and the negligible positive effects of the Mexican Revolution on the Indian whose human dignity she tries to protect. A fusion of history and *intrahistoria*, her novel reveals "la transformación dentro de realidad en mito."[33]

Luis Spota (1925-) states the sordid motivations and the savagery of the military caudillo in *El tiempo de la ira* (1960).

La pequeña edad (1964), the first of a planned tetralogy, tells of the tragic days of Huerta's betrayal of Madero. La carcajada del gato (1964) has a protagonist eventually murdered by the very ones he hopes to protect from a corrupt world. And so Spota continues his tales of corruption and sexual excesses in novels like Los sueños del insomnio (1966), a second person interior monologue about the artificial artistic circles of Mexico, and Lo de antes (1968).

Sergio Galindo (1926-) and Sergio Fernández (1926-) share first names and birth years. Galindo's novels, largely about Xalapa, Veracruz, include El Bordo (1960), about the guilt-ridden search for identity, and La comparsa (1964), about a hypocritical town during a frenzied Carnival where people ponder the meaning of sex and search for roots and their own authenticity. Fernández' En tela de juicio (1964) is about the marriage of a man to a woman carrying another man's child and the existential alienation suffered by most Mexicans. Los peces (1968) concerns a woman's neurotic preoccupation, and the meaning of guilt and the drive for salvation in the contemporary world.

Josefina Hernández (1928-) in La plaza de Puerto Santo (1961) satirizes the adventures of six voyeurs; in Los palacios desiertos (1963) she dwells on a love-hate relationship, suicide and murder; in La cólera secreta (1964), La primera batalla (1965), La noche exquisita (1965), and El valle que elegimos (1965) she handles a variety of themes, revolutionary Mexico and Cuba, the absurd and fruitless lives of lesbians, homosexuals, and misfits, and the artificial world of actors in Mexico City. In La Memoria de Amadís (1967), she treats of the generation gap, the fears and frustrations of the Mexican middle class, and specifically of an irresponsible husband, a homosexual army officer, and a suicidal son.

Carlos Fuentes (1928-), the best known Mexican novelist, conveys the "totalidad geográfica étnica y social de la nación"[34] in La muerte de Artemio Cruz (1962). Filled with interior monologue and multiple points of view, it shows, through the memories of its protagonist who is dying in a hospital, the role of the Revolution in Mexican life, and his own empty marriage and climb to power. He is Mexico itself, a victim of its own decisions to follow false materialistic goods, trapped by an existentialist fatality from which there is no escape. Zona sagrada (1967), a mixture of mythology, fetishism, suggested incest and sodomy, and sexual transformations, involves oneiric imagery and the role of woman as mother and destroyer. Cambio de piel (1967) tells of depersonalized man in a cruel, superstitious, absurd world. A kind of allegory of Mexican history, the novel attacks Western civilization as it seeks to balance man's duty to society with that of his own freedom. Fuentes, with a macabre humor, creates a "fictional joke," if one can speak of the Spanish conquest, American beatniks, and Nazi genocide as something humorous.[35]

The best known Venezuelan novelist of his generation is Salvador Garmendia (1929-), especially noted for his poetic passion and conception of reality, "no solo en el poder explosivo de su significado sino en el peso, el olor, en la densidad de las mismas palabras."[36] Los habitantes (1961), although it has no particular alienated hero, reveals modern man's futility and inability to communicate. Día de ceniza (1964) again seeks to understand humanity through a failure, an obsessed man who cannot accept his reality. La mala vida (1968) attempts to interpret man's chaotic world, and the protagonist takes a masochistic pleasure in his own frustration in a world of fecal flundering. Garmendia describes a sordid sensual world, relating childhood punishment to a moment in the present and a particular impotence in a whorehouse to the general impotence of mankind.

Uruguay's Angel Rama (1926-) and Jorge Musto (1927-) have produced excellent fiction, but Mario Benedetti (1920-) excels them both. He used interior monologue to convey his existentialist preoccupations, especially the metaphysical anguish of ordinary men who lead sad and humble lives of sexual and spiritual frustration. La tregua (1960) is about the momentary respite of a fifty year old man from the loneliness of life. In Gracias por el fuego (1965) a son plots to kills his powerful and important father but commits suicide instead. He and his generation, cast adrift, are unable to face life's problems. The other characters, much like ordinary Uruguayans, are also victims of life's ambiguity, their time, and the inevitable consequences of their individual choice.

Among other novelists born in the 1920's, the Peruvian Julio Ramón Ribeyro (1929-), concerned about his country's culture and past, deals in Crónica de San Gabriel (1960) with adolescents, sordid sexual appetites, and the melancholy process of becoming an adult in a hostile society, and in Los geniecillos dominicales (1965) with the theme of alienated man. Pedro Juan Soto of Puerto Rico concentrates on his countrymen's inability to adapt to changing conditions in Ardiente suelo, fría estación (1961) and offers a subjective view, in El francotirador (1969), of Cuban and Puerto Rican realities. Joaquín Beleño (1922-) of Panama writes about a mestizo's love for a white girl in Los forzados de Gamboa (1960) and continues his social preoccupations in Curundú (1963). Oscar Barbery Justiniano (1928-) of Bolivia in El hombre que soñaba (1964) and

El reto (1967) also reflects on the continuing corruption of his country.

Younger Novelists

In Chile, Jorge Edwards (1931-), who belongs to the so-called "Generation of 1950," in *El peso de la noche* (1965) discusses the lack of authentic values in contemporary Chile, but Juan Ventura Agudiez (1933-) seems quite removed from American preoccupations. In *Las tardes de Thérèze Lamarck* (1964), an analysis of history and fable untouched by social, ethical, or political material, he reflects the universal consciousness and the cosmic totality of animate and inanimate things, employing esthetically pleasing and sensation evoking imagery to weave a peculiarly rhythmic thematic texture.

In Argentina Marta Traba (1930-) in *Las ceremonias del verano* (1966) analyzes man's isolation, and the protagonist recalls four summers which fail to relieve her frustrations. *Los laberintos insolados* (1967), filled with oneiric imagery, is an Odyssean story of a world traveler, a victim of a siren's song. Daniel Moyano (1930-) wrote *Una luz muy lejana* (1966) and *El oscuro* (1968), about a jealous colonel and his inability to understand his fellow human beings. Manuel Puig (1933-) wrote *La traición de Rita Hayworth* (1968), about the fantasies of a young boy, and *Boquitas pintadas* (1969), an attempt at popular literature and a reflection of the vulgar in Argentine life. Néstor Sánchez (1935-), a disciple of Cortázar, deals with the discovery of love by a young boy through the aid of a pimp and some prostitutes in *Nosotros dos* (1966). *Siberia Blues* (1967), about a strange set of characters in a Buenos Aires bar, and *El amor, los Orsinis y la muerte* (1969) are his other novels.

In Mexico Tomás Mojarro (1932-) in *Bramadero* (1963) and *Malafortuna* (1966) tells of lonely, frustrated, and alienated people in a hopeless and stagnant world. Salvador Elizondo (1932-) portrays an anatomist and a woman who identifies dissection and death spasms with a love orgasm in *Farabeuf o la crónica de un instante* (1965). *El hipogeo secreto* (1968) promotes the idea that the world exists only in the mind. Vicente Leñero (1933-) concentrates on man's guilt, lost identity, mental disintegration, and the search for God. *La voz adolorida* (1961) is about a hypocritical maiden aunt who causes her nephew's insanity. *Los albañiles* (1964), through the police testimony about the supposed murder of a night watchman, shows us the sordid private lives of the suspects. *Estudio Q* (1965) treats of the television industry and an actor's alienation and suicide. *El garabato* (1967) examines the enigma of existence and a manuscript whose author is both protagonist and critic. Fernando del Paso (1935-) author of a complex and obscure novel,

José Trigo (1966), combines magic and myth with a search for identity. Including the story of railroading and a chaotic confusion of past and present, the novel views Mexico as a fusion of Indian and Spanish elements with modern technology. Gustavo Sainz (1940-) uses tape recordings to tell a tale of attempted seduction in Gazapo (1965). His other novel is Obsesivos días circulares (1969). Sainz excels at portraying the disturbed lives of Mexican adolescents. José Agustín (1944-) in his novels La tumba (1964), De perfil (1966), and Abolición de la propriedad (1969) exposes the generation gap among the wealthy and gives a nihilistic view of teen-age sex and absurd and abnormal youths.

The Cuban writers reflected both revolutionary fervor and esthetic interests. Edmundo Desnoes (1930-) wrote No hay problema (1961), about the Batista years, Memorias del subdesarrollo (1965), about a misfit sunk in an existential well of despair, and El cataclismo (1965), about the effects of the Castro revolution. Lisandro Otero (1932-) examines the Cuba of 1951 and 1952 in La situación (1963) with special attention to the hypocrisies, the myths, smells, and colors. His La pasion de Urbino (1966) is about a priest overwhelmed by his sister-in-law's physical attractions.

Severo Sarduy (1937-) published Gestos (1963) and De donde son los cantantes (1967), the first an objectivist account of Cuban night life in pre-revolutionary days, and the second about a magic world of hallucination and symbolic transformations. Mortal Pérez, the protagonist of the second novel, in his roles as general, politician, and double for Christ, reveals the Chinese, Negro and Spanish components of Cuban existence. Reynaldo Arenas (1943-) writes about a grotesque rural world as seen in the interior monologue of an idiot boy in Celestino antes del alba (1967), and alternates first, second, and third person narrative to show us Fray Servando Teresa de Mier, "Tal como fue, tal como pudo haber sido, tal como a mí me hubiera gustado que hubiera sido" in El mundo alucinante (1969).

Peru's Oswaldo Reynoso (1933-), in Los inocentes o Lima en Rock (1964), discusses the government-run high schools and the disturbed inhabitants of the rock and roll world. En octubre no hay milagros (1965) is about the rebellion of a youth against the religious hypocrisy of the system. The author details the incredible corruption, middle-class homosexuality and immorality, and shows the general alienation of an entire generation. The best Peruvian novelist of the century, Mario Vargas LLosa (1936-), in La ciudad y los perros (1963) examines the lives of a number of cadets (the perros) at the Leoncio Prado military academy of Lima. Filled with multiple perspectives, alteration of time and space, and interior monologues of various kinds, the novel takes us behind closed doors and into the secret corners of the mind to show us the hypocrisy and evil which lurk there. Bestialism, masturbation, and murder take place in the rigid and stratified society, a microcosm of the outside egotistical one without moral values. The cadets eventually become conformists to the empty Peruvian world, but Vargas Llosa has managed to exorcise the forces of brutality and expose the face of evil which conscience must repel.

His La Casa Verde (1965), a monument to collective jungle memories, "has sweep, beauty, imaginative scope, and a sustained eruptive power that carries the reader from first page to last like a fish in a bloodstream."[37] Vargas Llosa uses a variety of interior monologues, disorienting dream states, and frozen dialogue, He sees time as overlapping fragments of a multidimensional framework. The action occurs in a green colored bordello, first on the outskirts of Piura and later in its tin shack district known as La Mangachería, and in Santa María de Nieva, a jungle rubber trading post, a place of contrabandists and white slave traders at the mouth of the Marañón river. Los cachorros (1967) concerns the effects of castration and includes themes of homosexuality, machismo, and erotic frustration in a kind of poetic parable about social integration and the change form adolescence to adulthood.[38] Conversación en la Catedral (1969), through Cayo Bermúdez, depraved defender of the status quo, shows us the typical government figure. He is but one actor among many in a world peopled by lesbians and homosexuals. Santiago Zavala, typically bourgeois, rejects respectability for the bohemian life, and it is through his conversations that we discover the tale of dictatorship and murder.

Edmundo de los Ríos (1944-) in Los juegos verdaderos (1968) gives us a first person recall of university days, life in prison and the hopelessness which lack of freedom brings. He is the Peruvian counterpart of equally fine young novelists like Fanny Buitrago (1944-) of Colombia, author of El hostigante verano de los dioses (1963), about the boredom of modern life whose emptiness is unrelieved by attempted vice, and El hombre de paja y las distancias doradas (1964); and Jesús Urzagasti (1941-), a Bolivian, who explores existential themes and the search for identity in Tirinea (1969). Among other important novels of the sixties one may mention País portátil (1968) by the Venezuelan Adriano González León (1931-) and Los fundadores del alba (1969) by the Bolivian Renato Prada Oropeza (1937-). The Venezuelan novel takes place during one day on a bus but at the same time presents the history of the country. The Bolivian novel was apparently inspired by the activities of Che Guevara, and explores the apparatus of guerrilla warfare in Bolivia.

The Spanish American novel of the 1960's used universal symbols and myths, framed at times in a local setting. Side stepping the epic view of a social reality, for the most part, it turned ever more inward. Masters of techniques to which many arrived quite late, these novelists are now producing a final fusion of esthetic and formal aspirations with a continuing concern for the individual and the problems of human destiny.

Notes

[1] Luis Alberto Sánchez, Proceso y contenido de la novela hispanoamericana (Madrid, 1955), p. 51.

[2] See James E. Irby, La influencia de William Faulkner en cuatro narradores hispanoamericanos (Mexico, 1957).

[3] A. A. Mendilow, Time and the Novel (London, 1952), p. 234.

[4] Guillermo de Torre, "Para una polémica sobre la nueva novela," Mundo Nuevo, 34 (1969), 85. See also Mundo Nuevo, 33 (1969), 70-82.

[5] Carlos Fuentes, "Situación del escritor en América Latina," Mundo Nuevo, 1 (1966), 17.

[6] Emir Rodríguez Monegal, "Diaro de Caracas," Mundo Nuevo, 17 (1964), 22-23.

[7] Julio Ortega, "Néstor Sánchez: La novela del lenguaje," Imagen 30 (August 15, 1968), 6-7.

[8] Ernesto Sábato, "Realidad y realismo en la literatura de nuestro tiempo, " Cuadernos Hispanoamericanos, 60, 178 (1964), 5-20.

[9] Alejo Carpentier, Tientos y diferencias (Mexico, 1967), p. 116.

[10] Angel Flores, "Magical Realism in Spanish American Fiction," Hispania, 38 (May 1955), 187-92.

[11] Luis Leal, "El realismo magico en la literatura hispanoamericana," Cuadernos Americanos, 26, 153 (1967), 230-35.

[12] See Robert G. Mead, Jr., "Miguel Angel Asturias and the Nobel Prize," Hispania, 51, 2 (May 1968), 330.

[13] Jean Franco, The Modern Culture of Latin America (New York, 1967), p. 281.

[14] Luis Harss and Barbara Dohmann, Into the Mainstream (New York, 1967), p. 27.

[15] Mario Castro Arenas, "La nueva novela peruana," Cuadernos Hispanoamericanos, 46, 138 (1961), 317.

[16] Mario Vargas Llosa, *Times Literary Supplement*, 3 (November 14, 1968).

[17] Alexander Coleman, "Why Asturias?" *The New York Times Book Review* (November 19, 1967), p. 89.

[18] Borges has since declared that he is tired of labyrinths. See his interview in *Mundo Nuevo*, 18 (1967), 25.

[19] G. Suárez Rendón, *La novela de la violencia en Colombia* (Bogota, 1966).

[20] Humberto Bronx, *Veinte años de novela colombiana* (Medellin, 1966), p. 25.

[21] José Miguel Ullán, "Carlos Fuentes, Salto mortal hacia mañana," *Insula*, 22, 245 (1967), 12.

[22] Mario Beneditti, *Literatura uruguaya, siglo xx* (Buenos Aires, 1963), p. 110.

[23] Emir Rodríguez Monegal, "Cara y cruz de Martínez Moreno," *Mundo Nuevo*, 10 (1967), 79-85 has a good dicussion of this point.

[24] Alfred J. MacAdam, "Cortázar, novelista," *Mundo Nuevo*, 18 (1967), 38-42.

[25] For an elaboration of this point see Martha Paley de Francescato, "Julio Cortázar y un modelo para armar ya armado," *Cuadernos Americanos*, 28, 3 (1969), 235-41.

[26] Manuel Valledeperes, "Evolución de la novela en la República Dominicana," *Cuadernos Hispanoamericanos*, 59, 206 (1967), 311-25.

[27] See Urte Lehnerdt, "Ensayo de interpretación de *Hijo de hombre* a través de su simbolismo cristiano y social," *Revista Iberoamericana*, 65 (1968), 67-82. See also, Seymour Menton, "Realismo mágico y dualidad en *Hijo de hombre*," *Revista Iberoamericana*, 33, 63 (1967), 55-70.

[28] Emir Rodríguez Monegal, *El juicio de los parricidas* (Buenos Aires, 1956), pp. 136-37.

[29] Hernán Godoy Urzúa, "El ensayo social en Chile," *Anales de la Universidad de Chile*, 118, 120 (1960), 81.

[30] Emir Rodríguez Monegal, "El mundo de José Donoso," *Mundo Nuevo*, 12 (1967), 77-85.

[31] Ariel Dorfman, "Perspectivas y limitaciones de la novela chilena actual," Anales de la Universidad de Chile, 124, 140 (1966), 110-67.

[32] Ebel Botero Escobar, "La gran bestia, el sin madre y el amatista. Intimidades de la novela de Rojas Herazo," Boletín Cultural y Bibliográfico, 10, 11 (Bogotá, 1967), 127-36.

[33] Joseph Sommers, "Rosario Castellanos: Nuevo enfoque del indio mexicano," La Palabra y el Hombre (enero-marzo 1964), 83-88.

[34] Rosario Castellanos, "La novela mexicana contemporánea y su valor testimonial," Hispania, 47 (May, 1964), 223-30.

[35] For a good discussion by Fuentes of his own novel see "La situación del escritor en América Latina," Mundo Nuevo, 1 (1966), 5-21.

[36] Emir Rodríguez Monegal, "Salvador Garmendia, la visión y el lenguaje de un novelista," Imagen 31 (August 15, 1968), 4-5.

[37] Harss and Dohmann, p. 364.

[38] Julio Ortega, "Sobre los cachorros," Cuadernos Hispanoamericanos, 75, 224-25 (1968), 543-51.

THE THEME OF SUICIDE IN REPRESENTATIVE
SPANISH AMERICAN NOVELS

In the real world self-destruction may be classified as egotic, a self-denigrating depression involving doubt or fear; dyadic, based on deep unfulfilled needs and wishes pertaining to a love object; or ageneratic, which causes feelings of alienation.[1] Psychoanalysts, emphasizing the frustrations and anxieties involved in parental relationships, stress that the suicide often expiates his guilt and mollifies his super-ego through his self-murder. Freud contends that the death instinct, a primary aggression, is present from the very beginning of life. Blending with a love instinct, it accounts for ambivalent, destructive and libidinal attitudes toward various objects.[2] Nonetheless, as Gregory Zilboorg declares, "It is clear that the problem of suicide from a scientific point of view remains unsolved. Neither common sense nor clinical psychopathology has found a cause for even a strictly empirical solution."[3]

One of the major themes of Spanish American fiction, suicide reflects the tortured and chaotic world in which the novelists and their characters live. Although political motivations contribute greatly, the external misery so prevalent in Spanish American novels plays but a small role in the fictional deaths. Universal factors of fear, frustration, sexual difficulties, alienation, and insanity play a large role in the self-destruction, but the Spanish American, prey to a profound sentiment of solitude and need to know his origins, embarks more readily on an ardent search for death, the final mask against the outside world. As Octavio Paz states, "Nuestro culto a la muerte es culto a la vida, del mismo modo que el amor, que es hambre de vida, es anhelo de muerte. El gusto de la auto-destrucción no se deriva nada más de tendencias masoquistas, sino también de una cierta religiosidad."[4]

Suicide was an integral part of romanticism: "Death was the great inspirer and great consoler. It was they who made suicide fashionable . . ."[5] Vicente Riva Palacio, who almost singlehandedly created the Mexican historical novel, in Monja y casada, virgen y mártir (1868), has Blanca de Mejía throw herself over a cliff into a raging torrent to escape the advances of Guzmán. Other self-immolations occur in the Venezuelan novels of Fermín Toro, Eduardo Blanco, and Julio Calcaño. Toro's Seyde, in La viuda de Corinto, stabs himself when his beloved Atenais dies, and Blanco's Laredán, in the novelette Claudia, jumps into the Seine. Calcaño's Blanca de Torrestella (1865) has a heroine who poisons her lover's murderer and then herself with a Borgia ring, hoping, like Melibea, to join her beloved. Deprived early of maternal love and educated by a severe and indifferent father, Blanca suffers emotional crises diagnosed as "una sobreexcitación del sistema nervioso, como si hubiese sufrido algún susto prolongado."[6]

Of all the romantic novels, Santiago Vaca Guzmán's Días amargos (1886), subtitled "Páginas del libro de memorias de un pesimista," examines suicide the most extensively. Although Enrique Finot claims that no real analysis of the protagonist's psychosis appears,[7] one is more inclined to agree with Juana María Gorriti, who believes it to be "un estudio psicológico profundo. . ."[8]

The plot concerns Daniel Neltson, an illegitimate young Bolivian who learns, at the age of sixteen, of his mother's sexual indiscretions. He longs for his half-sister who has come to represent for him a symbol of purity and possible salvation: "la he conceptuado siempre como un anillo que me ligaba a la vida . . . que su presencia en el nublado hogar de mi madre . . . lo regeneraría . . ."[9] To protect her current happiness, he has to acknowledge her as dead.

Retained by Adela Velázquez Derteani as a lawyer against her philandering and embezzling husband, Neltson in shocked when the husband accuses him of adultery with his wife. Adela's daughter, Hortensia, with whom Neltson is madly in love, is forced by her father to marry a rich old man. Neltson's mother, meanwhile, attacks her son as an imbecile for refusing to go to his father's death bed to inherit the family fortune. Justice finally triumphs, but Adela, on her death bed, begs Hortensia to avoid adultery with Daniel, who shoots himself through the heart.

When Neltson discovered that his mother, whom he had loved almost as a saint, had had various lovers, he was unable to handle his new ambivalent feelings. Recalling a happier childhood, he introjected his mother, identifying with and assuming her guilt. At twenty-four, a neurotic, melancholy, and somber, "alma enferma de desencanto, siguiendo la senda nublada que la suerte le deparaba, con paso vacilante, desconfiado y tembloroso,"[10] he sees in Hortensia the good non-sexual mother (and lost sister), combined with the not-so-good sexual woman (she betrays him by marrying another). When Hortensia, his mother surrogate, rejects him, he is lost and driven to punish and be punished. His mother's reproaches also intensify his guilt feelings. He refuses to accept his father's bequests because he unconsciously wished for his death.

From a psychological viewpoint childhood impressions of moral standards "obtained from parents are all the more lasting and potent because they become unconscious. Even impressions received long after the infantile period--at ten or twelve years or even later--exert a distinct effect in determining the emotional attitude of the individual."[11] Neltson, a victim of emotional deprivation and deep-seated hostilities against both parents, reinforces his guilt feelings and consciously indulges in self-criticism and self-condemnation, to which he himself alludes as "esta especie de invencible condenación."[12] As he distorts the meaning of incidental events, his own sense of worthlessness increases. When Hortensia issues her final rejection, he, feeling without hope and unable to bear up under this final blow, seeks "en el regazo de la nada compasivo amparo a mi dolor postrero."[13]

Many realists make positive if primitive attempts to explain the psychological bases for their characters' suicidal actions. Alberto Blest Gana, who in several of his novels dwells on violent or tragic death, was "un psicólogo avezado, profundo, admirablemente dotado para ver las almas de los hombres por dentro . . . logró componer en sus obras una imagen psicológica tan coherente y profunda . . ."[14]

In two of his early novels, Una escena social (1853) and Los desposados (1855), Blest Gana deals with self-destruction. In the first novel Caroline's supposed husband expresses "un inmenso, pero tardío dolor por haber destruido la felicidad, por los dolores de que he llenado tus días,"[15] and prefers to die rather than endure a miserable existence. In the second novel Clementina Dunoye and the young revolutionary Luis d'Orville whom she marries both jump into the Seine after her father disowns them and denounces the young man to the police.

In El pago de las deudas (1861) Blest Gana depicts a melancholy hero who wants to "buscar la causa de mi mal."[16] Luciano, torn between love and economic necessity, marries Luisa, a rich young widow. He continues to love Adelina, who eventually rejects him. Unable to bear his loss of love, guilty about Luisa, and overwhelmed by money problems, he throws himself into the sea. In a letter to his friend Pedro he comments on the futility of life and shows that suicide, which he views as "un amigo triste pero seguro,"[17] is the culmination of a long series of inadequacies and guilt feelings of which Adelina's rejection, destroying his fantasy of idyllic love, was simply one among many.

In Rastaquoère (1889) by Alberto del Solar, the foolish Polish prince Paul de Kantaski, overwhelmed by gambling debts, commits suicide. In Blest Gana's quite similar Los transplantados (1904) it is the prince's wife who destroys herself. Don Graciano Canalejas's family, which has moved from Chile, is soon seduced by the false aristocratic French values.

Mercedes, one of the daughters, in love with Patricio Fuentealba, her childhood sweetheart, is forced into an alliance with Prince Stephan de Roespingsbrück. A weak-willed girl who accepts blindly that parental respect is a precept of the Church, Mercedes, her hopes destroyed, remains in a semi-stupor. Her despair, combined with fear of her husband, makes her believes she has to die, a conviction which takes on "las proporciones de un mandato del destino. Ningún temor de piedad cristiana protestó contra ese desesperado pensamiento aceptado como una fatalidad. Su muerte . . . no sería culpa de ella, sino de los que la habían sacrificado."[18] Exaggerating in her mind the abjection she has undergone, and exhausted by lack of sleep and emotional tension, she finally rebels against her Christian resolve, viewing her death as loyalty to her one true love. Although she asks Heaven's pardon, she tranquilly turns on the gas oven and fixes her final thoughts on Patricio.

Carlos María Ocantos in Quilito (1891) presents us with a moody Argentine protagonist who plays the stock market and loses. He cannot replace some borrowed money and believes his only salvation is suicide. He play-acts his death in front of a mirror, thinks of throwing himself into a river, but finally, filled with remorse and guilt, fires a bullet into his head.

Rafael Delgado's suicidal heroine in La Calandria (1891), simple, young and beautiful, temporarily succumbs to the charm of rich young Alberto, even though she truly loves honorable but inflexible Gabriel. He cruelly disdains her, and she poisons herself. Again the rejection is the culmination of a long struggle, in her case against poverty, misery, and hunger. Feeling that she has been pursued by fate from the cradle on, without parents or moral force to sustain her, she cannot overcome her essential weakness: "linfática por herencia que oculta el germen de la incurable enfermedad . . . cierta indolencia felina y cierta vibración del cuerpo rítmica y sensual."[19]

Nicolás Heredia's Leonela (1893) tells the story of a passionate and proud young Cuban girl, Leonela, and her less vehement and more sentimental twin sister, Clara. John Valdespina, a visiting engineer, in love with Clara, does not realize that Leonela has taken her place at an assignation. To save the family's honor, Clara pleads with John to marry her sister. Leonela, hidden in the room, overhears John's vehement rejection, and with "un heroico sentimiento de desdén hacia la vida . . . hundió en el seno virgen las tijeritas de reflejos acerados y brillantes que . . . había tomado del costurero . . ."[20] Spanish American fiction has a plethora of passionate suicides, but few have died with more rage than this rejected protagonist.

Gonzalo Picón Febres dedicated El sargento Felipe (1899) "al honrado y laborioso pueblo de Venezuela," so in a sense he depicts a social suicide. Felipe Bobadilla, a good husband and father, is forced to leave his loved ones for army service. During his absence his wife dies, and the landlord, Jacinto Sandoval, seduces his daughter. Hastening home, Felipe, disillusioned and dishonored, kills the landlord and jumps off the cliff. Before he leaps, he crosses himself three times, an appeasing gesture to be repeated by a number of his fictional counterparts.

In the naturalistic mode of tragic destiny and environmental and hereditary victims, a variety of pathological characters are often analyzed with pseudoscientific zeal. Beba (1894) by Carlos Reyles and Sin rumbo (1885) by Eugenio Cambaceres typify this kind of novel.

Reyles, fascinated in many of his works by suicide, stressed what he called "estados de alma y los espejismos interiores; . . . la psicología arbitraria: en vez de la realidad las posibilidades de ella y el campo infinito de las alteraciones de la personalidad bajo la acción de los poderosos reactivos del tiempo . . ."[21] Beba, whose own father had killed himself, does not find in her husband, Rafael Benavente, the strong personality she is seeking. She visits her childhood country surroundings and her uncle, Gustavo Ribero. When they are isolated by a raging river, they rediscover and consummate their love. Rivero, obsessed by the possibilities of improving the blood lines of the stock on his ranch, blames his failure on his relationship with Beba, whom he abandons.

Beba, a narcissistic, neurasthenic creature, cries without motive, reads romantic novels and the poetry of Bécquer, and creates dream fantasies of love and passion. She is "romántica y soñadora . . . quería un hombre que la amara . . . capaz de morir por ella . . . El desengaño le trajo crueles pesares; se juzgó ofendida, engañada, y este convencimiento la hizo cometer mil extravagancias, dañinas todas."[22] A succession of boy friends cause continuing defeats and deceptions. Disillusioned by her wedding night and the social conventions of the day, she suffers from a black melancholy: "Siempre me sucede lo mismo: al menor disgusto, y como vigorizados por ellos, tornan a poseerme doblemente amenazadores, los desabrimientos no bien definidos, que ahincaron el venenoso diente en mi alma . . ."[23] Yet she continues to create images of herself not in harmony with reality, a self-deception which helps cause the tragedy. She might have survived the stillbirth of her monstrous son, but she is unable to endure her lover's rejection, the final blow to her dream life. Preferring death to solitude, and asking God's pardon, she throws herself into the sea.

Andrés, the hero of <u>Sin rumbo</u>, is frustrated and bored by his empty life. His rebelliousness, pessimism, and skepticism stem in part from his early upbringing and education by women, especially by an overly permissive mother. Idle, irresponsible, and given to sudden enthusiasms of one kind or another, he also undergoes abrupt alternations of manic and depressive states. He cannot believe in anything, rejects human contact, and "insensible y como muerto, encerrado dentro de las paredes mudas de su casa, días enteros se pasaba sin querer hablar ni ver a nadie . . . pensando . . . en la miseria de vivir . . ."[24]

His love for his illegitimate daughter changes his previous cynical attitudes, but her death, at the age of two, plunges him into a private hell from which he cannot escape. His dark despair, reinforced by God's indifference to his prayers, causes him to open his abdomen in the sign of a cross. When his death does not take place at once he yells, "¡Vida perra, puta . . . yo te he de arrancar de cuajo! Y recogiéndose las tripas y envolviéndoselas en torno de las manos, violentamente, como quien rompe una piola, pegó un tirón."[25] Andrés' self-crucifixion, a Christian symbolism reversed, may be interpreted as his guilty atonement, not for the sins of humanity, but for his own. One critic contends that he crucifies himself by not accepting his Creator and that the "moral would appear to be that as he had lived by his own will, so would he die."[26] Not a believer, Andrés, unable to escape the agonizing question as to life's purpose, defiantly reverses the most sacred belief of his father's faith. In his rage he commits a symbolic self-murder and thus rejects both his own existence and a Christian salvation, triumphing, in his own way, over life through a voluntary death.

In spite of their aesthetic preoccupations, Modernist novelists indulged in a good bit of psychological introspection, typifying what they conceived to be the artistic temperament through any number of abulic and alienated protagonists. Pedro César Dominici forgets his native Venezuela in <u>El triunfo del ideal</u> (1901) whose María kills herself when she loses her beauty and thus the interest of Count Carlos de Cipria. José María Vargas Vila, irresistibly attracted to death, treats of suicide in several novels, especially in his own favorite, <u>Ibis</u> (1900), in which he claims that suicide "es siempre una virtud . . . La rebeldía a Dios; eso es el suicidio."[27] The novel supposedly caused as many as seventeen suicides among those who read it.[28] Teodoro, overcome by loneliness and sexual passion for Adela, his adulterous wife whom he has discarded, shoots himself through the heart. Pedro Prada in <u>Alsino</u> (1920)

describes a poor winged victim of society and his unpleasant encounters with humanity which result in his being wounded, imprisoned, and blinded. Unable to enjoy a pure and free life, Alsino embarks on a final feverish flight and allows himself to burn up by falling through the atmosphere.

More substantial suicide studies may be encountered in Augusto D'Halmar's La pasión y muerte del cura Deusto (1924), Enrique Larreta's Zogoibi (1926), and especially in Manuel Díaz Rodríguez' Sangre patricia (1902). Tulio Arcos, in Díaz' novel, belongs to an aristocratic family with a long tradition of service. Overwhelmed by family history, he dedicates himself to an empty past and to dreams of heroic activity whose failure reinforces his feelings of worthlessness. The fact that Belén Montenegro, his beautiful fiancee and proxy bride, dies and is buried at sea, simply intensifies his frustration, moral disintegration and neurotic withdrawal. Filled with aesthetic preoccupations about Belén, his ideal woman, he recreates her in his mind, speaks to her, and becomes more and more lost in fantasy. The trauma of losing his father and mother at an early age created personality difficulties for him, and he had always been considered queer, "un hombre original y muy extraño . . . un cierto extravío de cerebro."[29] Tulio, whose life lacks final metaphysical justification, becomes more and more attracted to the idea of death, which he relates to water symbolism. Unable to overcome his alienation, and the victim of bad dreams, hallucinations, stupors, and drugs, he finally throws himself over the ship's railing into the sea.

Díaz Rodríguez, interested in subconscious motivations and death, again treated the theme of self-destruction in Peregrina o el pozo encantado (1922). Peregrina, her love not returned by Bruno, jumps into a raging stream, not to die immediately but later of fever and miscarriage. Since she receives the Church's last rites, officially she is not a suicide.

In Larreta's novel, Federico de Ahumada, in love with Lucía, a simple Argentine girl who represents his ideal of purity, integrity, and dignity, lusts for Zita Wilburns, another man's wife. While he and Zita are together one night, Federico kills an intruder dressed in gaucho clothes. Upon discovering that he has killed his beloved Lucía, he throws himself on his long knife point to die. Despair over responsibility for the death of a loved one under these dramatic and tragic circumstances and his temporary insanity seem self-explanatory. Nonetheless, Federico suffers from broader guilt feelings which have been with him for a long time. He is alienated and neurotic, prone to easy jealousy and violent emotional reactions: "Era Federico . . . uno de esos hombres soberbiamente confiados, a quienes su arrogante falta de cautela suscita, con frecuencia, enojosos conflictos."[30] Aside from the immediate responsibility, he needs to punish himself for choosing evil over good, a symbolic expiation he achieves by mixing his victim's blood with his own on the same murder weapon.

Augusto D'Halmar, also fascinated by death and self-destruction, traces, in La pasión y muerte del cura Deusto (1924), the relationship between Igancio Deusto, a Basque priest, and a Sevillian gypsy boy, Pedro Miguel. The priest, jealous of Pedro's amorous assignations, finally discovers, to his horror, that his feeling for Pedro, who had tried unsuccessfully to commit suicide, is a homosexual one. He allows himself to be killed by a speeding train, by walking heedlessly between the rails. Just before his death Ignacio suffers a kind of feverish delirium, an attenuated elucidation of his dreadful act, the worst prejudice to his religious principles. Suicide, normally a positive violent action involving muscular energy, in this case results from Deusto's negative attitude of abstention from activity, which has the same consequence, for his refusal to save himself must end in his death.[31]

Twentieth-century suicides derive from the loss of a love object, insanity, alcoholism, drugs, political motivations, hostility and guilt, often toward one's mother, sexual difficulties, and alienation. In some novels a combination of factors leads to the protagonist's suicide.

Otto Miguel Cione of Uruguay in Lauracha (1906) analyzes the psychology of a hysterical heroine who kills herself when Carlos, the man she loves, rejects her. A more intense treatment of Uruguayan rejection may be found in Carlos Reyles' El terruño (1916). Reyles, as we have seen in Beba, was preoccupied by psychological states. In his La raza de Caín (1900), Julio Guzmán has an almost religious belief in self-murder, although the novel's planned suicide pact never materializes. In El terruño, Primitivo is betrayed by his wife and half-brother. He suffers both mental and physical (Jaime knifes him in the face) anguish. He takes to drink and kills Jaime. After his wife's death, he undergoes an accelerating degeneration, incapable of channeling his predisposition to kindness into productive attitudes in the face of life's brutal reality. His silent sorrow and frozen emotions finally yield to a fit of madness. He sets fire to his ranch, and drunk and blinded by the flames, cuts his throat in a scene reminiscent of Sin rumbo.

In Ricardo Güiraldes' novelette, Rosaura (1922), Rosaura Torres of the little Argentine village of Lobos falls madly in love with Carlos Ramallo, the son of a rich hacendado she has seen several times at the train window. Bored with her dull village life, she sees in him and the train freedom from her existential prison. When he marries another, she, overwhelmed by despair, throws herself under the train's wheels.

Benito Lynch's heroine in El inglés de los huesos (1924), Balbina Fuentes, is a beautiful young adolescent on "La Estaca" ranch where James Gray, an English archeologist, is engaged in scientific research. A capricious and impulsive creature, Balbina has ambivalent feelings about Gray but gradually falls completely in love with him. He decides to return to England, and she hangs herself from a tree.

Balbina, alternating between hope and despair, suffers from "ilusiones disparatadas" and a "profunda depresión de espíritu."$_{32}$ Ignorant and half-savage but softened by love and her dream of happiness, she tries to bind Gray to her through witchcraft. Rejected by him, she commits suicide with a rope which, symbolically, since it cannot tie him to her, will unite her with death.

Love object loss contributes to the demise of Blanca, Campito, and Darío. Blanca, the Uruguayan heroine of Adolfo Montiel Ballesteros' Castigo de Dios (1930), loves a man who, she later discovers, is married. Road builders destroy the cemetery where her beloved mother lies, a final loss she cannot endure. Campito loves Aurora, a Colombian guaricha, in Rafael Jaramillo Arango's Barrancabermeja (1934). She dies in a brawl, and he, unable to bear his loss, jumps from a boat into the river. In Rafael Maluenda's Armiño negro (1942) Darío, the son of María Raygada de la Paz, whose own uncle had cut his throat with a razor, longs for a father. He believes he has found one in Felipe Unzuaga, his mother's boyfriend. Upon discovering that his mother is a prostitute and that he cannot have a father, he shoots himself through the neck.

Political and altruistic or idealistic motivations influence some early twentieth century suicidal heroes, among them Pantaleón of El terruño and Gaspar, the liberal young student who fights the forces of religious repression in Armando Chirveches' Casa solariega (1916). Gaspar, the Bolivian dreamer, finally realizes that the world belongs to the success worshippers. Leaving a tear-stained letter for his survivors, he puts a bullet through his brain. Pantaleón, a martyr to the revolution, commits suicide for a patriotic ideal, allowing himself to be dragged to death by his horse.

Three novels of the 1940's, José Tombe (1942) by the Colombian Diego Castrillón Arboleda, Sobre la misma tierra

(1943) by Rómulo Gallegos, and Los animales puros (1946) by the Ecuadorian Pedro Jorge Vera, reflect varying degrees of political idealism. José Tombe, the Indian fighter against whites, finally defeated in his quest for freedom for himself and his people, jumps to his death from a church tower. Demetrio Montiel, in Gallegos' novel, deals in contraband goods and slaves and briefly contemplates incest with his daughter, Remota. Sensual and unethical, he feels a growing depression because at fifty he finds life worthless: "Nada que valiera la pena al cabo de ellos . . . Solo le quedaba el triste descenso de allí adelante . . .¿Ya para qué? Por delante no le quedaban sino los años yermos del envejecimiento. . . ."[33] General gossip has it that he killed himself because of his incestuous feelings. Nonetheless, his one positive act of bravery in saving victims of a fire leads him to realize too late that he might have been the moral leader of his people and a truly positive force for his country. Whatever his sensual or depressed feelings may have been, this realization is what prompts him to seek a watery grave. Otherwise it is hard to justify Gallegos' sympathy for Demetrio, "al cual, el autor aunque en secreto, quiere más que a todas sus otras criaturas que viven en el volumen."[34]

Los animales puros contains three suicidal characters. David Caballero, a puritanical young patrician, whom Benjamín Carrión labels "un pobre Hamlet conceptualista,"[35] dedicates himself to the Marxist revolution. A romantic intellectual, he admires the supposed inflexible revolutionary fervor of fellow workers like Luis Rojas. David's ideals result in his father's death and in his abandonment of his pregnant wife. Finally, unable to live up to his self-imposed purity and temporarily insane, he jumps into the river. Bolívar Merizalde, condemned by the ultra-pure Rojas for stealing some books and unable to contemplate the possibility of expulsion from the Party, shoots himself. Carlos Suárez, incapable of total commitment to his revolutionary ideals, also gives up his life.

Other suicides for an idealistic cause include Miguel Angel Asturias's Gaspar Ilóm of Hombres de maíz (1949), who fights the invaders who reject the sacredness of corn. Whatever his god-like attributes, finding himself poisoned, "se arrojó al río. El agua que le dió la vida contra el veneno le daría la muerte."[36] In El papa verde (1954), another Asturias character, Mayarí Palma, kills herself rather than betray her people. Carlos Martínez Moreno, in El paredón (1963), presents us with incidental characters, Baltasar Brum and Eddy Chibas, who destroy themselves over political frustration or national corruption.

Balta Espinar, the protagonist of César Vallejo's striking novelette, Fabla salvaje (1923), is typical of the insane victims. An anguished, depressed and paranoid peasant, he suffers from auditory and visual hallucinations, seeing and hearing people who are not there. Unable to sleep, the victim of nightmares and a growing unfounded jealousy of his wife, Adelaida, he, brushed by an imaginary presence, jumps off a cliff. Another psychotic, Julián Pardo, the frustrated businessman of Jenaro Prieto's El socio (1928), invents a mythical partner, the Englishman Walter P. Davis, who gradually acquires more reality than his creator. In hallucinatory states Julián carries on conversations with his creation, about whom he suffers paranoid delusions of persecution. In order to obtain vengeance, Julián blows his brains out, arranging his death in such a manner that Davis will be arrested for his murder.

Santiago, known as Juan Cocoliso, the protagonist of Mariano Azuela's La marchanta (1944), succumbs to alcohol. An orphan whose father had committed suicide, he feels scorned by society. After he accidentally inherits a treasure trove, he becomes an indolent drunkard. His dissipations and absurd passions trigger his inherent character weakness for which he needs more and more alcohol. He finally drinks himself to death, with the pistol he planned to use lying in front of him on the table.

Drugs rather than alcohol cause the death of Alvaro Díaz, in Coca (1941) by Raúl Botelho Gonsálvez. Alvaro, an aristocratic veteran whose nervous system has been shattered by the Chaco War, lives for a time with María Boa, an Indian girl, whom he eventually abandons for another unsatisfying love. He later tries to reestablish his relationship with María, but loses her to a gringo. Sensual and neurotic, he acquires the drug habit, and temporarily insane, jumps off a cliff, to drown in the river. An intellectual type, like Tulio Arcos interested in literature and philosophy and victimized by the memory of past family glories, he cannot bear the despair of a meaningless existence.

Spanish American fictional heroes feel very keenly the disparity between their achievements and goals, with concomitant depressions and drives to self-destruction. Victims of an inferiority complex which neither drugs nor alcohol alleviate, they often adopt masks with which to face life. Thus Prieto's protagonist lives a lie by having a fictitious creation take his place as an authentic being with a superior existence. In this way Julián hopes to be able to free himself from a feeling of his own futility. This sense of failure leads many protagonists to reject the possibility of ultimate coherence or logic in an absurd world. At times suicide itself becomes random. Gálvez in Juan Carlos Onetti's El astillero (1961) throws himself off a ferry boat, one more grotesque gesture in an absurd existence. The anguish of one's lonely trip toward death removes any possible meaning from life itself.

In La ciudad junto al río inmóvil (1936) Eduardo Mallea, stressing the transitory aspect of life, treated the theme of suicide in "La causa de Jacobo Uber, Perdida." In Todo verdor perecerá (1941), Agata Cruz, the motherless daughter of a weak Bible reading father, marries without love and finds temporary relief from her anguish in an affair. Abandoned by her lover and pursued by her own frustrations, depressions, and interior fury, she goes mad and one night disappears. Although in the novel she does not kill herself, Mallea implies that she will. As she rushes off into the darkness, he states that "hubiera querido morir."[37] He stresses this drive toward death throughout the novel: "Pensaba que lo que ella quiso fué morir" (p. 87); "Lo que nos manda matarse no es la muerte sino la vida. La parte más misteriosa del suicida no es su coraje, es su resignación" (p. 40); "Atención y memoria alcanzaron al fin en Agata un estado de muerte" (p. 144); "¿No le había sido siempre la vida una extranjera?" (p. 122).

Salvador Garmendia, in Los pequeños seres (1959), analyzes another alienated protagonist. Mateo Martán, finally achieving his longed-for promotion, finds life without meaning. His chief's death triggers his own psychic disequilibrium, repressed for many years. He wanders through the city, gets drunk, visits a whorehouse, and indulges in a recall of the ridicule to which he had been subjected as a youth. He is disoriented, uncertain, and fearful, and the author implies that his neurotic alienation will lead him to commit suicide.

Julio Cortázar in his short story "Todos los fuegos el fuego" portrays an abandoned girl who succumbs to an overdose of sleeping pills. His Horacio Oliveira, the protagonist of Rayuela (1963), is an absurd and alienated middle-class intellectual who seeks for ultimate values in life. His search for authenticity doomed to failure, Oliveira finds a kind of reality in his final jump to his death. Although Cortázar claims that he does not know "himself whether Oliveira really jumped out the window and killed himself or simply went completely mad,"[38] in the novel he refers several times to self-destruction. Maga thinks about killing herself. Oliveira contemplates jumping to his death down an elevator shaft, and Adolfo Abila Sánchez, ex-soldier, poet and linguist, a victim of alcoholism and mental illness, commits suicide.

Sexuality plays a large role in fictional self-murder. Estela Canto's El hombre del crepúsculo (1953) presents us with the neurotic Francisco Lérida, whose homosexual leanings toward Paula Feller's lover causes him to push her to suicide. He exacerbates her guilt feelings with his deceitful moral preachments in a compulsive rage at his own impotence. In Fernando Robles' La estrella que no quiso vivir (1957) a provincial girl who becomes a revolutionary and then a film star, true to her conservative Catholic upbringing, poisons herself rather than surrender her virginity to the evil dictator, Calles. In Luisa Josefina, Hernández' La noche exquisita (1965), Teresa Esteban, provoked by Rebeca Aguilar, undisputed ruler of a circle of homosexuals, lesbians, and philanderers, takes an overdose of sleeping medicine.

A number of homosexual protagonists end their lives as a consequence of their sexual aberrations. José María Vélez Gómara in El ángel de Sodoma (1929) by Alfonso Hernández Catá suffers from the incomprehension of the world which persists in emphasizing the immoral aspects of his behavior. The oldest of four children of an alcoholic father who deliberately killed himself in a car wreck, he is tortured by his homosexuality: "Entre todos los pecados posibles el suyo sería el más hediondo, el más denigrante."[39] Determining that only death can bring him the purity he craves, he jumps off a platform to be crushed by an approaching train. A more complicated homosexual, Julián García, the protagonist of Marta Brunet's Amasijo (1962), chooses death as preferable to a meaningless life. Smothered as a child by mother love, he views all women as his mother. Sex becomes destructive rather than fulfilling, arousing guilt feelings and self-reproach. Repelled by sexual acts with women and by the sinful nature of homosexuality, he kills himself.

Sexual hang-ups and alcohol cause the suicide of Delfino Valdelomar in Poniente de sirenas (1937) by Flavio Herrera. Anxious, neurotic, and frustrated, Delfino cannot overcome his hostility toward his wife: "Mi anafrodisia se tornó en hostilidad y, al fin, en hastío hasta la repulsión."[40] He falls madly in love with Mrs. Allan Vane, herself a victim of deception and despair, on board a ship. Even the news that his wife is with child cannot sway him from the woman who has come to be the very center of his existence. Obsessed by the sea whose "maleficio" he cannot escape, he drowns, together with his sweetheart. Although his sexuality triggers his suicide, he had always been considered a bit abnormal, given to mad transports, "extravagante . . . chiflado . . . padecía una de esas psicosis . . ."[41]

Sobre héroes y tumbas (1962) by Ernesto Sábato analyzes the suicide of Alejandra Vidal Olmos. Dominated by her father Fernando, who seems to covet her incestuously, she suffers from epileptic fits. For a time during her adolescence she undergoes a kind of religious mysticism. Manic and depressed in turn, she dreams that she is doomed to solitude. Constantly overwhelmed by a sense of guilt and of being immersed in filth,[42] she seeks sexual fulfillment with Marcos Molina, who rejects her because of his own fear of mortal sin. She equates the need for spiritual purification with physical destruction, which leads her to murder her father and destroy herself in the fire she sets. Her immolation purifies her and shakes off her father's evil shadow, cleansing her of the filth of accumulated generations of her family and symbolically giving her country, the authentic Argentina, a new chance to survive. Alejandra is overwhelmed by her obscure sense of worthlessness. She kills herself in order to give some significance to her life through a meaningful death. She cannot see the image of the past projected toward the future. By turning her death wish against her father, the object with which she identifies, she is able to go through with her self-destruction as an act of punishment, sacrifice, and salvation.[43]

Hostility as symbolic murder misdirected against a "self-other," the introjected love object, focuses to a great degree on motherhood in the Spanish American novel. Amasijo offered us one helpless victim. Alfonso Hernández Catá in El bebedor de lágrimas (1926) presents another classic victim in Luis. Embittered, envious, unable to find satisfaction in love, he had a frivolous, vain, social butterfly mother who spent little time with him. He seeks revenge on all women for the love she never gave him. Atilio Vidal in Gabriel Casaccia's La llaga (1963) is an immature, sullen and jealous Paraguayan youth who resents his mother's relationship with others. His father had killed himself in a whorehouse in order to protest, the son believes, his mother's faithlessness. Atilio denounces one of his mother's friends to the authorities for political activities. Identifying with his father, and guilty about his denunciation, he performs the only positive act of his life and shoot himself.

In Luisa Josefina Hernández's La memoria de Amadís (1967), Benjamín's family interrelationships are the central motive of his unconscious life. He hates his parents, repressing and transferring his guilt over real or fancied wrong-doing into a need for punishment. His father, a frustrated writer and womanizer, does not understand him. His mother, after a series of miscarriages and too many births, represents for him the filthiness of life. He sees in all physical functions nothing but shame and humiliation: "¡Qué vergüenza comer, lavarse, defecar! ¿Cómo mirar a los otros después de haberse lavado los dientes ¡Qué sucio todo!"[44] Nauseated, he wears the same clothing for days on end, repelled by his own bodily functions and contact with others, a reaction to a series of youthful interruptions by him of the primal scene and his parents' insensitivity. His hostility toward his parents turns inward, and he finally drowns himself.

Jacinta Medinar, the sensitive young girl in Estela Canto's El estanque (1956), feels unloved by her mother, Manuela. An imaginative girl, she thinks of dying: "Quisiera no molestar a mi madre, no estorbar su camino."[45] She begins to suffer from hallucinatory states, finding peace and contentment in a hidden pond. Believing more and more that she must die, she jumps into the pond.

Miguel Angel Correa's La ciudad cambió de voz (1938), Adolfo Bioy Casares' El perjurio de la nieve (1944), Clemente Palma's XYZ (1935), José Osorio Lizarazo's El pantano (1952), and Gabriel García Márquez' La hojarasca also deal with self-murder. In numerous novels, like La última niebla or Cien años de soledad, the protagonist attempts suicide. If one includes the kinds of death we find in Carlos Mazzanti's El sustituto (1954), where the protagonist willingly accepts another's crime and is hanged, or in Mario Vargas Llosa's La Casa Verde where Seminario kills himself in a game of Russian roulette, the theme become truly endless.

The thematic network of fictional suicides in Spanish America reflects the insecurity, feelings of inferiority, distrust of the outside world, love deprivations, and obsessive fears of local hero-victims. A surprising number of suicides lost one or more parents early in life. The fictional creations shoot themselves through the heart, neck, or head; hang, poison, stab, or burn themselves, throw themselves under train wheels; and jump from high places. Transcending the sociology of suicide, the writers reveal the impotence of personal religious beliefs in a menacing modern world where eternity and time, the grotesque and the absurd, depersonalization and dehumanization have intensified the anxieties of solitary beings to unbearable limits. Suicide becomes an acceptable starting point for the hero who sees life as insignificant, senseless, or even mad.

The novelists have intuitively penetrated the emotional wellsprings of their fellow countrymen, and through their instinctive and yet perceptive judgments have given special aesthetic form to a universal problem. Grand passions apparently play no greater role than the universal neuroses which beset us all in an uncertain and hostile universe. Yet Spanish American suicide seems essentially romantic, the result of the continuing duality between reality and desire. The depressing and devitalizing process of living in Spanish America blends intimately with that of dying; it follows that the instability and anguish of existence may be resolved by the one meaningful, decisive action that can bring both peace and freedom.

Notes

[1] See On the Nature of Suicide, ed. by S. Shneidman (San Francisco, 1969), pp. 13-15. José Asunción Silva, Horacio Quiroga, Armando Chirveches and José María Arguedas are among well-known writers of Spanish American fiction who took their own lives.

[2] Sigmund Freud, "Thanatos and Eros," The Standard Edition of the Complete Psychological Works of Freud (London, 1961), XIX, 42.

[3] See Patterns of Self-Destruction, ed. by Kurt Wolff (Springfield, 1970), p. 53.

[4] Octavio Paz, El laberinto de la soledad (Mexico, 1950), p. 21. What he says about Mexico, with minor changes, may be applied to other Spanish American countries.

[5] A. Alvarez, The Savage God (New York, 1970), pp. 211-12.

[6] Julio Calcaño, Blanca de Torrestella (Caracas, 1901), p. 86.

[7] Enrique Finot, Historia de la literatura boliviana (Mexico, 1943), p. 191.

[8] Santiago Vaca Guzmán, Días amargos (Rosario, 1891), p. 8.

[9] Ibid., p. 67.

[10] Ibid., p. 33.

[11] C. P. Oberndorf, "Child Parent Relationship," in Psychoanalysis Today, ed. by Sandor Lorand (New York, 1944), p. 85.

[12] Días amargos, p. 62.

[13] Ibid., pp. 316-17.

[14] Raúl Silva Castro, Alberto Blest Gana (Santiago, 1941), p. 590.

[15] Alberto Blest Gana, Una fascinación. Una escena social (Santiago, 1947), p. 19.

[16] Alberto Blest Gana, El pago de las deudas (Santiago, 1949), p. 204.

[17] Ibid., pp. 165-66.

[18] Alberto Blest Gana, Los transplantados (Santiago, 1935), p. 405.

[19] Rafael Delgado, La Calandria (Mexico, 1931), p. 148.

[20] Nicolás Heredia, Leonela (Havana, 1930), p. 365.

[21] Carlos Reyles, "Arte de novelar," in Incitaciones (Santiago de Chile, 1936), pp. 54-55.

[22] Carlos Reyles, Beba (Santiago, 1936), p. 52.

[23] Ibid., p. 161.

[24] Eugenio Cambaceres, Sin rumbo (Buenos Aires, 1953), pp. 18-26.

[25] Ibid., p. 166.

[26] Phyllis Powers Beck, "Eugenio Cambaceres: The Vortex of Controversy," Hispania 56 (1963), 758.

[27] José María Vargas Vila, Ibis (Paris, 1947), p. 229.

[28] Arturo Escobar Uribe, El divino Vargas Vila (Bogotá, 1968), pp. 35-36; 165.

[29] Manuel Díaz Rodríguez, Sangre patricia (Madrid, 1916), p. 25.

[30] Enrique Larreta, Zogoibi (Buenos Aires, 1926), p. 102.

[31] See Emile Durkheim, Suicide, a Study in Sociology (Glencoe, Illinois, 1965), pp. 42 ff., for an elaboration of negative suicide.

[32] Benito Lynch, El inglés de los huesos (Buenos Aires, 1940), pp. 185; 261.

[33] Rómulo Gallegos, Sobre la misma tierra (Buenos Aires, 1968), p. 79.

[34] Ulrich Leo, "Sobre la misma tierra," Revista Nacional de Cultura, no. 51 (1945), 69.

[35] Benjamín Carrión, El nuevo relato ecuatoriano (Quito, 1950), p. 257.

[36] Miguel Angel Asturias, Hombres de maíz (Buenos Aires, 1949), p. 25.

[37] Eduardo Mallea, Todo verdor perecerá (Buenos Aires, 1951), p. 163. Further citations in the text are to this edition.

[38] Luis Harss and Barbara Dohmann, Into the Mainstream (New York, 1967), p. 233.

[39] Alfonso Hernández Catá, El ángel de Sodoma (Madrid, 1929), p. 115.

[40] Flavio Herrera, Poniente de sirenas (Guatemala, 1937), p. 33.

[41] Ibid., pp. 14-18. For his neurotic and ecstatic sea states, see pp. 50. 57, 58, 92-94, and 141.

[42] See Karl Abraham, On Character and Libido Development (New York, 1966), p. 79. It is natural to expel the introjected father object and destroy him. Her compulsive need for cleanliness involves sublimated sadistic instincts as well.

[43] For a discussion of suicide as punishment see William R. Roalfe, "The Psychology of Suicide," Journal of Abnormal and Social Psychology, 23 (1928), 59-67. See also Wilhelm Stekel, "On Suicide," American Journal of Urology and Sexology (August, 1918), 335-50.

[44] Luisa Josefina Hernández, La memoria de Amadís (Mexico, 1967), p. 12.

[45] Estela Canto, El estanque (Buenos Aires, 1956), p. 83.

HOMOSEXUALITY AS A THEME IN REPRESENTATIVE CONTEMPORARY SPANISH AMERICAN NOVELS

Perversions of various kinds were treated in Spanish American Modernist and naturalistic novels, but homosexuality as a theme, with a few notable exceptions, played a relatively small part in Spanish American fiction until the 1950's. Enrique Gómez Carrillo in Del amor, del dolor y del vicio (1898) and Manuel Díaz Rodríguez in Ídolos rotos (1901) allude to homosexuality. Rafael Arévalo Martínez, too, masks such a relationship in El hombre que parecía un caballo (1915), but it was Augusto D'Halmar, about whose own sexual aberrations much has been written, who concentrated in an artistic way on the subject. D'Halmar describes a somewhat veiled sexual deviance in La sombra del humo en el espejo (1924) and focuses on the topic in Pasión y muerte del cura Deusto (1924), about young Pedro and a parish priest, Ignacio Deusto, who commits suicide upon discovering his homosexual attachment for the boy. Alfonso Hernández Catá's El Angel de Sodoma (1928) has as its perverted protagonist the unfortunate José María Vélez Gómara.

In the 1930's and 1940's many prison reform novels touched on the sexual perversions inherent in prison life. Three such novels are Carlos Montenegro's Hombres sin mujer (1938), Antonio Arraiz' Puros hombres (1938), and Alfredo Pareja Diezcanseco's Hombres sin tiempo (1941). Among other novels of this period which portray homo-eroticism are José Díez Canseco's Duque (1934), whch deals with the relationships of Teddy and Carlos Astorga; Eduardo Zalamea Borda's Cuatro años a bordo de mí mismo (1934), which introduces the theme of lesbianism; and Juan Carlos Onetti's Para esta noche (1943), which reveals the tortured feelings of Morosán, the bisexual police agent.

As one approaches the contemporary period the subject achieves a more legitimate fictional status. Salvador Reyes describes homosexual dives in Valparaiso, Puerto de Nostalgia (1955), and Hector Murena portrays a sapphic nurse in Las leyes de la noche (1958). In the 1960's Marta Brunet, in Amasijo (1961); Mario Benedetti, whose Gloria Caselli fruitlessly falls in love with a sexual invert in Gracias por el fuego (1965); José Revueltas; Guillermo Cabrera Infante, whose Tres tristes tigres (1967) is loaded with homosexuals and their haunts; and José Lezama Lima, who makes of homsexuality the centerpiece of his great novel Paradiso (1966), through subtly shaded connotations or candid revelations give artistic representation to previously limited fictional material. Among the additional plethoric portrayals of the theme, one may also mentions those of Juan José Arreola, Luisa Josefina Hernández, Oswaldo Reynoso,

Mario Vargas Llosa, Renato Pellegrini, Julio Cortázar, and Carlos Martínez Moreno.

Aside from novels which present perversion as their central preoccupation, many give it peripheral treatment. The characters reflect, in varying degree, the scientific dimensions of homosexuality, which apparently as yet has no definitive explanation, along with a number of common fantasies. The new interest among writers may, in part, stem from a new awareness of the psychological factors involved, brought about by the widespread popularized discussion of the subject in recent years. In Los muertos andan solos (1962) by Juan Arcocha, one of the characters, Jorge, has a fixation on his nymphomaniac sister. His mother had died when he was four years old, and he considered his father to be his enemy. His sister became his mother surrogate, and he found it difficult to live without her or away form her. His homosexuality is passive and veiled, but he likes the "buenos mozos" of the Varadero, "los hombres mejor parecidos de Cuba . . ."[2] In Julio Cortázar's 62: Modelo para armar (1968), a study of the interactions of humanity in search for individual meaning and of antagonistic forces of art and life in an absurd world, the lesbian incident between Helene, the anesthesiologist, and Celia, in love with Austin, adds a new dimension to the novel. The specific physical act here is done with some discretion: "no alcanzaba a librar la boca o la garganta cuando ya la caricia bajaba por el vientre . . . las manos se aliaban y se desanudaban entre sollozos y balbuceos, la piel desnuda se abría a látigos de espuma, los cuerpos enlazados naufragaban en su propio oleaje; se perdían entre cristales verdes . . ."[3] In Mario Vargas Llosa's Conversación en la Catedral (1969), Fermín Zavala, a successful business executive and Ambrosio, his mulatto chauffeur, are homosexual lovers. Fermín, a good family man, is ashamed of his activities, but he cannot break his relationship with Ambrosio and others. Another character, Hortensia, known as La Musa, has a number of lesbian lovers, among them Queta. Their lovemaking is more forcefully depicted than was the case in Cortázar's novel: "Sólo las cinturas y nalgas se movían . . . Queta estaba ahora de espaldas y Hortensia se veía pequeñita y blanca, ovillada, su cabeza inclinándose con los labios entreabiertos y húmedos entre las piernas oscuras viriles que se abrían . . ."[4]

Marta Brunet's Amasijo (1962) is a psychological study in depth of a homosexual. Wealthy but lonely Julián García, a dramatist, is physically incapable of loving any woman, all of whom come to represent his mother. Ill and confined to her bed as the result of a car accident, she smothered her child with love, keeping him next to her day and night. Julián had crawled late, walked late, and had difficulty in speaking. His mother wanted him to spend all his time with her: "la manía de la señora de tenerlo siempre[5] a su lado, junto a ella, en una absurda vida de encierro."[5] Defrauded of almost every normal activity and chained by her tears, he finally attends school, largely through the efforts of an understanding priest. His mother died when he was eight years old, but by that time he was unable to accept the language or cultural shock of the outside world. When he became an adolescent, "surgía imperioso desde mis entrañas. El deseo; el mandato del sexo, sostenido y lacerante. La necesidad de fundirse a una mujer y el horror a ese acto . . . Porque la mujer en potencia, la mujer, así genéricamente, en cuanto se materializaba—jadeó—y era una mujer junto a mí . . ., era . . ., se convertía . . ., era . . .--'Ella'"[6]

This revulsion led him to see sex as destructive rather than fulfilling, causing his self-reproach and eventual suicide. Unable to be with women, he returns home to live with an old servant who constantly reminds him of his debt to his mother, renewing and reinforcing his guilt feelings and belief that he cannot possess a woman without possessing his mother. When he becomes a homosexual he simply substitutes one nightmare for another. Repelled by sexual acts with women and by what he feels is the sinful nature of his homosexual proclivities, he finally kills himself. Brunet presents us with a textbook case of repression, shame, and guilt associated with the emotional attachment for one's mother which, in this case, renders the protagonist incapable of any feeling at all of attraction for the opposite sex. To him "all women are as forbidden as his mother. This may declare itself in pronounced misogyny or even, when combined with other factors, in actual homosexuality . . ."[7]

Asfalto (1964) by Renato Pellegrini, filled with obloquy, cruelty, and sensuality, verges on the pornographic in its extremely frank and explicit descriptions of a variety of libidinal arrangements. Nonetheless, the coarse utterances do not disguise the problems of real people. Eduardo, known to his friends as Ales, is a sixteen year old juvenile delinquent who has a variety of homosexual encounters both before and after his arrival at the capital. In spite of his homosexual activities, he does not consider himself to be a sexual deviant because he is not actively or consciously pursuing this role: ¿Qué era en verdad un homosexual? No seguramente uno de esos putos de mierda que andaban buscando encamarse con media humanidad. ¿Entonces? ¿Tenía ya algo de común con ellos? ¿Me parecía, aunque más no fuera, en algo . . . a los tipos del asfalto, a Ricardo? Estaba seguro de que el contacto físico con ellos, con todos ellos, me había disgustado. ¿Entonces? Me había abandonado, solo por placer o mejor dicho sin placer, por ansias de calor humano, de compañía. ¿Puede ser uno homosexual, así como soy yo?"[8] When he meets Julia, for whom he feels a sexual attraction, he abandons homoeroticism for heterosexuality. The author gives us forthright and precise descriptions of physical relationships: "Su brazo rodea mi cintura . . . Voz anhelosa: 'Querido' . . . Ojos fuera de las órbitas . . . Labios en mi cuello . . . Su mano de dedos ágiles, inquietos, desbrocha mi bragueta, busca el sexo. Le dejo hacer, sin resistirme . . . Luego lentamente, lleva mi mano hacia su propio sexo. Zanja. . . Su cosa se hincha a punto de estallar. Líquido caliente, pegajoso, a borbotones. Olor a engrudo podrido . . ." "Su respiración, fatigosa, me asustaba. Deseaba que terminara pronto y me dejase tranquilo. Su mandíbula crujía, al besar, cual desencajada. Mezcló nuestros sexos, hipando. El suyo duro, erecto; el mío, lánguido, sin fuerzas."[9] In other incidents Ales is attacked by two perverts who attempt to rape him and by an old man in the washroom of a cafe.

Eduardo finally encounters Ricardo Cabral, a more sophisticated Argentine, who discusses and explains the nuances of homosexual language: "Homosexual es aquel que mantiene relaciones sexuales con personas de su mismo sexo." "El invertido." "No precisamente, El invertido es generalmente lo que la gente llama marica o puto. Resultan, en verdad, algo así como la degeneración del homosexualismo. Por culpa de ellos, el vulgo no establece distingos. Llama putos a todos y se acabó."[10] Ricardo, a pederast or boy lover, believes his activities are the normal ones and is convinced that heterosexual love is a perversion. He and his pederastic society feel compassion for so-called normal men obliged to indulge in gross and grotesque heterosexual activities. They would not change under any conditions. Pellegrini, through Ricardo, in addition to describing a range of types from transvestites to sodomites, lists famous homosexuals of history, among whom we find Achilles, Plato, Julius Caesar, Vergil, Frederick the Great, Rimbaud, Proust, and Gide. In spite of the sadism, sexual lust, and anxieties professed by the characters, he reaffirms that "el homosexual verdadero es un santo."[11]

Oswaldo Reynoso's En octubre no hay milagros (1965) describes Don Manuel, an active homosexual and a possessive, jealous old man who from youth on had indulged in so many sexual encounters that their very memory nauseated him. Conceiving a passion for Tito, whom he more or less adopts, he brings him into the circle of former lovers, among them a servant and a black chauffeur. He feels the need for the fresh youth of Tito whose resistance only spurs his passion: "Había que soportarlo hasta que llegara el tiempo del asco, del aburrimiento, y, entonces, lo botaría como a un perro . . ."[12] In this antagonistic relationship, not uncommon among homosexuals, Tito achieves his vengeance by destroying Manuel's prize ceramics before he runs off.

Luisa Josefina Hernández in La noche exquisita (1965) analyzes a nasty, gossipy, bohemian group of frustrated individuals, headed by Rebeca Aguilar, a forty-five year old whose house is always filled with lesbians: "Que todas las lesbianas que frecuentaban la casa de Rebeca Aguilar lo hacían con la secreta esperanza de que ella les correspondiera porque estaban enamoradas de ella."[13] Other characters are Xavier Enríquez, very well known in homosexual circles; Efraín, another sodomist, who refers to his masculine lovers as "personas"; Pedrito, smothered by mother love and seeking in homoeroticism the purity he cannot find in her promiscuity; Ramón, his lover, affected by a puritanical upbringing, who transfers faithfulness to his mother into exciting relationships with boys; Rolando Esquivel, and his lover-companion, Eduardo, whose own possessive mother, delighted that she has no female rival, is not distressed that her son is a "fugitivo de una clase que va a enterrar su homosexualidad a un mundo encantado."[14] These crippled people, whose emotional obstacles prevent their interest in members of the opposite sex, view an enduring homosexual relationship as a special kind of defense against repressed anxieties about heterosexual relationships.[15] Hernández sympathizes with her group of perverts, claiming that "hay lugar en el mundo para los ladrones, las prostitutas, los homosexuales . . . para los que hacen su camino confuso y alcanzan sus ideales secretos."[16]

Manuel González Astica, known as "La Manuela," the tormented transvestite in José Donoso's El lugar sin límites (1966), is the fairy father of the madam of a brothel. He had earned his livelihood as a pianist in a number of whorehouses and considered himself to be a professional showman: "Maricón seré, pero degenerado no. Soy profesional."[17] He shares the classic fear of the vagina dentada and ensuing castration, convinced that he will "quedar mutilado, desangrándome dentro de ella."[18] Nonetheless, he is tricked into accidental parenthood, even though he thinks of himself as a woman and refers to himself as "ella." A grotesque figure, dressed as a woman and beaten by the men who frequent the whorehouse, he tries to relive his pathetic moments of past terpsichorean glory but finds only destruction and death.

Arnulfo Ayala, an army general passionately in love with Alberto, a twenty-five year old man who lives with him, is the tragic homosexual of Luisa Josefina Hernández's La memoria de Amadís (1967). Arnulfo's fixation on his mother and then on his sister Adelina, a mother surrogate, had resulted in an incest barrier. A lonely and solitary personality, Arnulfo saw in his sister's grace and conduct the constant image of his mother, which in his case blocked all possibility of heterosexual relief. This type of relationship with his mother and later with his sister, exceedingly common,[19] normally helps boys find their way to other women, but he could not escape the thought of mother and sister as erotic objects. The resulting incest barrier was carried over into his contacts with other women.

Arnulfo's friend and former classmate, Samuel Macías, had lost his position because one of his fellow workers denounced him as a homosexual. He had become a pimp for rich homosexuals, among them Arnulfo. A fairly secretive sexual deviate, Samuel feels trapped by his perversion: "Si vive con muchos, malo; si vive con uno peor; si no vive con nadie, muchísimo peor."[20] Yet he takes up with a younger man whom he meets in his travels as a messenger for the homosexual subworld, exhibiting both sexual and paternal drives. The perverts he meets run the gamut from those like Federico Rodríguez who do not enjoy their activities to those like Alberto Bárcenas who can conceive of no other human condition.

Homosexuality as a theme in Paradiso (1966) by José Lezama Lima created a mild polemic between Mario Vargas Llosa and Emir Rodríguez Monegal. The former contended: "Mi sorpresa fué grande al leer el libro y comprobar que este tema ocupa en realidad, un lugar relativamente modesto en la novela . . . y que junto con él hay cuando menos una veintena de temas . . . Esta obra . . . puede ser considerada muchas cosas distintas, como toda creación mayor pero, en ningún caso, un tratado, un manual o una apología del homosexualismo."[21] He contends that homosexuality has nothing to do with literary evaluation and is merely a matter of personal taste. Rodríguez Monegal, although he agrees that Paradiso contains much more than the homosexual aspect, proves that the novel has an "aspecto francamente homosexual." Lezama Lima, he says, spends almost a third of his novel discussing homosexual relationships and defending them. Furthermore, he lists a series of homosexual episodes, among them those of Leregas, Baena Albornoz, various episodes of sodomy in which Farraluque takes part, and the debates between Foción and Fronesis about various aspects of homosexuality, which take up about a hundred pages. Rodríguez Monegal concludes that "lo que determina la naturaleza centralmente homosexual de una parte muy considerable de este libro . . . es todo el sistema de alusiones y de metáforas que constituye la trama lingüística del libro . . . no hay capítulo en que, con un motivo u otro, no aparezca muy destacada alguna imagen fálica . . ."[22]

This insistence on phallic symbolism and glorification of genitalia (one path to homosexuality lies through narcissism and love of one's own genitals) is a constant note throughout the novel. Lezama carries on at length about Leregas' incredible phallic extension and Farraluque's priapean rituals, among which are the sodomizing of a mestiza cook, the ejaculation on to her little brother's breast, the fellatio performed by the lady of the house, and Farraluque's homosexual encounter with her masked husbad. Marincillo, el flautista, known as "La monja" and "La margarita tibetana" by his blond little companions, "prerrafaelista y femenil,"[23] has artistic friends who reproduce a gigantic penis on his door with appropriate ithyphallic commentary: "Pon las manos en la columna Luxor—y su fundamento en dos ovoides.—Pon las manos en larga vara de almendro—, donde dos campanas van" (p. 36).

Lezama provides us with a number of homosexual fantasies along with scientific discoveries about the subject. A simple psychogenic explanation is that the individual becomes fixated upon his object choice because of gratification in early childhood or even adolescence.[24] George, a homosexual whom Foción meets in New York, can enjoy a longed-for incestuous relationship with his sister only by being possessed homosexually, an inversion of more common sodomizing tendencies and a recreation of mother and father roles. Ricardo Fronesis, for whom Foción feels an overwhelming desire, believes that homosexuality is a manifestation of a kind of ancestral memory, preserved in childhood, a golden age, lacking in sex discrimination. In some men, he says, this stage of innocence lasts all their lives and those fixed on this period "tienen siempre tendencia a la sexualidad semejante, es decir, a situar en el sexo la otredad, el otro semejante a sí mismo" (p. 330). Shrouding the formative experiences of a child's life in mystery establishes a pattern, and in some cases, through introjecting the parent of the opposite sex, a "young man will feel an inclination towards male persons because he has assimilated his mother by means of a psychological process of incorporation and consequently reacts to male objects in the way that she would do."[25]

José Cemí, the protagonist of Paradiso, relives many of Lezama's own experiences. The author's father, a colonel, died in a flu epidemic when Lezama was nine years old. He, too, moved to his maternal grandmother's house, suffered from asthma, and had a close and mutually dependent relationship with his mother. The greatest blow in his life, her death in 1964, apparently freed him to project his conscious and unconscious feelings in this novel.[26] Cemí has a never fully verbalized emotional fixation on Fronesis but dislikes Foción. Both disappear from his life, but his spiritual resurrection is furthered through the higher type of love he feels for Fronesis, perhaps a reflection of the perfect Platonic love visualized by the Greeks. Cemí's homosexuality is implied through a number of oblique references.

The central homosexual figure in the novel, Eugenio Foción, had suffered a sexual crisis which "se revelaba en una falsa y apresurada inquietud cultural, que se hacía patológica ante las novedades de las librerías y la publicación de obras raras" (pp. 315-16). An old friend of the family took advantage of his pathological fears: "Foción tenía por el abstracto desarrollo de su niñez y adolescencia, el complejo de la vagina dentada, veía la vulva de la mujer como una inmensa boca que le devoraba el falo" (p. 426). Undoubtedly, his fear of castration as a child led him to assume that girls had been punished by losing their penes, and their genitals had become phobic objects which reminded him of that anxiety. As Fenichel states, if anxiety on this subject is strong, it may override and repress any erotic interest in the opposite sex and leave only homosexual objects as safe ones.[27] Foción's fear of castration, a passive feminine fantasy, is also augmented by the madness of his father. His guilt feelings and need for punishment in return for sexual satisfaction and his inability to slake his insatiable desire for Fronesis eventually lead to his own madness and self-destruction.

The interminable debates about homosexuality between Fronesis and Foción focus on Greek concepts, on Japanese belief that homosexuality was a "privilegio de esa casta guerrera" (p. 337), and ideas of the Middle Ages, voiced by Thomas Aquinas who contended that "El adulterio, el estupro, el rapto, el sacrilegio, contrarían más la caridad del prójimo que el acto contra natura . . ." (p. 359). They discuss the relationships between Góngora and the Count of Villamediana, alluded to by Quevedo, and comment on the deviance of Socrates, Julius Caesar, Pascal, Nietzsche, Novalis, Barba-Jacob, Oscar Wilde, and André Gide.

In these Spanish American novels, along with almost casual and unimaginative sexual descriptions, we find perceptive analyses of the conflict of mutually hostile opposites, along with sound character development and convincing and artistic structures. Some of these novelists, attempting to utilize Freudian psychology, describe pederasts, lovers of father figures, and homosexuals fixated on their mothers. Others, still unable to escape a general feeling about the immorality involved, believe that homosexuality causes an irremediable soiling, leading to suicide in many cases. Lezama Lima, almost unique in his portrayal of phallic puissance, makes of his study an object of intellectual intuition rather than a sensuous perception, combining the physical and the metaphysical with intuitive genius. The homosexual theme is but one aspect of the novelists' search for new realities in old human relationships. The associations, obscene or untenable, vitiating or debasing, alleviating or assuaging, all form part of contemporary existence in a fragmenting universe where one's most anguished and secret world becomes the subject of artistic evaluation. Some of the novelists are over-intellectualized; others reveal great tolerance for human weakness. In assessing group tendencies or arbitrary ideals without pompous moralizing or emotional mawkishness, they all seem to understand that one's duty to one's fellow man transcends incidental anomalies and that we are all in need of a spiritual regeneration.

Notes

[1] See Hernán Díaz Arrieta, *Los cuatro grandes de la literatura chilena* (Santiago, 1963), pp. 20, 36.

[2] Juan Arcocha, *Los muertos andan solos* (La Habana, 1962), p. 170.

[3] Julio Cortazar, *62: Modelo para armar* (Buenos Aires, 1968), p. 183.

[4] Mario Vargas Llosa, *Conversación en la Catedral* (Barcelona, 1969), p. 36.

[5] Marta Brunet, *Amasijo* (Santiago de Chile, 1966), p. 66.

[6] Ibid., p. 119.

[7] Ernest Jones, *Hamlet and Oedipus* (New York, 1954), p. 89.

[8] Renato Pellegrini, *Asfalto* (Buenos Aires, 1964), p. 89.

[9] Ibid., p. 14; p. 63.

[10] Ibid., pp. 84-85.

[11] Ibid., p. 146.

[12] Oswaldo Reynoso, *En octubre no hay milagros* (Lima, 1965), p. 115.

[13] Luisa Josefina Hernández, *La noche exquisita* (Xalapa, 1965), p. 47.

[14] Ibid., p. 163.

[15] See Robert W. White, *The Abnormal Personality* (New York, 1948), p. 411.

[16] Hernández, p. 179.

[17] José Donoso, *El lugar sin límites* (Mexico, 1966), p. 73.

[18] Ibid., p. 109.

[19] Ernest Jones, pp. 157-58.

[20] Luisa Josefina Hernández, *La memoria de Amadís* (Mexico,

1967), p. 143.

[21] Mario Vargas Llosa, "Sobre el Paradiso de Lezama," Mundo Nuevo, no. 16 (1968), 89-91.

[22] Ibid., pp. 91-92.

[23] José Lezama Lima, Paradiso (La Habana, 1966), p. 34.

[24] See Robert F. White, p. 410.

[25] See Karl Abraham, On Character and Libido Development (New York, 1966), pp. 87-88.

[26] For further insight into these matters consult Armando Alvarez Bravo, Lezama Lima (Montevideo, 1968).

[27] See O. Fenichel, The Psychoanalytic Theory of Neurosis (New York, 1945), pp. 328-41.

FROM PRISONER TO WARDEN IN
TWENTIETH-CENTURY SPANISH AMERICAN FICTION

From El Periquillo Sarniento on, jail experiences have comprised a basic ingredient of Spanish American fiction. Manuel Payno, dedicated to the need for jail reform and prison rehabilitation, treated these topics realistically in his romantic novel, El fistol del diablo. José Martí, in El presidio político en Cuba (1871), eloquently describes the degrading and dehumanizing "cementerio de sombras vivas,"[1] prison scenes endlessly duplicated in the fiction of the twentieth century.

A number of twentieth-century novelists spent time in jail, among them José Rafael Pocaterrra, Rufino Blanco Fombona, Nelson Himiob, Enrique López Albújar, Juan Seoane, Ciro Alegría, César Vallejo, Ernesto Montenegro, Heriberto Frías, José Revueltas, Alfredo Pareja Diez-Canseco, Gustavo Valcárcel, and José María Arguedas, all of whom reflect personal prison experiences in their novels as they attack those who would betray the human condition.

Ramón Díaz Sánchez, Arturo Uslar Pietri, Miguel Otero Silva, Manuel Rojas, Carlos Droguett, Hugo Blym, Gabriel Casaccia, Martín Luis Guzmán, Rafael Bernal, Fernando Benítez, Carlos Luis Fallas, Joaquín Beleño, and Manlio Argueta also describe prison life in their novels. Perhaps the high point of such fiction is Miguel Angel Asturias' El señor presidente (1946), which, while more than a prison novel in its almost nightmarish evaluation of human degradation suffered under Manuel Estrada Cabrera, shows us the physical atrocities practiced in horror-filled cells.

One of the earliest prison novels, Mercedes Cabello de la Carbonera's El conspirador (1892), set the tone for future Peruvian prison novels, among them those of "Serafín Delmar" (Reynaldo Bolaños), author of the bitter evocation of prison life, Sol: están destruyendo a tus hijos (1943), and La tierra es el hombre (1943); Juan Seoane; Gustavo Valcárcel; José María Arguedas; and Edmundo de los Ríos. In Cabello's book Jorge Bello, an imprisoned revolutionary, reflects on some of the problems of prison life,[2] and the final homily about the need for public morality and a new idealism reappears in different form in later novels.

The novels, reflecting the infringment of human dignity and perversion of justice, concentrate largely but not exclusively on political aspects of imprisonment; primarily social instruments intended to sensitize the reader to the sorrows of humanity, they are, nonetheless, more than mere ideological manifestos to jab at our conscience. The lonely, isolated, often irrational prisoners and self-torturing intellectuals indulge in typical human aspirations, even though they lead anguished lives as victims of a closed and sordid universe where mortality and brutality are the only norms.

My purpose, rather than to explore the aesthetic and stylistic qualities of the works I have chosen to discuss, is to contrast two types of novels. The earlier fiction represents the continuing utopian view that the protagonist may be able to overcome the basic inhumanity of man. The novelists convey, through their passion, a concern for the dignity of society's victims. Rejected by a number of critics who feel these novels stress immediate issues over invariables, they authentically portray human illusions and moral anguish. The more critically acceptable fiction written later in the 1970's may reflect an aesthetic experience, but it glorifies the decadent tyrant, presented sympathetically in his human dimension to the detriment of his depersonalized victims and human compassion.

The novels of the earlier period include La llaga (1910), by Federico Gamboa, which serves as a prototype for later Mexican treatments of the subject; Hombre y rejas (1936) by Juan Seoane: Hombres sin mujer (1938) by Carlos Montenegro; Puros hombres (1938) by Antonio Arraiz; Hombres sin tiempo (1941) by Alfredo Pareja Diez-Canseco; La prisión (1951) by Gustavo Valcárcel; El Sexto (1961) by José María Arguedas; Los juegos verdaderos (1968) by Edmundo de los Ríos; and Perromundo (1972) by Carlos Alberto Montaner.

The authors of these novels, passionately involved in combatting official injustice, expose the exploitation and cruelty of their society in a sincere and spontaneous if highly subjective manner, reinforcing the idea that we all owe a commitment to our fellow human beings. Since almost all of these novels are autobiographical accounts, their authors are in a unique position to document and articulate the state of moral degeneration of their Spanish American world, Gamboa insists that whatever the individual responsibility, society itself must assume the blame for "la llaga nacional: éranlo las autoridades, que hacía siglos pasan junto al pueblo y no acaban de abrirle los brazos." Juan Seoane, who was falsely accused of conspiring to kill Peruvian General Sánchez Cerro and as a result spent a year in solitary confinement and some time on death row, relates the horrors of his prison life and the cruelties, tortures and pressures applied to political prisoners. Carlos Montenegro in Hombres sin mujer, based on his own twelve-year imprisonment in Cuba, concentrates on the prisoners' sexual frustrations, rivalries, and perversions and states in the prologue that he seeks to "desenmascarar la ignominia que supone arrojar al pudridero a seres que más tarde o más temprano han de regresar al medio común . . ."[4] The Venezuelan Antonio Arraiz, in his advertencia to Puros hombres, acknowledges: "Este es un libro brutal, desarrollado en un ambiente sórdido y violento, entre personajes primitivos. He sentido tanto escrúpulo al escribir muchas de sus escenas como ardorosa tristeza un día al presenciarlas."[5] Pareja Diez-Canseco describes his own imprisonment in Quito's García Moreno prison viewed as a "cárcel . . . llena de terror sórdido y helado."[6] Gustavo Valcárcel treats of Peruvian life under the dictatorship of Manuel Odría during which he himself was jailed. José María Arguedas, fictionalized as a student protagonist in El Sexto, relates his own Peruvian prison experiences under the dictatorship of General Benavides. Edmundo de los Ríos' Los juegos verdaderos is yet another first person narrative of prison life, and Montaner deals with the consequences of rebelling against the repressive and dictatorial forces which, unfortunately, still control so much of the world.

These novels, filled with a kind of external intensity in their revelation of the morbid and brutal reality of prison life, use memoir or diary form. Episodic accounts rather than tightly structured narratives, most offer us vignettes of prison life and the various characters residing there, often accompanied by a series of soliloquies and digressions which augment the central presentation. Intensely personal, the novels are often crude, dramatic, and anguished; in most instances the principal character recalls former happier days. All these novels, whether lineal narratives or technical, temporal, aesthetic mosaics, objective recalls or subjective reinterpretation, serve as spontaneous testaments to one of the circumstances of our time.

The characters, since they represent symbolic and ethical imperatives as well as aesthetic and psychological ones, whatever the ring of authenticity of the author's unique vision, seem individually underdeveloped, but the cumulative composite created by the basic repetitive patterns somehow enables them in their daily existence to transcend a fixed time or place and to remind us of the irrational in human behavior. Emilio Viezca of La llaga, an army officer imprisoned for strangling his wife, attempts to adjust to normal life with another woman after his release. Gregorio, a young newspaperman, searches for lost ideals. In Montenegro's novel Pascasio Speek, the primitive man, fights prison customs but eventually succumbs to his sexual need for "La Morita." In Hombres sin tiempo Gabriel Pérez Portilla, a thief, rapist, murderer, and habitual offender, kills for pleasure and revenge against a corrupt and unjust society, and black Jaramillo hides his feelings of inferiority beneath an outward show of violence. In Gustavo Valcárcel's La prisión, Froilán, a student falsely accused and imprisoned for terrorist activities, succumbs to the spiritual and physical tortures, a solitary victim of man's inhumanity. The novelists, whatever their artistic shortcomings in integrating the momentary with the eternal, attempt to convey the humanity of their characters, which they share through identical experiences, even though they come from a different cultural milieu.

The delirious unnamed protagonist of Los juegos verdaderos and Montaner's Ernesto Carrillo are the most completely elaborated characters. The former, in order to preserve his sanity, recalls his childhood companions with their model planes and make-believe games, his later sexual adventures and revolutionary idealism. Ernesto Carrillo, a philosophy teacher turned terrorist in Perromundo, relieves his meaningless existence of torture, thirst, cold, and loneliness by recalling his sexual relations, his "conspiracy against the State," and the murder which brought him to jail. Carrillo, resisting the brainwashing and other indignities which rob him of his humanity, refuses to reject his previous philosophical code. Alienated though he may be, he still has the freedom to determine his course of action, to rebel at all costs and to proclaim his free will, even in the face of death. Montaner and Ríos have situated themselves in the skins of their protagonists to recreate their special interior reality and their human dignity in the face of governmental oppression.

In spite of the horrors beyond belief which they portray, at some point the novelists extol the prisoners' human qualities and moral vigor, or at the very least, their solidarity brought on by a common agony. Aside from glimmers of goodness, we see a reaffirmation of human values and idealism, of hope rather than hate. The novelists, through the victims, identifying themselves with unversal imperatives as well as with their immediate social and historical situation, voice their ultimate concerns for brotherhood, peace, and the survival of personal liberty. The protagonists, projections of the novelists, dream that some day, in spite of all the degradation, man may triumph over his worst instincts, a facile philosophy not borne out by the novelistic situation but nonetheless a reflection of human aspiration.

Unsavory prison conditions play a large part in these novels, and the novelists paint page after page of horrific, disagreeable, and offensive scenes of human degradation. In La llaga the food consists of "líquidos sospechosos" (p. 11); in Hombres y rejas it is a kind of "vómito de un perro";[8] In La prisión some of the men are forced to eat "excremento de caballo."⁹ In all of the novels food is withheld or given to pressure political prisoners, who live without mattresses or sanitary facilities in filthy jail cells covered with feces and urine. Most of the jails are described as dark, dank places infested by rats, where men perform their bodily functions in the cells and, victimized by flies, lice, and bed bugs, live in their own filth.¹⁰ Some of the convicts brutalize themselves and others through drugs and homosexuality, and the authorities do all in their power to degrade their prisoners.

Each novel delineates a series of physical tortures, among which we find: "Entonces me hicieron parar sobre un banco y me amarraron las muñecas con unas sogas . . . por la ranura de una polea . . . Ya me iban a colgar otra vez . . . se me rompían los brazos; se me abrían los cartílagos de los huesos en la caja del cuerpo . . . Los bárbaros me habían estrujado los testículos . . ." (Hombres y rejas, p. 198); "Se azotaba con largos látigos por cualquier falta pequeña . . . al rebelde se lo ponía en el cepo, o en cuclillas, entrabados brazos y piernas por un fusil. Y los que morían en los suplicios, eran arrojados a una gran fosa, en el patio triangular. . ." (Hombres sin tiempo, p. 53); "Tubo algo más grueso que un dedo. . .; en el ano de los interrogados . . . hay dos alambres de corriente eléctrica. . ." (La prisión, p. 163). In Juan Seoane's novel the alienated prisoners engage in self-deception as to their future, despair, and finally fall victims to a kind of abulic boredom. Many attempt suicide; others go mad. They become mechanical spectators at their own funeral in the special silence and solitude of prison life which inhibits their human feelings. They suffer nightmares, dream states and hallucinations during which the very walls seem to come alive, " como bocas abiertas de gigante . . . pintadas de alquitrán que van rindiéndole el espíritu, nutriéndolo de deseperación con su frialdad y sus chirridos espantosos . . ." (p. 126). Seoane, disoriented, sinks into a semi-stupor during which he encounters himself outside his sleeping body. Recovering, he discovers "Se han pasado las horas, muchas horas . . . no he sentido nada . . . no he pensado, y, sin embargo, he estado lúcido y despierto" (p. 68).

In Hombres sin mujer the men, obsessed by sex, participate in perversions; after long years of imprisonment "el hombre privado de mujer . . . acaba por descubrir en otro hombre lo que echa de menos, lo que necesita tan perentoriamente que aun en sueños le hace hervir la sangre, y despierto le coge todos los pensamientos . . . apuntando a lo anormal, a la locura" (p. 16). Homosexual rivalries in Puros hombres also lead to suicide and murder, and are resisted or accepted in Perromundo as part of life, but not without accompanying psychological damage.

In Pareja's novel the environment of the cold, gray cells gradually affects the prisoners' mental life. Margarita, the ex-prostitute, becomes a religious mystic with a passionate fondness for prayer. Ramírez manages at first to stay half sane through his work and his conversations with Margarita about God and other subjects and in the recall of happier times, but gradually becoming almost an automaton, encloses himself more and more in a fantasy world and becomes a timeless creature in an endless sea of solitude where "el tiempo era una noción que no me pertenecía ya . . . no me sirve de nada . . ." (p. 131). In one of his hallucinations he sees himself as a corpse; when he is released from prison he cannot survive beyond the walls.

In Valcárcel's novel the protagonist at first remembers happier days and sexual adventures, but the homosexual, syphilitic, drug-ridden prison environment makes him forget the outside world and his humanity. Seized by a kind of recurring delirium and nightmares, he suffers some disorientation, as do the other prisoners: "etapa intermedia entre la vigilia y el sueño, donde se vive un instante cierta irrealidad para luego, volver a ser lo ya sufrido" (p. 27).

For the protagonist of Los juegos verdaderos only the morning withdrawal of the rats indicates that another day of life yet remains to him. Disoriented and delirious, he hallucinates two columns of marching lice and, in a kind of phobic displacement, sees his body as a foreign object belonging to his cellmate. He lives on the vain hope of an impending transfer, and at the end is but "un bulto de carnes purulentas, inflamadas, descompuestas, que se retuerce y convulsiona de dolor" (p. 272).

A continuing concern in these novels focuses on authority in general and specifically on prison officials, few of whom exhibit human traits. In Hombres y rejas, for example, the sadistic warden deprives the prisoners of visits and bathing privileges. The authorities "solo sirven para torturadores de políticos. . ." (p. 259). The guards, returning the sullen hatred of the inmates for whom this emotion becomes the subterranean force waiting to explode at any moment, replace their customary indifference with sadistic pleasure. In La prisión, the prison authorities embark on a deliberate and ruthless destruction of Froilán's human personality. Perromundo's authorities, more sophisticated and psychologically oriented, continue punishments further to darken the lives of the victims of political discrimination and to stifle remaining rebellious sparks: "Eso era fácil regresando de la celda de castigo con la cabeza rota y en andrajos. Ahora usted regresará a su galera sin un rasguño tras haber conversado un buen rato con el Alcalde, y con un aliento a buen coñac que se lo descubrirán antes de dar dos pasos. Así es difícil convocar a la rebeldía."[11]

Surprisingly, in many of these novels, in spite of the brutality of prison authorities and sadistic prisoners, the attempts to destroy human dignity and dehumanize the prisoners succumb to their human traits, temporarily inhibited by the forces of evil. In La llaga Eulalio will use his love for Nieves as a key to regeneration and a promise of hope for the future. Even the most amoral prisoners maintain memories of former illusions and lavish on a pregnant rat and her litter the only affection which they can project. In Hombres y rejas the shared suffering and enforced subservience bring out feelings of human compassion, for the prison unites the men "como una matriz a la que vuelve la vida desnuda" (p. 255). And in this process, overcoming their moral and physical apathy in spite of years of imprisonment, somehow they constantly reinforce their spiritual resources by their will to live and to resist: "La voluntad del hombre no puede estancar la fuerza vigorosa de la vida . . . El sufrimiento tiene poder de exaltación. El sufrimiento nos irá haciendo duros" (pp. 203-204). The victims in Hombres sin mujer seek to give meaning to their lives through acts of sacrifice, attempting to maintain or to rediscover their human aspect, succumbing to sexual aberrations but always hoping and striving for human liberty, which no exploitation and cruelty can fully undermine.

In Puros hombres Ibarra, through his strong sense of justice and final immolation, helps his fellow sufferers ascend from their animal existence to be truly "puros hombres." In spite of the incredible circumstances surrounding their lives, the political prisoners in El Sexto, overcoming doubt and despair, also maintain their spirit and fight for their ideals of justice and freedom: "la voluntad de luchar, de no retroceder nunca . . . "; "Luchamos por un Perú sin criminales, sin explotadores, sin caciques, sin soplones, sin privilegiados" (pp. 124, 133). In Los juegos verdaderos Humberto Marín and the others who are being transferred must assume the responsibility for their actions and be prepared to accept the consequences of their idealism. In defending his conscience, Ernesto of Perromundo also justifies his existence and human essence, the most we can expect in this "perromundo," making an existential choice in the face of doubt and disenchantment, refusing to escape into the madness and alienation of others. He resists and decides to "proteger mi dignidad de ser humano contra todas las tentativas de ultrajarla (p. 39). In these novels the prisoners think constantly of freedom but also muse on the meaning of moral guilt and responsibility.

Twentieth-century Spanish American novels about prison, startlingly similar, describe unjust incarcerations, political repression, brutality, tortures, escape attempts, psychological problems, dreams and hallucinations, homosexuality, suicides, and murders. The novels, polemical and provocative, although usually based on eyewitness accounts, offer us a misleading photographic intensity and realism; however true to life the situations may appear to be, they are but a symbolization of the authenticity of the personal involvement of the protagonist in his absorbing chronicle. At the same time the author includes episodes about other prisoners in order to convey more broadly the horror and compassion of the moment. He probes the mind and soul of the prisoners, but at times his immediate emotional bias or social preoccupation impedes introspective interpretations. On one level of reality these writers produce excellent novels, but some substitute the philosophical preaching of the protagonists for a sound substratum of universal artistic concern. Yet a writer like Seoane may achieve more emotional involvement from the reader through his very brutality than that obtained by those who attempt a more artistic and experimental novelistic form. In any event, whatever the word games of modern writers, ". . . the true originality of Latin American art . . . has kept alive the vision of a more just and humane form of society and it continues to emphasize those emotions and relationships which are wider than the purely personal."[12]

Unfortunately, in the 1970's, the focus has shifted from the prisoner and victim of social rape to the rapists. The less technical earlier novels attacked tyranny and oppression and, fusing ideology with the emotions and experiences of human beings, gave us a glimpse, however imperfect, into the soul of man. The more aesthetically acceptable fiction of today, rather than indicting political persecution, uses myth and symbol to commemorate private ambition. Many of these novelists promote a kind of perverse glorification, albeit a disguised one, of the dictator in works like El recurso del método (1974), Yo el Supremo (1974), and El otoño del patriarca (1975), one more distortion in a dangerous and disintegrating cosmos.

Alejo Carpentier, always ambivalent about his political beliefs, supposedly opposed Machado and Batista but managed to be away when the real fighting took place. In his portrayal of the Frenchified "Primer Magistrado" in El recurso del método, he burlesques his own writing through the dictator's speeches, conveying the idea that the ruler is a typical Latin American who loves good food, sex, literature, and music. Although Carpentier mentions cruelty to Indians, a general strike, a corrupt collection of funds, ostensibly to help disaster victims, and death, he treats these subjects humorously. Only when he denounces the United States does the humor cease;

indeed, he pictures positively the dictator's fruitless attempts to stop the gringos.

In this novel Carpentier reveals the polarity of love and hate. The "Mayorala Elmira," faithful servant, loves the dictator, but he, incapable of true love, seeks through prostitutes to satisfy his desires and fantasies. The ruler is tired of having to put down uprisings, and even sex and liquor fail to cheer him up: "Un enorme cansancio lo invadia ante el género de esfuerzo que había tenido que desplegar cuatro veces desde los inicios de su gobierno . . . y habría que perseguir por tales tierras al General Hoffman . . . ponerlo de espaldas a una pared . . . y tronarlo . . . No había mas remedio. Era la regla del juego. Recurso del Método."[13] His own severest critic, the dictator uses slogans such as "liberty," "loyalty," and "independence," even though he knows they cannot do away with the evil in the hearts of men.

Betrayed by everyone, his daughter, his generals, his aide, Peralta, the Americans, and at the end known simply as "El Ex," the dictator dies alone, lacking even the consolation of his one real wish, being buried in the earth of the land from which he came": ". . . Ofelia, pensando que la Tierra es una y que la tierra de la Tierra es tierra de la Tierra en todas partes . . . había recogido la sagrada tierra, perennemente custodiada por los cuatro emblemáticos jaguares, en una platabanda del Jardín de Luxemburgo."[14]

Luis Leoncio Martínez, president after the fall of the "Primer Magistrado," cannot solve the real problems of the people either. The socialistic "El Estudiante," instrumental in dethroning the dictator and without a workable program, sees little difference between the two. Carpentier appears to be saying that one cannot rely on revolution to remedy a negative political situation and that all governments are equally ineffectual.

Augusto Roa Bastos' Yo el Supremo provides us with the semi-mad ravings and reflections of Dr. José Gaspar de Francia, Paraguay's "Dictador Perpetuo" between 1814 and 1840. Shortly before his death, Francia recalls the events of the past, dictating notes to his personal secretary and writing in his secret diary. Unaware at times of the boundaries between reality and fantasy but with keen insight into his own motivations, he justifies his foreign and domestic policy on the grounds of helping his people and in the name of peace and prosperity.

By allowing the dictator to monopolize center stage, Roa Bastos gives his word enormous weight which appended condemnatory footnotes cannot overcome. Furthermore, the dictator refutes accounts of jailings and torture as the gossip of malcontents,[15] and he is always eager to forgive errors except those which are dangerous "para el orden en que viven los que quieren vivir dignamente . . . No tolero a aquellos que atentan contra . . . el orden de la sociedad, la tranquilidad pública. . ." (pp. 180-181). Even conspirators receive unmerited leniency: "Menos de un centenar de ajusticiamientos en más de un cuarto de siglo, entre ladrones, criminales comunes y traidores. . ." (p. 354). Scrupulously honest, the dictator allows neither government workers nor himself the luxury of a family or possessions: "Ni ustedes ni yo podemos poseer bienes de ninguna naturaleza . . . Guerreros, magistrados, ayudantes, especie de santos armados, sin bienes propios ni vida familiar, están obligados a defender los ajenos con desprecio de toda otra mira" (p. 396). Indeed, when he took over he discovered that the country was bankrupt, and he had to take care of the most minute details "en mi afán de sacar al Paraguay de la infelicidad, del abatimiento, de la miseria en que ha estado sumido por tres siglos" (p. 382).

Francia reiterates that he wanted only to create a free, independent country (p. 37); end the unjust exploitation of the Indians (p. 47); grant freedom of religion, insisting on the true meaning of good works and charity (p. 356); and do away with the caste and class system which had led to the slavery of the masses for the benefits of the few (p. 315). His secret notebooks seem to bear him out, and he sincerely believes that his rule "ha sido . . . la más justa, la más pacífica, la más noble, la de más completo bienestar y felicidad, la época de máximo esplendor disfrutada por el pueblo paraguayo en su conjunto y totalidad, a lo largo de su desdichada historia" (pp. 268-69). And exterior testimony also supports him: "a la verdad, debo decir, dice el francés, que por todo lo que veo aquí los habitantes del Paraguay gozan desde hace 22 años de una paz perfecta bajo una buena administración" (p. 285). Throughout, the dictator contrasts favorably his own achievements with those in other less fortunate American countries, as he talks of "presente bienestar, el futuro progreso de nuestro país . . . que quiero proteger, preservar; si fuera posible, hacer avanzar más aún" (p. 320).

The Perpetual Dictator also reiterates that he rules only with the consent of the governed: "Esta no existe sino como voluntad soberana del pueblo, fuente del Poder Absoluto . . ." (p. 47); "un mandatario elegido por el pueblo de por vida" (p. 92); "me ha elegido la mayoría de nuestros conciudadanos . . ." (p. 135); " me habéis elegido y me habéis entregado . . . el gobierno y el destino de vuestras vidas" (p. 345); "puesto que el pueblo me ha hecho su potestario supremo" (p. 180). He admits that he has made mistakes and realizes that he will in the end be held accountable: "Tú . . . eres quien debe dar cuenta de todo y pagar hasta el último cuadrante" (p. 455).

The dictator is by no means perfect. He refuses to attend his father on his death bed. He can be ruthless. Sexually frustrated and unhappy, an enchained subjective self striving for expression in a world of frigidity and destruction, and at the end, lonely and rejected even by his dog, he dies in isolation. Roa Bastos in his final compiler's note states that he has only copied down faithfully what others had composed but that the dictator had "el derecho de una existencia ficticia y autónoma" (p. 467). Unlike his previous works where he denounced corruption and stressed the need for social justice and an end to political abuse, the author in Yo el Supremo seems to abandon his personal morality; for by pretending that the novel comes from official documents he leaves the impression that he approves the dictator's interpretation of history.

Gabriel García Márquez, in El otoño del patriarca, gives us a nightmare vision evoked by the rambling memory of a dying dictator, another view of tyranny seen by the tyrants themselves. His protagonist, a mythic and mysterious composite of many dictators, lives for more than a hundred years. The Patriarch's mother was a prostitute; his father was unknown. He himself fathers thousands of children but without pleasure and must satisfy fantasies with school girls who turn out to be prostitutes. Never loved, he sees his vision of happiness, Manuela Sánchez, beauty queen, escape his power; his wife, Leticia Nazareno, unloving, uses his power. Although he cleverly creates an inefficient government bureaucracy whose members fight each other instead of him, he lives in terror, obsessed by thoughts of death. His whole life is a lie, as his double, Patricio Aragonés who pities him, states: ". . . yo soy el hombre que más lástima le tiene en este mundo porque soy el único que me parezco a usted . . ."[16]

While it is true that the ruler assassinates his rivals, kills the husband of newly wed Francisca Linero so that he can have her, and dynamites a boatload of children, the tragic events become almost humorous. The horrors, as handled by García Márquez, become "happenings," rather like television programs, not to be taken seriously. Bad as the dictator is, he is better than Ignacio Sáenz de la Barra, the cultured sadist, and other followers who, unlike the dictator, are not victims of their own power. Indeed, the Patriarch contends that "hay órdenes que se pueden dar pero no se pueden cumplir" (p. 116). And the pueblo itself does his bidding: ". . . todavía me queda el pueblo . . . el pobre pueblo de siempre" (p. 239). He is an evil despot, but his solitude overshadows his wickedness.

A victim of his own power he cannot relinquish, a "monarca ilusorio en la casa del poder" (p. 220), he becomes a blind, depersonalized impulse, compelled by forces he cannot control. Frightened by everyone, reduced to one room, he lives at the end in a dung-filled palace, occupied by buzzards, chickens, cows, and cobwebs. Weary, sick, physically decayed, he is a mythical, solitary shadow, a tragic figure whose suffering and death evoke sympathy. At the end, after years of sterile illusions, he realizes that he has not lived and that the people, for all their suffering, have been happier than he. He had struggled in vain to mitigate his incapacity for love through the solitary vice of power, but he remained only with lies, for "la mentira es más cómoda que la duda, más útil que el amor, más perdurable que la verdad" (p. 270). He became only an uncertain vision, pitiful eyes seen through dusty train windows, "un anciano sin destino que nunca supimos quien fué . . . un tirano de burlas que nunca supo donde estaba . . . con el dulce silbido de su potra de muerto viejo tronchado de raíz" (p. 271). A paradigm of the dark forces at the very center of existence, the dictator represents the collective sense of the pueblo, their own mythic creation, a product of a land, says García Márquez, which needs a stabilizing force which democratic societies cannot provide.

Carpentier, Roa Bastos, and García Márquez, neither condemning nor revindicating, nonetheless cause the reader to empathize with the sad end which awaits these ruthless entites because of a thrust for power, love, or glory. They cause the reader to shift from a merited condemnation—at least for those who believe in Western ideas about democracy and social justice—to an acknowledgment of and almost a justification of their humanity. The current crop of non-thesis novels succeeds in breeding compassion for the villains, something previous thesis novels were unable to do for the victims. For today's supposedly sophisticated critic the complex narrative structure and aesthetic niceties of the modern novel become more important than the human values extolled in the more simplistic documentaries of earlier decades.

The murders, horrors, tortures (even anthropophagy occurs) become happenings, subordinate and explicative of the dictator as a collective need of the Spanish American pueblo. Paradoxically, the latest novels, avoiding the structural deficiencies and moral indignation of the past, fail in their mythical expressions and aesthetic niceties, unlike their sociologically oriented predecessors, to come to grips with the most important concern of all, the reaffirmation of human values and human dignity in a world sadly quite deficient in freedom which continues to implement, in ever more esoteric manners, man's inhumanity to man.

Notes

[1] José Martí, *El presidio político en Cuba* (New York: Ediciones Islas, 1968), p. 46.

[2] Mercedes Cabello de Carbonera, *El conspirador* (Lima: E. Sequi y Cia., 1892), p. 5.

[3] Federico Gamboa, *La llaga* (Mexico: Ediciones Botas, 1947), p. 319. Further citations in the text are to this edition.

[4] Carlos Montenegro, *Hombres sin mujer* (Mexico: Impresora Azteca, 1959). Further citations in the text are to this edition.

[5] Antonio Arraiz, *Puros hombres* (Caracas: Cooperativa de Artes Gráficas, 1938), p. 5. Further citations in the text are to this edition.

[6] Alfredo Pareja Diez-Canseco, *Hombres sin tiempo* (Buenos Aires: Editorial Losada, 1941). Further citations in the text are to this edition.

[7] José María Arguedas, *El Sexto* (Lima: Editorial Horizonte, 1969). Further citations in the text are to this edition.

[8] Juan Seoane, *Hombres y rejas* (Santiago: Ediciones Ercilla, 1937), pp. 22-23. Further citations in the text are to this edition.

[9] Gustavo Valcárcel, *La prisión* (Mexico: Ediciones Cuadernos Americanos, 1951), p. 150. Further citations in the text are to this edition.

[10] A typical jail is that of *Los juegos verdaderos* where prisoners live "entre ratas, debajo de ratas . . ." Edmundo de los Ríos, *Los juegos verdaderos* (Havana: Casa de las Américas, 1968), p. 12. Further references are to this edition.

[11] Carlos Alberto Montaner, *Perromundo* (Barcelona: Ediciones 29, 1972), p. 85. Further references are to this edition.

[12] Jean Franco, *The Modern Culture of Latin America* (New York: Frederick A. Praeger, 1967), p. 282.

[13] Alejo Carpentier, *El recurso del método* (Madrid: Siglo XXI Editores, 1974), pp. 120-121.

[14] Ibid., p. 343.

[15] Augusto Roa Bastos, *Yo el Supremo* (Buenos Aires: Siglo XXI Editores, 1974), pp. 153-154; 326-328. Further citations in the text are to this edition. The documents by Bel-Asco, Ventura, and Robertson are cited but explained away in the footnotes themselves and labeled defamatory, distorted, or apocryphal.

[16] Gabriel García Márquez, *El otoño del patriarca* (Buenos Aires: Editorial Sudamericana, 1975), p. 29. Further citations in the text are to this edition.

TWO FACES OF FEMINISM IN THE 1920's

The standard view of Spanish American culture emphasizes its machismo and the traditional role of Spanish American fictional heroines as submissive housewives and mothers, but early twentieth-century Spanish American fiction has produced a glittering array of aggressive, daring, and forceful females, Rómulo Gallegos' Doña Bárbara among others. Many women, following a long tradition established in colonial times, assume masculine fighting roles in defense of liberty.[1] In Eduardo Acevedo Diaz' El combate de la tapera, the protagonists, Ciriaca, "criolla maciza vestida a lo hombre,"[2] and Catalina, "una mujer fornida y hermosa" (p. 182), armed to the teeth, accompany a fifteen-man patrol, unload munitions, and fight ferociously. Catalina attacks a wounded enemy soldier and "muda e implacable, introdujo allí el cuchillo, lo revolvió con un gesto de espantosa saña y luego cortó con todas sus fuerzas" (p. 191). The women's relationships to the soldiers, in spite of some sensual contact, seem more " man to man" than womanly or sexual. Similarly, during the Mexican Revolution, La Pintada of Los de abajo, Pensativa, in Jesus Goytortúa's story of the cristero revolt, and Angustias, Francisco Rojas González's heroine, indulge in pursuits normally assigned to men. In some instances the women seem to be men with feminine names, for they are lacking in the special compassion usually associated with womanhood. At times they serve as sexual objects, but, for the most part, male dominance is not the principal factor. Indeed, in some novels the man becomes the victim of female sexual advances, a process which accelerates in Spanish American fiction from the 1960's on.

In spite of such heroines, signs of a Women's Movement arose only sporadically until recent times in Spanish American novels, dominated by a continuing concept of machismo. A plea for equality in love and even superiority to men became more apparent in Spanish American poetry written by women authors like Alfonsina Storni, but few standard Spanish American heroines appeared even remotely touched by themes of liberation. Two novels of the 1920's, somewhat ignored by critics, which concentrate on this ignored subject of women in society and feminism as a movement, La tragedia de un hombre fuerte (1922) by Manuel Gálvez and La mujer y la guerra (1926) by Roberto Andrade, provide us with a dimension of reality which at times flouts the traditional codes of behavior and the whole sexual apparatus of society. In these novels some women abandon their assigned secondary roles to engage actively and successfully in the political world, in Andrade's novel without losing their feminine characteristics as mothers and wives, and in Gálvez' work as activists in the battle of the sexes.

Roberto Andrade (1851-1938), an ardent liberal, believed that Ecuadorian women, subjected to a spiritual and political slavery, needed emancipation. His novel, a modern version of Aristophanes' theme in <u>Lysistrata</u>, received negative reviews from Benjamín Carrión, who characterized its author as a pamphleteer who practiced "la polémica política en forma de novela,"[3] and Angel F. Rojas, who agreed that Andrade's novels served to "volcar su pasión política tremenda; sus ímpetus literarios, su desprecio por las tiranías."[4] Alejandro Andrade Coello, on the other hand, discovered in him "gracejo, espontaneidad, talento, estilo nervioso deleitable."[5]

<u>La mujer y la guerra</u>, inspired by the ideas of the "Confederación Femenina de la Paz Americana" and dedicated to its president, Maximina Olmos de Giménez, primarily concerns Isolina, the wife of the chief executive of the Republic, a mediocrity who allows his country to drift toward war over a boundary dispute. Believing in the power of education and reason, his wife unites the leading women of the town to try to save the lives of their men. They decide to convince the legislature to renounce war; otherwise they will abandon their husbands in the broader cause of peace. Attacked by conservatives and priests as dangerous anti-establishment forces, the ladies lobby for their position and elicit support even from some chauvinist males who at first look upon the whole project as a joke. A leading general, fearing the growing support for the new cause, launches a surprise attack. The women redouble their efforts and adamantly refuse to have children to be cannon fodder. The counterparts in other countries follow their lead, and the new movement finally achieves its universal peace.

Andrade, throughout his life, had been actively supporting women's rights, pleading for new education to substitute for outmoded religious instruction. Seeing woman's role as primarily that of mother, he nonetheless realized her need for a good secular education and freedom to search for her own identity. He himself helped create a school of <u>artes y oficios</u> for women in 1907, stressing their potential escape from the strict societal ties binding them in Ecuador. He believed that the early education of the child by the mother was vital in creating good citizens and "si la facultad de la mujer como madre es mejorar la estirpe o depravarla, la primera obligación de todo director de pueblos, debe ser perfeccionar la educación de tal sacerdotisa . . ."[6]

The novel, which in spite of its lyric descriptions never neglects its message, contains a number of statements about the solidarity of women in the movement: "Ya sabes que con las mujeres no cuentan los hombres, cuando se trata de la inmolación de su sexo . . .";[7] "en el caso del propósito [Isolina's husband's justification in the name of national priorities] pertenezco a mi sexo" (p. 49). Andrade, attacking the various corruptions implicit in Spanish American power politics, believes that women, who carry men in their wombs, and educate them, may help transform their society by assuming a more active political role. In a sense, says Andrade, men are really women's charges, and teachers should not allow themselves to become victimized by negative chauvinistic opinions voiced by the Lord Chesterfields of this world.

Andrade decries the discrimination as a sex object to which woman has been subjected since biblical times and her enslavement and exploitation throughout the world. At best men patronized her as an inferior and child-like being. Now, in the twentieth century, woman must assume her rightful role as a peer: "Vamos a aparecer en un nuevo proscenio de la vida: la mujer es digna de él, y en él debe resplandecer, como no ha resplandecido hasta el día" (p. 57). She must protect her investment as an equal partner by claiming her rights, forming societies with other women, and try to teach men the proper meaning of love. Unfortunately, the Church, a principal factor in denigrating woman, has frustrated Jesus's own desire for equality between the sexes. But in spite of this opposition, the feminist movement, in order to implement its program and refute traditional Spanish American anti-feminism, should seek a new path: election to the legislature where it may press for constitutional amendments to insure for its members equal rights as fully participating citizens of a progressive society.

For the most part Manuel Gálvez' fictional heroines, governed almost completely by conventions which they may break only with dire personal consequences, reflect that author's male chauvinism, something he continues in La tragedia de un hombre fuerte in spite of its long discussions of women's rights. Gálvez describes women as either idealistic or sensual and apparently prefers them in a dependent domestic role. Women, he believes, represent tenderness, delicacy, sacrifice, contemplation, and passivity in contrast with action, a superior quality which pertains to the masculine: "La fuerza es cualidad viril. Y el don de crear, y la energía . . ."[8]

In assigning women an amatory role subordinate to that of men, Gálvez depicts them throughout as unable to resist masculine attraction: "no la imaginaba resistiendo a una mano hábil e insinuante y a unos tentadores labios masculinos" (p. 113); "eran raras las que resistían al amante" (p. 189). Even though Gálvez admits the hypocrisy, Víctor Urgel, his protagonist, justifies his love-making to a married woman because "la había dado los únicos recuerdos de poesía que iba a tener ella en sus años de madurez (p. 171). Because he sees women as sex objects, he describes them constantly in terms of amorous voluptuousness: "Clota entornaba los ojos con cierta voluptuosidad . . ." (p. 64); "Aurelia . . . ojos de pasión . . . sensuales" (p. 139); "Adela vestía un blanco traje . . . liviano, voluptuoso" (p. 112). Gálvez overemphasizes this sensual quality he perceives in women and their need for masculine physical attentions. Women who do not follow this pattern, he states, are either peculiar or abnormal: "la animadversión hacia los hombres es siempre artificiosa o anormal en las mujeres" (p.64). Víctor believes that Genoveva, Rauch's sister and the leader of a woman's rights group, must be an exception because she has political preoccupations which women normally lack; furthermore, he finds what he terms lack of sentiment only in those women "de temperamento masculino, es decir: poco mujer" (p. 242).

Women in Gálvez' novel, easily hurt in their search for happiness, nonetheless exhibit their superior ability to sacrifice. Urgel's wife, Asunción, loving and long-suffering, cannot compete with more liberated types. His sister, Virginia, whose husband mistreats her shamefully, remains submissive because she believes her Christian duty involves respect "a su dueño y su señor, seguirle adonde el fuese, ser sumisa para con él y rogar por él a Dios" (p. 41). The women in Víctor's home town, sexually and socially repressed by fathers and husbands, dressed in black, attended Church, and conversed about births, deaths, engagements, and marriages. Though the men concede that women have more feeling and emotional capabilities, for the most part the masculine protagonists believe them to be "ignorantes, sin espíritu, sin almas . . ." (p. 69).

Yet Víctor, even sharing his creator's prejudices, comes to admire "la fe . . . en las mujeres feministas. . ." (p. 131). Genoveva, the activist leader of the group of women professionals, doctors, teachers, writers, and painters, resents the inferior position to which Argentine society had tried to condemn her. Reiterating that women are slaves, she insists that they must fight for ". . . nuestra liberación, tenemos el deber de consagrarnos a esa obra" (p. 65). Devoted to that cause, she and other feminists place the movement above religious concern but at the same time scorn sensual women. She claims that the only way to avoid domination by men is to remain chaste. Víctor, on the contrary, believes that women will be truly free only when they can give themselves to any man. Genoveva includes husbands and lovers in her condemnation: "ésos son los tiranos de las mujeres" (p. 230). She laments that the husband who killed her friend, Clota, will go free because the laws exist to oppress women and protect men; even though married couples swear the same vows to Church and State, women suffer heavier consequences for breaking those vows.

Considering men culpable rather than superior, she and several other women in the novel see men as mediocre and ignorant. Lucy, another liberated woman, contends that men, easily dominated, should really be considered the weaker sex. In spite of her feminist views and rejection of all social conventions, Víctor does not consider her to be a marimacho. She, on the other hand, disappointed when Víctor wants to make an honest woman of her, abandons him as one more man lacking the will to live free of social prejudice. Genoveva, ferociously feminist, concedes, somewhat sadly, that some women are responsible for their own state because "eran cobardes y se dejaban dominar y engañar por los hombres" (p. 270).

The feminists, almost all socialists, believed in reforming the Civil Code which provided that married women needed their husband's permission for most legal transactions, in equality for all children, legitimate or not, in absolute divorce, and in the right to vote. Almost all were single and hated the thought of marriage. Some of them wore men's suits and ties and suppressed all perfumes and cosmetics. Revolutionaries, they did not seek simply to modify society but rather to transform it completely and bring about a new kind of family unit and a "cambio esencial en la situación de los sexos" (p. 126). Many non-feminists in the younger generation accepted their ideas, united to them in joint sentiments of protest against the dominant ethic of their society. Not content with meetings, many feminists, devoting themselves to literature, founded magazines and created a new audience of literate women readers.

Víctor carried on long conversations with his male friends on the subject of women's rights. Rauch contends that Christianity bears a great share of the responsibility for keeping women in a state of slavery. He believes that it is a matter of some urgency "establecer la igualdad de los sexos. Las leyes, las morales, las religiones, han sido hechas por los hombres, en beneficio nuestro, y en perjuicio de las mujeres" (p. 196). Eduardo Iturbide notes that modern woman, morally superior to her grandmother, must escape the outworn moral codes binding her to her husband. If men and women had equal opportunity under the law, women would prove themselves the equal or even the superior of men in certain areas. Some of the men are even willing to admit that women play the role to which they have been assigned at birth. Flesh and blood creatures with the same feelings and desires as men, they are victims in the majority of cases of "unos cuantos prejuicios que les han inculcado desde la infancia" (p. 282).

Gálvez, who views with some trepidation the political activities of liberated women, believes that the newly freed feminist spirit corresponds to the disintegration of the family and the Catholic Spanish tradition. The loss of religious beliefs, promoted by precedent-shattering movies and a tragic world war, allowed women to accept freer sexual relations with men. These women, restless and individualistic, reject social sanctions, choosing love or a man through curiosity, desire, or vice. No longer economically dependent on men, they feel that they are free in body and spirit and that "nadie posee el derecho de pedirles cuenta de lo que es privativo, íntimo de ellas " (p. 221).

Astonished at the existence of a feminist group of restless, tormented women, Víctor salutes their intellectual and metaphysical capacities: "sufrimientos metafísicos y . . . deseos de vivir libremente y por curiosidades sin límites. . ." (p. 116). But, as demonstrated by his lecture on "La mujer y la guerra," he assigns them a much more passive role than Andrade was willing to accept. Víctor believes that women represent conciliation, peace, and love. Because of these special attributes with which nature has endowed them, women should refrain from sending their children to fight in wars.

The speeches, manifestos, and discussions at times seem to make the plot merely a vehicle for a message, but the novels, technically and aesthetically a half-century removed, describe a drive for equality surprisingly close to the current feminine world-wide pluralistic movements, programs, and points of view. The American woman, for the most part, appears in early twentieth-century fiction as an aesthetic and romantically idealized rather than real projection or, on the contrary, as a promiscuous type like the oddly named Pura, the sensual dancer of El embrujo de Sevilla (1922). In countless novels Spanish American women also appear as prostitutes. Juana Lucero (1902), Santa (1903), Nacha Regules (1919), El roto (1920), and La carreta (1929) are but a few of the outstanding novels which deal with woman as whore and harlot. Manuel Gálvez, who wrote about these women in many of his novels, considers them to be the counterpart of the feminists as a reflection of the anomie of collapsing social structures. More importantly, both Andrade and Gálvez in the novels examined in this paper, emphasizing one aspect of woman's realistic capacity for love, present her also, without a radical metamorphosis, as both symbol and flesh and blood creation capable of militant action and self-scrutiny as a contributing citizen in the context of her society. Rejecting the standard Spanish American view of "hommes a femmes" that women are sexual objects which exist to afford them physical pleasure, thus denigrating that relationship, both authors, in fairly modern terms, create a neo-cultural dialogue in their description of woman's concomitant feeling of impotence and need for communion as an equal with other human beings. Gálvez, more prone to conservative and intellectual sexist evaluations about the sexual, social, moral, and political character of women, fears the change which Andrade potentially promotes. Andrade's women are more aggressive; those of Gálvez more alienated. Gálvez reflects the ideas of a segment of his society; Andrade seeks to help form new ones. But what is clear in both novels is that modern woman, regardless of her role as mother and wife, in order to reinforce her identification with and higher love for the total humanity to which she belongs, transcending regional limitations, must question drastically the social values which have circumscribed her, and, with exceptional energy, try to defeat the forces of hostility, indifference, and ridicule which frustrate her just claim to freedom.

Notes

[1] See Alicia Vidaurreta de Tjarks, "Participación de la mujer en el proceso histórico latinoamericano," *Revista de la Universidad Nacional de Córdoba*, 10 (1969), pp. 153-180.

[2] Eduardo Acevedo Díaz, *Soledad y El combate de la tapera* (Montevideo: C. Garcia, 1931), p. 179. Further references in the text are to this edition.

[3] Benjamín Carrión, *El nuevo relato ecuatoriano* (Quito: Casa de la Cultura Ecuatoriana, 1950), p. 354.

[4] Angel R. Rojas, *La novela ecuatoriana* (Mexico: Fondo de Cultura Económica, 1948), p. 109.

[5] Alejandro Andrade Coello, *Motivos nacionales* (Quito: Escuela de Artes y Oficios, 1927), p. 76.

[6] See Manuel Aparicio Suárez, *Roberto Andrade, su tribu, su época y la República del Ecuador* (La Habana: Impresora Modelo, 1958) p. 15.

[7] Roberto Andrade, *La mujer y la guerra* (Quito: Imprenta de la Universidad Central, 1926), p. 7. Further citations in the text are to this edition.

[8] Manuel Gálvez, *La tragedia de un hombre fuerte* (Buenos Aires: Editorial Tor, 1938), p. 326. Further citations in the text are to this edition.

SEXISM IN THE SPANISH AMERICAN NOVEL (1965-1975)

In spite of all the emphasis of late on the liberation of women, Spanish American novelists of the last decade, refusing to welcome them as equal partners in the difficult and tension-filled world of today, have reinforced their age-old machismo and intensified the battle of the sexes. A study of many of the best-known novels of this period reveals that in them neither woman's social status nor the Spanish American male's assessment of her sexual role has changed for the better. Indeed, these novelists deliberately attempt further to degrade women and the sexual process. Relying at times on the Jungian concept of the Terrible Mother and ancestral fear of woman and her sexual apparatus, the authors reinforce the male's neurotic fixations, not as momentary circumstances but as ineluctable verities. Obsessed by sexual compulsions and frustrations, they suffer from feelings of impotence brought on by the predominance of physical over spiritual love as a defense against the probability they will live a full life without an exemplary woman. As a result, both men and women become psychological victims of an absurd society, inarticulate prisoners of ever more rigid modes of thought.

Carlos Fuentes sees hypermanliness historically as part of the Arabic influence but attributes it psychologically to two factors. The first relates to the fear of women (in Mexico Aztec goddesses are more apt to devour or kill); thus men tend to overemphasize strength and power which subconsciously they really attribute to the female. The second factor involves the Spaniards' violation of Indian women to people the continent with illegitimate offspring who knew their mother but not their father. The children, seeking to recapture the image of the violating father, an impossibility, repeated his act by violating somebody else and creating more bastards.[1]

José Donoso explains in The Obscene Bird of Night (1970) that when a gentleman had illegitimate sons by the women on his lands "persons cling with a certain pride to the brand of the patron's bastard son . . . but when it's a gentleman's daughter who gives birth to a bastard, her son immediately loses all vestiges of identity, every trace of his lofty origin disappears . . . there's no son here; nothing's happened here.[2] The double standard needs no commentary. Where there is no child there is no father, and therefore no vengeance is called for. The emphasis on having a son, as though daughters were non-existent, clearly reveals the author's own unconscious sexist prejudice.

The old medieval ideal of courtly love persists in Spanish America where woman must be either saint or whore. Indeed, in

Mario Vargas Llosa's The Green House (1965), which portrays both nuns and whores, the two worlds impinge directly upon one another. In Juan José Arreola's La feria, Concha de Fierro, a virgin after three months as a prostitute, seeks a change of status with the aid of Pedro Corrales' sword. In El recurso del método (1974) by Alejo Carpentier, the all-powerful dictator fulfills one of his fantasies in a special house by fornicating with a young lady dressed as a nun. Others, dressed as brides, also indulge in role playing to satisfy the men's desires.[3]

In spite of the incredible sexual happenings in the contemporary Spanish American novel, nothing has changed the moral imperative of a rigid Catholic interpretation that sexual intercourse occurs only after marriage and for procreation. Since the male must constantly prove his sexual superiority because of the same tradition which enforces a girl's chastity, associations with prostitutes offer a temporary way out.[4] For Onetti in Juntacadáveres (1965) prostitutes are as indispensable as "the doctor or barber";[5] for Vargas Llosa in Pantaleón y las visitadoras (1973) they are as important as "lawyers or priests."[6]

Conversely, though man's most vital aspect may be his "erotic and licentious thirst, his liberation from taboos,"[7] as Julio Cortázar insists in Libro de Manuel (1973), he also needs passion, vision, and a love object beyond mere physical desire. Javier, one of the protagonists in Calos Fuentes' A Change of Skin (1967) wants Elizabeth to become, in the darkness of a dance floor, his dream image in order to have his conquest. He believes that one woman can satisfy his hunger for many women.[8] Similarly, Toñita, the deaf mute totally dependent upon Anselmo in The Green House, represents his impossible dream, a kind of fulfillment of his masculine desire for complete possession. Even the incredible old dictator in El otoño del patriarca (1975), who has thousands of concubines, becomes enamoured of Manuela Sánchez, a beauty queen, his unattainable ideal. Overcome by his all-powerful passion and desiring her with such intensity, he begs his astronomers to invent a fireworks comet because the appearance of an earlier comet had caused her for a fleeting moment to touch his hand. When she escapes, his wounded pride will never let him rest, and he remembers her as a vision for the rest of his life.[9] The masculine characters in La vida breve, Sobre héroes y tumbas, El túnel, Rayuela, Los pasos perdidos and other earlier novels similarly seek uncorrupted women to fulfill their dream image.

The double standard involves practices which echo the age-old pundonor concept of Spanish Golden Age theater with its perennial dichotomy between hymenolatry and Don Juanism. In The Green House Sergeant Lituma almost rapes Bonifacia but needs to know that she is a virgin, "That she had never known anyone til now,"[10] Lituma feels he must maintain his status as a male, for him synonymous with prestige and honor. When Lituma's friend, Josefino, causes Bonifacia's degradation, Lituma blames her: "he pushed her down onto the sand with a shove, and he was kicking her, whore, tramp, insulting her until he lost his voice and his strength" (GH, pp. 171-172). Typically, in Ernesto Sábato's Abaddón el exterminador (1974), when Nacho's sister, whom he apparently loves incestuously, has an affair, he feels his masculinity and honor are threatened. Where no father exists the brother must protect the family, and the author, exhibiting the usual cacography of the contemporary novel, describes how Nacho tears off her clothes and "crying and shouting spits on her: first in her face and then on her sex."[11] A surrogate father figure, he protects but exploits her as an extension of his own gestalt.

One aspect of the artificial and exaggerated code involves the husband's provincial view of his wife's exclusively maternal responsibilities. In The Obscene Bird of Night Jerónimo blames his wife for their lack of children. It never crosses his mind that the fault may lie with his own sterility, because such a thought is imcompatible with his superior dream image of himself as very manly. He insists: "your useless womb exterminated . . . betrayed by the incapacity to give me a son" (OB, p. 280). Since Inés has failed her assigned task as a servant, that is, to give birth to a son to carry on his cherished family name, Jerónimo looks elsewhere for a solution. Iris Mateluna, a psychotic orphan girl, lends her body as a vehicle for the birth of a monstrous male offspring. The protagonist refers to her as a uterus surrounded by unimportant flesh because he sees her, not as a person, but only as a womb to carry children: "But what am I to do with Iris' shell, the useless container that encloses her womb, once she's carried out her specific function of giving birth?" (OB, p. 101). Even the insignificant Humberto Peñaloza considers her to be a blob of primary existence "wrapped around a fertile womb that's so much the centre of her being that everything else in her is superfluous" (OB, p. 58).

These conscious and unconscious anxieties and motivations, whatever their ontogenetic origins, help create childish attitudes toward sex. Irony aside, the vile language and gleeful comparisons of what masculine and feminine organs are called in various countries, for example, reveal a juvenile attitude toward the sexual process. In The Obscene Bird of Night the characters do "nanay" or "yumyum"; in Libro de Manuel they don't make love either; they do "pudu-pudu". Both synagamic acts seem far removed from love or even violation. More zoographically, the deadly serious but psychologically adolescent hipsters in A Change of Skin describe the true dream in pejorative terms as time enough for "at least one more cup of coffee and one last piece of ass" (CS, p. 430).

For Latin American authors the female archetype, fragile, submissive, maternal, sacrificial, and obedient, is a subordinate creature.[12] In Libro de Manuel, which supposedly seeks a new revolutionary society, the protagonists maintain that women must be treated aggressively, and Heredia expresses the innate masculine assumption that women cannot resist them. The feminine characters in almost all the new novels implement the models established for them by the primacy of a masculine world in which, whatever a woman's moral persuasions, she will give in to the skillful sexual technician. In most of the sexual encounters described, the women willingly accept a subordinate if not always passive role: "You fell on your knees before him . . . He standing before you, you kneeling before him, you embraced his legs harder and harder and moved your hands up his waist" (CS, p. 80).

Carrying the idea of submissiveness one step further, the contemporary Spanish American novelists reduce the female to an object whose primary purpose is to serve as a sexual vehicle for the male. The more than hundred treatments of the theme of prostitution of various types and descriptions in the twentieth-century Spanish American novel testify to the prevalent propaganda about man's needs. A contemporary analysis occurs in Pantaleón y las visitadoras (1973). Pantaleón Pantoja, a career officer, accepts the task of providing prostitutes to various armed services on duty in th jungle. Soldiers' sexual needs are such that they are attacking women in Church, even though the army has prepared a special diet which "without decreasing necessary proteins, debilitates the libido of the soldiers by eighty-five per cent" (PV, p. 85). Nonetheless, the army decides that it must give ". . . these hungry soldiers something to eat" (PV, p. 20).

But another dimension in the contemporary novel involves the non-professional and man's pursuit of sexual pleasure. In El mundo alucinante (1969) by Reynaldo Arenas, Servando's guide possesses one woman after another and exclaims that "a man's pleasure should not be lacking at any time."[13] The old dictator in El otoño del patriarca kept more than a thousand women around for his sexual pleasure. In the darkness "he would take one at random by assault without undressing her . . . without closing the door" (ODP, p. 12). In spite of wars, changes of power, and customs, the First Magistrate, another dictator, in El recurso del método submits that whatever the changes of values, "I found the only permanent things to be more breast or less breast . . . a common language universally understood" (RM, pp. 369-70). All the women serve as merchandise to be bartered. In The Green House Lalita, who comes to Fushía as a virgin, passes from his hands to those of Reátegui, Nieves, and finally Pesado. Meanwhile, Fushía steals young Indian girls to satisfy his needs.

Since women serve as sexual property, their needs are not important; in One Hundred Years of Solitude (1967), Aureliano, during the war, takes advantage of the custom of sending virgins to the bedrooms of soldiers in the same way that hens were turned loose with fine roosters. He fathers seventeen bastard sons, but, in addition, he maintains a retinue of women whom he calls to his hammock and from whom he obtains a rudimentary satisfaction. None of these women leave a "trace on his feelings . . . they were nothing but a touch of fatigue in his bodily memory."[14] Carlos Fuentes claims that the macho Mexican is merely an onanist. If he could have intercourse with himself he would do it. The woman he takes is no more than "an object that happens to be necessary" (CS, p. 121). Elizabeth, in Fuentes' novel, says that men become furious on seeing the birth of a love in which the woman is just as free and just as much a person as the man.

Siete lunas y siete serpientes (1970) shows us yet another dimension of rampant sexism concerning women as a sexual vessel. Candelario throws his spurs on women, single or married, on the grass or on horseback, whenever the urge takes him. Seeking a cure for his supernaturally acquired impotence by marrying Dominga, represented as having rampant breasts and rhythmic hips, be believes: "For what other reason were women born."[15] Candelario's preconceptions preclude his accepting females as human beings. Aguilera Malta, his creator, describes him as having testicles on his forehead which orient him like a pilot fish to a hungry shark. In the same novel the personified sexual male attacker who seeks Dominga wants to mount her "only with his sex. Without using his hands. Nor his arms. Nor his mouth. Only with his sex." (SL, p. 11). Cándido, the priest, also maintains that women are only what they have between their legs.

Inevitably then, the relationship between man and woman becomes negative, and the male authors and their protagonists describe women pejoratively, presenting us with a panoramic perspective of degraded and debased sexual activities without any spiritual implications. The women implement a mechanical process to afford the men physical pleasure and to enhance their superiority complex. In El mundo alucinante, though women are plentiful, sailors attack a young girl, each waiting a turn to enjoy her body, insulting her time and time again (EMA, pp.

50-51). In <u>Siete lunas y siete serpientes</u> Chalena forces the town women to undress before him so that he can laugh at them.

This scorn for women, a leitmotif in all the novels, a defense mechanism to screen out childish fears, quite often is associated with the manifest homosexuality of some of the characters. In <u>Paradise</u> (1966) Foción extols the androgynous state in creation before Eve's destructive appearance on the seventh day. Throughout the novel, woman's sexual apparatus is described in disparaging terms. Since men fear the sexual encounter, they attempt to denigrate it in some way. Fronesis recalls with nausea and disgust his one heterosexual contact. He cuts, out of the back of his undershirt, a circle, and in the centre of that he cuts a hole. Until he is certain that he has covered her sex with the wool, he cannot perform.[16] Many of the relationships are not only degraded but sadistic. Mario Cobián (<u>Los errores</u>) is one brutal example among many: "The point of his shoe struck the humiliated face of the woman with sharp brutality, making her fall obliquely and noiselessly, twitching on the wooden floor."[17] In <u>The Obscene Bird of Night</u>, Inés explains that in her sexual encounters with her husband it was "always rape, every single time, from our wedding night on, always a matter of being taken by force" (OB, p. 376). The ancient dictator in <u>El otoño del patriarca</u> tells his double Patricio Aragonés that if he wants a woman, "I'll put her by force in your bed with four soldiers to hold her feet and hands while you dispatch her with your great spoon" (OdP, p. 16). Javier, in <u>A Change of Skin</u>, violates Isabel anally; Andrés also similarly degrades Francine in <u>Libro de Manuel</u>, adding insult to injury by insisting that she enjoyed it: "I did not besmirch you; it all went away in the shower" (LM, p. 327).

The need of men to justify themselves leads them to the conclusion that women really like and even demand what they are receiving, for they constanly need man's sexual attentions. Men, in this way, can rationalize also their own sexual shortcomings and their very real terror that they may not be able to satisfy a woman whom they basically fear and who may lower their status by seeking sexual fulfillment elsewhere. In <u>Epitalámica</u> (1969) by Héctor Murena, Africa Pedrada cedes her favours to three sweethearts in a row, but unfulfilled by them or her husband and overcome by the fever or "stinging between her legs", she becomes a popular prostitute to satisfy her desires.[18] The dictator in Carpentier's novel describes Caribbean women as "born with the Demon between their legs" (RM, p. 179). Lady Hamilton in Reynaldo Arenas' novel needs three men at the same time to ease her sexual fire. In <u>The Green House</u> Lituma explains that jungle women are so demanding a man has to keep fighting them off (GH, p. 230). Josefa of <u>Siete lunas y siete serpientes</u> forces Candelario to have interminable

sex with her every night. In The Obscene Bird of Night all
women, young and old, normal and deformed, ceaselessly seek sex.
Peta lives with lecherous desire. Emperatriz is constantly
aroused, her genitalia "slippery and excited" (OB, p. 233). In
A Change of Skin Isabel, when Javier begins to philosophize,
tells him: "All I'm looking for is orgasms" (CS, p. 279). Lupe
the maid used to pay a peso for admission to a dark room where a
man would possess her standing (CS, p. 118). Elizabeth, always
obsessed by thoughts of sex, acknowledges her lasciviousness and
enjoys it; to extirpate her sensuality she must satiate it. For
her, sex, like money, has value only if it is spent: ". . . I
could hardly wait, control myself . . . you wanted the promised
reward, that he would take you, and. . ." (CS, pp. 244-45).

The women seem to live for the pleasure given them by a
man's sexual prowess. When Aureliano makes love to his aunt
Amaranta Ursula she barely has time to use a towel as a gag
between her teeth so that "she would not let out the cat howls
that were already tearing at her insides" (HY, p. 366).
Francine in Cortázar's novel is unable to restrain her moaning
and shouting when Andrés begins his sexual stimulation. The
authors also accept the almost universal myth that the size of
the male organ relates directly to the pleasure received by the
woman. Demetrio Aguilera Malta's Tin-Tines who want to
impregnate Dominga are composed of nerves, muscles, and a giant
sex organ. These Tin-Tines are replaced by Equis X-Rabo-de-
Hueso, a modern serpent who changes into a gigantic phallus.
The First Magistrate in El recurso del método recalls how his
wife used to fondle a young army official, famous for the
exceptional proportions of his nature (RM, p. 216). In El mundo
alucinante a group of noble ladies want to enjoy the attentions
of the monumental artefact of a priest (EMA, p. 74). In A Change
of Skin a similarly endowed character's phallus elicits a
similar desire and adoration among the women: "Ay what a shaft,
what a baseball bat." (CS, p. 404). Unable to resist, they
decide to hold a raffle to see who will be lucky enough to enjoy
him. Ursula's son, José Arcadio, in A Hundred Years of
Solitude, so well-equipped for life that he seems almost
abnormal, exhibits his unusual masculinity, covered with tatoos
and foreign languages, as the women besiege him with offers of
payment. Iris, in The Obscene Bird of Night, gives herself
eagerly to any man who wears the phallic cardboard head.

Paradise dwells inordinately on phallic size with a
concomitant commentary on woman's worshipful reaction to large
masculine organs, for example Farraluque's, which elicits a
"pleading ecstasy" (P. p. 203), and Leregas', with a phallic
power equal, says Lezema Lima, to Aaron's staff (P. p. 198).
The high point of this worship occurs during a parade of an
enormous phallus (on a cart with a face in the form of a

vulva), surrounded by a double file of aristrocratic ladies, each bearing a wreath which they deposit on the quivering phallus.

But Priapus, the Greco-Roman god of procreation, does not always receive a joyful welcome from a few women, unable to accept men's findings that women are instinctively lascivious. These, according to the male authors, are products of a neurotic cultural background or unconscious inhibiting processes which make them fear sex. In A Hundred Years of Solitude, Ursula wears sailcloth bloomers reinforced with leather straps to maintain her virginity. Fernanda, in the same novel, wears a white nightgown which reaches her ankles, with a large round buttonhole, delicately trimmed, at the level of her lower stomach (HY, p. 198). Similarly Javier's grandmother, in A Change of Skin used to sleep with a nightgown down to her ankles, with an embroidered hole in it for sex (CS, p. 85). In these novels, the Spanish American male associates his sexuality with ideas of competence, worth, self-esteem, and superiority. He unconsciously fears his lack of masculinity, thus creating a corresponding terror of the female recipient of his most prized possession. Spanish American fiction is replete with man-eaters like Rómulo Gallegos's Doña Bárbara, José Eustasio Rivera's Zoraida, or Francisco Rojas González' Angustias. Ernesto Sábato believes that during intercourse the woman, by retaining the semen within herself, becomes a full person, but the man, through his discharge, suffers "separation, splitting, disorientation."[19] These associations of castration with the female reveal profound hostilities. The myth, universally entertained by men and repeated by Sábato and others, is that women reduce men's strength, because seminal fluid is the source of masculinity.[20] Sandor Ferenczi related the serpents and the Medusa head to the phallic woman, "the terrible symbol of the female genital region" associated with the absence of a penis and the frightened impression made on the child by the penis-less castrated genital.[21] The loss of the masculine organ, then, is a kind of death. Dominga in Siete lunas y siete serpientes strangles and buries her phallic serpent. Josefa, in the same novel, freezes Candelario's testicles and threatens to bite them off (SL, p. 364). Clotilde invites men to mount her and then "with a single chop cuts off their testicles" (SL, p. 92). Her sex possesses "coffee-blue teeth. Teeth which bite, like dogs bite the moon reflected on the water . . . To be with her had a price. To leave their virile parts in her hands" (SL, p. 94).

Other novels detail the death a woman can deliver. Celita, Foción's mother, attempts to seduce her husband's brother who dies in the embrace. Foción's wife remains a virgin because Foción suffered from the complex of the vagina dentata and saw a woman's "vulva as an immense mouth that devoured the phallus" (P. p. 319). Remedios the Beauty of One Hundred Years of Solitude possesses powers of death. To spend a night with her would cost a man his life.

Even though relations with women may not kill, say the authors, they enervate and affect creativity. Javier blames Elizabeth for his inability to write because she has worn him out sexually by making excessive love demands on him: "you have always wanted to exhaust me . . . you'll never understand the ways you destroy me . . . You were a princess with the lust of a bull. And you made me into a sterile ruin. I didn't marry a woman. I married a tigress" (CS, pp. 325-28). Elizabeth believes that Mexican women invented the myth of the macho male as a kind of compensation for his subjugation to daughters, mothers, and wives, "all the devouring women who impose their values on him " (CS, p. 178).

Women rule not only sexually but politically. In the Ascoitía family of The Obscene Bird of Night the women snare men with their whispering, "with their bedtime kiss, with a farewell smile that makes or breaks reputations and traditions" (OB, p. 37). In El otoño del patriarca Leticia Nazareno, the novice nun, used her bed to rob the dictator of his power (symbolically) both sexually and politically.

As one reads the contemporary Spanish American novel, one concludes that male authors are unable to express themselves in terms of their sexuality, as free and independent beings. The thrust for woman's liberation has aroused a fearful and neurotic response. Whatever their admittedly formidable acquired cultural veneer, in which they take such pride, they and their protagonists react as abnormal primitives plagued by self-doubts; their self-proclaimed desire for social renovation, even in the supposedly anti-burgeois novels of García Márquez and Cortázar, reflects, where woman is concerned, standard middle-class ideas of their society. Illuminated by an overly aggressive and neurotic hostility towards women, the men have attitudes which may stem from painful dynamics of personal experience or special realities of their Spanish American world, inherited from Spanish-Arabic ancestors. The combined insistence on overactive heterosexual behaviour may be a defense against incestuous or other subconscious proclivities, as love cedes to sensuality, eroticism to erotomania. The novelists, through their imagery and situations, seem to reflect intrapsychic conflicts, destructive impulses and unconscious motivations, but they have managed creatively to transpose them into a universal framework which, unfortunately, neither envisages a relation of togetherness nor the redeeming power of love. Their novels refuse to acknowledge woman as other than subservient or destructive, thus maintaining social values which have circumscribed her, in their attempts to defeat and frustrate her just claim to freedom.

Notes

[1] See "Machismo in Mexico: Carlos Fuentes Talks", *Johns Hopkins Magazine* (September 1976), 4-6. Typical of the search for the father are the sons in Juan Rulfo's *Pedro Páramo* and Gabriel García Márquez' *Cien años de soledad*.

[2] José Donoso, *The Obscene Bird of Night*, trans. Hardie St. Martin and Leonard Mades (New York: Alfred A. Knopf, 1973), p. 288. Further citations in the text are to this edition hereafter listed as OB.

[3] Alejo Carpentier, *El recurso del método* (Havana: Editorial de Arte y Literatura, 1974), pp. 12-13. Hereafter cited as RM.

[4] See W.A. Luchting, "Constantes en la obra de Mario Vargas Llosa," *Razón y Fábula*, 12 (1969), 36-45.

[5] See Juan Carlos Onetti, *Juntacadáveres* (Montevideo: Editorial Alfa, 1964), p. 87.

[6] Mario Vargas Llosa, *Pantaleón y las visitadoras* (Barcelona: Seix Barral, 1973), p. 286. Hereafter cited as PV.

[7] Julio Cortázar, *Libro de Manuel* (Buenos Aires: Editorial Sudamericana, 1973), p. 8. Hereafter cited as LM.

[8] Carlos Fuentes, *A Change of Skin*, trans. Sam Hileman (New York: Farrar, Straus and Giroux, 1968), p. 230. Hereafter cited as CS.

[9] Gabriel García Márquez. *El otoño del patriarca* (Buenos Aires: Editorial Sudamericana, 1975), p. 85. Hereafter cited as OdP.

[10] Mario Vargas Llosa, *The Green House*, trans. Gregory Rabassa (New York: Harper and Row, 1968), p. 158. Further references in the text are to this edition hereafter cited as GH.

[11] Ernesto Sábato, *Abaddón el exterminador* Buenos Aires: Editorial Sudamericanca, 1974), p. 494. Further citations in the text will be listed as AE.

[12] See Hernán San Martín, "Machismo: Latin America's Myth-Cult of Male Supremacy," *Unesco Courier*, March 1975, pp. 29-30.

[13] Reynaldo Arenas, El mundo alucinante (Buenos Aires: Editorial Tiempo Contemporáneo, 1970), p. 84. Hereafter cited as EMA.

[14] Gabriel García Márquez, One Hundred Years of Solitude, trans. Gregory Rabassa (New York: Avon, 1971), p. 167. Cited as HY.

[15] Demetrio Aguilera Malta, Siete lunas y siete serpientes (Mexico: Fondo de Cultura Económica. 1970). p. 161. Hereafter cited as SL.

[16] José Lezama Lima, Paradise, trans. Gregory Rabassa (New York: Farrar, Strauss and Giroux, 1968), p. 288. Cited as P.

[17] José Revueltas, Los errores (Mexico: Fondo de Cultura Económica, 1964). p. 158.

[18] Héctor A. Murena, Epitalámica (Buenos Aires: Sudamericana, 1969), p. 189.

[19] Ernesto Sábato, Obras: Ensayos (Buenos Aires: Losada, 1970), p. 326.

[20] Wolfgang Lederer, The Fear of Women (New York: Grune and Stratton, 1968), pp. 51-52.

[21] Sandor Ferenczi. "On Symbolism of the Head of the Medusa", Further Contributions to the Theory and Technique of Psychoanalysis (New York: Basic Books, 1952). p. 360.

THE WHOREHOUSE AND THE WHORE
IN SPANISH AMERICAN FICTION
OF THE 1960s

Spanish American fiction, from its earliest moments, has emphasized the whore as a reflection of society and the basic drives of human beings. José Joaquín Fernández de Lizardi's protagonists associate with numerous prostitutes, and one of them, Don Catrín de la Fachenda, works in a whorehouse. Other nineteenth century whores include the sentimental one in Eugenio Cambaceres's Música sentimental (1884) and the idealistic one in Mercedes Cabello de Carbonera's El conspirador (1892).

Twentieth century Spanish American fiction is replete with man-eaters like Gallegos's Doña Bárbara, Rivera's Zoraida, Rojas González's Angustias, and with promiscuous types like the oddly named Pura, the sensual dancer of El embrujo de Sevilla (1922). The prostitute as protagonist, however, enters the century through Augusto D'Halmar's Juana Lucero (1902) and Federico Gamboa's now classic Santa (1903). A poor, seduced, and abandoned country girl, Santa becomes first a high and then a low-class prostitute in brothels and bordellos. For all its supposed lasciviousness, the novel exudes a moralistic and religious note. Augusto D'Halmar's detailed description of whorehouse life in his novel, aptly subtitled "Los vicios de Chile," rivals that of Gamboa.

Among the approximately 100 treatments of the theme in the first fity years of the twentieth century, one should emphasize those of Manuel Gálvez, Joaquín Edwards Bello, Enrique Amorim, Francisco Espínola, and Guillermo Meneses. Gálvez, who wrote his dissertation on the white slave trade, analyzes a number of fictional prostitutes. He sentimentalizes Nacha Regules, the prostitute of El mal metafísico (1916) and the protagonist of Nacha Regules (1919), as he describes the low sections of Buenos Aires. Joaquín Edwards Bello fills his novels with whores and whorehouses about which he constantly moralizes. In La cuna de Esmeralda (1918) and its more famous elaboration, El roto (1920), he narrates the sentimental biography of a boy born in a brothel and the various prostitutes who lived there. Enrique Amorim, almost obsessed by the subject, portrays the Uruguayan "quitanderas" (circus folk whose cart serves as a travelling bordello) in La carreta (1929). His final novel, Eva Burgos (1960), about a beautiful prostitute, attacks legalized prostitution but shows great compassion and understanding for the women involved. His compatriot, Franscisco Espínola, empathizes with the unfortunate brothel dwellers of Sombras sobre la tierra (1933), an amalgam of the beautiful and the sordid. Meneses's magical evocation of a black prostitute in La balandra Isabel llegó esta tarde (1934) is the best poetic treatment of the subject. His short story, "La mano junto al muro" (1951, about the murder of a whore in a whorehouse, is credited by some critics as beginning the new novel in Venezuela.

Spanish American novelists have overwhelmed us with fictional portraitures of these ladies. Chilean harlots include the mawkish one in Eduardo Barrios' Un perdido (1917) who refuses to contribute to the moral and physical deterioration of Luis Bernales; the beautiful young girl in Salvador Reyes's Valparaiso, puerto de nostalgia (1955); and those who inhabit the red light districts of Concepción in Los túneles morados by Daniel Belmar. Cuba has given us the sensual whore in Jesús Castellanos's La conjura (1908), the broad-minded one of Miguel de Carrión's Las impuras (1919), the delicate one of Carlos Loveira's La última lección (1924), the long-suffering one in his Juan Criollo (1928), and the one in Alejo Carpentier's El acoso (1956).[1]

Contemporary Spanish American whores are often as sentimental, hostile, or neurotic as their literary ancestors, but they also project vital attitudes which enhance value judgments and enable the novelist to be both national and universal by associating abstract and symbolic relationships of this segment of society with the religious, psychological, sociological, and philosophical preoccupations of humanity as a whole. In spite of the world of brutality and betrayal it inhabits, prostitution as a fictional theme affords us glimpses into the true relationships of men and women and an existential dimension of reality. It furthers the possibility of man's self-understanding and of his impotence as well as his inability to escape the absurdity of life through the continuation of traditional codes of behavior.

The Houses

Spanish American fictional prostitutes practice their profession in hotel rooms, huts, canteens, and houses of prostitution which double as places of entertainment, complete with dance floor and orchestra, to help escape the boredom of daily life, "to amuse oneslf for a while by talking . . . or taking a drink . . . or playing a hand of monte or bezique in a gay but safe atmosphere . . ." (Donoso, 1966: 68). Often the whorehouse itself appears to be the raison d'être of the novel, the center from which all other plot threads radiate.

Physically, the houses vary widely. In El lugar sin límites (Donoso, 1966) the wind whistles through the cracks of the old house without electricity but complete with Victrola and stack of records: "With the passing years, without quite knowing how, and almost imperceptibly, the level of the facing kept on rising while the floor of the room, perhaps from so much sprinkling and tamping it down to make it suitable for dancing, kept on sinking" (Donoso, 1966: 18). As a result the floor was soon streaked with stained hollows, marred by burnt matches, scraps of leaves, buttons, and chewing gum wrappers. Anselmo's house in La Casa Verde (Vargas Llosa, 1965), has a large first floor room and six small upstairs bedrooms furnished in spartan fashion with beds, wash basins, and chamber pots. As business prospers, additions have to be made. The bar is expanded and the initial four occupants eventually have sixteen fellow workers. Existing at the very edge of the desert on land bought from the city, the house is finally burned down by the "decent" townfolk.[2] After the destruction of the first green house, Chunga, Anselmo's daughter, expands a restaurant bar into a new whorehouse, first located in a filthy alley in back of the slaughterhouse near the river, and later, reestablished in a chalet with garden and balconies and with walls covered with hearts and arrows.[3]

The presence of the houses profoundly affects the society of which they are a part. In spite of the economic gains which La Casa Verde, almost a tourist attraction, brings to Piura, Father García finally incites the citizens to burn it down. In other novels conforming members of society complain that their families cannot accept scandals and activities associated with "women of ill repute" (Otero Silva, 1961: 156) and that "prostitution is the cancer of society" (Arreola, 1964: 80). Father Bergner, in Juntacadáveres, inspires letters to the families of Larsen's customers until the powers of righteousness finally prevail and the house is closed down on orders from the governor himself.

Although reactions of citizens have certain political repercussions, resulting in the occasional closing of houses and periodic sweeps through red light districts to make arrests,[4] the owners and managers continue to prosper. One such owner, Barthe, a local pharmacist, his plans approved by the town commission, collects $500 a month which Larsen, the manager, hopes to recoup by charging ten dollars a visit; justified, he feels, because people need prostitutes "as much as visits to the doctor or barber" (Onetti, 1964: 87). One mayor takes credit for having cleaned up the town, but the houses, in a new district, prosper even more, as "the owners of the business receive benefits from the move" (Otero Silva, 1961: 170-71). María la Matraca, a decent woman, bought property and invested money in prostitution because "strumpets were so plentiful there they seemed to rain from the skies" (Arreola, 1964: 76).

Religious Significance

In addition to their social and economic importance, the whorehouses relate to primary considerations about life itself, especially religious ones, for home life and internal associations cannot be isolated from community life and external ones. Anselmo builds his house lovingly, as though it were a living creature, baptizing it (Vargas Llosa, 1966:96) and guiding its growth (1966: 101). Vargas Llosa's comparisons between the convent in the green jungle and the green house in the city indicate a deliberate religious-sexual mix. The whores in Juntacadáveres constantly make the sign of the cross, and La Magnífica is so named because of her custom of constantly repeating "the first phrases of the Catholic prayer" (Revueltas, 1964: 43).

Some of the whores, aware of the paraphysical and spiritual implications of their act, associate sex with God, reflecting a primitive respect for phallic properties: "First of all, I grab his imp in this way and make the sign of the cross with it two times on my belly in order to free myself from rot; because a man is clean, but a woman has damaged stuff in her: (Garmendia, 1968: 71-72). In Hijo de hombre, the Paraguayan Magdalen, María Rosa, is purified by her belief in Gaspar Mora as a virginal Christ figure and by her love for him. Another redeemed Paraguayan prostitute, María Encarnación, who used to entertain soldiers in her "dark little hut on the bank of the river" (Roa Bastos, 1967: 213), stopped being the enfermadora and became an enfermera. Having known men only as dehumanized and bestial creatures, she is saved through her pure love for Cristóbal Jara, a rehabilitation which occurs in the deepest recesses of her soul: "she must have felt her virginity revive like a gland, reborn and purified by this new and devastating sentiment: (1967: 214).

Officially, Catholic Spanish America forbids premarital sex for young people as an act severely punished through psychological and social ostracism (Sepúlveda Nino, 1970: 76). The current fragmentation of the Church and diverging views on everything from the rosary to birth control have, nonetheless, not shaken the essential fears or moral imperative imposed by traditional Hispanic views that sexual intercourse is to take place only after marriage and for the purpose of procreation. A young man's machismo impels him to prove sexual superiority, but tradition enforces a girl's chastity. Proponents of the double standard contend that men, being more highly sexed than women, need sexual partners before and after marriage. Although Saint Jerome stated that "everything which bears within it the seeds of sensual pleasure is poison," Saint Augustine approved of prostitution as a sexual outlet (Henríquez, 1965: 13-16). The male thus can enhance his masculinity by his associations with prostitutes, who usually belong to lower levels of society (Luchting, 1969, emphasizes this point). Spanish American orthodoxy also accepts the Victorian stridencies of William Acton and others that women fundamentally do not enjoy sexual intercourse, a concept somehow associated with the idea of the Virgin Mary as the chaste mother of God, which reinforces the view that extramarital sexual relations are a greater sin for women than for men. What in many parts of the world has become an insignificant physical event is, in Spanish America, a tragic one. Given the emphasis on virginity and lack of experience in the woman, it might prove difficult for some husbands to experience satisfactory relationships within marriage, where sexual enjoyment, in any event, is viewed as sinful. By seeking out a prostitute, condoned by the Church, sexual enjoyment may be possible (Henríquez, 1965: 214-215).

This concern with chastity and "hymenolatry" continues in the whorehouse itself. Concha de Fierro of La feria, still a virgin after three months in her profession, wants to remedy the situation through an operation. The horrified madam pleads with her not to change, not only because Concha's virtue is an attraction for which she can charge double but because Concha, technically unsullied, can end her life as a lady. With the aid of the bullfighter, Pedro Corrales, and his sword, Concha changes status. Yet so powerful is the virginal imperative that after that night it is rumored that Pedro and Concha have married. García Lorca expressed an aspect of this Hispanic dichotomy quite simply in his "Romance de la luna, luna": "and she shows, breasts hard as tin, erotic and pure" (1946: 9). Even in death one custom provides that when one of the girls dies, her friends or the madam of the house "in which she sinned, ask around for the dress of an honorable girl so that they may bury her in unsullied clothes" (Arreola, 1964: 166). The religious prohibitions on lustful procedures and continuing strictures become, then, peripheral parts of the process of prostitution itself.

Psychological Themes

The contemporary fictional prostitutes of Spanish American, no longer principally symbols of social abuse,[5] are, like all humanity, happy or sad, depressed or elated, and, more often than not, victims of loneliness and alienation. Many of them have special sobriquets: La Barco Sereno, Greta Garbo, La Magnífica, La Jaiba, La China, La Japonesita, La Luciérnaga, La Ranita, La Mariposa, and La Selvática. Whatever the sometimes absurd or grotesque connotations of the appellations, the women, unlike the whores described by Oscar Wilde as having "lips of flame and heart of stone," need love and understanding.

In many instances the prostitutes are psychological victims, not only of society, but of their own insecurities and anxieties. Lucrecia, a cabaret bar girl and inarticulate prisoner of life, was the product of an alcoholic father and a mother who first tried to abort her and later abandoned her. She suffered from a constant feeling of revulsion which clouded her actions and left her almost indifferent, a dehumanized being from another world, "without hate, love, or any sentiment whatsoever" (Revueltas, 1964: 159). Overshadowing her search for meaning in life is her knowledge that she is driven by natural forces and that she is "very much a whore . . . it was a question of a natural disposition, a kind of gift" (1964: 160). The whores in El lugar sin límites are also victims of life. Unattractive Clotilde has customers only when they are drunk and sexually frustrated. She sublimates her emotional turmoil through constant physical labor in the house. Lucy, although she reveals a good sense of humor, has no purpose in life. Off duty, "her feet smeared like those of a dog, she would throw herself into bed and spend all afternoon between the dirty sheets, eating bread, sleeping, and getting fat" (Donoso, 1966: 16). The unattractive eighteen-year-old madam, La Japonesita, who had rather unique beginnings as the daughter of a bawd and a fairy, is prepared to sacrifice her virginity to the brutal Pancho Vega. Nelly and Irene, disillusioned and pessimistic, willingly face the hatred of the town on their free day, accepting their weekly humiliation because it makes them feel alive and important enough to arouse emotion. Otherwise the world for them is completely depersonalized and peopled by "furtive and nocturnal males" (Onetti, 1964: 85).[6]

Yet, in spite of their problem, Spanish American fictional whores, on the whole, seem more loving, sympathetic, and compassionate than their U.S. counterparts. In some instances they cook for their favorite clients or accompany them on outings. Unfortunate rather than depraved, they often have mutually satisfying sexual experiences with their visitors: "She renewed her work expertly up to the small, panting climax, which this time, surprising concession, was mutual" (Garmendia, 1968: 190). Many have a strong sense of honor and dignity, even pride, in a job well done. Hortensia Colón, one of the prostitutes in Oficina número 1 (Otero Silva, 1961) proudly acknowledges her four years of honest service in her career when she enrolls her son in elementary school. Lucrecia "never took a customer to her own apartment" (Revueltas, 1964: 113).

Most prostitutes feel they are fulfilling a positive function by offering themselves to the men who come "to forget the scarecrows to whom they are married" (Donoso, 1964: 48). In many instances the girls, though victims, live in a fairly normal social environment. La Japonesa, when she had great crowds, would appeal to her friend, La Pecho de Palo, who would willingly send her "two back-up whores" (Donoso, 1966: 66). Even under her daughter's rule, a spirit of informality reigned, and the prostitutes could have both privacy and friendship with the owners. Larsen, too, thinks of his whores as one big family: "They were a family, he, María Bonita, and the two girls, united by the common goal of making money." (Onetti, 1964: 157).

Many of the prostitutes show great resourcefulness and resilience. Susana, an aging Frenchwoman, succeeds by painting a sign on the wall to the effect that "Susana has a Secret" (Otero Silva, 1961: p. 85). Every night men paid her, as much to learn the secret as to share her charms. La Japonesa, of El lugar sin límites, won her bawdy house by betting she could turn La Manuela, a homosexual, into a man through her techniques and charms, agreeing to cede him half ownership for his cooperation. Greta Garbo, who had to overcome a special kind of problem, achieved an even greater triumph. Having been subjected to a painful cure for syphilis, she was terrified at the possibility of reinfection. She works on the stiff-necked Charlie Reynolds, heir of an important New Orleans family, until he first builds a special house for her and eventually, to the dismay of his American society, marries her.

La Selvática, an Indian girl, known as Bonifacia before her entry into the green house, also overcomes physical and psychological difficulties. Captured in an expedition against the Aguaruna Indians and turned over to some nuns in a jungle convent as a servant, she fears men because one attempted to rape her when she was twelve years old. Lituma, an army sergeant to whom she loses her virginity, is jailed over a shooting incident. Pregnant, she takes up with some of his friends, one of whom convinces her to have an abortion. She supports them for a time before becoming a member of the whorehouse. Basically religious, compassionate, and kind, she is unable to adjust to civilization and high heels. Nonetheless, she survives because she still has primitive contact with some eternal values which transcend the artificial ones of contemporary Peruvian society.

Some of the prostitutes are extremely sensual. Generously endowed by nature with physical attractions, Africa Pedrada ceded her favors to three sweethearts in a row. After her marriage, unfulfilled by her husband and overcome by the fever or "stinging between her legs" (Murena, 1969:189), she becomes an attractive, popular prostitute, satisfying her sexual desires in a beautiful home whose rooms are filled with clients. La Magnífica, a very well-constructed girl with long hair, is "completely enchanting, with erect, youthful breasts and buttocks precisely adjusted to her body with graceful and impressive harmony" (Revueltas, 1964: 149). Viewing submission and fulfillment as synonymous, she associates the sexual act with that of voluptuous abandonment. After making love, motionless and pale, she cries with silent pleasure, "Stretched out naked . . . unaware of her tears . . . dead, dead with happiness" (1964:156). Lucrecia has a suggestive face, pronounced cheekbones, and beautiful lips. Her arousing hips point up her "cat-like smoothness, soft, slippery, and silent" (1964: 14).[8]

Lust, Indifference, and Hostility

Although love and lust may be coequal parts of a closed circle, two people, to be as one, must have the same spiritual as well as physical capacity. Sartrians contend that in the conflict between self and the other, one must be object and the other subject, that is, unequal (Sartre, 1956: 364). In a professional sexual situation male dominance reinforces this existential interpretation. Most Spanish American fictional heroes are "hommes a femmes" who view women as sexual objects which exist to afford them physical pleasure without spiritual implications, thus insuring later pessimism, anguish, and self-doubts, whatever their momentary ego boost, and denigrating the relationships of men and women. In some instances a man, impotent with his wife, can copulate with a prostitute only because the association is degraded,[9] for his money justifies contumely without, thereby, curing his basic insecurities and feelings of guilt. Since he pays her, the man need not preoccupy himself with affording her pleasure; he thus protects himself from potential feelings of sexual inadequacy. Impotence is routinely handled by one of the whores in La mala vida "with an indifference which seemed to me in no way disdainful or hostile, since surely my fault had not been so great and in any event was a frequent thing which must have happened many times" (Garmendia, 1968: 242). Since she is not interested in her client's sexual prowess, the prostitute fulfills a therapeutic function.

The dualistic reality of the world of whores reinforces ambivalence in those who associate with them. Mario Cobián, a not untypical victim of the matriarchal Latin tradition, reacts ambivalently to that world: "The presence of women of ill fame produced in him the joyful sensation of innocent immodesty and liberty of one who finds himself facing something which he rejects and censures but which at the same time he can penetrate at will without having to alter the normal patterns of his life" (Revueltas, 1964: 144). Mario associates Lucrecia with his sacred mother. As his love for her grows, he becomes increasingly resentful of her services to other men. He rationalizes his robbery of a loan shark as necessary to save her from a life of sin. Yet he feels a sadistic desire to beat her along with his urgent desire to possess her. He is even more sadistic with the other whores. In his imagination he knocks La Jaiba down in order to "enter her, beating and kicking her, until she is ready for the dung heap" (1964: 135-136). With La Magnífica, he is even more brutal: "The point of his shoe struck the humiliated face of the woman with sharp brutality, making her fall obliquely and noiselessly, twitching on the wooden floor" (1964: 158). Cobián's sadism seems to reflect several insecurities, including the fear of being devoured by a woman--that is castrated. Miguel Vera views death itself as an "insatiable whore . . . obscene and transparent . . . whose serpent eyes search out and elect her lover for the new copulation" (Roa Bastos, 1967:202). The menacing female image and the reference to serpents make this a plausible interpretation here also. Ernesto Sábato (1970: 326) believes that during intercourse the woman, by retaining the semen within herself becomes a full person, but the man, through his discharge, "implies separation, splitting, disorientation . . . In the woman, on the contrary, it implies union, fusion." These associations of castration fears with the female reveal profound hostilities toward the mother, and, in Cobián's case, explain his obsessive interest in prostitutes.[11]

Contemporary Spanish American fiction emphasizes the sexual straitjackets and insecurities of modern man. Indeed, at times it seems that contemporary novelists are obsessed by the subject, for their protagonists are inevitably tormented by sexual compulsions and frustrations, which, for the most part, they are unable to resolve, and which reinforce the absurdities of the world in which they are trapped. Prostitution, by reemphasizing the concomitant feelings of impotence and need and the continuing trauma of an apparent predominance of physical over spiritual love, affords the authors an area of operation in which they can treat eternal verities of human behavior. The emphasis on the whore also underscores the mestizo aspects of Spanish American life and the alternating hostilities it engenders. Spanish American man's personal relationship to nature and his myths seem more important to him than similar associations are for his Northern counterpart. The whorehouse helps symbolize the accelerating process of alienation.

Sexual arousal for the Spanish American males is exacerbated by their daily exposure to women who have "brown, soft thighs . . . hungry hips and a round belly" (Garmendia, 1968: 16, 17). In order to satisfy their sexual needs they troop to the "house of the prostitutes, fat and lascivious stallions all of whom neigh at their neighbor's woman" (Arreola, 1964: 92). Men without a woman "go about like madmen" (Otero

Silva, 1961: 136), and with "glances lit up by alcohol, and spurred on by sexual abstinence" (1961: 174). In this presence of male lust, often associated with violence, the prostitutes more often than not reflect the anomie of collapsing social structures. Their profession, almost uniquely, implies an ambivalent attempt to engage in antisocial activities, but the illegality is less emphasized than the lack of love or need for belonging. The light ladies, less insecure and threatened than their clientele, though they fit no easy pattern, often truly love and are loved, refuting their demeaning relationship with men as an expression of concupiscence.

Just as La Selvática-Bonifacia reveals the dualistic role of reality, so other prostitutes want more than mere money or erotic satisfaction. They hope to escape from their alienation and to find communion with other human beings through transcending the limits of self (Fromm, 1956: 9). They find their self-expression and release from the tension of conflicting forces through sex. Feeling themselves chained to an absurd world without dignity, the protagonists, unable to personalize or humanize effectively, increasingly desire to achieve identity through sex. In the absence of spiritual feeling and the impossibility of a higher love, man strives in vain for its illusion through physical relations. As Ernesto Sábato (1963: 88) states, "Sex, for the first time in the history of literature, acquires a metaphysical dimension." Unfortunately, the world, which debases other areas of human personality, also degrades the love of man and woman to a mechanical, scientific level, augmenting rather than alleviating alienation. The novelists of contemporary Spanish America, not insensitive to contemporary values, use the whorehouse and the whore as particularized artistic selections proportional to an inner world. Through these cross sections of current life they afford us panoramic perspectives of humanity which transcend formal stylistic diversity, revealing mankind's common susceptibility to suffering, despair, and hope, all aspects of the human condition.

Notes

[1] The whore as martyr, as mentally deficient, as unfulfilled, or as of limited illusions may be seen in the Peruvian novels of Rosa Arciniega, José María Arguedas, Enrique Congrains Martín, and Mario Vargas Llosa. Poetic, redeemed, unredeemed, degraded, or exalted prostitutes are characters in the Ecuadorian novels of Gerardo Gallegos, José de la Cuadra, Demetrio Aguilera Malta, Alfredo Pareja Diezcanseco, and Humberto Salvador; the Colombian fiction of Jaime Buitrago, José Antonio Osorio Lizarazo, Augusto Morales Pino, and Gabriel García Márquez; the Mexican novels of Xavier Icaza, Martín Gómez Palacio, Mariano Azuela, Agustín Yáñez, Luis Spota, and Sergio Galindo; the Chilean fiction of Alberto Romero, Benjamín Subercasseaux, Rafael Maluenda, Juan Marín, Nicomedes Guzmán, and Enrique Lafourcade; the Uruguayan novels of Juan Carlos Onetti and Angel Rama; and the Argentine works of Manuel Peyrou, David Viñas, and Néstor Sánchez.

[2] Several of the houses are distinguished by their color. In Juntacadáveres the author refers constantly to the "blue Venetian blinds" (Onetti, 1964: 118).

[3] Typical of lower class centers, the houses in La mala vida have downstairs rooms, a cheap bar, and a few linoleum covered tables. Located at the end of an alley near a chapel, they have discolored doors of faded rose or green. Inside the cell-like rooms, complete with cheap mirror, one is always overcome by the odor, "strong and bittersweet, a sticky vapor, reeking of human nakedness and the bathroom, which impregnates everything in each house" (Garmendia, 1968: 68, 189, 224).

[4] The police efficiently round up the "usual nocturnal foray . . . they shouted curses from the barred windows of the police van" (Revueltas, 1964: 215).

[5] Nonetheless, some age-old social problems exist. Hookers, worn out by work and illness, continue to be associated with the only life open to them: "She grew to be fat and toothless and, since no man would seek her out with such looks, she had to retire from the profession. Nonetheless it was impossible for her to live in any other environment" (Otero Silva, 1961: 134). Many of the underpaid streetwalkers must fight each other for survival: "they come out of all the doors shrieking. They fall all over me, shaking their breasts and stomachs" (Garmendia, 1968: 67). No matter how hard they work some always face hard times: "the treatment which poor prostitutes who live in third class hotels receive . . . They come and go, work the street . . . Anybody could believe that in their weariness and desperation at not finding a customer they

pay for their room, as a last resort, by sleeping with the manager" (Revueltas, 1964: 12).

[6] Among the other psychologically troubled prostitutes are La China of La mala vida and María Bonita of Juntacadáveres. La China, always tired and in a bad humor, has a mind fragmented by ideas like pins in a felt pincushion. Although she professes to adore outings and simple pleasures, she is unhappy and longs for a man with whom she can settle down. María, prudent but immoral, has occasional intercourse with her old friend Larsen. Feeling that she is growing old, she needs a few minutes at the end of each day in order to dream and forget the cold image she can no longer recognize in her bedroom mirror.

[7] Other family-like situations occur. In La Casa Verde the prostitutes lavish love and affection on Toñita. They bring her candy, dress her, comb her hair, and amuse her, as though she were their own younger sister or daughter.

[8] Many other sensual whores can be found, among them the imported Rosita of the "soft little rump, pure affection" (Donoso, 1966: 70); María Rosa of "rounded forms . . . dark pupils" (Roa Bastos, 1967: 24); and Rosa Candela, with hard round breasts and "a magnificent mulatto rump," fit into a skin-tight dress (Otero Silva, 1961: 172).

[9] Although, as we have noted, many of the prostitutes are quite sensual, others are physically ugly and described in pejorative terms. La Tora, a madam with thick lips, false teeth, and a cruel and heavy face, is in charge of "humiliating cadavers . . . bent and deformed bodies, worn faces, grotesque . . . four obscene remains of women . . . the cadaver on duty, dirty, fat, short, with sleep and paint stains on her face, drooping and beaten" (Onetti, 1964: 75). Even Larsen's three women, in the same novel, viewed somewhat more sympathetically, are described as old, ugly, and grotesquely dressed. One of the whores of La mala vida has large flat feet and "nipples . . . dry wrinkled figs, like baby bonnets sewn to the flesh" (Garmendia, 1968: 67). Another is "squat, fat . . . the thick rouge on her face bringing to mind the image of recently retouched dough" (1968: 237-238). Yet their physical deformity and apparent dehumanization cannot alter the fact that they are, indeed, human.

[10] Sandor Ferenczi, relating the serpents and the Medusa head to the "terrible symbol of the female genital region," associates them with the absence of a penis and "the frightful impression made on the child by the penis-less (castrated) genital" (see Ferenczi, 1953: 360).

[11] Karl Abraham says of one of his patients, that prostitutes "represented his mother in a derogatory sense--his mother who had let his father understand her sexual desires by means of certain looks and gestures. In comparing her to a prostitute he was revenging himself for having been disappointed by her. His reproach was meant to say, 'You are only a sensual woman, not a loving mother.' On the other hand, his nocturnal perambulation of the streets represented an identification with the prostitutes (his mother)" (see Abraham, 1966:112).

References

ABRAHAM, K. (1966) On Character and Libido Development. New York.
ARREOLA, J.J. (1964) La feria. Mexico.
DONOSO, J. (1966) El lugar sin límites. Mexico.
FROMM, E. (1956) The Art of Loving. New York.
FERENCZI, S. (1953) "On symbolism of the head of Medusa," p. 360 in Further Contributions to the Theory of Technique of Psycho-analysis. New York.
GARCIA LORCA, F. (1946) Romancero gitano. Buenos Aires.
GARMENDIA, S. (1968) La mala vida. Montevideo.
HENRIQUEZ, F. (1965) Prostitution in Europe and the Americas. New York.
LUCHTING, W. A. (1969) "Constantes en la obra de Mario Vargas Llosa." Razón y Fábula 12:26-45.
MURENA, H.A. (1969) Epitalámica. Buenos Aires.
ONETTI, J.C. (1964) Juntacadáveres. Montevideo.
OTERO SILVA, M. (1961) Oficina número 1. Buenos Aires.
REVUELTAS, J. (1964) Los errores. Mexico.
ROA BASTOS, A. (1967) Hijo de hombre, Buenos Aires.
SABATO, E. (1970) Heterodoxia. Buenos Aires.
SABATO, E. (1963) El escritor y sus fantasmas. Buenos Aires.
SARTRE, J.P. (1956) Being and Nothingness (H.E. Barnes, trans.).
SEPULVEDA NINO, S. (1970) La prostitución en Colombia. Bogotá.
VARGAS LLOSA, M. (1965) La Casa Verde. Barcelona.

ANTISEMITISM IN MODERN ARGENTINE FICTION

One of the minor constants in Argentine fiction concerns the Jewish problem in general and the Jewish character in particular. Aside from paranoid antisemites like Julián Martel and Hugo Wast, authors of the stature of Alberto Gerchunoff (1884-1950), Manuel Gálvez (1882-1962), Bernardo Verbitsky (1907-), and David Viñas (1929-) have handled the theme. The relationships between Jews and non-Jews, in both city and countryside, reflect Jewish soul struggles to accommodate a universal prophetic vision to a national, narrow survival. Attempts to integrate Jewish customs and culture into a new way of life reveal that fictionally, Jews may have adopted Argentina, but Argentina, with rare exceptions, has not really accepted the Jews.

The cacoethes of viewing the Jew in some of the novels as a demonic archetype depends on the oligarch's need to have a scapegoat for national political shortcomings. The middle classes in Argentina, as well as the oligarchy, through their resistive reaction to immigrants, reaffirm their own indigenous values and beliefs. As Gladys Onega points out: "xenophobia has served in our country, since immigrants and their descendants became the political majority, as a pretext for the defense of the most conservative and antipopular values and interests."[1] The exploding Jewish immigration during and after the 1880s, accelerated the antisemitic wave of feeling.

Antisemitism continued in spite of many Jewish organizations such as the Centro Juventud Israelita Argentina, founded in 1909, which later developed into the Sociedad Hebraica Argentina. The motto of the Juventud group, as early as 1912, was: "Youth, Jews, and Argentines,"[2] but their Christian counterparts refused to accept the triad, even though the Jewish group used its journal to help celebrate Argentina's centennial in 1916.

Part of the presentation, by friend and foe alike, concerns the Christian perception of the Jew as a somewhat unsavory stereotype. Thus even positive virtues, such as the concept of a tightly-knit family, become, in Argentine eyes, a plot against Christian society; a viewpoint held, not only by such outright antisemities as Hugo Wast, but also by Manuel Gálvez, for instance, a supposed admirer of the Jews. Many Argentines, among them the famous poet, Leopoldo Lugones (1874-1938), rejected the _Protocols of the Elders of Zion_ as "malignant and imbecilic,"[3] but he and Gálvez accepted other myths about Jewish control of banks and newspapers. Part of this credulous seeking after conspiracies may stem from ancient Christian perceptions of Jews as money-changing materialists in the temple.[4] In Argentina, as early as 1908, Jewish schools in the agricultural colonies of Entre Ríos had been attacked by Catholics. Schools used antisemitic textbooks, and, at various times, priests viewed Argentine Jews as traitors, triggering attacks on them at the Universisty of Buenos Aires School of Medicine. Extreme right wing Jesuits sponsored the Tacuara antisemitic group to which cousins of Che Guevara belonged.[5]

The increasing Nazi influence in Argentina after the Second World War (in 1946 Ludwig Freude opened a store to distribute antisemitic propaganda) helped spread the age-old myth of Jewish domination to such an extent that it became an article of faith to most Argentines. Jordan Bruno Genta, an Air Force official, gave a series of lectures in which he blamed all of Argentina's problems on the Jews; and when Eichmann was kidnapped, the government condoned[6] an ever-increasing antisemitic campaign through the 1960s. The situation in the 1970s has not changed and "Jews will have to bear the burden of economic chaos . . . and antisemitic repercussions."[7]

Bartolomé Mitre and Domingo Faustino Sarmiento, both as nineteenth-century presidents of Argentina and as writers of essays, expressed ambivalent feelings about Jewish immigration, which were shared by members of the literary generation of 1880, such as Eugenio Cambaceres (1843-1888), Francisco Sicardí (1856-1927), and especially Miguel Cané (1851-1905). The first important antisemitic novel, La bolsa (1891), was written by José María Miró (1867-1896), better known by his pseudonym, Julián Martel. A business reporter for "La Nación," he labels his work a "social study," viewing the Stock Exchange as a monster which will destroy his country. Considered to be one of the principal founders of the Argentine novel,[8] he defends the cosmopolitan, aristocratic Argentine society against the coarse Jews, viewed as long-bearded moneylenders with sordid international connections. Having attributed to the Jews a set of repulsive characteristics, Martel finds it credible to blame them for the Stock Market crash which so adversely affected the "better" elements of society. The theme of Jewish speculators who control the money supply and cause the ruination of innocents was undoubtedly influenced by Edouard Drumont (1844-1917) whose notorious La France Juive (1886) sees Jewish bankers as an overwhelming threat.

Martel includes all of the classical antisemitic arguments used by Drumont. Through his alter-ego, Doctor Glow, Martel accuses the Jew of being aggressive and submissive at the same time; of perverting the native Christians; and destroying their religious and moral virtues through international machinations. The two principal Jewish characters, Filiberto Mackser, whose young correligionist, connected with the white slave trade, writes biased news reports in favor of Jews, and Jacob Leony, have almost no redeeming features. Mackser, an exponent of hypocritical humility, according to Martel, had the special characteristics of the Jewish race--small eyes, a curved nose, and ostentatious attire--which marked him as lacking the good taste of his Aryan counterparts. Jacob Leony, who practiced "intrigues and vileness of every kind," lived in a sordid den--a center from which he consistently charged usurious rates of interest.

Doctor Glow, a famous Argentine lawyer, abandons his career to speculate in the stock exchange. Although he engages in fraudulent liquor and real estate dealings, pure and innocent, he falls victim to the demonic Jews who influence him badly. Glow, elegant, friendly, and democratic, has a circle of Christian friends who share his fear that the Jewish syndicates will monopolize the principal productive resources of Argentina; that "they are going to invade us surreptitiously, and if we are not vigilant will end up by monopolizing everything" (p. 22). The Jews inspire Glow with "loathing and horror" (pp. 92, 106-107). Granulillo, the only "native" who defends the Jews, is himself evil. He deceives and eventually helps ruin Glow.

Martel views Mackser as a secret envoy of a Universal Jewish Alliance which will use gold to destroy Argentine values. Refusing to enter the Christian society which shelters them, Jews, destroying the very people who debate about social justice and progress, gradually control the press, the schools, and eventually the government itself. The Jew can never become a true Argentine citizen, for all Jews stick together against Christians, in a union of secret conspiracy, called the "vampire of modern society" (p. 116). Eventually everyone will become first Jewish, then socialistic, and then revolutionary. Even though Christian genius outshines Jewish contributions to society, without eternal vigilance, the Jew will triumph. Martel accepts other immigrants such as the English and Italians, portrayed as hardworking or daring but doomed also to be victims, "a fate reserved for everyone who has the bad fortune to fight against the Jews" (p. 34).

Aside from the virulently antisemitic, modernist writer, Angel Estrada (1872-1923), the next antisemite of some importance was Gustavo Adolfo Martínez Zuviría (1883-1954), who wrote under the pseudonym of Hugo Wast. An internationally known novelist and the winner of various literary prizes, he had written an early novelette, El judío, which nobody wanted to publish. He occupied various government posts, became the director of the national library, and, an ardent Catholic, received a commendation from the Pope. His two volume antisemitic novel, El Kahal, Oro (1935), part of which he first published under the pseudonym, Juan Timbú, supposedly represents his Catholic viewpoint.[10] Israel Zeitlin (1906-), better known as César Tiempo, called Wast "fluent, fecund, and feculent,"[11] and his stand against him elicited the comment from one of José Chudnovsky's Jewish characters that "it was a real k.o. Wast won't say any more . . . . Who had time for antisemites, anyway?"[12]

Wast's El Kahal and its sequel Oro concern the rivalry of two Jewish banking groups. Zacarías Blumen, who by dint of shady smuggling had achieved a position of prominence as a banker, wants his son to convert to Christianity in order to be able to marry into the rich Adalid family. He thus rejects Thamar, the daughter of his rival, Mauricio Kohen, as a wife for his son. Denounced for the conversion, both father and son defend themselves as always remembering the Jewish goal of corrupting gentiles. Unimpressed, the Kahal, or ruling body of the synagogue, exprels them both. Thirty years pass and the son, now a candidate for high office, manages to lift the excommunication and eventually becomes the president of the synagogue. His daughter, Marta, falls in love with Mauricio Kohen, Junior, who enlists her as an ally against her own father, to whom her grandfather, Fernando Adalid, owes a great sum of money. Julius Ram, a chemist, apparently changes base metal into gold and uses the process to save Adalid. The international bankers, alarmed by the threat, plan to murder him. Eventually, we learn that the Bank of Argentina had paid Adalid's debt and that he and Mauricio had combined to destroy the Rheingold banking interests of which Blumen was a leading member. The gold remains in Jewish hands, but Mauricio and Marta, finally realizing spiritual regeneration, convert to Christianity.

Wast, in order to justify his diabolical caricature of the Jew as a sleazy stereotype, points out that Jewish separatism prevents them from becoming reconciled to their fate or from forgetting their own ethnic background: "this ferocious fidelity to his nationality makes of the Jew an unsociable and unassimilable being in a foreign country."[13] While this separatism has accounted for Jewish survival, it also accounts for the universal hatred in which Jews are held. Wast's members of a secret cabal and their shadowy, squinting associates follow what Wast contends has been the Jewish plan from Biblical times--to take over the money supply of any country they inhabit: "Fatal fetishism, a true Jewish trap. It is impossible to take over the total welath of a country. But it is not so difficult to control its business, if you control the money supply" (p. 12). Quoting at times from the Protocols of the Elders of Zion, Wast proposes that part of the Jewish process involves the destruction of Christianity. He laments

Argentine apathy at the appearance of mysterious Jewish schools and fears that Buenos Aires, "without traditions, too much mixed with foreign customs, may become . . . the capital of the future kingdom of Israel" (p. 19). He stresses that the strange Kahal, a secret organization within the synagogue, controls financial dealings in coordination with secret daily meetings by Jewish international bankers. Aided by their control of news agencies, banks, and the best authors, the Jews not only seek political control but also deliberately promote new customs to corrupt Christian women. Fernando Adalid explains the "vast Jewish maneuver to drown Christian civilization" (p. 92), and Marta Blumen exposes the Kahal's plans to drag all govenments "with chains of gold into a universal war from which will emerge the super kingdom of Israel . . . the immortal throne of the Antichrist" (pp. 250-51). Wast holds out hope in a somewhat contradictory fashion. At one point he exclaims, through Marta: "The day that a Jew falls in love with a Christian girl heaven and earth will unite" (p. 198), but the spirit of God overcomes that of gold, as both Marta and Mauricio, in love, convert to Christianity.

Jewish authors from Alberto Gerchunoff to José Chudnovsky treat the antisemitic theme, though some of their characters refuse to succumb to the prevailing sickness. In a few cases, Argentines speak favorably about Jews and their efforts to conform to Argentine modes of behavior, but, for the most part, friendship, decidedly ambivalent, involves the implicit understanding that acceptance means becoming more Argentine and less Jewish. Martiniano Leguizamón, in his prologue to Gerchunoff's Los gauchos judíos (1910) in which the Jews promote exhaustive agricultural colonization, talks about the "classic old Jew of large beard and acquiline nose, with his sad women, and his face marked by deep furrows of suffering," but at the same time he implies criticism of "their severe precept which prohibits them from loving those who are not of their race." In one of Gerchunoff's stories, the colonists lose their rabbi, killed by a gaucho peon, which was a re-creation of the tragedy which befell the author's own father.

Manuel Gálvez believed himself to be the friend of Argentine Jews, though he constantly deplored their association with what he considered dangerous, left-wing movements. He boasted about his many Jewish friends in Amigos y maestros de mi juventud (1944) and, on many occasions, denied that antisemitism existed in Argentina. Yet, in another context, he maintained that if Jews wished to remain in Argentina, "without conspiring against our nationality nor against our religion, they can be sure that nobody will do them any harm."[14] He believed that because he was a good Catholic, it was impossible for him to be antisemitic; but his ambivalence seems readily apparent.

Gálvez deals specifically with Jews in two of his novels: El mal metafísico (1916) and La tragedia de un hombre fuerte (1922). In the former, in which his friend, Alberto Gerchunoff, plays a large role as Abraham Orloff, he speaks of him in positive terms. Nonetheless, Orloff has vague, small eyes, a large nose and a certain bovine tameness, and Gálvez refers to a "talmudic beard," for, one would suspect, other than descriptive reasons.[15] Víctor Urgel, the "strong man" of the second novel, reacts negatively to two Jewish intellectuals, even though his friend, Rauch, tries to convince him that they will be strong assets for the new Argentina about which Víctor is always declaiming. Víctor reacts with astonishment and then anger when the Jews insist that Argentina is antisemitic. His anger turns to fright when his friend claims that it is logical for Jews, religiously passionate about intellectual matters, to dominate Argentine life. Eventually, without really liking them, "he, who admired . . . feminists, could hardly fail also to admire the Jews."[16] Intellectually, a progressive thinker because of his political persuasions, Víctor, nonetheless, is unable to overcome his inherited, if not overt, bias toward the creative Jewish presence.

In Fiesta en noviembre (1938), by Eduardo Mallea (1903-), Lintas, outraged at the death of a Jewish bookseller at the hands of some fascist types, nonetheless describes him in physically unflattering terms: "small and sickly, yellowish skin:"[17] "red nose . . . that face of a fearful mouse" (p. 124).

The Jewish authors, with the exception of Gerchunoff, seem less ambivalent in their position,[18] but they present some sympathetic gentiles among the Argentine antisemites. Duarte, in Es difícil empezar a vivir (1941) by Bernardo Verbitsky, wishes he had been born a Jew. When Pablo Levinson, the Jewish protagonist appears surprised, he explains: "If I had been born a Jew . . . I would have been born with your sensibility. . . . If I were a Jew I should know the secret of colors. . . ."[19] Although Duarte insists on the superiority of Jewish sensitivity and critical facilities, and another non-Jew, Viera, "did not put obstacles in the way of Jews being admitted [to medical school] . . . they say he even appreciates them" (p. 343), Pablo, himself, at first rejects the tales of Hitler horrors against the Jews. Argentine Nazis, together with the discovery of his own Jewish essence and religious respect for life, lead him finally to identify as a Jew.

In David Viñas' <u>Un dios cotidiano</u> (1957), Moshe Mendel, the son of a Jewish family, endures both obscene comments and physical torture in his Catholic School. The other boys disrobe him, mock his circumcision, cover him with shoe polish, and cut his hair. One of the priests indirectly defends the action through his praise of the novels of Hugo Wast. The boy's father has a pointed talmudic beard, a flashy red tie; and the daughter has bovine eyes (Jewish women's eyes seem to fascinate all Argentine authors). In <u>Dueños de la tierra</u> (1958), Viñas' Vicente Vera thinks of Jews in pejorative terms, although he insists he has nothing against them: "Jews weren't pretty, but what could one do? . . ."[20] When Yuda Singer, his Jewish girlfriend, asks him what he thinks defines a Jew, he replies that, "Jews were some lamentable oldsters with dirty beards . . . ." (p. 125). Ironically, when he sides with the workers, the crowd attacks him as a Jew, for them the supreme insult. Meanwhile, the "white guard" breaks synagogue windows. In <u>Dar la cara</u> (1962), Pelusa almost innocently affirms: "To be homosexual was worse than being a Jew."[21] The youths, alienated politically and sexually, imitate the authorities, for whom Jews are "shit" (p. 453).

José Chudnovsky's two perceptive novels, <u>Dios era verde</u> (1963) and <u>Pueblo Pan</u> (1967) discuss a wide range of Argentine-Jewish relationships and what it means to be an Argentine Jew. Surprisingly, both have little to say about antisemitism. The father recalls Russian pogroms, the fires set in synagogues, "so that fear might burn [in Jewish breasts] together with the sacred books . . .",[22] but neither he (after an intial encounter with an Argentine who takes advantage of him) nor his son experience discomfort at the hands of ambivalent Argentine officials: "That's the way it is . . . if they jew me I jew them without nausea . . . but to take advantage of those black birds, is not for me, I assure you" (p. 178). The major area of friction stems from the Argentine perception of Jews, especially right after World War I, as politically radical. Old and young Jews suffered, says Chudnovsky, when "people we grew up with yelled 'Jews' at us and beat up on people wearing beards" (p. 237).

Pedro Orgambide (1929-), in his novel <u>Los inquisidores</u> (1967), deals with discrimination of various kinds against blacks and political rebels. The author describes Nazi camps such as Treblinka, with their mass murders in which the living had to throw the dead into mass graves and then lie atop them also to be killed. One of the protagonists, Efraín Azevedo, a Spanish Jew persecuted by the Holy Inquisition of Lima, from whose documents the author quotes, refuses to convert to Christianity and suffers the consequences.

Marcos Aguinis, author of an interesting work on Maimonides, in Refugiados (1969), takes up the Arab-Israeli dispute. The novel, essentially a poetic as well as political projection, discusses historical, cultural, and religious stereotypes. The heroine, the beautiful Myriam Miersohn, is killed by a surviving Nazi criminal who fears she is seeking vengeance for her father's betrayal at his hands. The good Germans, such as Ingrid Beickert, who had protected Myriam and her parents in Nazi Germany, are a decided minority. The author discusses the trials and tribulations of Jews in their exodus from various European countries and the lack of charity or even sympathy which they received from supposedly democratic western governments. The young Arab protagonist protects Myriam from his fellow Arabs, even though for him "the word Jew had an irritating meaning and the word Israel was a synonym for enemy."[23] Rejecting his own acquired generalizations about Jewish exclusiveness and togetherness against non-Jews, he sees, after Myriam's tragic death, the possibility of Jewish understanding.

One of the incidents re-created fictionally in most of these novels, is the Semana Trágica, which occurred between 7 January and 12 January 1919. During a strike at the Pedro Vasena factory, some of the workers died. The govenment believed that the "maximalist" movement, largely dominated by Russians, anarchists, and communists, was responsible. Since many Jews had been active in workers' movements since their arrival in Argentina, the government, petrified by the Russian Revolution, dreamed up a Jewish plot to install a Soviet in Buenos Aires. Government officials did not discourage attacks on Jews by civilian groups such as the "guardia blanca." In addition to semi-official pogroms, groups such as the Liga Patriótica Argentina attacked and burned Jewish homes and shops, beat old people, and raped Jewish girls.[24] The government later called for the expulsion of all foreigners but especially Jews.[25]

Arturo Cancela (1892-1957), in Una semana de holgorio (1922), a satiric treatment of the theme, reflects that all true Argentines belonged to the Jockey Club. In his story, Argentine "patriots" stone the "commercial houses, the names of whose proprietors abound in consonants. Why do they hate consonants so much?"[26] Verbitsky, who refers to the tragedy as "la semana de enero," mentions the fury against the "maximalistas" and the pogroms against the Jews: "La Liga Patriótica, master of the situation, hunting old Jews in the streets, and shooting them, after burning their beards" (p. 175). Recalling the events ten years later, Pablo's fading memory of those dreadful doings implies a subconscious compromise made by other Argentine Jews to forget the past--hopefully to be accepted by non-Jews. The more realistic David Viñas shows how difficult it is to change, as Vicente, in Los dueños de la tierra, attempts to rationalize the 1919 events. In Dar la cara, Viñas uses the tragic week to bolster his belief that Jews should continue a commitment to ethical values and to the rejection of evil. The fascist types who attack Bernardo Carman's friend and insist that Jews must leave, consider themselves to be "the owners . . . those who decided who might stay and who had to be eliminated . . . .The Jews were bothersome . . . the Jews stank and nobody could stand them . . . Jews were everyone except themselves . . . Demoralizing Jews . . . who were always asking questions" (p. 585). Finally, in José Chudnovsky's novels, which concentrate on rural living, the 1919 week troubles, but does not horrify, the Jewish author.

Some of the novelists and their characters reveal a continuing concern for all humanity; but for the most part, Argentines, as reflected in their fiction and their basic, unchanged attitudes toward Jewish citizens, refuse to consider them in a new and meaningul way. In Argentine fiction, many citizens with a real or dream image of themselves as good cannot counteract the failure of the decadent, middle and upper classes to accept their Jewish fellow citizens nor can they really understand their problems and preoccupations. At times, Argentine attempts to gain victory over their worst instincts simply create an antisemitic parody. The Jewish characters either find or continue commitments, in some way, to their Jewish heritage; in many of the novels, the synagogue continues to be a central institution in their lives. Eventually, most come to terms with themselves and their continuing persecution and realize the fruitlessness of trying to forget what cannot be forgotten.

The self-justifications and aesthetic pretensions of the Argentine antisemites in their portrayal of invidious stereotypes fail to persuade ethically or aesthetically, as one senses their feelings of frustration, impotence, and inability to love. They represent the continuing presence in modern life of the monstrous in a ruthless and repressive universe; but their novels and those of their Jewish antagonists reveal that as long as human beings continue to fight against their own evil, both Jews and the rest of humanity will survive.

Notes

[1] Gladys Onega, La inmigración en la literatura argentina, 1880-1910 (Santa Fe, 1965), p. 132.

[2] See Manuel Bronstein, "Orígenes de la Sociedad Hebraica Argentina," Davar, No. 119 (1968), 70.

[3] See Davar, No. 118 (1968), 146.

[4] Claire Huchet Bishop, How Catholics Look at Jews (New York, 1974), pp. 52-54.

[5] See Juan José Sebrelli, La cuestión judía en la Argentina (Buenos Aires, 1968); see also Victor A. Mirelman, "The Semana Trágica of 1919," Jewish Social Studies, 37 (1975), 61-73.

[6] Sebrelli, pp. 21-31. Genta reiterates the relationship between religion and ideology in Libre examen y comunismo (Buenos Aires, 1960) and Guerra contrarevolucionaria (Buenos Aires, 1964).

[7] Victor A. Mirelman, "Attitudes Toward Jews in Argentina," Jewish Social Studies, 37 (1975), 220.

[8] Ricardo Rojas, La literatura argentina (Buenos Aires, 1925), p. 680.

[9] José María Miró, La bolsa (Buenos Aires, 1905), p. 193. Further references in the text are to this edition.

[10] See Juan Carlos Moreno, Genio y figura de Hugo Wast (Buenos Aires, 1969), p. 199.

[11] See Davar, No. 88 (1961), 50.

[12] José Chudnovsky, Pueblo Pan (Buenos Aires, 1967), p. 46. Further citations in the text are to this edition.

[13] Gustavo A. Martínez Zuviría, El Kahal (Santiago, Chile, 1935), p. 10. Further citations in the text are to this edition.

[14] Sebrelli. La cuestión judía, pp. 98-102.

[15] Manuel Gálvez, El mal metafísico (Buenos Aires, 1962), p. 42.

[16] Manuel Gálvez, La tragedia de un hombre fuerte (Buenos Aires, 1938), pp. 130-31.

[17] Eduardo Mallea, Fiesta en noviembre (Buenos Aires, 1942), p. 10. Further references in the text are to this edition.

[18] Gerchunoff later became less ambivalent in his defense of the moral and spiritual heritage given the world by Jewish culture. See Manuel Bronstein, "Orígenes de la Sociedad Hebraica Argentina," Davar, No. 119 (1968), 75.

[19] Bernardo Verbitsky, Es difícil empezar a vivir (Buenos Aires, 1941), p. 188. Further citations in the text are to this edition.

[20] David Viñas, Los dueños de la tierra (Buenos Aires, 1958), p. 68. Further citations in the text are to this edition.

[21] David Viñas, Dar la cara (Buenos Aires, 1967), p. 221. Further citations in the text are to this edition.

[22] José Chudnovsky, Dios era verde (Buenos Aires, 1963), p. 130.

[23] Marcos Aguinis, Refugiados (Buenos Aires, 1969), p. 16.

[24] Mirelman, "The Semana Trágica," pp. 61-73.

[25] Onega, La inmigración p. 131.

[26] Arturo Cancela, Tres relatos porteños (Buenos Aires, 1923), p. 166.

THE JEW IN TWENTIETH-CENTURY ARGENTINE FICTION

Jewish personalities and problems have played a large but not fully documented role in the development of Spanish America. As Pedro Orgambide says, ". . . judíos españoles (confesos u ocultos detrás de la armadura de la Cruz y la Espada de la Conquista) cayeron con una flecha en el pecho o fueron decapitados, conquistadores que llegaron con los cristianos viejos a estas tierras de América . . ."[1]

In Argentina since colonial times Jews formed "uno de los elementos más decisivos en la constitución de la sociedad rioplatense . . ."[2] At the very height of Spanish persecution, "no pocos hebreos . . . penetraron furtivamente en la Argentina radicándose en Buenos Aires y en diversos pueblos del interior."[3] Much later, in the 1880s, with the help of a German philanthropist, Baron Hirsch, European and especially Russian Jews began arriving in Argentina in great numbers, and with the dawn of the new century they formed the largest Jewish population in Spanish America. Their pronounced agricultural success, according to one source, opened South America to Jews in general.[4] In spite of their rustic environment, they inculcated their children with a continuing thirst for culture together with a certain mental restlessness. Jews in Entre Ríos province played a large part in Argentine life and letters. Alberto Gerchunoff, in his short stories, Los gauchos judíos (1910), dedicated to Baron Hirsch, deserves special mention for his depiction of these pioneers, but many other works, among them Lluvias salvajes (1962) by Natalio Budasoff, and Dios era verde (1963) and Pueblo Pan (1967) by José Chudnovsky, also deal with the same theme. The prospective colonists at first find it difficult to accept the reality of the New World, and one of them in Pueblo Pan tries to explain: "Se hablaba mucho de un país de un nombre largo y raro . . . Arguentine, o also así."[5] The Rabbi explains to those who worry about religious observances and their reception in the strange land: "Iremos y como siempre nos llevaremos a Dios con nosotros" (p. 26).

Partaking of the intellectual ferment of their new country, Jews founded periodicals like Vida Nuestra and Babel, the most successful of which proved to be Davar, published by the Sociedad Hebraica Argentina from 1945 on and edited by Bernardo Verbitsky, whom Roberto F. Giusti called "el talentoso narrador amigo."[6] Many other non-Jews wrote for the journal, among them José Ingenieros, Enrique Banchs, Marta Lynch, and Jorge Luis Borges. Leopoldo Marechal contributed his last short story, about a Rabbi and man's spiritual values, to Davar.[7]

Aside from the anti-Semitic examinations of Julián Martel and Hugo Wast, the Jewish theme fascinated non-Jewish writers like Leopoldo Lugones, Ernesto Sábato, Manuel Gálvez, and Eduardo Mallea who to a greater or lesser degree manifested their comprehension of Jewish character. The most devoted Argentine partisan of the Jews, Jorge Luis Borges, always captivated by Jewish culture,[8] includes many Jewish characters and treatments of Argentine anti-Semitism in his short stories. He sees the Jew as "un hombre encarcelado y hechizado, un hombre condenado a ser la serpiente . . . un hombre que es el Libro, una boca que alaba desde el abismo la justicia del firmamento . . . un hombre que se obstina en ser inmortal . . ."[9] Commenting on Jewish themes such as nostalgia, and "cierto coraje judío también, que no estaba en la poesía de la estirpe,"[10] he concludes that it is possible to be proudly Argentine and profoundly Jewish at the same time.

Many Jewish writers contributed to Argentine culture, among them Samuel Eichelbaum, one of Argentina's best dramatists; César Tiempo, whose real name was Israel Zeitlin, poet and dramatist; Carlos Grünberg, author of Mester de Judería; Samuel Glusberg, better known as Enrique Espinosa and a friend of Lugones, Martínez Estrada, and Horacio Quiroga; and Alberto Palcos, literary critic. In fiction Alberto Gerchunoff's short stories gave rise to a dozen later collections about the Argentine Jew, among them those of Arminda Ralesky, Elias Marchevsky, and Samuel Pecara. Jewish authors like Max Dickman and Luisa Sofovitch tended to avoid the subject, but Bernardo Kordon, Arturo Cancela, Eduardo Gudiño Kieffer, Bernardo Verbitsky, Pablo Orgambide, David Viñas, Marcos Aguinis, and José Chudnovsky examine, in their novels, various aspects of Jewish life and culture.

Jewish novelists create characters who suffer a variety of persecutions from Russian pogroms, Nazi horrors, the Spanish Inquisition, Arab youths, and Argentine fascists. One recurring incident in the novels concerns the Semana Trágica, between January 7 and 12, 1919, when, as a result of a strike at the Pedro Vasena factory, some workers were killed. The government blamed the "maximalistas," Russian anarchists and communists (to some synonyms for Jews), and several civilian vigilante groups, playing on the difference between Jewish and Argentine customs and the canard that Jews wanted a Soviet in Argentina, burned Jewish stores, raped Jewish women, and murdered Jewish men.[11] Arturo Cancela, Bernardo Verbitsky, David Viñas, and José Chudnovsky all deal with this sad event.

For non-Jewish novelists the anti-Semitic theme constituted an intrinsic ingredient of Argentine-Jewish relationships from La bolsa (1891) on. They paint Jewish characters as black caricatures, making them objects of ridicule or Jungian archetypes of evil. Their Christian presentation, stemming from ancient perceptions of the Jew as a money changer in the Temple,[12] promulgates the belief that Jews controlled Argentine finances and media outlets. In La bolsa, José María Miró, a business reporter for La Nación who wrote under the pseudonym of Julián Martel, portrays the Jews as perverting native Christians and destroying their religious and moral virtues through international machinations. But Martel's disparaging description pales before the pejorative poison of Gustavo Adolfo Martínez Zurviría who used the pen name Hugo Wast.

In his two-volume novel, El Kahal. Oro (1935), Wast drags up every unpleasant myth from the Protocols of the Elders of Zion and other anti-Semitic tracts to picture the Jew as the Antichrist who seeks to undermine Christianity,[13] "vasta maniobra judía para ahogar la civilización cristiana." César Tiempo,[14] who called Wast "Fecundo, facundo y feculento," became a hero to the Argentine Jewish community. A character in José Chudnovsky's Pueblo Pan elucidates: "Lo dejó nocaut. Ese no habla más. ¿Quien tenía tiempo para los antisemitas?" (p. 46). Hugo Wast's Jewish characters, romantically projected stereotypes, are products of the author's pathological prejudice of what Jews should act like in order to conform to his preconceived notions. His consistent attempts to dehumanize them detract from their development as living creatures and destroy any possibility of an effective literary portrayal. Wast achieves his deformation through descriptive nuances and by outright denunciantion, using rhtorical jargon and stock slogans about a Jewish international conspiracy to control the world.

In El Kahal Zacarías Blumen, money lender, banker, and smuggler, plans to marry his son into a Christian family to further his designs to control Argentine society and conquer the country for his descendants. Not adverse to bribing local officials, Blumen, expelled from the synagogue because of his son's conversion, nonetheless venerated the Torah and "conservaba el espíritu del Talmud" (p. 64). Disguising his inward pride of race behind a bland and humble exterior, he accepts criollo laughter at his language, secure in the belief that he and Israel will some day rule the world. Zacarías' only son, driven by love of gold, shivers with pleasure when he touches the metallic dust: "sintió . . . aquel calor delicioso en la sangre, aquel deleite que su raza sentía desde cinco mil años atrás, al contacto del oro" (p. 252). The other characters, Mauricio Kohen, compatriot and rival banker, and his daughter Thamar, dedicated to destroying Christian civilization, are not even good stereotypes. The younger generation carried on old hatreds and rivalries, but young Mauricio falls in love with old Zacarías' granddaughter, Marta Blumen, who, in spite of her ancestral drive to rule, finally joins Mauricio in converting to Christianity.

Manuel Gálvez, who boasted about being a friend to the Jews,[15] reacts negatively toward them in La tragedia de un hombre fuerte (1922). His protagonist, Víctor Urgel, a member of an old aristocractic family, recognizes Jewish talent but describes Jews he meets as physically repulsive: "Uno de ellos, horroroso, tenía una nariz grande y gruesa en la punta, unos ojillos duros y una expresión fría y desagradable."[16] He believes they are dangerous and capable of taking over the intellectual life of his country. Gálvez's portrait of Abraham Orloff, a fictional and thinly disguised Alberto Gerchunoff, is more positive, if ambivalent at times. Orloff, the son of a Polish Jew, often went without sleeping, but "jamás desestimaba las ocasiones de alimentarse."[17] As a young man Orloff held strong revolutionary positions and "despedía ironías, sarcasmos, y violencias por todo el cuerpo" (p. 122). Gálvez obviously prefers the later Orloff, the successful editor of La Patria. Yet Gálvez describes him as loyal and generous to a fault, especially when his friend Riga falls on evil days. Riga defends him as a Jew against the attack of others: "Orloff es un judío. ¿Y que? Tendrá sus méritos . . . que era un muchacho lleno de méritos y de talento" (p. 138). The other Jewish character in the novel, Goldenberg, the business manager of the magazine on which Orloff works, is simply "el judío," described as a man who understands adversity. Eduardo Mallea, also apparently friendly to Jews, in his otherwise sympathetic portrait of Jewish suffering in Fiesta en noviembre (1938), cannot avoid describing the Jewish bookstore owner as having a "cara de ratón temeroso."[18]

The other central Jewish theme in Argentine fiction concerns the subject of dual loyalties to separate cultures. In general non-Jewish novelists, hostile toward the separate ethnic entity in their midst, interpret negatively Alberdi's dictum, "gobernar es poblar." Members of the literary generation of 1880 like Cambaceres, Sicardí, and Cané, together with antisemites like Martel and Wast, saw the socially active Jew as a threat to bourgeois values and to Argentine traditions. The oligarchy, equating high social status with large land holdings, created restrictive codes which formed part of the national consciousness. As Gladys Onega points out: "la aristocracia criolla . . . estaba teñida de desdén . . . por el trabajo manual y por el comercio, reservados a las clases inferiores y a los judíos . . ."[19] Ricardo Rojas, paladin of Argentine literary criticism, viewed Jewish separateness as a danger because "al traer sus fanatismos nos traen el germen de una cuestión semítica . . . el hijo criollo del inmigrante semita prefiere ser judío en vez de argentino. . ."[20]

Twentieth-century Argentine fiction reveals a historic animosity to all foreigners but especially to Jews. Gálvez, who respects their existence as human beings, resents their presence as Jews. Víctor Urgel more readily accepts other immigrants who, "venidos desde lejanas tierras europeas abrieron los surcos, echaron la semilla, hicieron hijos sanos, se incorporaron a la patria" (p. 37). He concedes the Jews' role in Argentine theater, education, and medicine, and their positive transformation of the spiritual physiognomy of Argentine, but he resents them anyway because "no olvidaban nunca su condición de judíos" (p. 130). In Pedro Orgambide's Los inquisidores, a collage of twelve characters marked by tragic fate, Efraín Azevedo, a Spanish Jew in the New World, refuses to convert in order to save his life. He exclaims: "Yo soy judío, señores del Santo Oficio; y así lo digo ante este Tribunal sin arrepentimiento. No juro por el falso dios. No denunciaré, tampoco, a hermano y prójimo de mi fe" (p. 12). For Orgambide, his protagonist's statement assumes supreme importance. Even Gerchunoff, who in his short stories presents a romantic view of an idyllic Argentina where Jews live the gaucho life, indirectly admits the separate status because: "Es el judío quien roba el objeto desaparecido en la vecindad y es el autor de todos los crímenes imaginables porque peina barba extensa, no tutea al peón . . ."[21] Indeed, the colonists lose their Rabbi, killed by a gaucho peon. Gerchunoff's Talmudic ideas apparently later overcame the criollo traditions, for he declared that Argentine Jews had maintained a distinctive personality, as they contributed to the country's common intellectual creation, "al poner en contacto la cultura argentina . . . con las expresiones de una cultura milenaria que iluminó el mundo con el sentido de lo moral y el principio de lo social."[22]

Some critics assumed, nonetheless, that the Jews inevitably would become more and more Argentine and less and less Jewish. They believed that a separate Jewish sub-culture and social cluster were anachronisms, to be superseded by archetypal Argentineans, inextricable threads in a total national fabric. Vicente Blasco Ibáñez maintained that unlike all others in the world, Argentine Jews were uniquely national: "Argentina es el único país del mundo que vence esta tendencia al aislamiento del judío. . . . A la segunda generación apenas quedará visible el origen israelita."[23] Martiniano Leguizamón, in his introduction to Los gauchos judíos, admires them as a new kind of Jew who will avoid the synagogue, abandon traditional ways and who, after the disappearance of the older Jews, will become "argentinos por la fusión de la sangre" (p. xiii). Even the older hard-working colonists appear to be more interested in fighting locust plagues than in maintaining their racial and religious identification. Not isolated types, and more Argentine than Jewish, they are represented in later fiction by Lonstein, in <u>Libro de Manuel</u>: "Sos un gaucho judío y a la hora de entender ciertas cosas primero las boleadoras y después el Talmud."[24]

For the most part the fictional Argentine-Jewish equation, at least for Jews, does not so easily succumb to empirical formulae or Aristotelian principles. Some Jews identify with the life of the <u>criollos</u> and hope to escape into anonymity; others persist as a separate ethnic entity, intensely Jewish but also fervently Argentinean. The Jewish characters inevitably suffer as an inextricable segment of a cultural entity which wants to reject them, leading to conflictive Jewish interactions concerning their own interdependence and dichotomizing them as either committed or self-betrayed. This constant conflict between ancestral, almost instinctive judgments and contemporary commitments, as portrayed by the writers, reflects a reality discussed as early as 1909 by the Centro Juventud Israelita-Argentina, an organization which at first sought to solve the problem through a deliberate process of "incorporación de los judíos al medio ambiente, abandonando todo vestigio de su peculiaridad."[25] Soon thereafter, in a dramatic change, the group adopted the motto, "jóvenes, judíos y argentinos,"[26] feelings reinforced by Eichelbaum and Gerchunoff in their denunciation of the Semana Trágica in the first two issues of <u>Martín Fierro</u>, published in March and April of 1919.

Bernardo Verbitsky depicts through his protagonist the difficulties inherent in the drive for integration and the determination of one's identity. Pablo Levinson, the central character in <u>Es difícil empezar a vivir</u> (1941), a hardworking student and newspaperman, had been in love with a Jewish girl and had met a number of Jewish authors, but he hardly thought about Jews as such. He believes at first that "en nada diferían los judíos de quienes no lo eran. ¡Qué absurdo, qué contrario a la razón sería agruparlos de ese modo!"[27] His uncle Silver, described as "un judío perfectamente acriollado" (p. 59), also refuses to advertise his Judaism, but his fellow Argentines attack him anyway because "no era argentino como decía, sino judío" (p. 59). Rediscovering the synagogue and Jewish traditions, Pablo laments not being able to read Hebrew. Attempting to analyze his urge to fast on Yom Kippur as a kind of sacrificial penance, he realizes that, for a Jew, God exists in all men. He also comes to understand the Jew's devotion to learning, "esa milenaria devoción judía hacia el que sabe, aspirando que ese saber llegara también a los hijos" (p. 197). He perceives the Jewish essence, the opposite of fascism, as respect for both learning and life, and he knows that the Jew, in spite of centuries of humiliation and suffering caused by a bestial world, will survive, perhaps "como una herida, como carne viva en la cual sufre toda la humanidad" (pp. 313-314). Truly touched and moved by his new understanding, Pablo suffers a metamorphosis which enables him to face his Jewish problematic future with tranquility.

In Dar la cara (1962), David Viñas's protagonist Bernardo Carman at first rejects his identity: "Pero si yo no siento ni medio de todo eso,"[28] he replies when his father tries to talk to him about Israel and Jewish traditions. Feeling himself to be an Argentine, he cares more about sex and student activities than about Jews. He is willing to accept the demeaning platitude of his friend Nacho: "Claro, mi viejo, vos sos distinto, pero cuando yo te hablo de judíos, me refiero a los que no saben qué es el país ni lo sienten. . ." (p. 221). After the fascist attacks against fellow Jews, Carman realizes that integration is impossible: "Y los que no se sentían extranjeros para nadie, judíos también, puercos y peligrosos judíos. Los que querían hablar con cualquiera por la calle, los que querían amar . . . los que estaban dispuestos a pelear por otro y por otros por supuestos judíos. Y judíos los arrojados y judíos los generosos y judíos los amantes" (p. 586). Carman recognizes that Buenos Aires, not the center of the world, serves as but one more battleground for his people. Viñas himself appears briefly in the novel as "medio judío. Judío a medias, mazorquero a medias" (p. 99).

Yuda Singer, the Jewish freethinker of Viñas' Los dueños de la tierra (1958), neither sure of herself nor of her beliefs and open and frank to a fault, is politically aggressive and possesses a direct and startling vocabulary. Vicente Vera, her lover, concludes that she is different because: "¿sera porque es judia?"[29] In spite of her memories of the pogroms which first caused her family to emigrate to the New World, she is willing to have the child of a non-Jew and marry him in the name of advanced political thought. Still, aware of Jewish ideas, she also insists that "tenemos que quejarnos los judíos, si no, perdemos carácter" (p. 133).

José Chudnovsky presents the most detailed description of Jews, their spiritual solidarity, and their assimilation into the mainstream of Argentine life. In Dios era verde (1963), about the magic process of growing up as an immigrant boy in Argentina, Abraham, Pajarito de Plomo's father, seeks to live in peace and harmony with his Christian neighbors. He informs his son that he cries with patriotic fever whenever he reads the Argentine constitution. Yet, reflective of his own uncertainties, he also tells him: " . . .¿acaso puedo hablarte como a un judío? Pero debes saber que el Talmud es una serie de libros, una larga obra de nuestros antepasados para explicar la ley de Moisés."[30] The son, not really understanding the conversation, shows more interest in the alfalfa crop and the neighbor girl than in Judaism. Nonetheless, even though he cannot understand Yiddish, that language for Pajarito will always bring back positive memories of gefilte fish, candles, and prayers.

Chudnovsky, a highly articulate interpreter of personal values rooted in his own ethnic background and emotions, integrated his aesthetic and emotional commitment in Pueblo Pan, the most complete statement of Jewish-Argentine relationships and the meaning of being an Argentine Jew. He analyzes the Jewish adjustments and the ambivalence many of them felt when they first arrived. In spite of glowing promises, the tailors, butchers, and others escaping from Russian pogroms, victimized by uncertain contracts, indifferent intermediaries, and anti-Semitic administrators, tried to adapt themselves to the agricultural way of life and succeeded in fulfilling Baron Hirsch's dream of becoming "derechos, erguidos, fuertes, en los vírgenes países de América" (p. 64).

Drawing strength from their Bible, they allowed nothing to dampen their drive for acceptance in the new land and proudly, if ambivalently, acknowledged the government's praise "que ya no son hebreos, es decir, extranjeros de la orilla opuesta, sino ciudadanos argentinos" (p. 196). Abraham names the local library for Bernardino Rivadavia instead of for Baron Hirsch and believes that his fellow Jews should not bring to Argentina "esos ritos arcaicos. . . . Aquí los judíos deben aportar su tenacidad, su apego a la cultura, su cohesión familiar" (p. 210). And some of the colonists' children neglect their origins. As one of these descendants states: "Yo elegí ser argentino . . . y di brazos, hijos y trigo a la patria" (p. 235). Abraham's own son, Pajarito de Plomo, reflects that the older generation spoke with borrowed book words and not those of men who dance the tango and that ". . . sabemos que el país como a al hembra hay que quebrarla en un abrazo para que nos dé toda su entraña" (p. 88).

Abraham, overcoming Russian persecutions and pogroms and early hardships in Entre Ríos, fails to keep the Sabbath or celebrate Yom Kippur. Yet he has his eldest son circumcised and feels it his duty to help build a synagogue near the school. Although he vows: "Seré argentino hasta mi muerte" (p. 162), he leaves a spiritual message for coming generations and answers queries about the Talmud. For him being a Jew means helping others; his solidarity with fellow Jews is secular and moral rather than theological, but he knows that all Argentine Jews will continue to seek their Hebrew roots, to find out "de donde venían, quienes fueron mis antepasados" (p. 246).

A special area of friction for Jews and non-Jews alike involves Argentine perception of political persuasions of Jews and the relationship between religion and ideology. Many of the characters have socialist leanings which, far from showing an affinity for Russian causes, reflect an age-old prophetic tradition and concern for social justice which transcends country, a philosophy equally anathema to the Argentine oligarchy. During the Semana Trágica one of the justifications of the Jew haters was that they were all "Maximalistas." The Jewish socialists, on the contrary, seem somewhat parochial in associating ethnic ties with political beliefs and have their own bitter quarrels and schisms. Yet even Gálvez in La tragedia de un hombre fuerte claims that Jews " eran casi todos socialistas, y . . . el éxito del bolcheviquismo los había hecho revolucionarios" (p. 128). World War I drove the Jewish colonists to splinter into various groups. Some older Jews denounced the young radicals; others joined the Zionist cause; but young and old alike suffered when, in Pueblo Pan, "gente con que crecimos juntos de pronto nos gritó: judíos y golpearon a algunos barbudos!" (p. 237).

In spite of all ethnic problems of identity or integration, Marcos Aguinis joins Chudnovsky in expressing a hope for the future. In Refugiados (1969) Ignacio Nassif, an Argentine Catholic, defends Israel against Arab attacks. Though the discussion in this novel is about Arab-Israeli relationships, those associations are also relevant to the Argentine scene. Ben Aaron reminds the Arab doctor who saves his life that two peoples, both of whom have suffered injustices, should be friends. In spite of feelings of rage and hate, accommodation and understanding may be possible. The author hopes to find a human solution, as the young Arab medical student falls in love with Ben Aaron's beautiful adopted daughter, Myriam. Unconvinced by her arguments, but astonished by her tranquility, he finally views Jews as fellow sufferers, "tanto los árabes como los judíos fueron aplastados por la misma bota."[31] He also comes to accept his affection for Jorge Silverman, the Chilean Jew with whom he lives.

Most of these novels reveal an almost atavistic antagonism against Jews who for many Argentines will continue to be invaders who can never become completely integrated into the national culture.[32] Non-Jewish authors cannot understand the Jew's obdurate solidarity nor his moral and ethical posture. The Jewish authors' ethical positions transcend national boundaries. Azevedo's torture in the sixteenth century equates with that suffered by Jews in Russia and at Nazi hands. Pablo

Levinson discovers that we still live in a world of executioners and victims. Moshe Mendel, in David Viñas' Un dios cotidiano (1957), seeks conversion but finds only rejection. At the same time we see Judaism defined in terms of prophetic commitment. The Jews' reverence for life makes them responsible for the fate of other Jews and by extension for all fellow human beings. They see themselves as progenitors of a spiritual, moral, and literary defense of intellectual freedom.

The Jewish novelists show us suffering and terror but rarely do they attempt an irrational accretion in support of their group interest and rarely do they repudiate directly the repugnant beliefs of the Argentine oligarchy. Attuned to the Jewish essence, they reaffirm and rediscover a Jewish commitment as they explore ethical considerations involving spiritual freedom and social conscience in a society where they hope Jewish aspirations and culture may survive and even flourish. Whatever their transitory doubts or dedication to transcendental meaning, they continue to reaffirm their dual identity and hope that the Jew, the Argentine, and mankind may eventually form a mutually symbiotic nourishment. Typically, Abraham and the generations he forms, however patriotic or Americanized they may become, will continue to profit from their moral and ethical inheritance.

In the final analysis the Jewish theme is but one aspect of other essential human problems, but ritualistic reenactment of Jewish experience remains an important element of some Argentine fiction. Not really thesis novels, these works reveal that though Jewish writers may have based their argentinidad on an over-confident view of humanity's goodness and nobility of spirit, the Jew, estranged but not disaffected, will continue to survive both in the real world and as a literary figure together with his concepts of compassion and universal brotherhood, whatever the perils of a fading faith or the evils certain Argentines might wish to visit upon him.

Notes

¹Pedro Orgambide, <u>Los inquisidores</u> (Buenos Aires: Editorial Sudamericana, 1967), p. 71. Further citations in the text are to this edition.

² José Ingenieros, <u>La evolución de las ideas argentinas</u> (Buenos Aires: Elmer Editor, 1956), I, 19.

³Juan José Sebrelli, <u>La cuestión judía en la Argentina</u> (Buenos Aires: Editorial Tiempo Contemporáneo, 1968), p. 77.

⁴Peter Wiernik, <u>History of the Jews in America</u> . . . (New York: Hermon Press, 1972), p. 441.

⁵José Chudnovsky, <u>Pueblo Pan</u> (Buenos Aires: Losada, 1967), p. 21. Further citations in the text are to this edition.

⁶See <u>Davar</u>, No. 100 (1964), p. 311.

⁷<u>Davar</u>, No. 124 (Winter, 1970).

⁸See Martin Stabb, <u>Jorge Luis Borges</u> (New York: Twayne, 1960), p. 73.

⁹Jorge Luis Borges, "Israel," <u>Davar</u>, No. 114 (1967), p. 3.

¹⁰See "Homenaje a Carlos Grünberg," <u>Davar</u>, No. 119 (1968), p. 30.

¹¹See Victor A. Mirelman, "The Semana Trágica of 1919," <u>Jewish Social Studies</u>, 37 (1975), pp. 61-73.

¹²Claire Huchet Bishop, <u>How Catholics Look at Jews</u> (New York: Paulist Press, 1974), pp. 52-54.

¹³Gustavo Adolfo Martínez Zuviría, <u>El Kahal. Oro</u> (Santiago de Chile: Ercilla, 1935), p. 92. Further citations in the text are from this edition.

¹⁴See <u>Davar</u>, No. 88 (1961), p. 50.

¹⁵Juan José Sebrelli, pp. 98-102.

¹⁶Manuel Gálvez, <u>La tragedia de un hombre fuerte</u> (Buenos Aires: Editorial Tor, 1938), pp. 129-131. Further references in the text are to this edition.

[17] Manuel Gálvez, El mal metafísico (Buenos Aires: Espasa-Calpe, Coleccion Austral, 1962), p. 48. Further citations in the text are from this edition.

[18] Eduardo Mallea, Fiesta en noviembre (Buenos Aires: Losada, 1942), p. 124.

[19] Gladys Onega, La inmigración en la literatura argentina, 1880-1910 (Santa Fe: Universidad Nacional del Litoral, 1965), p. 13.

[20] Juan José Sebrelli, p. 85.

[21] Alberto Gerchunoff, Los gauchos judíos (La Plata: J. Sese, 1910), p. 127. Further references in the text are to this edition.

[22] See Manuel Bronstein, "Orígines de la Sociedad Hebraica Argentina," Davar, No. 119 (1968), p. 75.

[23] Vicente Blasco Ibáñez, Argentina y sus grandezas (Madrid: La Editorial Española Americana, 1910), p. 100.

[24] Julio Cortázar, Libro de Manuel (Buenos Aires: Editorial Sudamericana, 1973), p. 342.

[25] Manuel Bronstein, p. 65.

[26] Ibid, p. 70.

[27] Bernardo Verbitsky, Es difícil empezar a vivir (Buenos Aires: Losada, 1941), p. 313. Further citations in the text are to this edition.

[28] David Viñas, Dar la cara (Buenos Aires: Editorial de América Latina, 1967), pp. 48-49. Further citations in the text are to this edition.

[29] David Viñas, Los dueños de la tierra (Buenos Aires: Losada, 1958), p. 125. Further citations in the text are to this edition.

[30] José Chudnovsky, Dios era verde (Buenos Aires: Editorial Goyanarte, 1963), p. 131. Further citations in the text are to this edition.

[31] Marcos Aguinis, Refugiados (Buenos Aires: Losada, 1969), pp. 239-240.

[32] Ernesto Sábato, nonetheless, postulates the Jew as one of the three basic entities of the new Argentina, "resultante de tres grandes fuerzas, tres grandes pueblos: españoles, italianos y judíos." See <u>Abbadón el exterminador</u> (Buenos Aires: Editorial Sudamericana, 1974), p. 212.

Two Contemporary Hispanic Views of Israel and the Jews

Carlos Fuentes, Mexico's leading novelist, respected for his ardent search to overcome the legacy of corruption of the Mexican Revolution, and Juan Goytisolo, Spain's best known contemporary novelist, make no secret of their sympathies for the Palestinian cause and for the political and economic independence of Arab countries.[1] Indeed, Goytisolo believes that a conspiracy exists between Israel and the United States to crush the Lebanese and the Palestinian resistance as part of a United States agreement with Russia to maintain military equivalence between the two powers. For him the raid on Entebbe was a practice blitzrieg, "destined to defend the sacrosanct values of our Christian civilization."[2] Fuentes, equating Zionism with imperialism, strives to distinguish between Jews in Germany as victims, and Jews in Israel as executioners. Far from viewing Israel as a vindication of Jewish emancipation, Fuentes equates the country with the rebirth of Nazi mentality; the Jews are the Nazis, the Palestinians the Jewish victims who oppose the evidence of their inexistence to all the unjust existences because they were denied theirs (CH, p. 269). Fuentes adds Moscobiya, Ramallah and Sarafand to Dachau and Treblinka, and he justifies anti-Israel terrorism by pro-Israel terrorism of previous decades at places like Deir Yassim (CH, p. 223). Fuentes promotes the PLO argument of one culture, Jews and Arabs together, but extols ancient Palestinian values over Israeli material progress. In any event, Palestinians had inhabited the region for centuries.

At the same time both Fuentes and Goytisolo proclaim their sympathy for the Jews as a people. Goytisolo sees no dichotomy between calling, on the one hand, for the "rejudification" of Spain, "on whose effects we should congratulate ourselves,"[3] together with his empathy with Jews as victims of Spanish theocracy,[4] and, on the other, for the condemnation and perhaps disappearance of the State of Israel. A self-proclaimed ardent pro-Semite, shocked at Spanish persecution of the Jews, he cannot, nevertheless, whatever his feelings about the Holocaust, find the sympathy or warmth for Israel he professes to hold in his heart for that entity called Jews. Fuentes in his novels, A Change of Skin (1967) and Terra Nostra (1974), talks respectively of Nazi and Inquisitional horrors and protests his love for Jews. Indeed, he claims that A Change of Skin was forbidden in Spain for being pro-Jewish and anti-German.[5] He examines, with an apparent sympathy, the plight of the Jews during the plague years of the Middle Ages when they were charged with poisoning wells and put to torture: "Bishops and the lords of Imperial cities agreed to annihilate their Jews, burning them, stabbing them, drowning them and always, of course, expropriating their property."[6] In Terra

Nostra Fuentes comments that Columbus's trip was made with money expropriated from three Jewish families, a few of the many from whom property was stolen and perhaps the least of the Jewish problems. The Jews were viewed as the greatest evil in the Spanish realm, and few believed in their conversion to Christianity. Considered a Judaizing animal, forced to eat pork, and victimized by pogroms, the Jew had to wear a round yellow patch over his heart and was forced to live in one section of the city.[7] Yet for each of his apparently sympathetic descriptions Fuentes manages to cloud the issue. In his discussion of the Jews in the Theresienstadt ghetto and those outside who decided to join their bretheren, he proclaims: "No one forced them. They went into the ghetto voluntarily" (CS, p. 223). As Herr Urs, the satanic representative, exclaims: "The ghetto has contaminated all of you. And the infection of the ghetto is real infection . . . Neurosis was born in the ghetto. By fear out of ridicule . . ." (CS, p. 444).

Although both Fuentes and Goytisolo show dichotomies in their treatment of Israel and the Jews, their positions are ultimately quite different. Juan Goytisolo, accepting the uniqueness of Spanish history through a fusion of Jewish elements with Moorish and Christian ones, elaborates on Américo Castro's thesis concerning the irritation of the power structure at the superiority of Jews in liberal arts, science, and medicine. He points out that some of the complexes and the dreams of glory found in the Spanish character stem from "a scarcely hidden desire to diminish or negate the impact of Semitic traces and to embellish, on the contrary, their Visigothic and Roman inheritance" (OI, p. 73). Spain's neurotic and almost psychotic insistence on spiritual purity, says Goytisolo, prevented capitalism in Spain, given the myth that commercial and banking interests were Jewish. The power structure in sixteenth century Spain extolled honor over the accumulation of riches which might reflect on Spaniards' status as "Old Christians"; wealth came to be associated with Jewishness and thus with something negative. Spain's entry into the modern world, part of the "rejudification" of Spain, presages the acceptance of the physical but not yet the intellectual and spiritual contributions of the Jews (F. , p. 183).

In the 1970's Goytisolo became increasingly interested in fifteenth, sixteenth, and seventeenth century conversos as major factors in determining modern Spanish cultural, psychological, and sexual components. As part of his reexamination he analyzes three important literary works which, according to him, never received a proper critical evaluation by Spanish critics because of Jewish elements the works exhibited. Accepting as decisive

Stephen Gilman's interpretation of the subversive quality of La Celestina, Goytisolo sees its author Rojas, a convert from Judaism, as part of a vast community of New Christians "whose conflictive situation we see reflected in a great number of literary works of the period" (D., p. 14). The Jewish converts, surrounded by suspicion both from within and without, lived in a world in which they could not trust any human relationship because one unpremeditated expression might cause disaster. Thus their existence became one of disguises and masks. The change which occurred in Jewish lives with the decrees of expulsion of 1492, "signified a cataclysm without precedents whose lasting consequences pursued them generation after generation with implacable tenacity" (D, p. 20). Under the nightmarish conditions imposed, it is easy to imagine that the sincerity of many of these conversions was open to question.

Goytisolo postulates the Jewish lineage of Francisco Delicado, author of La lozana andaluza, because of the tremendous number of references to and intimate knowledge of Jewish customs as well as that author's fierce attack on the idea of lineage and pure blood. Delicado portrays the heroine as "sharp," a code word in those days for Jew, and stressed in documents of the Inquisition as a distinguishing feature (D., p. 41). Another method to determine Jewishness involved "baconphilia and baconphobia, which in Golden Age literature marks the dividing line between Old and New Christians (D., p. 42).

Estebanillo González, hombre de buen humor (1646), a subversive attack on the established values of reactionary Catholicism, gives us a self-portrait without lectures or spurious sermons, in the best picaresque tradition. Irreverent, sarcastic, satirical, Estebanillo inverts the mythology of Spanish honor, virtue, respect for women, and bravery. The book's episodes are ostensibly violently anti-Semitic. Estebanillo sadistically pulls a tooth from an unhappy victim because "he is a Jew and his friends are all Hebrews. I did it on purpose and not because I don't know my job" (F., p. 72). These anti-Jewish outbursts, in their violence and crudity, differ from those of fellow picaresque novelists. For Goytisolo, Estebanillo seems to be saying that the Jewish enemies attacked by the cristianos viejos were, in reality, themselves.

The Jews, according to accepted authors of the day, were portrayed in a constantly unflattering light as Spaniards solved their inferiority problems by persecuting, robbing, and expelling Jews to protect their immaculate purity, a racism which endured for centuries (L., p. 120). José María Blanco White, whom Goytisolo identifies as a spokesman for his own feelings (OI, p. 98), points out that the slightest mixture of Hebrew blood tainted the family in its totality to the most remote descendants. Documents were maintained through the years in order to establish purity of blood. And so, centuries after the statutes of purity were promulgated, the prejudices of the Old Christians showed no signs of weakening (OI, p. 75). In the 1970's anti-Jewish propaganda was still being taught in the schools. Lectures stressed the necessity for Spanish Catholic purity and the elimination of "Jews, Moors, Lutherans, Encyclopedists" (OI, p. 6). On a psychological level, the persecution of Jews was deliberately designed to enclose them in straitjackets which would incapacitate them from functioning as free adults, and Goytisolo attributes the lack of critical thought in Spain through the centuries in part to the "antisemitic and intellectual persecution" (D., p. 171). Indeed, the experience started by the Inquisition gave twentieth century Spanish censors an enormous storehouse of precedents from which to work. Goytisolo finds what he calls a "morbid phobia against Jews" in many of the current standard histories of Spanish literature (D., p. 139).

Spaniards from the sixteenth century on have adopted the mask of the Christian myth at the expense of their Jewish reality, one reason for the continuing reaction of the Catholic Church and the "pure" Spaniards, a strange mixture of hate, fear, and scorn, to the potential pollution of their Christian orthodoxy. In extreme cases, even in the twentieth century, certain bigots maintain that "a Christian Jew is as Jewish and dangerous as a Hebrew Jew" (D., p. 148, f.n. 9). Goytisolo rejects this part of Spanish history which kept Spain in the Dark Ages even during the Enlightenment which swept the rest of Europe. He implies that in Spain, with the exception of a work or two like Don Quixote, it was the Jews and Arabs who sought to enlarge the human mind. In spite of his rejection of Spain's false values, he accepts the reality of Semitic culture as the best part of his country. In order to recreate the real Spain, says Goytisolo, Spaniards must reject the historical lies and proudly acknowledge their Semitic heritage.

Carlos Fuentes appears more ambivalent about even non-Zionist Jews. One may, indeed, read A Change of Skin as a defense of Nazism: "The Nazis are congratulated for enacting 'that true freedom to accept all, not only what man is but what he may be'."[8] Fuentes insists that he was writing parody through one of the characters who sported "all the self-justifying cliches of the Third Reich." Furthermore, says Fuentes, what a protagonist says may not always reveal what an author thinks.[9] Fuentes, it is true, documents twentieth century Nazi tyranny. Through ex-Nazi Franz's cognitive matrices burgeoned with visual input, he describes the concentration camp, painting the living conditions in minute detail. A hundred and twenty women used a single basin in a damp cell. Prisoners lived among garbage heaps; their children, suffering from diarrhea, scampered about excrement-smeared floors, filled with fleas and lice, and dead from typhus, were thrown into a common pit with the adults where guards with pliers and knives picked out gold-filled teeth. But Fuentes defends Franz, a student of architecture. He met Hanna Werner, a musician, held hands, went to concerts, and fell in love. At first he laughed at the Nazis but later joined them. In the midst of destruction he welcomed the opportunity to build. When the crematorium was finished, he drew up plans for the construction of a new cell block. He contends that he could not have helped Hanna and that furthermore: "History never flowed through me . . . I just happened to be around" (CS., p. 354). In a mock trial directed by Hanna's son Jacob, Franz says that he simply obeyed orders, that he tried to build a new world, to destroy modern mediocrity. He had searched for Hanna, but she was an anonymous victim in the mausoleum of all anonymous victims. Furthermore, the narrator observes: "the trial of Franz has not convinced me of his guilt or of the justice of the punishment they intend to impose" (CS, p. 449). Even Jacob admits: "I shall shout with them that you must not be pardoned, for to pardon you would be to deny forgiveness of all meaning. Only later will I insist that you didn't deserve to die, that you have paid the price of whatever may have been your crime, paid with twenty-five long years of decency and honesty." Indeed, what Franz did or didn't do makes no difference to anyone. He must die because "he is the old, and we are the new. . ." (CS, pp. 450-51). Essentially Fuentes blames the world and not Franz for Auschwitz, contending that for man, incapable of accepting truth, certainty is impossible. He recalls that many Jews came to Mexico City during the war and afterward many Germans. They never "talk about those things, they've forgotten them, old trunks, suitcases, boxes tied with string . . . Nazi flags and armbands. . ." (CS, p. 80). Fuentes implies that Jews, too, should forgive and forget.

Whereas Fuentes finds a kind of justification for Franz, at least pathognomically appropriate, he sees no such mitigating circumstances for Elizabeth Jonas. Fuentes describes her as a passionate Jewish girl and through Javier, his hypermanly Mexican protagonist, violates her much as Spaniards violated Mexico's Indian women. Like them Elizabeth, too, willingly accepts a subordinate role. Indeed, she exults in her passivity and power of surrender, much as the Jew, implies Fuentes, "surviving entirely by abstention, once again in your universe, your vicus Judaerorum . . . your Judengasse, your damned ghetto (CS, p. 32). Elizabeth, whose family had suffered discrimination in New York, becomes Franz' lover, even though she recognizes the barbarism of Treblinka, Buchenwald, and similar places. Fuentes reduces the Holocaust from a unique event to an acceptable historical one, for after all, claims Fuentes, antisemitism has been around for a long time and in a number of places.

Similarly, in Terra nostra, which depicts the inevitability of despotism and the recurrence of historical discrimination against Jews, he claims he cannot be held responsible for his protagonists' conclusions. Again one senses feelings not fully parodic. Fuentes believes that the Jews saw the crucifixion of Jesus as a way to reduce Roman power much as Pilate sought to balance Jewish and Roman power. Yet, in discussions about Jesus's death, the Jews receive direct condemnation (TN., p. 96), and as dregs of humanity are ineligible for the redemptive sacrifice of God the Son (TN., p. 276).

In La cabeza de la hidra we see even more clearly that Fuentes's interpretation of Hispanic culture involves his own anti-Jewish categories. Fuentes certainly paints a pejorative picture of Jewish protagonists. Doctor Leopold Bernstein, a sloppy Polish Jew and Nazi hunter, helps usurp Arab lands. Abby Benjamin's wife, an Israeli agent, like Elizabeth for Fuentes a sexually insatiable Jewish stereotype, has "black and humid pubic hair . . . smell of an unsatisfied and sensual Jewess" (CH., p. 122). Ruth, another pretty Jewish girl, participates in a murder and is a "Hebrew Geisha, a Madame Butterfly with the decalogue of Sinai in her arms instead of a son" (CH, p. 45). Fuentes's symbol, the hydra head, represents treason, violence, insidiousness, subterfuge, and an illegal Judaic activity inspired by nationalism. He believes that espionage, blackmail, sabotage, bribery, and murder are normal instruments of Israeli state policy. He compares the threat against Mexico to the betrayal by Malinche, Cortés's lover, and associates it with the Plumed Serpent's return for vengeance. Israel, a modern Malinche to the Jews, helps manipulate the Mexican economy (did not the Jews boycott Mexican tourism on Israeli orders? [CH, p. 198]) and impedes Mexico's true search for identity and control over her own natural resources.

Fuentes makes his usual ambivalent obeisance to Nazi victims. Sara, the good Israeli, discovers that her country has eliminated the existence of the identity of Palestinians and their culture. When Sara's Arab friend is tortured, Sara protests that the Jews, victims of the Nazis, could not repeat the same horrors of their own executioners, in effect becoming the new Nazis: "Our suffering imposed now on weaker beings than us . . . we did not know how to be masters without new slaves. We ended by being executioners in order not to be victims. We found our own victims in order to stop being victims" (CH, p.

108). Admitting that Israel appears to be a nation where all may seek justice, Fuentes points out that this is but an illusory ethical surface. Sara is killed, when she tries to proclaim the truth, by wicked Jews and their conspiratorial Jewish friends in the United States. Indeed, the fact that Sara suffered at Auschwitz makes his meaning even more clear, if there were any doubt, that the state of Israel is the modern Auschwitz, the reverse of the normal connection between the two entities, and he proclaims that unless Israel changes, Jews will again be "hated and persecuted" (CH, p. 131).

Fuentes denigrates the suffering of the Jews in pre-War Germany: "But while the Jews were only rich bankers, prosperous merchants, and prizewinning intellectuals in pre-Nazi Germany, the Palestinians were already victims, exiles from the very land which only they, in reality, inhabited" (CH, p. 204). Fuentes sees Zionism, advancing the Jewish national state, as a prolongation of Western colonialism, as the Jews obliged the Arab world to pay the price for the Nazi ovens.

Carlos Fuentes at times seems to be writing the history of the Holocaust from the point of view of the murderer. Although he uses the customary Christian expressions of compassion for the victims (that is, if we accept his statements in defense of the Nazis as ironic), he reiterates that the Jews of Israel are themselves the new Nazis and that his defense of the German Nazi point of view is done in "the old tradition of Latin satire".[10] But a treatment of Nazi genocide repels as a fictional joke. In La cabeza de la hidra he promotes the idea of monstrous tortures practiced by Jews and tries to Procrusteanize the Holocaust with Israeli policies toward the Palestinians and fellow Jewish victims. While on the one hand he acknowledges the Holocaust, on the other he stresses Palestinian rights as superior to the survival of Jews in Israel. Like Mexico, a kind of spiritual wasteland, Israel stands in need of purification.

In his passion for an emotional cause, Fuentes, usually anything but a precisian, has allowed his bias to show. In his exprobration of the Jews, less objective than his fellow Hispanic novelist, he has substituted for a former concern for the brotherhood of man a synchronic denunciation verging on the malicious, disguised as a parodic search for truth. Goytisolo, on the other hand, whatever his association with Arab causes, strives for artistic and moral integrity, not indifferent to the anti-semitism of the world, in spite of his irrational accretion of "facts" in support of Palestinians. He may be opposed to the politics of Israel, but he excoriates the persecution of Jews at the hands of a ruthless world. For Jews his distinction may be somwhat subjective and romantic, though we live in a cruel world where we can all share inevitable burdens of guilt.

Notes

[1] See Juan Goytisolo, *Disidencias* (Barcelona: Seix Barral, 1977), p. 299. Further references in the text are to this edition hereafter cited as D. See also Carlos Fuentes, *La cabeza de la hidra* (Barcelona: Librería Editorial Argos, 1978), p. 105. Further references in the text are to this edition cited as CH.

[2] Juan Goytisolo, *Libertad, Libertad, Libertad* (Barcelona: Anagrama, 1978), p. 117. Further references in the text are to this edition hereafter cited as L.

[3] Juan Goytisolo, *El furgón de cola* (Paris: Ruedo Ibérico, 1967), p. 183. Further references in the text are to this edition hereafter cited as F.

[4] Juan Goytisolo, *Obra inglesa de D. José María Blanco White* (Buenos Aires: Ediciones Formentor, 1972), p. 97. Further references in the text are to this edition hereafter cited as OI.

[5] See Daniel de Guzmán, *Carlos Fuentes* (New York: Twayne, 1972), p. 162, f.n. 28.

[6] Carlos Fuentes, *A Change of Skin*, tr. Sam Hileman (New York: Farrar, Strauss, and Giroux, 1967), pp. 236-37. Further references in the text are to this edition, hereafter cited as CS.

[7] Carlos Fuentes, *Terra Nostra*, tr. Margaret Sayers Peden (New York: Farrar, Strauss, Giroux, 1976), p. 505. Further references in the text are to this edition hereafter cited as TN.

[8] David Gallagher, "*A Change of Skin*" New York Times Book Review (February 4, 1968), p. 41.

[9] Carlos Fuentes, New York Times Book Review (March 3, 1968), p. 16.

[10] Carlos Fuentes, "Cambio de piel en Italia," *Mundo Nuevo*, no. 21. (1968), p. 21.